Legacies, Logics, Logistics

Legacies, Logics, Logistics

Essays in the Anthropology of
the Platform Economy

JANE I. GUYER

The University of Chicago Press
Chicago and London

Jane I. Guyer is the George Armstrong Kelly Professor Emerita in the Department of Anthropology at Johns Hopkins University. She is the author or editor
of numerous books.

The University of Chicago Press, Chicago 60637
The University of Chicago Press, Ltd., London
© 2016 by The University of Chicago
All rights reserved. Published 2016.
Printed in the United States of America

25 24 23 22 21 20 19 18 17 16   1 2 3 4 5

ISBN-13: 978-0-226-32673-3 (cloth)
ISBN-13: 978-0-226-32687-0 (paper)
ISBN-13: 978-0-226-32690-0 (e-book)
DOI: 10.7208/chicago/9780226326900.001.0001

Library of Congress Cataloging-in-Publication Data

Guyer, Jane I., author.
  Legacies, logics, logistics : essays in the anthropology of the platform
economy / Jane Guyer.
      pages ; cm
  Includes bibliographical references and index.
  ISBN 978-0-226-32673-3 (cloth : alk. paper) — ISBN 978-0-226-32687-0
(pbk. : alk. paper) — ISBN 978-0-226-32690-0 (ebook)   1. Economic
anthropology.   2. Economics—History—21st century.   3. Economic
anthropology—Africa.   4. Africa—Economic conditions—1960–   I. Title.
  GN448.2.G89 2016
  306.3—dc23

                                                    2015017229

Remembering
My father
Walter Wright Mason
1911–1985

My brother
Timothy Wright Mason
1940–1990

I am very fortunate that there is interest in publishing these papers, all but one written over a period of fourteen years from 2000 to 2014, as a single collection. They all arose out of intellectual and collegial engagements, rather than from an overarching research project or a concentrated theoretical reworking. All were written as response papers to invitations, with respect to particular topics, so each had its own purpose and interlocutors, who had provoked me to search further into the relevant empirical and theoretical sources than I would otherwise have done. While attempting to pull out certain themes, which proves a very interesting intellectual challenge, I nevertheless wish to preserve the sense of ongoing engagement from which they came, where specific findings reach the provisional resting place of classical empiricism—*ataraxia*, equanimity—rather than certainty on every point. There is evidence and argument in these papers, but their form is definitive on some points while remaining open to the next engagement on others.

This means, then, that I could probably list every person I have talked to, or whose work I have read, over decades, as part of the acknowledgments. Let me first indicate my debt to my late older brother, historian Timothy Mason, to whom I dedicate the book under the title of "remembering" rather than "in memoriam." Extraordinary intellectual presence that he was, he and his influence came earliest in my life in scholarship and continue into the present. I thought of his exceptionally high standards as I worked. The craftsmanship he brought to the evidence, in concert with theoretical and life commitments, was exemplary. Early in my career, he taught me that theory was not the front portico and the back veranda of the architecture of an argument. It was the foundation that held up the entire construct. It might not be visible at all, or it could be indicated and strongly referenced. But the evidence had to stand up on the foundation, with its own power. I tried passing by him one of my first historical papers, on colonial taxation, and even hoped he would consider it for publication in *History Workshop Journal*, of which he was a cofounder. He indicated to me that there was still work to be done on it, even though I thought I had delved into all the sources I could find. His requirements for the combination of theory and evidence set a kind of "gold standard" toward which I still reach. I add my father to the dedication. Few women of my generation seem to have received such profound support from their fathers, for all of their endeavors, as I received from him, from the very beginning.

I next acknowledge, with gratitude for their provocation and attentive engagement, the colleagues who invited each paper, without whose instigation the papers would simply not have been researched and written. I acknowledged these colleagues in the published papers, but I add their names briefly here to highlight their importance, and I add the names of others for whom I wrote shorter pieces, which are not included, but whose reactions also provoked new thought.

I wrote " 'Toiling Ingenuity,' " in part 1, "Foundations," at the invitation of Ashraf Ghani, then at Johns Hopkins University, and it benefits from a previous paper (published in 1994) that I wrote for a conference organized by John Harbeson, Don Rothchild, and Naomi Chazan, on civil society in Africa. I wrote " 'The Craving for Intelligibility,' " included in part 2, "Public Economic Cultures," for a conference organized by Stephen Gudeman. I co-organized the newspaper archive on which it is based with LaRay Denzer, who collected its materials in Nigeria, along with students at the University of Ibadan, in particular Olatunji Ojo and Wale Adebanwi. I originally presented "Prophecy and the Near Future" as an invited lecture for the meetings of the American Ethnological Society in 2005, with particular instigation from Ida Susser, and then *Current Anthropology* published it as a forum. I thank those who responded to the paper. "From Market to Platform," the draft of chapter 5, was written at the invitation of Ariel Wilkis and Alexandre Roig, for a conference held in Buenos Aires in 2012. It was helpfully critiqued by Bruno Théret.

In part 3, "Cultures of Calculation," the paper on ordinality, "The Eruption of Tradition?," was first germinated by issues raised in my work in Africa, then was enabled by my collaboration with Naveeda Khan and Juan Obarrio, and eventually all the other contributors to the workshop and the publication "Number as Inventive Frontier," which was financed by grants from the National Science Foundation and the Wenner-Gren Foundation. For the paper "Percentages and Perchance," I am indebted for their invitation, interaction, and editing to Celia Lury, Sophie Day, and Nina Wakeford, at their conference "Materializing Number through Measure: Sensing, Knowing and Participating." Helen Verran, who attended the conference, critiqued the paper and has been an ongoing inspiration for many years.

I originally planned to start part 4, "Platforms," with a paper written for a panel called "Temporalities of Rationality," which included John Comaroff and Sally Falk Moore as panelists, for the annual meeting of the American Anthropological Association in 2001. Although I now include only a summary of this paper, in "The Themes of Legacies, Logics, Logistics," I thank these colleagues for their engagement. I wrote "Intricacy and Impasse" as a lecture by invitation from members of the Department of Anthropology, Indiana University, whose reactions are reflected in the final version. The paper on the consumer price index (CPI), "Indexing People to Money," owes its very existence to the challenge given by Keith Hart, longtime colleague and inspiration, for a conference on the human economy. It further benefited from adaptation and extension for a lecture at the biannual meeting of the International Market Studies Workshop in 2014, from interaction with the other participants, from help with French sources from Alexandre Mallard, from discussion about economic history with Angus Burgin, and from a further instigation by Keith Hart to contribute to a discussion of Thomas Piketty's book.

In the fifth and final part, "Toward Ethnography and the People's Economies," it was a conference organized by Keith Hart and Chris Hann, on Karl Polanyi, that provoked the writing of the paper on the ethnography of price, "Composites, Fictions, and Risk," and my experience on a World Bank oil project that made the oil economy accessible and stimulating, along with ongoing discussion with colleagues in Nigerian studies, particularly LaRay Denzer and Michael Watts. The final paper, "Is the 'Real Economy' Disaggregating, Disappearing, or Deviating?," grows out of discussions with Federico Neiburg, Ariel Wilkis, and Alexandre Roig, and benefits from exchanges with Michel Callon, Vincent Lepinay, and in several different contexts, with Horacio Ortiz. Also Beatrice Hibou and Laurence Fontaine. One section of that paper derives from work done for an invited presentation to a meeting of the group on "Monetary Plurality as the Normal State of Money," based in Paris and led by Jérome Blanc. Without these invitations, collaborations, and conversations none of these papers would have been written at all, or certainly reached their current form.

Other people from whom I have learned a great deal, over time, include: Hirokazu Miyazaki (and his meeting "Hope in the Economy"); Anneliese Riles; Bill Maurer (and my attendance at events at the Institute for Money,

Technology and Financial Inclusion); Katie Eagleton, then at the British Museum, for several meetings about African currencies; Max Bolt, Karen Sykes, and Chris Gregory, at Birmingham University and Manchester University; the Cultures of Finance group, with Arjun Appadurai, Ben Lee, and others at New York University. Akinobu Kuroda drew me into the international networks on multiple currency economies.

Other very long-term colleagues and friends have shaped many of these thoughts: Pauline Peters, with whom I worked on households in Africa over thirty years ago and whose work continues to inspire. Also Sara Berry and Paul Richards, and economists who have been willing to engage, such as Chris Udry. New colleagues and students at Johns Hopkins University have been important, opening new doors. Angus Burgin guided me to the new publications on the economic history of the twentieth century.

The introductory chapter, "The Themes of Legacies, Logics, Logistics," reflects all these inspirations, and more, woven together in ways that are no longer extricable. The one task that one particular person took up was a critique of the first draft. Caitlin Zaloom offered to read it and sent acute suggestions, from which I benefited a great deal.

David Brent, at the University of Chicago Press, encouraged a first submission of the whole collection, which two anonymous reviewers generously engaged, with helpful critical comments.

In expressing my gratitude to these people, I am "cutting a network" (to quote Marilyn Strathern) that leads ever outward to include many others, in fields and conversations that have overlapped many times, with enormously important influence. Those other influences were simply more indirect for these particular papers. My colleagues and students at Harvard University, Boston University, Northwestern University, and Johns Hopkins University, and in Africa, have been a source of ideas during my tenure on their faculties. My husband, Bernard Guyer, has been an ongoing stalwart presence in my life and career for far longer than the years it took to write these papers.

I am grateful to Cambridge University Press and Berghahn Books for permission to include papers that are already in print, and to the Peabody Museum at Harvard University for permission to reproduce the photographs in chapter 11.

The clarity of the text benefits from the careful formatting by Meg Wallace and editing by Jennifer Rappaport.

PART ONE

Foundations

ONE

The Themes of Legacies, Logics, Logistics

As the financial crisis of 2008 set it, the *Economist* published a brilliant cartoon on its cover, under the title "Redesigning Global Finance."[1] It depicts global finance as an intricate, and leaky, Heath Robinson or Rube Goldberg type of machine, complete with bellows, hammers, pulleys, candles, boilers, drive belts, and four tiny human attendants in lab coats with national flags on their backs, who are trying, with hectic gestures, to keep it synchronized and generally under control. And there are two other creatures: a pig, also in a lab coat, and a scientist with the American flag on his back. They are scrutinizing what looks like a very sketchy blueprint for the machine. The human-pig appears to be pointing out the place in the plan to which the American should devote attention. The whole thing is directionless, in that the mechanism simply drives a globe of the world up and down, again and again, on a kind of roller-coaster track. A boiler is labeled WTO. Some kind of large monitor box is labeled Bretton Woods. At the bottom, a spring propulsion lever, positioned for sending the globe back up again, is labeled IMF. And a small bucket-like container in the middle is full of banknotes which seem to be flying in from behind the Bretton Woods monitor box, but then just piling up, unattended by anyone.

Even in the centers of the economic public sphere, then, "the financial economy" was no longer being represented as a market, and its trajectory was not one of growth, although it was still a system, of sorts. But then there were no beneficiaries of this circuit, no indication of the rapidly differentiating situations of different populations, and as yet no obvious way in which the whole thing might just collapse into a useless and irreparable heap of junk. Both of these possibilities, growth with differentiation and collapse, were certainly intimated already by then, but the detailed works on differentiation in the age of finance capital (Stein 2010; Piketty

2014) and those envisaging possible imminent collapse (Harvey 2014; Amin 2011; Wallerstein et al. 2013) were mainly published subsequently. There was no "logic of capitalism" depicted here in the cartoon. It simply depicted a contraption from the first machine age, with inexpert experts trying to put out fires (Germany), fix gauges (France), and hammer an improbable-looking mechanism to start the ball—the globe—rolling (Japan). The whole globe was on the same roller coaster, rising and falling and stalling, as one.

The idea of a concatenation of "parts and labor," to take a craft image I will draw on later, is appealing, but the imagery has to be taken out of the realm of the ridiculous, the partisan, and the technologies of the first machine age. The advantage is that the image creates a space for imagining another, more workable, image for those of us who keep a focus precisely on parts, labor, and craftsmanship, but who also retain attention to the historical nature of the architectures, the central importance of differential access and control to both the structure and its outputs, the possibilities of localized chipping away and undermining rather than comprehensive collapse, and the need for an imagery better suited to the third machine age. "The platform economy." This was the title of the paper I developed in 2012 for a conference in Buenos Aires, in part provoked precisely by this cartoon. Clearly there is a structure of some sort to the global economy, but built out of a vast variety of moving components, constantly tinkered with, diverted and mined for advantage in some places and shored up against erosion in others. A platform can be a highly technical framework that can support many specific applications (but perhaps not all, or not at the same time); a stage for amplification of some voices and presences over others; a focus of close collective access and attention, by everyone; a way of enabling specific owners and engineers to reorient it for new purposes; and a place for announcing originality. And the platform as an image also evokes an architectural structure in the most literal sense: vulnerable to heedless neglect of the need for repair or updating; weakened by zealous hacking into its foundations and pillars; open to renovation and embellishment; and inviting to those finding advantage in perceiving it under the rubric of a commons, as this was depicted in Hardin's "tragedy of the commons" (1968) view: willing to divert apparently (to them) underused properties, in their own interests, for their own benefit. It could also be seen in terms of different localized structures, or with each one as part of a vast and interconnected network, each with its own platform qualities, especially in the globalized and Internet age. The historical fact is that many of the "parts" of our current economic platform(s) have endured for a very long time.

The recombinatory rebuilding and reconnecting process has involved the kind of tragedy, occasional insurgent improvement, and moments of demonstrative occupation that Hardin depicted for the medieval commons, where different groups inhabit it in their own way, and, in historically changing circumstances, sideline the access avenues, block or open up specific benefit routes, repair and restore, privatize, and so on.

A platform imagery also allows the notion that a particular performance or event in time depends on those past resources and successive occupations and is always one among several possible ones, on that particular grounding at that particular time. Which exact set of pulleys and levers will be mobilized, with what immediate effects and reparable retrievals from clumsy incompetence or deliberate sabotage, depends on which exact version of *A Night at the Opera* is occupying it, with which players. The structure, however, with all its pulleys and players, must be in the picture, somehow. Like any son et lumière act, it is powered through circuits of energy: in this case, by money. So a platform, as an image, may be hokey in its own way, but it necessarily draws attention to its own historical, structural, and variable properties. It is very basic in its fundamentals, highly adaptable in its components and capacities, and cannot be studied without all of its craftsmen, inhabitants, users, and viewers. I take up the analysis further in chapter 5, "From Market to Platform," but I introduce it here to indicate how some of the components of the argument that I draw out of these papers now fit together, retrospectively, as persuasive imagery as well as an eventual theoretical impulse toward detailed ethnographic research into specificities of current political economy and enactments in the formal sector; broad interdisciplinary engagement; and an open horizon, but not an ungrounded sense of orientation, toward the future, both in the world and in the discipline.

Many other colleagues in economic anthropology have been describing the novel component parts of this architecture and the applications they make possible: Maurer on mobile moneys (2012a) and "the payment space" (2012b); Hart on money in all its varieties (the MITMOWS network);[2] Graeber (2011) on the range of relationships implicated in what has become the ramifying field of debt (Han 2012, for a case study); in the expanding anthropology of finance, Zaloom (2010), Miyazaki (2013), Riles (2011), Lepinay (2011), and Ortiz (2014). And many others. Looking back over the themes in my series of papers on the West, collected for the first time here, I see that their own central concern has been with existing specific architectures, their inhabitation and retooling, and with our disciplinary methods for cultivating a close focus on striking phenomena, personnel and locations *within* this architecture, and its repertoire of operations. Hence the book's title, which focuses on moving parts: there are *legacy* components, brought forward by reprise or simply immovably present; *logics*, put forward theoretically and ideologically about the workings of the whole, but also, particularly importantly for us in anthropology, locking entailments together even in very small parts; and the *logistics* of making it work at all, in life, day-to-day, with or without blueprints, master scores, open access to the energy sources, and human or nonhuman guides. I have found these concepts parsimonious enough to be productive to think with, separately and together, in the concatenated relationships within and between different "devices" in platforms, and in their varied tensions in lived lives, under turbulent, and also slowly reshaping, conditions that encompass the situations and imaginations of ordinary people, at every level: from experts to all others.

This framing also allows me to engage theoretically with perhaps the most prominently novel approach in recent economic anthropology, namely the Actor Network Theory (ANT) group on economics, broadly taken, which has been pioneered by Michel Callon, who has also engaged analytically with my Africa work. As in my own work, the "composition" of "elements" is one key theme for the members of this group. For them, composition creates assemblages: a term they take from Gilles Deleuze and Bruno Latour. For myself, there are advantages to the approach, and at the same time there remain questions and lacunae, which I discuss later. My recent interactions with members of this group and my recently expanded knowledge of their work can explain the prominence that I give to their work in two sections: at the end of this chapter and at the end of chapter 12. None of the papers was engaged directly with this school of research at the time, although its initiatives were increasingly in the air over the period they were written and I brought out a possible engagement with their work in a precursor (Guyer 2007a) to the paper included here on ordinality. I argued there that the hybridity of modernity had been its normal condition in Africa, thanks to mercantilism and colonialism. My focus on ranking scales, their cultural-ideological bases, and the asymmetries at monetary interfaces provoked by, and rippling outward from, the "modern"/"traditional" interface might then be more pervasively relevant to the present phase of capitalism. This applies particularly to the "legacy" component of compositional dynamics. The political economy, social anthropology, Africanist, and people's history perspective from which I come, and which is explained in the next section, informs this engagement, in

ways that I hope can be analytically productive through identifying consonances, dissonances, and differences of emphasis and lacunae.

To pull these disparately written papers together, I offer here three
frames for the reader's connection to them: first, a "life and times" biography of the circumstances in which they were written; then the rationale
for their thematic organization here; and finally some particular theoretical engagements that arise. This last theme is picked up again at the end
of the collection, so in a sense the last section of this chapter and the last
section of chapter 12 could be read as a single argument. In my own situational and responsive style of thinking with respect to topics that do not
arise from my own research project, from which these papers result, the
two parts are best kept within the context that provoked them, which threw
specific aspects into relief. The reader can splice them together, as needed.

The next section is a chronological account, over almost twenty-five
years; the following section profiles the themes of the papers and their
grouping in the collection; the final section is analytical and theoretical.

Life and Times

I start from a rather full intellectual-biographical profile, since this alone
explains the sequence of the papers, the variety of topics, and their cumulative momentum. As I was writing these papers, my field and historical
research were still focused on Nigeria and Cameroon, while several other
professional commitments drew me increasingly into much broader arenas,
from about 1980 onward. So these papers on Western economic dynamics all arose from my own disciplinary and temperamental/experiential response to the world: both the intellectual world and the "world out there,"
in changing interaction with them over a particularly intense period of
global economic history. The period they cover saw the growing prominence of the policies generally grouped under the heading of "neoliberalism." This move toward applying theories of open markets and international trade to the entire world was initiated by policies of the international
financial institutions around 1980, as structural adjustment, and applied at
large to what was then still the "third world." These were the places where
much economic anthropological research—including my own restudy
of an urban hinterland over the twenty years from 1968 to 1988 (Guyer
1997)—was still undertaken. Many of us had already been drawn deeply
into oral historical, archival, and ethnographic-historical study by current theories of colonialism, especially for places and themes where the

necessary empirical work had not yet been undertaken. The neo-Marxist concept of the articulation of modes of production (Foster-Carter 1978) demanded deep immersion in the actual devices and processes by which articulation was crafted, maintained, and transitioned from one mode to another. The imagery of "articulation" could be taken as organic, mechanical, or expressive-performative, but the theory always assumed, foundationally, that differential political and social control of the elements, and of the processes of composition, would never be irrelevant to their mix and their application. My own first journal publication (Guyer 1978) was on the colonial history of food supply to the capital city of Cameroon, since, without this, no ethnographically based account and interpretation of the current food system seemed plausible to undertake. This then informed our edited collection of regional case studies of African urban food supply (Guyer 1987).

Expanding the scope of historical and political dynamics, in addition to ethnography, during the policy shifts of the 1980s, was a simple logical step, after the decline in the structuralism of the basic theory, by straightforward conviction of the importance of the empirical as a source of inspiration. The policy shifts of the 1980s, and their effects in local arenas, brought contemporary world economic dynamics yet more broadly and forcefully within the range of public attention. I brought into the response papers in this era a similar empirical sensibility and commitment to engaging with experience on the ground as anthropological training and practice had already instilled. Kathryn Barrett-Gaines (2004) entitled her introduction to a collection of historical essays taking off from my ethnographic book *An African Niche Economy* (1997), "A Keener Look at the Evidence." This has been exactly my orientation, and also my hope for the promotion of grounded analytical and theoretical engagement with others.

After 1989 and the dissolution of the "second world" as another system altogether, and then particularly in the twenty-first century, the political-economic philosophy of neoliberalism became more clearly enunciated for the "first world" as well as the rest, within an integrated theory of global markets. At each juncture, for those of us working back and forth between theory and evidence in European and African history and ethnography, emergent points of similarity and difference necessarily provoked our minds and opened up pathways from puzzlement to investigation of all kinds of relevant materials in domains that were relatively new to anthropology, such as macroeconomic debates in the public arena, government administration, and taxation, and formalized activities in new markets (such as currency exchange rates). Our early training in Bronislaw Malinowski's ethnography urged us to notice "inponderabilia of actual life," which now emerged at all interfaces between the people and an opaque and powerful formal sector, and kept our perceptions permanently open to a quality that I recently depicted by using Nigerian novelist Ben Okri's concept of "the quickening of the unknown" (Guyer 2013b).

In this context for my own work, then, when a situational request for my participation was made, I could use it as an opportunity to dig more deeply into a question or anomaly that I had archived in my mind, where the topic was compelling but my current state of knowledge was either thin or incidental. New books and collegial engagements also opened up new pathways and offered comprehensive new resources. Most recently, and not included here, the prominence of a new concept or reality—such as the expansion of "debt"—took me back to the classics (such as Marcel Mauss's *Essay on the Gift* [1925 in French; 1950 in first English translation]) and into new compendia (David Graeber's *Debt: The First Five Thousand Years* [2011], and Richard Hyland's *Gifts: A Study in Comparative Law* [2009]) (Guyer 2012c). The widening vista of my colleague in West African economic studies, Keith Hart, from informal economy to the study of money in general, and in particular his article "Two Sides of the Coin" (1986) and book *The Memory Bank* (2000), created momentum to go further into West African monies, which necessarily works back into the history of Western money and its transactional institutions more broadly. The monies of the slave trade have been discussed in my book *Marginal Gains*, but the place of the monetary *concepts* of the slave trade in Western history is a new topic I have engaged with, in the same call-and-response mode as the present papers, with colleagues I met through the efforts of Akinobu Kuroda on multiple currency systems, particularly in France (Guyer 2013a). I have folded some findings from this paper into the new one written for this volume, on the "real economy."

Several of the general points about compositions, which I would now emphasize, were already explicit in the first article included here, entitled " 'Toiling Ingenuity': Food Regulation in Britain and Nigeria" (1993). Little cited though it is, this paper remains a deeply meaningful piece to me, so I profile the elements that now seem embryonic, in retrospect, of my subsequent work in the present vein. " 'Toiling Ingenuity' " was written for a workshop called "The Politics of Consumption" in 1991, picking up on a provocation that arose while I was working for an earlier conference, organized by political scientists on civil society (Guyer 1994). In the sources on the Manufacturers Organization of Nigeria during the period of mandated indigenization of businesses, I had run across the puzzling and very contentious concept of "essential commodities." It turned out to be a construct created in wartime Britain, then exported to the colonies. Further exploration then became deeply personally meaningful, since I could use the occasion to draw British and Nigerian history together. I had grown up on postwar rationing and have vivid memories of shopping with a ration book in one hand, money in the other, and parental instructions to be very respectful to the neighborhood shopkeepers, on whose skill in managing both goods and customers we all depended. I remember their names: Mrs. Shuttleworth and Mr. Evans. I still have my last ration book in my possession, saved for me by my parents, and remember my visceral disbelief, as an undergraduate, when taught that the free market was somehow "natural." Premonitions, perhaps of the performativity of economic theory, and the collection entitled *Do Economists Make Markets?* (MacKenzie, F. Muniesa, and Sui 2007). Of course they do. But equally self-evidently, not alone. They began to do so in the enormously theoretically contentious ways identified by Burgin (2012) for the post-1918 period, in the context of European war and depression, and again after rationing. And national markets were "made" well before the twentieth century, as the detailed historical work of Laurence Fontaine (2014) on the "conquest" of the market brings to the fore. For an ordinary child of a rationing regime, like me, the fact of intricately local calendrical, calculative, and interpersonal conventions in marketing in Nigeria in the 1960s, in this case beyond direct state control, seemed much more familiar in its localized relationships than the impersonal market of Paul Samuelson's (1948) *Economics* textbook. Even Samuelson's imagery was an exotic performance, to me. I remember either the book, or a teacher, comparing market equilibrium to the movement of an olive in a martini glass!

At the time of writing this first paper, alongside the necessary reading in the official histories of the war and in colonial policy, I was able to draw on several recent initiatives in anthropology's expanding engagement with history, and with anthropologists' own growing concern about structuralism of all kinds. The 1980s had been particularly active in these domains. I could use works such as Appadurai's (1990) seminal paper on disjuncture in the neoliberal world, along with Cooper and Stoler's (1989) article on "tensions of empire." On food in history, Sidney Mintz's *Sweetness and Power* (1985) exemplified the creation and cultivation of global chains of commodities, currencies, and control systems, in their manufactured concatenations across the material-social spectrum. The idea that "tradition" could be "invented," as well as drawn forward from the past, had been launched by Hobsbawm and Ranger (1983). Also important as resources at that time, and referenced in the paper, were scalar nesting processes that could be addressed using Sally Falk Moore's (1986) concept of the "pyramiding" of organizational forms, developed within her expanded work on indeterminacy; John Comaroff and Simon Roberts's work on "rules and processes" (Comaroff and Roberts 1981); and Eric Wolf's "multiform plural" of social patterns "built up out of manifold elements" (1988, 758–59), in his work on "multiplicity" in "inventing society." My paper was defined as an attempt to take on Wolf's advocacy of anthropology's struggle "to free itself from theories of coherence and consensus," by "taking an ethnographic approach to modern governmental forms of multiplicity" (Guyer 1993a, 798). These scholars were already breaking out of holism, without, however, abandoning all reference to structures of power.

I was able to see the process that Wolf defined as "invention" as "toiling ingenuity" by simply taking a concept from the official history of British food control during World War I. It had been used by Lord Beveridge in his moving depiction of what remained of that system at the end of the war: "so many forms and circulars . . . instructions," and the records of a whole administrative nexus, which remained as "monuments of toiling ingenuity," and which he hoped would "lie mouldering gently into dust and oblivion—lie buried, please God for ever"; "little if anything learned in them can be of use again, save in a civilization bent again on self-destruction" (1928, 344). And yet they were used again, rethought and retooled repeatedly, in different times and places, as an archive for selective and enhanced reprise. This concept of "toiling ingenuity" contained embedded implications that went beyond the current more broadly inclusive concepts of "creative invention" and "performativity," which seem, in their present use, to invoke immediacy and openly invite frontiers of possibility. Beveridge's term combined exacting and repetitive work ("toil"), intelligence ("ingenuity")—in the context of compelling purpose (the defense of the home front in wartime), high stakes (a world war, and all the attendant dangers), and realization that the archive of this particular endeavor would remain, and either molder or get mobilized, depending on subsequent events. That combination was particularly powerful for the historical instances of the world wars. Its implications, however, have remained convincing foci of attention for me, even with respect to much smaller phenomena, in that—alongside the orientations already depicted—it compels me to look in detail at the work, the intelligence, the purpose, the stakes, and the longer entailments in all constructs or assemblages that shape definitions and distributions in economic life. And the case itself demands the suspension of any immediate ethical-critical stance, until these components have been excavated and assessed. My paper notes, for example, that war rationing fed the people while also enormously favoring the further entrenchment of the corporate sector in the food industry. If we were to critique this productively, to encourage subsequent awareness, we would need to know exactly how that was accomplished and with what constructs that may still lie buried in the archive, awaiting curatorial attention and selective redeployment.

The particular question became how the concept, as well as the practice of, "essential commodities," developed for food rationing in Britain during World War II, was, in fact, dusted off, redeployed, and morphed, as it moved to colonial and postcolonial Nigeria. There it became the focus of many confrontations, finally resulting in a dramatic episode in 1984, which was reported worldwide. The full repertoire of centuries of food regulation regimes in Britain was clearly a powerful archival legacy, each concept bringing its own sets of assumptions, experiences, regimes of implementation but also gaps in zones of application (depending on the exact food regime of the people targeted) and flexibilities for adaptation that could lend themselves to the creation of loopholes for manipulation (at all stages of the trade, including by British merchants; see Falola 1989).

The elements of that initial "toiling ingenuity" were combined "explicitly envisaging a connection between dimensions that were intimate and traditional, those that were technical and inventive and those that were political and unprecedented" (Guyer 1993a, 800). As a result, I noted, "politically motivated arguments were . . . openly contradictory and complicated." In the analysis, I draw out that the selectivity among the elements for policy was clearly shaped by "contentious dynamics in the international political economy." I identify three successive ideological models of the place of government in the food system of the population and note the potential for their partial replacement and the resulting incoherence: "Traditions are invented or selectively retrieved as a way of identifying constituencies or lobbies" (Guyer 1993a, 811) in a new framework that replaces the previous one. The last sentence of the paper plants a concern that we scholars may be implicitly conveying sectional interests if we do not pay sufficient attention to exactly how these political processes in the creation and deployment, across time and space, of what would now be termed assemblages or devices are constructed: in relation to which enduring frameworks of power and ideology, requiring what use of established platforms, and with what implications for populations.

"Essential commodities" is a small and defined topic on which to focus, given the magnitudes of economic theory and policy. Several of my other topics are just as small and defined, although the realities in which they partake may be vast. The topical focus may be somewhat similar in formal terms to the experimental cases now undertaken within assemblage and financial theory. Each of my own cases, however, speaks within the intellectual engagements of the time, in its own voice of that time. For example, coming from the inspirations of historical-political anthropology and the startling puzzles of the world in the 1980s, I found a powerful image in the historical-political processes of Equatorial Africa. Although this paper on difference, multiplicity, and the composition of "wealth in people as wealth in knowledge" (Guyer and Eno Belinga 1995) did not concern the modern formal sector, the example was very graphic: of situational composition, where elements could be disaggregated and then reaggregated according to need and purpose, which then included dynamics both for mobilization in action and for the cultivation of skill and difference during labile inactive phases, as I studied in papers on "self-realization" (Guyer 1994) and, much later, on personal "enhancement" (Guyer 2012a). The processes of this kind of composition remained in my mind to apply to other dynamics, if we are thinking in terms of repertoires of elements, of different kinds, that are created, archived, and mobilized for eventual combination. The question of the political processes brought out in "toiling ingenuity" then refers not only to putting elements into action but to dismantling the assemblage during quiescence, while still curating elements to be available for subsequent occasions, however complex that activity may be.

Following this conceptual train of thought linking anthropological history and political economy can then lead into a further aspect in this "life and times" section, in a biographical mode. Several of these papers are explicitly provoked by African stimuli, even where the eventual focus is not Africa. Probably the most prominent is the paper "Prophecy and the Near Future" (Guyer 2007b), where my long exposure to the rhetoric of structural adjustment in Africa made the monetarist rhetoric of the early 2000s, in our own economies, both familiar and puzzling. What makes the immediate and the distant future plausible as the main frameworks for prospective thought, for whole populations? It returned me to the question of "the craving for intelligibility" raised by Hayek in 1944 (p. 204), so also in wartime, which LaRay Denzer and I had addressed in our paper on Nigeria's trajectory of public discussion of the economy between the early 1980s and the mid-1990s: from public debate about terms, to nationalist invocations of unity, to "cacophony and silence" (Guyer and Denzer 2009). The convoluted and frustrating experience of the Nigerian people, so graphically expressed by the newspaper cartoons, then posed the general question of how a willingness to "submit to markets" could be fostered in *any* population.

Likewise, the chronologically first of the new phase in this series of papers, "The Life Cycle as a Rational Proposition" (Guyer 2001), emerged from my attention to household studies in Africa and a classic source on peasant Russia: the developmental cycle in domestic groups (Goody 1962), which was argued to depend on sociopolitical structures (in African societies); the domestic demographic cycle of dependency (Chayanov 1966), which depended on the stability of household membership criteria over the generations and the social capacity to redistribute parcels of land (in precommunist Russia); and the finding from my own Ghanaian household budget reanalysis that personal social status and relationships along a "social gradient" seemed more strongly relevant to expenditure than either household size or social category (that is, income quintile) (Guyer 2004). By contrast, the modern theoretical-economic proposition of a life cycle of personal economy that was somehow natural and rational differed profoundly. Clearly it was a construct of a particular economic regime, which was then designing and installing a whole gamut of institutional initiatives, *as if* they reflected a natural arc of life or could realize a natural aspiration. It obviously took the toiling ingenuity of probably tens of thousands of policy makers, businesses, implementers, economists, insurance companies, civil servants, and so on, over decades, to realize. Equally clearly none of these arcs of life was more basically human than any other, although Sahlins (1972) did take the Russian Chayanov model, applied it to Africa, extended it to "stone age economics" in general, and argued it to be somehow closer to human origins than any other. Since I was working from Africa, this seemed as implausible a logic as that of the "rational proposition." And finally, African calculation, which I studied for *Marginal Gains*, placed calculation on the empirical radar screen for me in ways that are reflected in the two papers that address the theme of numbers. I do not include the paper on the life cycle as a rational proposition in this collection, since the topic is enormously complex and deserves more attention than I could give it for a conference presentation. But revisiting those economic models, from Franco Modigliani and Milton Friedman's Nobel Prize–winning work, was instructive and influential.

As a result of this strong "life and times" influence on their writing, each paper reflects the intellectual "mood" of an ongoing conversation: challenging, grateful, illuminating, committed, while also including phases of incomprehension, impatience, and disagreement. And also limitation. In each paper, in this kind of mode, one gets to a point of being confident in what these "inponderabilia" are *not*, but perhaps not yet exactly what they *are*, or are most likely to be productively analyzed *as*. A new pathway is opened up, rather than a whole field plotted out and defined. In now seeking out the intellectual commonalities and cumulative import among the papers, I obviously have a certain poststructuralist and empirical-exploratory intention that I inherited from intellectual strands coming to fruition in the anthropology of the 1980s, when we were moving beyond both "social structure" and "modes of production," while focusing on specific configurations that still had import in linking bottom-up and top-down trajectories, and which never left power out of the picture. Clearly this is where the concept of, and debate around, "assemblage" would be provocative: not only as a theoretical corpus about the currently complexified world, whose cases and arguments one can mine for analytics, but also as an epistemological position with respect to a critical reflexivity about the terms and locations of provisionality in argumentation, and how this relates, as intellectual input and output, to the way in which the indeterminate provisionality that "assemblage" presumes actually takes place in the world.

There is one last criterion to mention, as a final biographical source. This is social-economic history and more broadly historical method, as "people's history," or "history from below," with particular attentiveness to the life and livelihood of the common people within larger political-economic contexts. Wages. Work. Money. Modes of coordination. Concepts of wealth and value. And the enormous dislocations of recurrent war and disruptive policy change. The expectation that "people's history" will always be richer than is available in the written sources, along with the conviction that a topic of study has to matter in a life-logistical as well as a theoretical-demonstrative way, comes from "life and times" in the most literal genealogical and historical sense, and from training during the era of Eric Hobsbawm, E. P. Thompson, Fernand Braudel, Frantz Fanon, and the two novel initiatives in British Marxist scholarship that were gaining momentum in the 1960s: History Workshop (founded by a group of socialist and feminist historians) and the Birmingham School of Cultural Studies (founded by the Jamaican scholar Stuart Hall). Their influence here is particularly marked in my choice of topic, already present in "'Toiling Ingenuity'": the source of the provocation being somehow in the lives of the people, thus creating the imperative of attentiveness to the stakes at issue, the necessity of doing my own "toiling ingenuity" to develop the sources and skills to do some justice to them, and some humility about how far I have managed to go.

While deeply committed to hearing how "the subaltern speaks," as all of us must be in anthropology, when it comes to very complex dynamics on which I have no opportunity to be ethnographic in the field, I am on stronger ground to address terminologies, measures, devices, materials, and actions than to probe the much deeper cultural meanings that can only emerge clearly through language, music, religious thought and practice (including private prayer as well as collective ritual), art, and their interpenetration in all expressive forms. I necessarily have had to choose topics, then, on which there is considerable evidence to be found, from different angles and of different types, without ethnographic work of my own. This is where "logistics" become crucially important: the life experience of living within, and trying to make sense of, assemblages largely created by others. I have also fallen short of making general theoretical claims of a macro-order because of a conviction that our classical thinkers in this regard—Adam Smith, Karl Marx, A. V. Chayanov, and onward to many other figures across the whole spectrum of importance—have based and backed their claims on a formidable empirical scholarship. The alternative of developing arguments entirely from philosophical propositions was simply implausible for one not comprehensively trained in philosophy. So this "life and times" account explains the array of particular unconnected topics addressed in these papers, to show how they were all triangulated through political economy, people's history, ethnography, and Africa, and all engaged with compositional dynamics.

The Papers

The following groupings of the papers in this overall collection now seem persuasive, given the punctual contexts of their writing. Although most are focused on the West, or general questions, I have kept two papers that address Africa as the central focus, as a way to not only reflect the intellectual stimulation mentioned above, but also to indicate specific connections made between national "platforms" in the globalizing economy. These connections are the tailoring of a common economic ideology to different places and populations, under the auspices of the International Financial Institutions (" 'The Craving for Intelligibility' "); and the implications of the international currency market after the abandonment of Bretton Woods in the 1970s ("Intricacy and Impasse"). " 'Toiling Ingenuity' " is explicitly focused on the passage of a device from Britain to Nigeria. Then African examples are used at the end of "From Market to Platform" and of "Indexing People to Money" to trace out implications that go beyond direct connections.

Public Economic Cultures

The papers grouped in part 2, "Public Economic Cultures," address economic theory, but mainly in its public guise. The intricacies of particular theoretical debates were not the sources that generated these response papers. While the ANT and performativity schools of thought have made the link between models and the enactment of the economy, or preferably, the process of economization (Çalişkan and Callon 2009, 2010), the papers in this group were focused, at the time, on a classic anthropological issue, which can be inferred from Hayek's concept of "intelligibility": how plausibility is "craved" and created. The first explores the different successive framings of the rhetoric of economic "intelligibility" in Nigeria from the early 1980s to the mid-1990s, under the policies of structural adjustment that emanated from a market-based, monetarist theory of development. What did the government rhetoric and policy focus on? What was the public commentary about (as far as it could go, under military rule) and how did its engagement play out over time? Certain contested constructs, such as "subsidy," rose from the sources. This paper paved the way for a return to intelligibility, and to the ethnographic questions it raises about the "who," "what," and "how" of economic understanding by the different constituencies that make up a "public," anywhere and at any phase of history. For Hayek, the "craving for intelligibility" raised the danger of a particular constituency creating a specialist preserve from which to enact its own aspirations. "There are fields where the craving for intelligibility cannot be fully satisfied and where at the same time a refusal to submit to anything we cannot understand must lead to the destruction of our civilization. . . . The only alternative to submission . . . to the market is submission to . . . an equally uncontrollable and therefore arbitrary power of other men" ([1944] 2007, 211–12). An ideologically promoted transition, under the last thirty-five years of monetarist-leaning policy interventions, moved the concept of the market prominently toward a market in assets, so beyond the goods and services that undoubtedly Hayek had in mind. This then drew my attention back to the locus of intelligibility at home, and new configurations in the imagery of time and prediction and prophecy in rhetoric and in public religious culture, and to what seemed to be a specific new *gap*: an approach to the "near future" that reduced it to calendrical and punctuated time.

The most recent paper in this series examines how economies are represented in the postcrisis period, since 2008. The concept of the platform economy arises from taking the ethnographic route into both the architectures of economies and public understanding, acceptance, and participation in them. Also arising, in particular spaces, are terms of resistance to rebuilding by others and perceptions of possible renovation, or as Harvey (2014) most recently put it, "revolutionary humanism." Hart, Laville, and Cattani (2010) advocate analysis in terms of a "human economy," which Hart carries forward into his work that envisages terms of public engagement on "the economy" in a more searching, ethnographically inclusive, comparative, and historical manner. Hart's argument has provoked several of the papers that culminate my collection. "Platform" has simply become a provocative image for keeping the current large architecture in the picture, as itself an assemblage of assemblages (as I discuss later), while entering the field from the vantage point of highly specific constructs within it.

Cultures of Calculation

The two papers in part 3, "Cultures of Calculation," grow from my Africa work, and from engagements that derive from the study of scales of value there. Helen Verran's (2001) ambitious theoretical work, which links the Western world of science to "an African logic," was a major provocation to go further, geographically, than her particular historical case, and collaboration with Naveeda Khan and Juan Obarrio (Guyer, Khan, and Obarrio 2010) provided the immediate stimulation and opportunity. To take on ordinality in our current value structures was an imperative that came from public life itself, at a time when CEO salaries were already becoming—a couple of years before the coining of "the 1% and the 99%"—a rising theme for concerned, if not scandalized, attention. The infusion of imagery that I saw there came from mythology and old traditions that were also on the rise in public entertainment and gaming culture. The "invention of tradition" concept could hardly do justice to the burgeoning of mythology of all kinds in the twenty-first century. Constructs of competitive ordinality, iconicity, and symbolic meaning were being created in all kinds of different contexts, which seemed mutually reinforcing. The conviction that this was a topic of enormous importance, which could be approached anthropologically, was then taken further on a different numerical concept, with its own long history, namely the percentage, and I examine its deployment in the present. It was through working on the sources that I apprehended the way in which the one hundred of the percentage began to stand in for "wholes" that were hardly imaginable in any other terms in a new age of uncertainty. These papers can connect to Callon's concept of *qualcul*: the combination of qualitative and quantitative measures and meanings.

Platform Economy

The concept of "platform" now seems, retrospectively, to work well in the title for part 4 as in the subtitle of the collection. It allows the macro-field to be in the analysis, as a replacement for the ideological "market economy" of neoliberalism, but without resort to its total denigration as a Heath Robinson contraption or a capitalist conspiracy (even though parts of it may best be interpreted, after empirical study, in comparable terms). Here, we can work with components and compositions, as assemblage theory does, without an implication of organic or mechanical completeness of the whole, but also without eliminating structure, power, and interdependence, including ongoing implications for the logistics of life. The platform imagery also has the great advantage for me that it allows us to see specific processes or acts of *de*struction as well as processes of *con*struction that are implied by assemblage theory and constructivism more broadly. As my "toiling ingenuity" topic taught me, there are destructs as well as constructs, and detritus, although these others have received considerably less theoretical attention than "construct," except in political-economic history.

I had originally intended to include here an unpublished paper written in 2001, entitled "The Life Cycle as a Rational Proposition," on the complex differences in economists' and anthropologists' approaches to life planning. Revisiting it, I realized that some analyses had already made their way into the chapter on household budgets in *Marginal Gains*, some is implicit in the paper on the consumer price index, and new work is being carried out on this topic, by Caitlin Zaloom. So I simply summarize the argument here, as a first illustration of the kind of construct that makes up the platform of the late twentieth-century economy and exemplifies the recurrent selective bricolage that keeps retooling it. The rational life cycle is as old a concept in economic thought as Thomas Malthus, who posited that, left to themselves, people lived for the moment, indulged in sex and indolence, multiplied out of proportion to resources, and succumbed to the lightning retribution of intermittent scourges. This fate could only be arrested by people's ability to "calculate distant consequences" (1992, 21). Thus did individual foresight's dependence on the predictability of conditions enter the sphere of economic thought. Rationality depended on order.

It is not until the unprecedented sustained economic growth after World

War II in the West that the life cycle became a fully developed rational economic model of the life course, formalized powerfully in economics in the mid-twentieth century. Milton Friedman (1957) developed the idea that households aim to smooth consumption, so that budgeting operates to produce that effect ("intertemporal utility maximization"). Modigliani's (1966) addition was to trace out characteristic savings patterns over the life cycle, in light of the permanent income hypothesis. In general, people dissaved in youth, saved in middle age, and dissaved again in old age. A vast public and private financial infrastructure of insurance, mortgages, student loans, retirement funds, and so on was built on these analyses, which then effectively tracked people into these channels and allowed their rationality to be deployed elsewhere, because of this platform, than in Malthusian struggles. My own adult life has been lived on this institutionalized platform: the theory of a cumulative career, family building, health insurance on a household-dependency model, retirement and pensions, and long-term mortgages. It is therefore, perhaps, the specter of its selective dismantlement and rebuilding in new ways for the next generation that further encourages the platform imagery. The theme of assemblage processes as creating selective "destructs" as well as "constructs" can be faced right here, in the now-presumed "natural" life course.

The papers I did include in this section bring gaps, loopholes, incoherence, and other "destructs" to the fore. The themes were not chosen for the purpose of representing this particular dynamic of economic process, but rather to respond to themes and events in the world. The invitation to write "Intricacy and Impasse" provoked a focus on a theme that inevitably runs through any work on African economies since the 1980s, namely the exchange rate for the national currencies in a newly created, and rapidly shifting, international currency market. With colleagues, I had coedited a collection on the popular responses to devaluation in Nigeria, entitled *Money Struggles and City Life* (Guyer, Denzer, and Agbaje 2002). The other paper in this section is the most recently written, indeed the only one rewritten for this collection. Head-on consideration of a major instrument of economic policy, in an anthropological way, was my response to Keith Hart's *Human Economy* project. I was invited to examine how humans were indexed to money, in some way. Having already worked on historical sources on poverty and demographic statistics in Britain, I thought the concepts that were brought to the consumer price index seemed a focused place to look. The CPI is an enormously intricate construct: created in the era of World War I (so alongside the livelihood depictions developed for food rationing); imposed worldwide under the International Labor Office/

International Monetary Fund regime of labor and economic reporting and governance in the postwar, postcolonial, and structural adjustment periods; placed under regular revision; and having implications across the board, from the calculation of trends in gross domestic product (GDP) to the adjustment of social payments in national systems. It is a much vaster topic than a paper can do justice to, but the detail of the record does allow the kind of empirical focus that ethnography demands. And here I was able to land on a topic both empirically accessible and illustrative of the destruct/construct process, over time, in a macro-context where household livelihood, national accounts, and international standing were all at stake.

Toward Ethnography and the People's Economies

The final section is more provocative of an ethnography for the future, in its classic sense of "being there," within the formalized economic world, than working in ethnographic *mode* from sources gathered from dispersed sources. The papers take single, crucial economic concepts—"price," "money," and the "real economy"—that are alluded to in all economic theory, over several centuries. What do they refer to now, and how are both ordinary people, and experts, understanding them? It was an uncanny finding, in the process of working on these papers, and another on the monies of the slave trade, that the "fictional" and the "imaginary" have been infused in the concept of the "real" for centuries. The price paper is a response to a workshop theme, on Polanyi's continuing relevance in general, and in my own case, to the creation of "fictitious commodities" in the present. The money paper is a summary of work on money, woven around my own trajectories, written to explain the anthropological approach to those outside the discipline. The "real economy" is a short, recent, programmatic piece that arises from the obvious slipperiness of the concept of "the real" in current life and thought. It links back to the history of the multiple currencies of Europe and outward to the place of this concept elsewhere in the world, as I have particularly discussed with Federico Neiburg. Since "the real," in relation to the economy, arises in economics as a discipline, in assemblage theory as a conceptual issue, and in conversation with colleagues in Latin America where economic crises are recurrent, it seems apposite to end the collection with this open frontier to both macro-theory and intricate experienced phenomena in the economic world.

As I have seen it, through the work for these papers on topics primarily in Western economies, which I have not been able to study in all the empirical detail they deserve, the study of the emergent global economy needs its many participants, with complementary expertise, localized experience, and the capacity to engage with each other. We are beginning to see this in economic anthropology, through the classic encompassing richness of the discipline itself, which now includes closely observed ethnographic expertise in areas that used to be off-limits: the financial sector, and government, the state, and the law (Riles 2006; Merry 2011, and other contributors to the *Current Anthropology* special edition on corporate lives; Partridge, Welker and Hardin 2011). These scholars' work, much more than my own, focuses closely enough on specific devices, in these powerful sectors, for the formal methodological and theoretical import to be transportable from one domain to another. In the more recent collaborative work (Callon, Lascoumes and Barthes 2009) of the ANT-Economics school, they advocate the importance of arenas where specialist and "wild" thought can interact. Reading this argument, I was reminded of a French colleague's comment that my own work was rather "sauvage." There is clearly potential in bringing the bricolage, in Lévi-Strauss's classic *The Savage Mind* (1966), into more explicit consideration, and into our own enactments.

What I will suggest that my own work can advocate, working from the various "elsewheres" that Mauss suggested as the necessary "points of departure" (1990, 56), is the compilation of the precision and methodological critique from the ANT-Economy group with other works and with suggestions that come from the present papers, for application to topics chosen precisely for their high stakes: in life and in theory. Laboratory-like instances may serve as grist for the precision of thought that philosophers and laboratory scientists depict in order to develop thought experiments. But all of my own paper topics were compelling for their own sakes, and other colleagues have taken on matters of yet more powerful import, such as detailed works on the place of concepts in African land law in the dynamics of dispossession (Peters 2013; Hammar 2014), and subsequent violence (Mokuwa et al. 2011). Asking why topics are compelling, and which terms to apply to their internal and external heterogeneity, would eventually return us to general theory of a more structural kind, and/or detailed historical framing. This orientation can be informed by Ben Fine's critique of Callon's making "a bonfire of macro-structures" (Fine 2003, 481), by focusing so closely on "the diverse bringing together of 'hybrids'" (Fine 2003, 479) that it results in systemic power being occluded rather than faced and combatted. Prospective theories that are implicit in the inclusive approaches of Maurer and Hart imply that new orders can be remade from below.

I remain convinced that much of our work in the new economic anthropology, from the vantage points of our different biographies and histories, can be compiled into theoretical and analytical conversations, as distinct from adversarial "debates" about positions, and that these can provoke novel configurative theoretical assemblages and trajectories for the future. Inevitably, all anthropological work is undergirded by some version of a theory of "form": whether terms, concepts, and "figures" that are repeated across contexts; practices that are recognizable, to both participants and observers, in different instances; institutions that remain stable over time; or complexes that can be compared across cases. As I will turn to next, it is the internal heterogeneity, external connectedness, provisionality, and lability of forms that assemblage theory brings to the fore. In my own work, as depicted in the previous playing out of "life and times," I treated all of the following in comparable terms: as internally composed of heterogeneous elements that were externally connected and labile in their combinatorial dynamics:

- "essential commodities" as a historical construct
- subsidy, temporal regimes, and imagery of "the economy," as created assemblages that themselves become components of a complex of economic "intelligibility"
- ordinality and percentage as calculative forms
- the "life cycle," the "currency market," and the CPI as fully established components of the formal economy
- "price," money, and "the real economy" as foundational and powerful concepts in the history of economic theory and practice, and in public culture, whose meanings and implications are shifting over time

What I had not yet done, until now, was think of all these instances, in a single frame, to extract the implications, for intellectual practice, of the landmarks I have depicted in "life and times" and the topics chosen and now grouped.

Complexity and Assemblages: My Own Framing

The final focus of this introduction to these papers' republication, together, is the potential for a more intense engagement between my own political-economic and historical-ethnographic approach to *specific phenomena* in our current economies, and the expanding economic work of Michel Callon, his colleagues and students, and others who are pursuing some version or another of assemblage and complexity theory. Callon himself has pointed out certain consonances in our approaches, although working from my engagements with Africa, namely in a series of generous personal communications and a published review (Callon 2008) of my book *Marginal Gains: Monetary Transactions in Atlantic Africa* (Guyer 2004). I have not yet responded in detail, although the development of this school of thought, alongside others, has doubtless been a growing influence within the crucible of discussion for which these papers were written. And certainly each paper does focus on the kind of specific phenomena that might otherwise be depicted as assemblages or devices, rather than primarily focus on macro-phenomena and general theory. If macro-dynamics come in, it is usually because the empirical topic leads me there. It remains, then, to tease out any cumulative ways in which these papers inform and offset each other with respect to general analytics and theory.

The poststructural focus on assemblages, derived from Deleuzian philosophy and Actor Network Theory's "disassembling the social," has some affinity with a major emphasis in the processual anthropology and political economic history that was informing my work on Africa from the beginning. Coming from the latter theoretical momentum, the key questions for me have revolved around how the phenomena to be placed under this kind of microscope are to be identified, accorded relative theoretical priority, described ethnographically, analyzed, and the results argued for as a contribution to theory and method with respect to the current world. The parallel that Michel Callon (2008) has seen between my own approach in *Marginal Gains*, devoted to African monetary history and practice, and that of the ANT-Economy group, can be examined retrospectively in relation to these papers about the West, providing the fulcrum to leverage my own thought onto a more defined general-conceptual level than any one of the papers aimed to achieve.

Some of the convergences seen by Callon and others, in the attention paid to specific phenomena as inventions, or constructs, or assemblages, doubtless result from the shared intellectual context of poststructuralism over the past thirty years. Where the ANT-Economy group parts company most obviously is in its own inheritance of science studies, where experiments can be contained within parameters and then treated as exemplary. "The market," as a shared topic for an insurgent scholarly innovation, was a brilliant move for taking on current economic theories of capitalism, and for incorporating work like my own that was about marketplaces on the margins of capitalism, while retaining the possibility for containment that comes from science studies. The ANT Economy group answers to the hegemonic pretensions of the neoclassical theory of the market, and its own form of holism, was to disassemble it, to undermine the assumptions about agency, and to break out of the modernism of binary distinctions. The financial world then offered a perfect domain for the ethnographic project on assemblages as themselves invented components, interacting with one another but not approached as an overarching configuration, beyond the ethnographic sites.

My own instances, however, come from the obstreperous world of enactment and composition in life-as-lived, where power is always actually or potentially at play. My analysis may be contained by focus and argument, but the topics themselves insist on their own parameters, which vary from one to another and manifestly lead further outward and inward, beyond what I could include in any single paper. New participants can suddenly emerge or equally suddenly be silenced. There can be no possible ceteris paribus here.

To focus my theoretical and analytical points, I draw first from Callon's (2008) appreciative and also critical review of *Marginal Gains*. He endorsed the orientation and findings in these terms: "My commentaries and reflections (focus) around a small number of concepts that JG proposes in order to take account of the transactions she is studying. These tools, I am persuaded, will be useful, and soon indispensable, for all those who are interested in markets" (2008, 1), since they "apply perfectly, it seems to me, to western economies themselves. Their context is even more fragmented, divided, dislocated than that of the economies of West Africa. Not only are disjunctures already omnipresent there, but their number and diversity are only growing, with the centrality of innovative activities and the growing role of financial speculation" (2008, 5–6). These key concepts are disjuncture, conversion, the multiplicity of value scales—in my own case nominal, ordinal and numerical—that are brought together in what he eventually calls *qualcul*, and tropic points at which such connections are most smoothly facilitated.

In criticism, Callon focused on the chapter on institutions, which he argued—also invoking Roitman (2005)—was misleading since it brought back the dualist thinking of formal and informal, which the rest of the book was undoing. Better, he suggested to profile another term for certain "forms" that I had used, namely "formulae," which could be pluralized in any way. This is interesting for two reasons. First, using *new* terms obviates the labor of dismantling the nexus in which a particular term, such as institution, is already embedded, as I had to do in order to be minimally precise about my own usage. And it also avoids the confusion of *not* dismantling it explicitly, thus dragging the whole aura of the old theoretical nexus into the new analysis. But secondly, and more importantly for moving forward here, it suggests that "assemblage," for Callon, is a category title, for which there may be many kinds or instances that are better analyzed under terms such as "formula."

This seems to me the clear frontier for thought, within an eclectic series of efforts to disassemble the old "social" in social theory, while also "reassembling" something in its place (Latour 2005). As DeLanda (2006) points out, Deleuze did not develop a fully defined theory of assemblage, and the idea itself would defy the bounding of forms by precise and authoritative criteria. And he suggests why it is that "elements" may not be precisely depicted: this would risk the essentialism that the whole endeavor is trying to escape, so that analysis can be in terms that go "beyond logic and involve causal intervention in reality" (DeLanda 2006, 31), and toward "possibility" rather than definition and constraint. It seems, though, that with this approach we meet assemblages "all the way down," so we would need an approach to *elements* as they present at the moment, and in the space (to use DeLanda's two key coordinates), at which they emerge for framing into an assemblage.

In this context, I find the ANT school, more broadly, most creative with respect to depicting relationships in the process of composition and *within* them, once composed. Callon himself argues for the term *agencement* as depicting "configurations that mix and imbricate textual elements, materials, forms of emotion, instruments . . . at different levels (micro and macro) as well as the links between these levels. They can be analyzed in terms of *path dependence* (*lock-in* and *lock-out*)" (Personal communication 2009). In the same note, he expresses no deep investment in one term or another, and certainly other terms have been used in this literature: entanglement, device, and, of course, assemblage itself, are widely used for what would otherwise be seen as an eclectic variety of phenomena. For example, William Connolly, in his recent book *The Fragility of Things* (2013), uses the term to designate the qualities of the writing itself, where the argument is neither a tight system of propositions and derivations, nor a dialectic, but "an assemblage of elements that lean on and infuse each other" (12), that express the nature of the subject matter, where "political economy is a moving assemblage . . . marked by loose joints, disparate edges, redundant noises and some-what open possibilities" (13). Here there are "bumpiness and frictions by which the open subsystems in which we participate are consolidated into larger assemblages with their own bumps, uncertainties, sharp edges, and fragilities" (19). The concept clearly fits many apprehensions of the present world, where one can see how implicitly varied the elements, external connections, internal "consolidations," and enduring processes through time, are taken to be.

Other scholars have found other terms for compositional processes and products, several of them coming from art and artisanship: refrain, code, resonance, entanglement. Even without precise definition, the theorists in this school have used such terms not only to depict the world as we experience it, but also to move past what Latour (2012) sees as the classic, and constantly deployed, mistakes of the "moderns," that have been assiduously cultivated in science and philosophy. The most important of these are the division between objective and subjective, society and nature, real and imaginary, the tendency to binary thought in general, and the assumptions about agency that are contained in theories of ontology. Ethnography, and more broadly the whole discipline of anthropology, are part of the method for breaking out. In his review article, John Law puts it thus: "The metaphor of construction—and social construction—will no longer serve. Buyers, sellers, noticeboards, strawberries, spatial arrangements, economic theories, and rules of conduct—all of these assemble and together enact a set of practices that make a more or less precarious reality" (2009, 151). For a domain such as economics and economic theory, permeated by presumptions about one preeminent ontological being that reasons, decides, and acts, but in an increasingly uncertain world, the imperative to grow the space for theories of human participation as performativity makes logical sense. This contextualizes how it is that Callon sees the compositional processes described in *Marginal Gains*, and my ethnography of a dramatic performance of the sale of petrol (gasoline), as particularly apposite, while any residual framing in binary terms, and any implicit reference to conventional holism, fall under critique.

Çalişkan and Callon (2009) have themselves pointed out the difference and complementarity of the direction in which my own works goes: "People are even more present and influential in Guyer's analysis than are the agents in Appadurai's and Thomas's because they are theorized to possess an intelligence of their interests." (2009, 387). From this, and implied in it, would emanate my reservations and suggestions about their treatment of the "elements": the "found objects" that the art theory of assemblage takes to be somehow lying around in a state of potential liberation. They either find each other, are found, or gravitate into each other's magnetic orbit, and are mutually repositioned, by a variety of means. In the reservations they express about importing "people" too strongly, one senses their circumspection about reintroducing the rational decision-making subject of the "moderns," by the back door. But then they do not yet systematically exemplify what "elements" are and do. Rather they reinsert the vernacular words of these same "moderns" themselves. For example, "*Anthropology* swiftly brings things and materialities back into the picture" (2009, 392; italics in the original) whereas economic sociology mistakenly "brackets off their material and technical dimensions or reduces these to generalized abstract notions such as 'resources' or 'capital.' This effectively evacuates all elements that cannot be qualified as social from the case, while inflating the analysis around those that can" (Çalişkan and Callon 2010, 4). Expanding the "things" that can be considered as elements of *agencements*, they then move to the kinds of framings that group them and retreat from making any advance identifications, since "the making of (new) agencies is an infinite and never-ending project; the classification of the different forms of agency is a finishing point, not a starting point of investigation" (2010, 10).

This, however, is relative to *agencements*, so *after* elements. In my own view, and as exemplified in my papers, the crucial questions of intelligibility, coordination, and the power to act, can, in fact, be approached through including greater attention to what become designated and included as "elements," in theory and in life, and to their provisional classification, to be applied once a compelling topic has been identified. In the case of my papers here, these are broader than the regional patterns, in localized transactions that were profiled in *Marginal Gains*, and than the "marketization" with which Çalişkan and Callon's and the ANT Economy group's project is primarily concerned. In several of these papers, it was precisely the impression made by an element or a consequence—a name for a policy, a receipt for an airline ticket, a contortion in the depiction of the foreign exchange "market"—that sent me in search of the compositions through which they passed. So I turn first to the operationalization of the implicit theory of elements and then to my own arguments.

What are "elements"? Law's list of the "elements" in *agencements* is drawn up as a poetic, parodic rendition of the heterogeneity of conventionally understood elements that are found and assembled in practice. Callon's list is also conventional, although in a different way: texts, materials, emotions, instruments. Interestingly, in his latest work on "composition," which is devoted to scholarship in addition to the world, Latour (2014a, 2014b) does not use the term "element," or another of his terms, *actant*, at all. A large tent (my term) is erected to multiply "diplomatic scenes . . . when . . . the inhabitants of the shrinking domains of life [find out] how to compose the common world that they are supposed to inhabit" (Latour 2014a, 306). "Inhabitants": so implicitly including everything. Possibly, "element" has been abandoned as a potential analytical concept, but this too would bow in the direction of a framing that he finds specific to us moderns, namely ecology. Fine (2003) also draws attention to "the almost total disappearance of . . . the idea of human and non-human (including physical) agents or *actants* as symmetrical" (2003, 480). This may be linked to his equal impatience with the relative disappearance of an ambition toward identifying causes and proposing explanations.

There is a comparable puzzle in the near disappearance of "element" as a concept in a paper by Callon and colleagues on what they call the "economy of qualities" (Callon, Méadel, and Rabeharisoa 2002). Here the "inhabitants" become mainly human, and one is not sure whether this is a function of a theoretical shift or a change in the phenomena under examination, namely segments of the market oriented toward consumers' experience rather than their generalizable commodity needs. It is striking that "groups" enter more forcefully into the argument here, "elements" fade from view, and the human factor is writ larger. "Elements" fade perhaps because the world is newly inhabited by the personal quests of a service economy, which encourages "the proliferation of the social," and a turn toward the place for collaboration between scientists and "wild (i.e., outside) thinking," in "hybrid forums" (2002, 195). This produces an "upsurge of reflexive activity" (2002, 212), which is most highly profiled in *Acting in an Uncertain World* (Callon, Lascoumes, and Barthes 2009, in English). Presumably only humans are reflexive, not other elements of assemblages, such as notice boards and strawberries, although these "objects" might be stubbornly recalcitrant, in their own ways, to being overenergetically or imaginatively manipulated by the reflexive members of the assemblage. So we have to think about whether agency has been shifted away from all "elements" and their compositional forms, for theoretical reasons, or because the subject matter simply works its assemblages differently, in different cases. If the latter, we are squarely in Malinowskian territory, using these particular moderns' depiction of their own world, "the native's point of view" (scientists, consumers, commentators), as analytical terms, and trying to figure out how they can be making sense.

This is troubled territory if one is looking for consistency. But I am inclined to retain the "element" as a component of analytical method, as a potentially richer concept than analogs such as entity, object, or thing, for working on all kinds of "assemblages that matter," anywhere, and as they erupt into action. It can be used in the "found object" sense, so any entity or being, as it is *to the parties at the time it is "found" (including itself)*, not what it is in any essentialist or objective sense to a third party, in presumed timelessness. The etymology helps, because the meaning has morphed over time and remains suitably ambiguous. The elements, in the classic sense of earth, fire, air, and water, became the "simplest component of a complex substance"[3] in the Middle Ages, and chemical substances in the nineteenth century. An element is always somehow basic, at the moment, and always combinable. We can therefore use it empirically, not only to describe what elements proclaim themselves—or are perceived—to be, but to examine how they have come to be, behaved up to now, and seem to promise to continue to behave: from Latour's (2014b) eels and water, to Callon, Lascoumes, and Barthes' (2009) individuals who make up hybrid forums, to existing assemblages that may be only partially adopted by others (shades of Marilyn Strathern's "partial connections" [2004]). In the larger turbulent world, we now find situations where participants and theorists are drawing explicitly on such concepts. In their comparative and historical analysis of chieftaincy in weak states, Derluguian and Earle (2010) describe "elemental power unbound." In popular culture, music, fashion, and commercial innovation, attention is increasingly being drawn to "remix." In a book entitled *Remix*, Lawrence Lessig offers a legal approach to "making art and commerce in the hybrid economy" (2008).

In light of this breadth of allusion, I would rescue the "element" as a promising concept for critical methodological use, especially as a locus for provoking exacting empirical instigation. This would be one important way of meeting Ben Fine's (2003) criticism. Through a more diligent and searching attention to elements as *actants*, explanation can be retrieved by working onward from the questions of "what" and "how," to the inevitably emergent questions of "why." They simply need to be approached through a keener look at the evidence.

To delve further into how "elements" have been addressed explicitly, I look at some examples from two main collections of empirical works and from two recent ethnographies of finance. If we turn back to Callon's first major collection, we see that Callon (1998a) approaches assemblage forms empirically through "framing as a process of disentanglement" (16) of "agents and goods" from prior relationships, which he acknowledges as impossible to achieve completely because it takes place through the mobilization of elements that stabilize, but by the same qualities, allow for "overflowing" and "leakage." With respect to markets, "framing puts the outside world in brackets, as it were, but does not abolish all links with it." (1998, 249). Indeed, citing Erving Goffman, he writes that, in any framing, "use is usually made of traditional equipment having a social history of its own in the wider society and a wide consensus of understanding regarding the meanings that are to be generated from it" (Callon 1998b, 250). Coming back to the example of the legal contract, Callon defines as the "crux" of the argument "each of these elements, at the very same time as this element is helping to structure and frame the interaction of which it forms more or less the substance, is simultaneously a potential conduit for overflows" (1998b, 254). As social scientists, our job is to "map . . . the trajectories." The argument then moves to "who is responsible . . . and who is affected" (257) and to the need to identify "devices" that define and control the borders between elements, and between elements and the outside. Elements themselves remain to be identified: either by the participants themselves or by the analyst. They are not identified ahead of time, by theoretical framing or predisposition, which risks to return us, faute de mieux—to criteria arising from theoretical holism and modernist binary thinking.

It is largely through the concept of "market devices" that some kind of specificity to the elements is brought in. Hence the collection with this title (Callon, Millo, and Muniesa, 2007). Market devices are "the material and discursive assemblages that intervene in the construction of markets" (2007, 2). The papers focus on specific "things," identified by the participants, that perform some "function" or other within and across the boundaries of the frames. Several identify moments, and means, whereby framing shifted, and some show how elements and/or devices were superseded and abandoned (Beunza and Garud 2007). Kjellberg notes that "there are many ways in which to work up . . . calculations . . . and many actors who are simultaneously trying to incorporate highly diverse ideas" (2007, 85). The elements therefore include those that the framing allows as participants, and the algorithms they either bring with them, favor most, or build within assemblage process. Barry (2007) presents a case where frames are set by the very wide range of the French national retail market and the compositional processes are explicitly seen as "struggle." This is important to contemplate in a theoretical orientation toward distributed agency: who or what is "struggling"?

The important contribution of the collection as a whole is that narrative cases of assemblage composition are recounted, in their specific details. For a general purpose, then, the remaining questions are, first, how should one choose a topic, in the sense of what defines salience beyond the opportunity to add another case? For example, should one choose a topic because it matters or because it helps to make a precise analytical intervention? And secondly, can we extrapolate by migrating the approaches of the authors in the collection to other topics and developing their applicability? In other words, how do the cases strengthen the *theoretical* assemblage? On the latter question, Lepinay (2007) offers the case of a deliberately "parasitic" financial product, which then draws attention to the quality of the elements that are already established enough, and in open and welcoming enough terms, for a parasite to be crafted to take hold and thrive. And inevitably the question has to asked: with what effect on the host? What already exists, and how innovations and innovators relate to that and to each other, possibly through "struggle," or else a term deployed by Callon, "negotiation," within powerful specific assemblages, seems to me to define a frontier on which to push forward.

So the critique that I would make is exactly symmetrical to Callon's constructive critique of my own use of "institutions." While rejecting ontology and the object/subject distinction, the "elements" of assemblage appear to be incorporated under terms that derive precisely from the native cultures of "the moderns" that Latour is attempting to "recall" (1999) and reform. For example, Çalişkan and Callon write of *agencements* being "designed to encompass the emotional, corporal, textual and technical elements" (2010, 22). Anthropologists can endorse the use of vernacular terms, but, as such, they also demand analysis: not only what they mean to the *actants*, but how that guides our research further into how they work, in practice.

Without this, attribution of the agency of elements risks being phrased in verbs that take the unspecific-collective form or are phrased in the passive voice or designated as in some sense emergent. This would short-circuit the relentless search for how they become "elements" in the first place; how they are made available; searched out, or thrown into the mix, or gravitate into assemblages; and, necessarily then, a search for what is available but *not* assembled, in part or in whole. Possible candidates to be elements can remain unnoticed, unliked, sifted out and neglected, forgotten or destroyed, or merged with others, and placed under a misleading title (see the paper on the CPI), as frames are drawn, redrawn, and struggled over. Externality should not be simply seen as assimilable to the "overflow" of elements that have been taken into the assemblage. Everything reflects the craftsmanship of the making. This makes the tracing of archives and curatorial practice a central empirical concern. The dynamics of the current turbulent world can offer the most literal of examples: museum collections picked over for circulation of objects into markets where profile and honor are crucial parts of price dynamics, in currencies subjected to legal and illegal exchange dynamics. "Toiling ingenuity" at work in many locations! . . . by many of the "elements" within layered assemblages.

The weakness I see here is that concepts such as leakage, overflow, and externality place most of the emphasis forward in the dynamics, to depict the fact that "elements" can continue to resist decisive containment within "frames," and hence the bounding of an assemblage is impossible and its internal dynamics of form have to be stabilized. Or the surpassing qualities of an element or assemblage capture novelty. The process by which elements move into the purview of assemblage in the first place is barely indicated in this particular instantiation of the theory. I would argue that these metaphoric images of entanglement and leakage, alone, are not sufficiently helpful in pursuit of full analysis of the assemblages within a broader conception of "economy" that is centered on livelihood and wealth. Elements do not just leak or overflow. Surely the "entanglements" that otherwise depict their continuing connections have been woven up already. The punctures that leak and the rims that overflow have been crafted: either purposely or clumsily or through accidents of inept preservation, as well as simply through "too-muchness." How are these elements lying around in the first place? I am reminded of all the literature descending from Walter Benjamin, on fragments, which implies breakage, loss, incompletion, and aspiration to some kind of *re*assembly to some semblance of integrity, such as the one yearned for, in puzzled mood, by Greek poet George Seferis (1967, 93), in a haiku I have used elsewhere in life:

> How can you gather together
> the thousand fragments
> of each person?

We also have Lévi-Strauss and others (such as Roger Bastide, 1970) on bricolage, where the elements are already ordered. Lévi-Strauss wrote of compositions created through what he, also, called a "heterogeneous repertoire" of "elements . . . collected or retained on the principle that 'they may always come in handy.'"(1966, 17, 18). The problem with this thinking for ANT theorists would be the implications of an ontology of subject-object, and of structures underlying the composition of the object categories in the first place. For Lévi-Strauss, the (human) bricoleur is assumed to be the most active party in "the dialog," as he "interrogates all the heterogeneous objects of which his treasury is composed" (18), in which "the elements which the 'bricoleur' collects and uses . . . already possess a sense which sets a limit on their freedom of manoeuver" (19). The elements already have a history, he writes, within structures of thought, from which they would not be liberated through a process like assemblage, because they do not possess their own agency.

For those of us still convinced that the histories and accrued qualities of elements are crucially important to analyze, we can identify ethnographic cases but also suggest approaches that would open up those directions of study. The ethnographic exploratory mode that I have depicted in here shares common characteristics with Marilyn Strathern's (1996; 2002) critiques of "externality" in Callon's work. In two sharply focused papers, she gives attention to two processes that create and re-create externality: the possibility of finding "the external" already within the ongoing "internal" (as the internal-external), since participants bring all their own histories; and the act of "cutting the network," as the frame is redefined. She offers empirical case material for the "external" being discovered "internally," hybrids serving as "boundaries to claims" (1996, 531).

The strategy that I took in these papers could certainly have benefited from deeper micro-analytics to depict some of the processes of assemblage formation and operation in sharable analytical terms. Where it differs from the ANT Economy approach, and perhaps hoes its own furrow (to use a vernacular image), is in two ways. The "economy" is not only "the market" or even "economization processes," and the financial sector as a site is very important but cannot be equated too closely with the concept of "the economy," as Fabian Muniesa seems to do in his book *The Provoked Economy* (2014). Economy has always comprised livelihood and wealth making, from its etymology in the *oikos*, the ancient Greek household, onward. Implications follow. We run into Hayek's "intelligibility" question all the time, but beyond the monopolistic experts, and located in suitably diffused times and places, for all participants, severally and together. Are A, B, and C phenomena actually possible to understand sufficiently for enacting any project, for all the different sentient, thinking, and responsive beings within assemblages? This is pragmatism and performativity within all the many, varied, and changing contexts, at all levels, in which quite different capacities mobilize "elements" into meanings and actions with respect to continuing in life and flourishing (livelihood and wealth making). The fact that "elements" are "at hand," available, mobile, open to interface, and have any other characteristics that qualify them for being noticed and included, and taken up without a fierce fight against other claimants, is a deeply complex process of creation and triage that may have a very long and intricate history that alone accounts for this availability, involving neglect and destruction as well as inclusion.

So classification can be useful: not to fix things, but to drive the research in imperative directions. My own classification is certainly provisional, arising from the composition of these papers. Its purpose for me has been to provide the incentive to pursue lines of empirical search, relentlessly.

In this way, the "heterogeneous elements" of all the kinds indicated by Çalişkan and Callon—"a panoply of entities . . . whether they are human beings or material and textual elements" (2010, 8)—can become demanding frontiers for scholarly effort. As with all the concepts implying engagement with the world, used by both Lévi-Strauss and the ANT theorists, the elements of the world can speak back when we pose questions and tell us to work harder, go further, don't give up yet, pay attention, don't retreat too quickly into abstraction, ask again, turn up and see for yourself, stop blathering, and so on; even, join in and enjoy yourself, or go away and come back when you're in better shape!

Without suggesting that the following categories would cover all possible types of elements comprehensively, I think that depiction in these terms has implicitly directed my thought and research in compelling directions toward the illumination of elements as well as processes. Neither are they completely mutually exclusive. Many models come as legacies, while other models are created in the moment. These are simply categories that can draw attention to, and drive an acute sense of, our responsibility for and accountability to, evidence about certain powerful *kinds* of relational processes that this school of thought has grouped together as "entanglements." The critical features I find salient here are duration, entailment, and practicability. I come to these terms with a similar combination of conviction and provisionality as Paul Kockelman brings to his *analytical* categories for bringing together Peircean semiotics and Marxian political economy, which are "best understood as a set of flexible and portable tools that are designed to interpret a wide-range of ethnographic data. . . . The issue then is not their truthfulness, but their usefulness" (2006, 85).

Legacies

I use the term "legacy" to draw attention to everything that, in the present, is seen as, or known to be, inherited from the past, which then gives it a certain aura of endurance: from the concept of the "household" in present-day national metrics such as the consumer price index, which comes into western political-economic enumeration from centuries-old taxation systems, to the development of the percentage in analysis and rhetoric. These elements cannot be depicted collectively as "traditional," since "tradition" implies coherence, coming from a particular phase of a fully theorized history where it is to be contrasted, qualitatively and completely, with "modernity." I needed a term that could be pluralized, legacies, that could be of any form, dimension, and value whatsoever, and that designates only what the present finds in archives inherited from the past, and has curated and protected, made available (or excised) in "repertoires" (to use a term from *Marginal Gains*), and infused with a quality of pastness.

These legacy elements may draw on tradition in the sense used by Max Weber, as a mode of legitimation. They may also take the form of long-established models (which I come to next), such as algorithms like Black-Scholes in finance, the "household" as the basis for CPI calculations, the forms to which new "parasites" (Lepinay 2007) can attach, and particular legal devices, such as those brought into the creation of *national* currencies and *international* money markets (clearing houses, and others), in the post-gold-standard era (see the paper "Intricacy and Impasse"). And they may also be matters of simple familiarity: people already know how to think and act skillfully in those terms, and it is tacitly assumed that they will continue to do so. It seems unhelpfully dismissive, to me, to consign all of this to "routine," as is sometimes done in the above-mentioned works, and in social theory more widely.

To take a totally mundane example: in the British culture in which I was raised we were taught how to "queue," which involved a bodily practice, an ethical assumption, a form of sociality and conversation, and so on. Breaching the familiar "code" was "jumping the queue": explosive, un-gainly, and unacceptable by the others in the line, that is, by peers and equals. In any situation, especially in the marketplace, everyone was sup-posed to be able to bring this encapsulated knowledge into instant action, as L.S. Lowry depicted in his painting of customers waiting for the grocery shop to open, in a working-class Lancashire town in 1943 (so under ra-tioning). Facing in both directions, chatting to each other, no one pushing, some trudging along to take their own places, all in hats: they still form a single line that conveys an understood decorum. The newly launched idea in American economic life, that people can pay more money to be moved to the front of a queue, would be deeply offensive here, even though a neoliberal theorist could logically claim that the monetization of physical access might bolster profits, enhance GDP, and raise indices of economic growth. Perfect! As I note in the paper on the real economy, "perfect" has leaked out and now overflows seriously from the concept of "the perfect market" as a theory, likened to the olive in the martini glass, into the phrase "in a perfect world," which can mean a world without taxes. We roll our eyes in fatigue. In this context, the concept of legacy is not just an in-strument but a provocation that invites, and then demands of us, exacting standards for a detailed archeology of the elements that are brought—or bring themselves—into assemblages and that bring their own past experience of distributed agency to the ongoing dynamics, in durational mode.

On a larger scale, attention to legacies would bring into the study of "making markets" the kind of detailed historical study, over centuries, by a scholar such as Laurence Fontaine (2014), who documents all the moves in the process she sees as "the social conquest" achieved by "the market" across the several centuries of the social life of the "moderns": so "making" in the sense of engagement, occupation, colonization, selective preservation and destruction, and pushing on.

The dynamics of legacies come into several of the papers: as fully developed mobile assemblage, like the "essential commodity" phenomenon; as imagery of the global financial system in the platform paper; as a foundational archive of text, emotion, and aspiration for selective deployment, in the paper on prophecy and the near future; and as the household in the paper on the CPI. The particular devices that I foreground in the two papers on calculation stress, not the novelty of cutting-edge equations and instruments, but the most ordinary, and surely among the oldest, of numerical concepts—ordinality and the percentage—as they have been most recently appropriated. The aura of pastness may continually infuse the assemblage in which it operates. It may be embellished, or it may be a cause of disagreement and debate among the *actants*, or it may be alternatively quiescent and active. The question of how legacy elements come into the equation, and then operate, opens up a large and important domain of study, especially for anthropologists with a historical orientation.

Logics

"Logics" directs attention to the components of assemblages that come with their own necessary entailments, so are taken into them with little or no internal flexibility, unlike logistics, for being reengineered. Already articulated and stabilized compositions, they are invoked and moved across time and space, perhaps reworked, but always presented as coherently unitary. Examples would include the legal devices of the kind studied by Anneliese Riles (2006), and the metrics that Sally Merry (2011) sees as created for measuring new phenomena in international contexts. Some numerical techniques, as algorithms, have this quality (Verran 2010). The particularity of my use of "logics," then, lies in attending to the complexity, and apparent necessity, of mutual imbrications and articulations of components that are made to be not just stable over time but also answerable to a logic that is expressed in "objective" formal terms, following the "moderns"' liberal logics of governance: so either mathematical or legal or rational-bureaucratic. They can be large or small elements: modular and internally coherent theories of whole economic systems, with all their derived logics, or specific policy configurations, with their own names, as I address in the papers on "essential commodities" and the consumer price index; or inventions that undergird necessary infrastructures, that hold together whole complexes of other elements, such as the theory of the life cycle alluded to in this chapter. Just how resistant the internal mutual entailments are anticipated to be, and then turn out to be, can come under scrutiny.

Logistics

"Logistics" refers to the points at which inponderabilia and questions of intelligibility arise most forcefully in life, where practicable solutions are required. Situations of confusion, incompatibility, and temporal logjam have provided several of my starting points in these papers. Different compositions, arising from different sites within economic formations, meet *each other* within "life on the ground," in ways whose *mutual* intelligibility is likely to be highly varied. Here one returns to "life and livelihood," where "the people" are triangulating—to use a much too limited geometric image (*only* three points?)—among the many elements within, and between, the compositions that frame and orient their economic lives. The kinds of "intelligibility" that *they* are searching for, finding, or missing, or indeed that we practitioners of our disciplines find provocative, can suggest points of departure. My paper on price composition starts from connecting a life puzzle about the representation of prices in the ordinary billing systems of daily life and in informational advertisements. I was provoked to write it by a conference on Polanyi, so I connected this conundrum to Polanyi's argument that the capitalist economy has excelled in creating "fictional commodities," and of course Marx's work on the fetish and concealment of relations by words. Even the classical economists' notion that "money is a veil," implied that money could be seen right through, to the real economy behind it.

This brings me to a final point that returns to the question of macro-structures and macro-theory. If we trace out the mutual imbrications of legacies, logics, and logistics in all their empirical complexity, asking "how" and "why" at every juncture, and about topics that matter to livelihood and wealth, the pathways will certainly return us to locations of power and to larger organizational dynamics. I would also note that these points of departure would perhaps mitigate the despair that Latour expresses with respect to the "moderns," that we have managed to lurch from indexing everything to one "utopia," ("the market") to another ("ecology") (2012, 35). In my own case, having theories of macro-power already in mind, even when the terms are not directly mobilized, has directed my empirical attention, alongside noticing the experiences arising from the lives of the people. I cannot do without such landmarks at the points of departure and the destinations of the arcs of study and argument, but they do not dictate the trajectory of the argument, as, for example, they do in more theoretically infused work, such as David Harvey's (2014) recent analysis of "seventeen contradictions and the end of capitalism."

Conclusion

These are my aspirations for publishing these papers together: that they illustrate a biography of intellectual life in which engaging in varied interactions has been crucial and in which I have much hope for its continuation in new ways within economic anthropology; that the themes connect to colleagues who are working on one or another of these topics and so can encourage and inform further efforts on engaging anthropology with the formalized economic world, and at its interface with the people; and that the whole collection can exemplify an analytics that demands a deep and demanding archeology of what it is that we treat as "elements," as well as an ethnography of their current compositional dynamics. Working on these papers over the years, and on this chapter in the present, has been a provocation to my own further thinking, as represented in the newly composed final paper.

TWO

"Toiling Ingenuity": Food Regulation in Britain and Nigeria

In one sense this article is simply an outline of key moments in the development of government food regulation in Britain and one of its colonies, before and after that colony's independence. It involves the careers of famous and infamous men such as Sir William Beveridge, John Boyd Orr, John Strachey, and Umaru Dikko. It covers the most traumatic world events of this century and the most tediously routine ones: the accumulation of "forms and circulars, reports and instructions, schemes and counterschemes . . . all so many monuments of toiling ingenuity," as Beveridge (1928, 344) depicted the physical remains of the World War I food-rationing program.

The purpose of this short article on such a vast historical and scientific topic, however, is to address specific anthropological issues. I use food regulation not only as a topic that is worthy in itself of anthropological analysis but also as a vehicle for addressing empirically the pervasive process of regulation: a process that frames intellectual approaches and helps to define the ethnic and national boundaries within which we work. I argue that the history of regulation reveals what Cooper and Stoler (1989) refer to as "break points of global significance [that] existed within the history of colonialism" and endorse their stance that the longer view can help to "clarify what they were about" (617). I then use the topic of food regulation as a challenge and as a crucible for the development of a systematic approach to formal sector models that extends beyond the colonial period and into the present. Those "break points" had, and continue to have, profound implications for local dynamics. But when we always look at them from the vantage point of other societies, they seem to come from such technical or hidden metropolitan sources and by such devious and indirect routes that their nature and even, one suspects, their very existence can be obscured. The "limits of naivety" (Gluckman 1964) pose a far more challenging problem for scholars of local arenas within "open systems" than do the "closed systems" that theory assumed in the past; the search for relevant connections needs to range beyond the local society and even beyond its interface with the formal sector, into processes that originate elsewhere.

One solution is to turn to direct examination of metropolitan processes, drawing on anthropological theory and addressing an empirical topic that has a clear connection to the local dynamics on which we generally concentrate. It is because of local familiarity that I have written this article on food and on Nigeria; this is a topic and a region with which I have already worked, always starting from the local arena (see, for example, Guyer 1987). But the regulation only glimpsed from that perspective is among the most important of global processes, one that literally inscribes boundaries on a world otherwise seen as "fundamentally fractal, . . . possessing no Euclidean boundaries, structures or regularities" (Appadurai 1990, 20).[1] And the vast edifice of regulation defines highly specific geographies now far more intricate and overlapping than a map of nations, even though national processes have been the major means by which it has been built over the past century and a half. Local arenas are pieces of a complex global mosaic of socio-technical models, constructed from diverse elements in one context, reconfigured for application to others, and subjected to constant amendment. They are punctiliously defined and redefined by technical terminologies and implemented by specialized functionaries.[2] Understanding any part of this process then, however small, entails an understanding of the dynamics of multiplicity without losing sight of the differential power that allows some intentions and definitions to prevail over others, some boundaries to hold strong and others to open up.

There are resources within anthropology for taking an ethnographic approach to modern governmental forms of multiplicity. Eric Wolf's critique of the concept of "society" traces anthropology's struggle to free itself from theories of coherence and consensus in order to devote itself to understanding "the multiform plural" of social patterns and cultural repertoires that are imaginatively and actively (toilingly and ingeniously, to borrow Beveridge's words) built up "out of manifold elements" (Wolf 1988, 757–58). In Wolf's own work, class and power are the forces that shape "manifold elements" into social and cultural forms.[3] By taking a social organizational approach to the problem of multiplicity, Sally Moore (1986) strengthens the ethnographic agenda; she assumes indeterminacy, focuses on regulation as a process, and studies empirically the historical layering of particular local organizational forms in a process which she refers to as "pyramiding." And Thomas Kuhn's (1962) study of scientific paradigms provides a different but stimulating resource for the study of the accretion of ideas in the modern era, and one especially relevant to the kinds of government regulation that depend on institutionalized science. Although he is concerned with the relationship between articulated conceptual models rather than with the social organization and cultural repertoires classically addressed by anthropology, his insights about historical succession in the production of multiplicity help to enlarge our vision over much longer historical periods than we usually address. Kuhn's main argument stresses the incompatibility of successive paradigms, but he also mentions the ways in which "an older paradigm is replaced . . . *in part,*" and a new paradigm can "preserve a great deal of the most concrete parts of past achievement" (1962, 91, 168; emphasis added).[4] Clearly he envisages structured accretion from one model to the next, as well as complete replacement of fundamental premises.

Kuhn's comments hold open a possibility that I argue is realized in the history of regulation, namely that older elements of knowledge and understanding remain available and selectively applicable, especially in a field like modern science that sees itself as progressive rather than revolutionary. Many older ideas remain in the repertoire of legitimated concepts and can be mobilized in new eras and different contexts. Technical and scientific ideas can be "pyramided," or more complexly recombined with social and political organizations, and shaped by the class interests focused on by Wolf. Part of the multiplicity of present open systems—and a multiplicity that is established separately from the complexities introduced by local populations' interpretations and domestications of foreign elements— can then be traced to the shape given to past accretions in the centers of power themselves and to the principles of their selective mobilization elsewhere.

Taking a historically long and geographically broad view of modern food regulation, we can see that multiple models have existed, and to some degree coexisted, in the British cultural and institutional repertoire, and that the coexistence has been ordered according to temporal principles. In Britain, models of regulatory frameworks have succeeded one another, each one largely replacing its predecessor without, however, totally delegitimating it as a potential resource. There are two plausible reasons for retention: each model is acknowledged as having been appropriate to its own time and circumstances, and each manifestly contributed to the development of the current model. This means that the entire sequentially structured metropolitan repertoire is available for selective use, especially in a colonial periphery defined in one way or another as behind in the sequence ("primitive," "underdeveloped"). The place of local populations in relation to the implicit narrative underlying the metropolitan repertoire is therefore one of the key issues at play. There is room for profound disagreement, each position entailing different and important implications for the way the fine print of regulatory frameworks are put in place.[5]

The characteristics of this pattern of structured accretion may be particularly British or perhaps typical of national traditions whose repertoires have not been transformed by revolution. British policy on issues defined as technical was extraordinarily, and perhaps uniquely, empiricist in explicit philosophy. It could take decades to construct a regulatory agency, piece by piece, and no measure—once put in place—was eliminated from the books.[6] Major decisions could be taken as if they concerned only the finest of fine print. Very occasionally abstract principles were publicly invoked to back them up. If general principles are kept largely in the background and the repertoire is treated as an accretion of elements, there is no logical inconsistency in pulling this or that measure out of its original historical and institutional matrix to put to a new use. Add to this Britain's uniquely long and geographically varied experience of colonial rule, and there exists the potential to preserve a vaster variety of usable rubrics than can be found elsewhere, even in other European contexts: in codes based on a revolutionary power that tried to replace past systems with newly formulated and internally coherent rubrics for government, or in cultures of governance that stand on a narrower basis of global experience than that of Great Britain.

Standing behind the "forms and circulars" that embody British empiricism, however, and giving them recognizable shape through the intervening screen of pragmatism, have been successive, legitimating rubrics of persuasive ideological power and impressive practical effectivity in a history of food regulation that is almost unbroken from the thirteenth century to the present. Ideological rubrics, however little invoked, do justify and give meaning to a set of associated principles, implementational structures, and detailed practices; they help to define whole complexes as models that can be invoked in toto or whose elements are recognizably attributable to one model or the other. At any given time, one rubric has been dominant in British history, but the achievements of its predecessors have not been negated. The acknowledged coherence and success[7] of older models keep them in the repertoire, as models and as separate elements, making them available as a resource for transposition elsewhere. Among the principles for transposition will be assumptions about the "place in history" of the people to whom it is to be applied and therefore their "match" against the metropolitan repertoire. And given the sheer length of preserved metropolitan experience, there are several possibilities. The assumption that the rest of the world belongs in the *same* era of administrative history as the metropolitan world implies that the models tailored for those contexts should duplicate the models dominant in the *current* metropolitan world as exactly as possible in all respects, including the ideas, institutions, rules, and practices. We might term this assumption "contemporary parallelism." The assumption that other administrative systems are at an *earlier stage* of development implies that measures should be taken from an *earlier phase* of metropolitan history. We might refer to this as "evolutionary parallelism." Both kinds of parallelism contrast with the assumption of complementarity—namely, that current differences should be recognized and that regulatory structures should reflect functional divisions of labor in the world. The last position is implied by the economic theory of comparative advantage, which advocates the organization of economies around the particular products to which they are most suited. It is rarely argued, however, as a general principle of government even when it clearly informs negotiations and the fine print of enacted regulation. For Britain in relation to Nigeria, the principles and practices from models of complementarity and from both kinds of parallelism have all been in play at once, characteristically promoted by different subgroups taking part in the intense engagements described in the article. One result, as Appadurai (1990) notes in another context is that "the politics of global cultural flows . . . plays havoc with the hegemony of Euro-chronology" (3). It is worth both endorsing and qualifying his comment: this muddling of history and mixing of elements clearly takes place *within* Western and corporate institutional contexts as they prepare for interfaces with other cultures, as well as at the interfaces themselves. We have, in fact, a certain embarrassment of riches in current Euro-chronology when it comes to the nuances of temporal concepts available to us: the self-consciously iterative time of cultivated nostalgia,[8] the sweepingly circular resurrection of old political-administrative measures indicated by Cooper (1989), and the intransigently progressive time that is appropriate to my subject here, technical knowledge and its implementation.

It may be that technical knowledge is the most temporally complex of all when it comes to the implementation phase. Successful realization, as distinct from conceptualization, means coming to grips with intimate human processes that are already built into entire technologies, philosophies, and rhythmic structures of life.[9] Certainly the architects of these plans and policies were themselves, in rhetorical moments, explicitly envisaging a connection between dimensions that were intimate and traditional, those that were technical and inventive, and those that were political and unprecedented. In their *Feeding the People in War-Time*, for example, Orr and Lubbock (1940) argued: "This war is very different; it will be lost and won in the homes of the people. . . . The health line of the Home Front may become as important as the Maginot Line" (8, 10). The simultaneous invocation of tradition and radical change, the intimate and the exposed, is just one of many ingenious maneuvers it must take to create new frameworks in the metropolitan system and then even more so to re-create them—complete with intended and unintended loopholes—at the interface with other polities and cultures.

Because anthropology has already struggled with the incongruity between Western-inherited models and non-Western cultures (see Cohn and Dirks 1988; Wolf 1988) and with the potential indeterminacies between principle and practices (Moore 1978), it is in a strong position to address "the heterogeneity and transformative nature of human arrangements" (Wolf 1988, 760) in the centers of power. While in some contexts a certain public model may predominate at a given time, as Foucault (1991) and Donzelot (1988, 1991) have powerfully demonstrated for France, the anthropological vision of structured multiplicity within models[10] and between them opens up the project of exploring how governance works, "toils," in its many different contexts. We need an approach to the coexistence of different models if we are to understand "multiple historicities" (Cooper and Stoler 1989, 617) and their implications. The intricate fractures in cultural and institutional constructions, in both political centers and at interfaces, may be a particular contribution that anthropology can develop in the study of the modern state and global processes.[11]

Certainly the foundations exist. The acceptable methods are probably still to be worked out. The present article was written entirely from published and archival documentary sources that inevitably highlight key moments, dominant symbols, and dramatic incidents. It cannot therefore meet the standards of the comprehensive and detailed descriptive mandate of anthropology. But by focusing on otherwise obscure connections between well-known dramas, it can encourage the study of more reclusive, and perhaps just as powerful regulatory processes at other interfaces. In many of the latter arenas, secrecy, technicalities of language, and convolutions of process may make the more traditional ethnographic method not only desirable for disciplinary reasons but also the only way to make headway at all.[12]

Food Regulation

In much of the history of food regulation, the details dominate the discourse. Politicians and administrators often present food control measures in reactive terms and justify them with convoluted, situational logics that seem to have no bold guiding metaphors. Reading the official literature from both Britain and Nigeria, one feels that there can be no topic on which politically motivated pronouncements are so openly contradictory and complicated.[13] The reason may lie in the moral dilemma of espousing a laissez-faire economic philosophy, while knowing that the ramifications of allowing the market to deliver the goods are not consistently, politically tolerable. The promise of enhanced legitimacy or straightforward functioning that can be achieved by the state's claiming some of the old responsibilities of paternalism is tempting and even politically imperative, but the possibility of unforeseen consequences is foreboding. "Canst thou draw out leviathan with a hook?" asks Hammond, the official historian of British World War II rationing, in discussing the "recalcitrance of real life in face of the planner with his blueprint" (1954, 22). Food regulations are a miracle if successful and a catastrophe if not, entailing complicated justifications to divert the public reaction: onto scapegoats if negative and in one's own direction if positive. As in early colonial Nigeria, a government can capitalize symbolically on a system that already works well (the South) or manage to fail to know about one that occasionally does not (the North, see Guyer 1987; Watts 1987). As a result, the panoply of interventions is often presented in terms such as those of R. H. Tawney, cited by Hammond, for the rationing system of Britain in World War I: "the impressive fabric of state control . . . not deliberately constructed at all . . . entirely doctrineless" (1954, 226). They are similar to Hammond's own terms for the rationing system of World War II that "proceeded by an endless process of trial and error, in which first principles had little place" (1954, 226).

Protestations to the contrary, moments of crisis have indeed provoked overriding images and even impassioned statements of political principle, so close can the threat to food supply come to the central emotive symbols of collective life. The successive rubrics under which food has been regulated in Britain are indicated by key ideas that were implemented through corresponding institutions and rules. In the premodern model, the Assize of Bread, was a *guarantor of fixed relationships* between the amount of flour and the amount of bread, between a loaf and a price, between the baker and the customer. The first modern model, involving the central state, translated a fundamentally religious concept of the state as *protector of pu-*

rity into scientific terms and was associated with a universalizable concept of justice, the basic—and eventually uniform—rights of the citizen. A second developed and flourished during World War II, when the state became *purveyor of welfare*, associated with a science and philosophy of the basic needs of the consumer. A recent third, which I will discuss briefly in the conclusion, defines the state as an *arbiter of social cost*, associated with calculations of the contributory capacity and willingness of the taxpayer. In the metropole, each model developed a characteristic set of basic principles, institutional alliances, and specific measures that differed significantly from its predecessor. The models did not, however, entirely replace one another, even though certain concepts and alliances were dropped at moments of critical transition. Rather, the terms, measures, and underlying moral frameworks remain available to be invoked and applied as appropriate. In colonial Nigeria, I will argue, application of the guiding imagery followed a pattern of evolutionary parallelism, with the Nigerian rubrics being selected from the model immediately previous to the one currently developing or fully operating in the metropolitan world. The selection of institutional and implementational *elements* at each stage, however, reflects the contentious dynamics of complementarity in the international political economy as well as the metropole's selective memory about its own past. As a result, the models as implemented in Nigeria have been internally inconsistent by the standards of those models as they once existed in Britain. Although each model probably does not represent the only or necessary combination and permutation of elements, each had once achieved validity, as both an idea and a social system. So when such a model is applied elsewhere, people expect it to work in a predictable and familiar fashion. If, however, the general rubrics are invoked while the transfer of elements is only partial, it is highly likely to produce unfamiliar dynamics. These dynamics then seem deviant, reflecting more on the actors than on the stage where they perform. The present history of food regulation is an extended illustration of these points.

British Food Control: Two Models and Their Formation

The history of food regulation in Britain is a long one. In 1266 the Assize of Bread was established, to be administered by the local justices of the peace. Only abolished six hundred years later, in 1836, the guidelines for the Assize "started with the legal liability of the baker to make 418 lbs. of bread out of every quarter of wheat," in three different qualities of the final product. Quantity and quality control were defined in combination, because adulteration could be defined as a breach of the weight ratios (Ernie 1961, 496).

In the free market of the mid-nineteenth century, the organized medical profession was gravely concerned that adulteration would become a general practice and that there was no clear way of prosecuting it. In his survey of the London food system, published in 1856, George Dodd reviewed the adulteration problem, finding, for example, that "the 'fast' Americans" occasionally made their flour barrels of unseasoned wood, which tended to "impart a disagreeable flavour to the meal"; that the bread was systematically adulterated with alum; and that medical investigators "rather to their own surprise, though of course to their satisfaction, . . . found 12 [out of 26 samples of milk] to be genuine" (1856, 186, 207, 299). Due to the pioneering efforts of a small lobby, the British Adulteration Act was passed in 1860 to prohibit "selling as pure and unadulterated what was in fact adulterated and impure" (Stieb 1966, 128). The British Sale of Food and Drugs Act was passed in 1875 and slowly amended to increase the power of the central state to the point that, almost forty years later, government was empowered to check on the uniform operation of the act throughout the country.[14] This body of legislation concerned with food purity and uniformity, accompanied by the various implementation structures of government and civil organizations associated with it (societies, journals, commissions, standards guardians), remained in effect until the interwar years. The concepts of purity and uniformity became the justification for state interventions.[15] Continuing an old European tradition of distrust of millers and bakers, the interventions focused on food processors and distributors.[16]

State concern with the larger question of the composition of the national diet was first faced under the food controls of World War I and the threat of industrial unrest. The rationed diet was thought of conservatively as a "basal diet," a "peasant diet" (Hammond 1954, 34), related mainly to the demands of manual work. The biological sciences contributed primarily to the calculation of per capita caloric requirements, and the social sciences contributed to the extrapolation of need from prewar consumption patterns. Sugar was the critical rationed food, one whose consumption was actually promoted and expanded under wartime conditions (Beveridge 1928, 122). Customary substitutions rather than technically defined alternatives seem to have been used to meet the essential bureaucratic task of grouping foods into categories for acquisition, pricing, and distribution.

The "basal diet" guaranteed to the citizen during wartime was justified in terms of basic rights, of justice under duress, in an elaboration and extension of an entire political culture of the state as the protector of basic uniform standards. Momentarily, the diet and the minimum quality of the commodities both came under the ideology of standardization. In perhaps the most eloquent enunciation of those principles, Beveridge described an entire political theory that lay behind food control and extended far beyond it:

> Meticulous pursuit of justice between places, classes and persons was one of the main factors in the success of food control. . . . Of the two master passions of democracy—the love of liberty and the love of justice—the latter is with the British people deeper and stronger. . . . To demand freedom at all costs in a crowded world is often mere crying for the empty moon. . . . Justice carries liberty on its back, but liberty does not carry justice. (Beveridge 1928, 234, 245)[17]

The enemy was the food distributor, bent on circumventing justice by profiteering and favoritism. In 1918 and 1919, there were more than fifty thousand prosecutions for offenses against food orders, mainly of dealers charged with raising prices, adulterating, or selling outside the official channels (Beveridge 1928, 235).[18] Reviewing the World War I system in 1940, Beveridge reminded the population that its designer, D. A. Thomas (Viscount Rhondda) had attributed its success to the fact that "he was, as he himself emphatically declared, 'on the side of the consumer *as against* the trader'" (Orr and Lubbock 1940, 80; emphasis added).

Ultimately, however, the official policy on food was as conservative in social terms as it was in its conception of the diet. During the war, all meats were priced uniformly irrespective of quality—that is, of cultural desirability—but the system was never intended to achieve a permanent alteration of the unequal distribution of consumption by social class. Uniformity of the diet had been abandoned by 1919, when price differentiation was restored, although the pursuit of standards and uniformity in other domains continued. Beveridge himself believed that nothing of any peacetime utility had been established by the wartime rationing. The moving, last paragraph of his book on the topic reads "Little if anything learned . . . can be of use again, save in a civilization bent again on self-destruction" (1928, 344).[19]

Associated with the era of purity and uniformity in food standards, then, was a concept of basic justice that could be extended—but only in wartime—beyond the quality of specific commodities to the general caloric adequacy of the diet. Those concepts were in turn associated with a science of standards, an explicit distrust between government and the food traders and a panoply of measures, such as licensing and regular inspection, to keep the traders under surveillance.

By World War II, the self-proclaimed empiricism of the food control measures of 1914–1918, which "grew like coral islands" (Beveridge, cited in Hammond 1954, 227), was no longer tenable, initially for administrative reasons. In preparation for war, the Essential Commodities (Reserves) Act was passed in 1938 to facilitate purchases of the old major staples: wheat, sugar, and whale oil (Hammond 1954, 14). By 1941, however, bureaucrats were faced with the allocation of thousands of commodities, rendering utterly impossible an attempt, as one official put it, "to steer a course from a mass of small bits of paper marked 'chocolate priority for Civil Defence' or 'Fats allocated to bakers'" (Hammond 1954, 156).

To simplify a vastly complex history (Hammond 1954), a passionately committed lobby of nutritionists (Orr and Lubbock 1940) altered the meaning of "essential commodities" in accordance with scientific findings about what they called "protective" and "energy" foods. They advocated using these as key terms of an operative taxonomy for judging a number of issues that went beyond the acquisition and distribution of a traditional diet. The new knowledge about nutritional composition translated into subsidies for various foods, promotion of the home production of some foods and the import of others, an emphasis on certain imports, and a more intricately differentiated distribution by age and state of health than had ever been envisaged during World War I.[20] Having written in 1936 that one-third of the British population was malnourished with respect not just to calories—the old World War I concern—but to "protective" foods and micronutrients, John Boyd Orr (1936)[21] was militant about the adoption of individual dietary standards along with rationing during World War II (Orr and Lubbock 1940). As it turns out, the national diet was primarily formulated on the grounds of what was believed good for the consumer rather than what was available or desired. Truly awful-tasting items appeared on the shelf, such as cod-liver oil from Iceland, a key source of vitamin A for children. It, and orange juice from Palestine for vitamin C, became defined as essential commodities. People did not enjoy the wartime diet: "The dullness of the national diet . . . was not made more acceptable by Government's rather tactless harping on calculations purporting to show that, on the average, people were better fed than they were before the war" (Hammond 1954, 220).[22] But the planned consequence was apparently achieved, namely the near eradication of the terrible deficiency diseases, such as rickets, that had scarred generations of the British poor.[23]

Far-reaching bureaucratic changes were associated with the change in conception of the diet, which was now envisioned in terms of nutritional components for consumers with varied needs rather than commodities for a uniform citizenry. First of all, the definition of adulteration could be—and indeed had to be—altered. During the serious shortages of the "austerity" period in 1943–1944, adulteration was rethought and partially unhitched from the morality of purity. Purity could not be sustained,[24] and the Ministry of Food set standards on what it now called "dilution"—determining, for example, how much potato flour could be added to bread and how much meat had to be included in sausages. Thus was created an entire enterprise of accurate product labeling that survived the end of the war intact (see Hammond 1951, chapter 24).[25] Through the politics and administration of wartime, a revolution in government regulation was put in place. Scientifically based permutations and combinations of ingredients became the standard of dietary adequacy, one that could be devised and implemented only with state intervention. Welfare replaced purity as the operative regulatory concept.[26]

Second, the rationing system was based on needs and therefore included additional subsidies and allowances for particular categories of consumers: pregnant women, nursing mothers, infants, and so on. On this basis, relationships were set up between the state and newly defined constituencies of people who had had no direct claim before. Again, the system survived the war, building the idea of subsidies in accordance with consumer need into the responsibilities of the state and building new client populations.

A less clearly intended outcome of the theory of *consumption*, but one entailed by it, was an almost revolutionary concentration of the control of *production* in the hands of large manufacturers. These corporations not only were more efficient to deal with when it came to complex regulations about ingredients and labeling, but also had been genuine partners in the Ministry of Food in London as well as in Lagos. The collaboration between government and organized interests in society was a classic case of corporatism, that is, one in which "the leaders of functionally organised interests negotiate[d] agreed policies with state officials and agencies" (Cawson 1986). As Hammond (1951) put it, one condition of success during World War II was "the existence of a considerable degree of organisation in the trades it was desired to control" (5). Very early, even before war broke out, Lever Brothers and Unilever were officially involved in working out a scheme for provision of oils and fat. Many leaders of the commodity divisions throughout the war came from the food industry and continued to be paid by it. And many industries had far fewer operators by the end of the war than at the beginning; small companies had gone out of business because they could not afford to meet the standards.[27] In Nigeria—to jump ahead—the United Africa Company, a division of Lever Brothers, emerges from the wartime archival records as one of the major cooperators with the governor general in developing product standards and trading with England. Nigerian traders were deeply angered, as were some of the midlevel colonial personnel. But I have the impression that consolidation of the power of major business was a general effect of the wartime configuration and was not restricted to colonial contexts. The food trader, explicitly mistrusted by government from the foundation of the Assize of Bread in 1266 through the food control of World War I, became a public ally under the welfare rubric.

The image of the state as purveyor of welfare, which replaced that of the state as protector of purity, was associated with a different set of institutions and measures: a science of ingredients, a reformer's approach to the national diet, an overt alliance between government and the food industry, new political constituencies, and implementation measures that now included routine reporting, monitoring, and active nutritional promotion.

The Colonies: Two Nigerian Models and Their Formation

The colonies felt food regulation from the other end of the producer-consumer link. The first regulations covered *only* products to be consumed in Europe. An ordinance prohibiting the adulteration of export produce, primarily palm oil, was promulgated in Nigeria in 1889 and reinforced with respect to cocoa in 1926. The idea of purity being guaranteed by the state was therefore introduced, but not for local consumption. In spite of the loss of markets that was the price of contravention,[28] the colonial government in Lagos reacted exactly as the British government had done in the late nineteenth century to the demand that it implement rules as well as pass them; at first it was very reluctant to claim that inspection necessarily fell within its own sphere of responsibility (Leubuscher 1939, 182n). Colonial officials raised the question of dietary standards for the ordinary colonial subject only for specific consumers such as government employees and prisoners (Guyer 1987). In some places the state shaped the consumption of private-sector employees as well, as in Tanganyika, where a market was being created for settler-farmer products (Bryceson 1987). The issue here was mainly calories and commodities by social category, paralleling the thinking in early twentieth-century Britain. But overall, while anthropologists and others who followed the nutrition movement in Britain took a lively interest in the "native diet" (see Culwick 1943; Firth 1934; Scott 1937),[29] government regulation was limited to the international market until well into the post–World War II period.[30]

The Nigerian cassava market during World War II exemplified the colonial politics this situation generated—one in which purity at the producer end catered to a consumer population now under a comprehensive and corporatist protection of its welfare. Cassava starch was to be produced for British laundry, glue, and confectionery needs,[31] in order to make up for the loss of Javanese produce. Interpretation of the meaning of purity, graphically represented in the rules requiring a "brilliant white" product, was contested by the potential participants in production and trade: state officials in London, large dealers, small producers, and colonial administrators with their own social and political agendas. Samples sent to England in 1940 seemed to pass muster, although the governor reiterated that the "question of quality is again stressed. . . . This will . . . involve a system of inspection and the introduction of regulations" (Governor of Nigeria 1940). A sample earned a "very favorable report" from analysis in New York in 1935, and in 1940 the Produce Department in London passed additional samples: "The Grade 1 starch is very nearly the quality of fine tapioca flour from Java" (Produce Department 1940). In 1941, the district agent for John Holt complained, however, of "a large tonnage of rubbish," adding, "from experiments conducted, we formed the conclusion that a blind man could tell 'brilliantly white' starch" (District Agent 1941). He alleged, in classic fashion, that the traders were mixing grades, whereas others contended that the large merchants were protecting their own interests by insisting on even higher standards than the government. As Falola (1989) writes, "The interpretation of 'good quality starch' constituted one of the persistent controversies during this period" (89). By extension, not only the traders but the producers themselves were eventually implicated in the lowering of standards. Misgivings about the ability of small (largely female) producers' starch to meet standards became one of the idioms in which concern was expressed about women withdrawing their labor from palm oil production. The government needed to keep palm oil production active, so it was not keen for the women to have a viable alternative in cassava starch production. The expressed concern about quality fed into the ban on starch production that was imposed first in eastern Nigeria and then in the whole country (Falola 1989, 92). The director of the Agriculture Department in Ibadan complained strongly about what one might see, in formal terms, as the contrast between evolutionary parallelism and complementarity:

> The work of my department has been built up on confidence . . . slowly gained over a period of 20 years. . . . I most respectfully suggest that the attitude of government to the cassava starch industry should have been not "how quickly can we kill this industry" but how can we help it survive under these difficult conditions. . . . What has happened in the case of cassava starch may at any time happen to any new industry which we have started or may try to start in the future. (Mackie 1943)

Even after the exigencies of wartime, the issue of quality again emerged to mediate the developing complementarities of zonal specialization in the world economy and the new corporatism of food policies. The director of commerce and industries in Lagos wrote to the chief secretary: "It is unlikely that hand-made cassava starch would fetch the price for first grade starch" (1948). The Colonial Office advisers were said to

> feel that for satisfactory development the only possibility is by means of mechanised production on a plantation basis, and that the industry would not be suitable for co-operative venture between the native growers and non-native interests with capital in the processing unit. (Creasey 1947)

The ultimate outcome of a complex history was this recommendation by the director of commerce and industries: "As regards long term prospects, I would repeat the view . . . that the introduction of modern methods of production are essential if Nigerian starch is to compete in the world's market. . . . I trust that due consideration has been given to the need for the projected factory" (Director of Commerce and Industries 1948).

African opinion was strenuously represented in critical newspaper commentary, but on the topic of the Nigerian share of production and trade rather than on standards. For example, an editorial note with respect to the United Africa Company's contract to supply *gari* to the military: "The gari contract given to this firm, has certainly been the subject of much bitter comment in the African community" (*Daily Service* 1942). Cassava standards were never a Nigerian domestic consumption issue. The quite abundant sources on the local cassava market seem to make no mention whatever of concern about what had intermittently been a quality problem: the cyanide content of artisanally produced *gari* for domestic consumption. In

1942, a contract for military supplies, for example, was discussed in terms of price rather than quality (e.g., Marshall 1942).[32]

Purity was a component of and an idiom in the politics of production: between countries in the colonial world, and between large- and small-scale producers on the domestic front. The struggle over Nigeria's share of a changed world market was being fought out in part over standards of purity. It was, however, being fought out in the context of the corporatism prevailing in the contemporary metropolitan political economy, where the higher levels of government were allied with large business, and the latter was far more concerned with producing complementarities than parallels. The Tanganyikan Groundnut Scheme was explained in quintessentially welfare-corporatist and complementary terms: the postwar minister of food, John Strachey, rushed to develop a vast and ill-conceived groundnut plantation in East Africa to ensure that "the harassed housewives of Britain get more margarine, cooking fats and soap" (Thomas 1973, 247) after the austerity of the war. Tanganyika was to fulfill the role of producer, quickly and on a scale and to standards that complemented the demands of the metropolitan "democracy of consumers," to use the Webbs' ([1922] 1963) term for welfare politics. In Nigeria, the lower levels of colonial administration and Nigerian society clung to their evolutionary models, championing the potential of the small farmer, processor, and regional Nigerian economy, advocating and demonstrating their capacity to meet the standards eventually.

Where the producer and the consumer populations were separated in the colonial political geography, and where one population was dealing with the purity model while the other with the full-fledged corporatism of the welfare model, the confusingly ad hoc application of measures and rubrics generated key debates about the one point of agreement between the two models: namely that quality was a legitimate issue. Great effort was poured into means of producing pure starch in Nigerian conditions. The nature of the standards and whether small producers could or could not rise to them were issues that various participants manipulated as the geopolitical ground shifted and the connections among the various plausible elements of policy were remade. For the vocal Nigerian population, the state's transparent manipulations in the apparent interests of business and foreign consumers made the people and the state open adversaries. The cost to the people was the loss of a potential small-holder industry and the waste of years of experimentation by colonial agricultural officers and Nigerian farmers.

Several inferences are worth making. The purity model itself was never fully developed in Nigeria, in that government treated the large traders as arbiters rather than enemies. And the rubrics did not apply to local consumption; there was no constituency of consumer advocates within Nigerian civil society demanding their own standards. The purity model was replicated but only partially. In its implementation it contended with the now-entrenched metropolitan welfare model, whose overriding concerns were best served by developing complementarities with the colonial world. And the result was incoherent by comparison with the model as it had once operated in the metropole; in the colony it led to a loss of resources and a loss of confidence in state functionaries.

My second Nigerian example centers on state involvement in standards of food for local Nigerian consumption.[33] Again the participants invoked metropolitan concepts, this time from the welfare era, but again by selectively combining elements of the welfare model and applying them in a complementary political-economic context. The key concepts, essential commodities and then austerity, leaped straight out of the British wartime lexicon. The initial institutions, however, were established not during wartime—in this case the Nigerian civil war from 1967 to January 1970—but in its immediate aftermath. First the government placed price controls on particular commodities in high demand,[34] and then in 1972 it established the Nigerian National Supply Company (NNSC), a government parastatal "for the purpose of making bulk purchases of scarce commodities," primarily on the international market (Oyewole 1987, 237).[35] The idea of "essential commodities" was soon brought in, the term applying to a motley collection of imported food, including salt, sugar, vegetable oil, name-brand baby formula (Cerelac), milk, and above all else, rice.[36]

Published analytical work on the essential commodities program is very limited and the original sources are too recent to be available, but there are three simple points to be made. First, except for salt, the foods in question were "essential commodities" in the Nigerian diet in a sense more similar to that employed in World War I Britain than in World War II Britain. They reflected a certain empirical demand, although one socially restricted to urban consumers. The list of commodities was defined by neither a theory of the diet nor a plan to enhance the country's productive potential.[37] The commodities were not in any theoretical sense "essential": the vast majority of the people ate some of them, but a relatively limited amount. All except salt were imported tastes as well as imported items.

Second, in terms of trader/state relations, the Nigerian system showed neither the profound distrust of private food business that still permeated the state in early twentieth-century Britain nor the overt corporatism of the midcentury. As a result, while the negotiated contracts must have been extraordinarily lucrative to the companies, all the public distrust and frustration that eventually developed were focused on other functionaries in the system. In fact, the large corporations were described in the newspaper as if they were benefactors, and all the inconveniences of price and supply were associated with what became perceived as massive corruption on the part of state officials.[38] The companies cannily managed to steer clear of the overt corporatism of the British essential commodities system and the entire welfare model, in which responsibility is shared. Lever Brothers was involved again, but this time in "trying . . . to sell to final consumers, without going through 'middlemen' who, in the public perception, are the major culprits of hoarding and profiteering," according to an article in the Nigerian press entitled "Food Locked in Warehouses" (*Concord Weekly* 1984d).

Third, and in striking contrast to the public support for the welfare model in Britain, by 1984 the public perception of the Nigerian essential commodities program could hardly have plunged to lower levels. Many newsmagazine articles about other grievances against the state were illustrated with photos of some stage or other of the disastrous system of essential commodities distribution. An article entitled "Economic Outlook: Recovery Still a Long Way Off" appeared under a photograph of a barrow boy hauling sacks, captioned "Essential commodities are vanishing as fast as jobs" (*Concord Weekly* 1984b). A critique of the military appeared under a photograph of a threatening soldier that was labeled "A soldier controlling crowds during public sales of essential commodities" (*Concord Weekly* 1984e). One article on the essential commodity system ended: "The sufferings of consumers, as it is now, can go on almost interminably" (Ezekiel and Otiono 1985). State officials found themselves enduring the classic moral opprobrium associated with food middlemen, mediating fluctuating prices that no one understood and openly getting rich doing so without a strong collective or theoretical justification and without the protection of corporatism. Welfare terminology had been borrowed, but without the situation, the elaborated theory, or, above all, the recognized political alliances of the British welfare model. The essential commodities program allowed major drains of Nigerian resources and became *the* key symbol of government corruption. In 1984, the former head of the program, Umaru Dikko, was found drugged in a packing case at a London airport accompanied by two Israeli guardians in a second packing case, apparently being involuntarily returned to Nigeria to face the public. This scandal was the last drama in what had already become a symbolic performance of prebendalism (Joseph 1987). Illustrating the moral fervor of the people's response, an article entitled "Dikko: Kidnapped, Drugged and Found" claimed that Dikko was "justifiably branded as the most wanted man in Nigeria" (*Concord Weekly* 1984a).[39] The terms of that response were varied but tended to resonate with religious motifs about the dereliction of public duty and collective culpability. Collective welfare is a concept that resonates with both old and new African traditions. The jacket of a record album entitled *Austerity*, made in 1984 by the endlessly popular musician Ebenezer Obey, includes a passage that slides unmistakably into the cadences and phraseology of the Anglican public confession:

> We have all in one way or the other contributed in the past in neglecting many aspects of our lives. . . . We totally neglected agriculture neither were we ready to patronise made in Nigeria goods. . . . We have left undone what we should have done. . . . Food is the priority of every man's life, both rich and poor. . . . God will bless us. (Obey and His Inter-Reformers Band 1984])[40]

It is quite clear from numerous sources that people do expect, on moral grounds, to have services provided by the state, but that they have little experience of the ways in which welfare provision as a political system, rather than a moral expectation, has worked in the metropole. The principles of selectivity are central: some elements have been replicated and others have not. The concept of essential commodities has achieved general validity in the English-speaking world, as have a whole series of images from the morality of the good war, such as the concepts of austerity and war applied to domestic peacetime programs; internationally we have the War on Want, and in Nigeria the military head of state General Buhari instituted the War against Indiscipline as an attempt to clean up public places when he came to power. But some concepts and practices have not been replicated. Why were some commodities defined as "essential" and others not, when nutritional theory was not replicated in the Nigerian context? And how were corporate interests involved when the familiar overt alliance of the metropolitan system was not publicly evident? These are questions about intention, about mobilization of the repertoire, and about consequences. The fine print of bureaucratic regulation in the former colonial world shapes the course of political change. Varied interests in metropolitan and local contexts negotiate a patchwork of measures from the existing repertoires whose specific gaps create channels for major resource flows. The failures create a vision of government as incompetent that deeply affects the moral claims the state can make on its people.

Conclusion

In this article I have addressed two topics: the history of food regulation itself, and more generally, the anthropological study of modern governance. My concluding remarks apply to the models rather than to food per se, and they include some speculations that guide my thinking about the most recent dynamics.

The development of bureaucratic models—their legitimation and succession within centers of power, and their replication and domestication elsewhere—is one of the most important political processes in the modern world. It is also extraordinarily intricate: the wording of guidelines is technical and arcane, the negotiations are often secret, and the intentions are masked. The volumes of fine print seem drier than the proverbial medieval debate about pins and angels. But like religious debate, the regulatory fine print expresses basic and highly emotive suppositions about society, the state, and their relationship, and it is a vehicle for political reconfiguration. The effects are powerful, even though their causes and conditions may be inaccessible to the ordinary public. These characteristics of regulatory processes—that they are produced by powerful, arcane, often secret processes, refer to symbolic models, affect intimate human needs, embody agency, and express negotiated meanings—are attributes to whose study anthropological theory and ethnographic method are ideally suited. What I suggest further in this article is that we should take the long view and search for systematic derivations from one model to the next, and from the model to the replication. The history of food regulation exemplifies the systematic nature of historical derivations if one looks at them over a long enough time frame, as distinct from the indeterminacy, convolution, and short-run strategizing that must strike the observer of specific events. The complex cultural "landscapes" (Appadurai 1990) of the twentieth century are the loci to which regulation is applied and in which their implications are sometimes dramatically ritualized in the kind of performative pastiche represented here by the Dikko affair. But the events often have long, and quite specific, antecedents in the past and long-term implications into the future. The history of food regulation suggests that administrative models have succeeded one another in the metropolitan repertoire over the past century but without the outmoded models disappearing from the cultural repertoire of modernity. They remain available, to be invoked and partially applied according to judgments about the match between the attributes of the populations or nations concerned and the attributes of past and present metropolitan populations.[41] The sequence of models, their critical symbolic and political differences from one another, the matching of models to populations, and the selectivity of specific measures can be seen as structured processes. The terms of struggle over the selection process on the part of different groups refer to recognizably different models. The flow of vast resources is guided by the fissures and dikes created by this process of model derivation within the metropolitan formal sector; in the micro-ecologies of the interfaces, conditions of life may be irreversibly altered. Since the beginning of the 1980s, we have been in the process of another shift of administrative models, whose links to the past and to the rest of the world are still being forged. A model of the state as arbiter of the cost to society is replacing the model of the state as purveyor of welfare. A complex cost-accounting calculation is placed before the taxpayer, overshadowing but not entirely replacing old images of state-society relations as involving citizens with rights or consumers with needs. The custodians of the national budget present the government's vast and largely incomprehensible expenditures to the millions of contributors as costs to be comparatively and competitively assessed and selectively afforded. Emphasis shifts from the quality control concerns inherited from the earliest model and the subsidies inherited from the second, to the direct and indirect costs of the regulatory bureaucracy itself to those who pay for it. The old issues of purity and welfare are incorporated, but into an entirely different idiom of public accounting in which the complex social costs of regulating are put before the taxpayer to be assessed against the equally complex social costs of not regulating. Citizens become categories of contributors and beneficiaries, whose political organization takes the form of constituencies relative to the budget.

The progressive opposition to the party line on the "cost to society" seems to accept the premises of the new model but argues that there are participants who cannot form political constituencies of taxpayers to protect their benefits and who therefore suffer from their costs and contributions remaining uncounted. These include, for example, children and future generations, unorganized subsections of metropolitan populations, workers, and consumers elsewhere in the world and forms of life in the natural environment. It is of special concern, then, to ensure that these others have a voice: in their own polities through democratization, in the world community through self-determination, and in the politics of the most powerful nations through representatives of their interests.

The meaning of "society" and its boundaries, and the conditions under which constituencies have a "voice," must then become among the most contested areas as the moral framework for this new model of regulation struggles into existence. For whose social costs is the national taxpayer responsible in the ever-increasing inclusions that cost accounting invites? Which of the many identities a person holds is most relevant to the creation of the boundaries of political constituencies? As in the past, the new model does not totally delegitimate its predecessor and in fact selectively borrows some of its images. Conservatism is still concerned with purity and welfare, but with respect to narrowly defined and culturally uniform constituencies. At another extreme is the global vision. Its adherents advocate that we "Think Globally and Act Locally," thus pitching the old welfare imagery at a global level and in a long-term time frame. They call for the mobilization of more complex and inclusive political constituencies, although the feasible bases of successful political organization in this mode are still rather a conundrum: the international network is volatile and the local constituency has little incentive over the long run to refrain from promoting its own sectional interests.[42] The contours and dynamics of a cost-accounting model of government regulation are still being fought out, both at home and abroad. There is perhaps a cumulative chaotic indeterminacy to this replacement/retention/selection process that will eventually constitute a challenge to all systematic analysis.[43] Still the derivation of one administrative model from another and the partial replication of models in new contexts must continue. However fractal the postmodern world becomes and however permeable some of the boundaries, the regulatory processes that create categories and boundaries are deeply institutionalized and have become seemingly inevitable facts of political and social life over the past two hundred years. The dominant model of regulation may shift, but it is impossible to conceive of a present world without some kind of formal regulation. The ways in which different models and their constituent practices are mobilized, and by whom, will constitute the substance of political competition, and the results will be a powerful practical expression of emerging theories of boundaries, difference, and multiplicity.

Anthropologists will necessarily engage with the ways in which the social cost model "plays in Lagos," that is, its application and implications in other political contexts. The state in the former colonial world may still be, as in the past, "one model behind": being encouraged to develop legitimacy on the basis of provision of services—one of which is "food security"—while the rest of the world is decisively moving on, and its representatives are pressing hard for the development of straight complementarity. The importance and the tangibility of these debates about regulation lend themselves to the application of ethnographic methods.

We need, in addition, to stand back and examine the model building and derivations themselves, in the present as well as in the colonial past. Appreciation of the depth, range, and internal structure of the Western regulatory repertoire allows anthropologists to address specific formal sector models, rather than to invoke a generic "occidentalism" (Carrier 1992). One can then envisage a political-administrative counterpart of Appadurai's study of the "shapes of culture (that are) less bounded and tacit, more fluid and politicized," and that offer "a new role for the imagination in social life" (1990, 19, 4). The constituencies of a "costs to society" model are constantly shifting as their members search for identities and organizations that can guarantee an effective political voice. If we develop workable models of such formal-sector processes, anthropology can bring its past work on multiplicity, tension, and contradiction to bear on situations where the agency, power, and negotiated meanings we usually study in microcosmic arenas—the "toiling ingenuity" of political actors—will have their most far-reaching effects on the future.

Finally, in addition to constituting a subject of study, the rise of this cost-accounting approach also helps, I believe, to contextualize the current concern in our own intellectual circles with defining "society": with questions of diversity, "multiple voices," the boundaries between "self" and "other," and the philosophical debate about universalism (see also Cooper 1989). If the idiom of governance is one of balancing costs, then the critical questions become, which groups form viable constituencies and who can accurately represent sectional interests. Traditions are invented or selectively retrieved as a way of identifying constituencies or lobbies—now increasingly referred to by the tradition-laden term "communities"—for a "cost to society" politics. By its focus on difference, the new model tends to undermine both versions of parallelism I have explored in this article, presentist and evolutionary, and to foster a theory and practice of complementarity, that is of competition relative to the costs communities have paid and the benefits they have enjoyed. By means that can often be difficult to grasp and explore, our own writing about difference may be part of the same process of defining constituencies as are the "forms and circulars" of food regulation.

Acknowledgments

This chapter was originally written as an article under the title "The Politics of Consumption," for the "Workshop on Commodities" held at the Johns Hopkins University, April 20–21, 1991, and chaired by Ashraf Ghani. The

archival work was carried out at the University of Ibadan while I was affiliated with the Institute of African Studies and the International Institute of
Tropical Agriculture, and it was funded by the National Science Foundation (BNS-8704188). The original article was written while I was a senior
fellow in the Department of Anthropology at the Smithsonian Institution.
I am indebted to Ellen Messer, Toyin Falola, and Vicente Navarro for their
comments on the first draft and to Achille Mbembe, Ashraf Ghani, Phil
Raikes, the anonymous *American Ethnologist* reviewers, and the editor for
their comments on the second draft.

PART TWO

Public Economic Cultures

THREE

"The Craving for Intelligibility": Speech and Silence on the Economy under Structural Adjustment and Military Rule in Nigeria

JANE I. GUYER WITH LARAY DENZER

Rhetoric and Intelligibility

I am concerned in this paper with what Friedrich von Hayek considered the grave dangers of "the craving for intelligibility" ([1944] 2007, 204) with respect to economic life. Hayek published *The Road to Serfdom* (1944) toward the end of a war that he saw as having profoundly entrenched centralized economic management in the state and in the hands of ideologues, with disastrous results for Germany and for the world. He argued not only against National Socialism but also against the Keynesian formula for selective state intervention, in favor of a return to markets as soon as the war was over. To "submit" to markets was by far the lesser of evils, as "the refusal to submit to anything we cannot understand must lead to the destruction of our civilization" (204).

In the new era of the post-1989 world, voices in the public sphere both in the West and in countries such as Nigeria are again searching for one or another set of terms that can offer intellectual and political traction on the state-people-economy relationship. How do economic and political leaders talk to their people? For what aspects of collective life are they technically and morally responsible? Are the people subjects or constituents with respect to those aspects? In what form can they or should they answer back? The theories and methods that are invoked at such times are compelling creations of their moment in history. And yet they also work out over time. It is to this working out of one economic theory and rhetoric over time, in one political-economic context, namely Nigeria under structural adjustment and military rule (1983–1999), that I turn in this paper. I draw on the remarkable coverage provided by the Nigerian newspapers over this period. Their journalists consistently reported on pronouncements and responses, mounted their own investigations, and raised their own critiques in spite of intermittent repression. What emerges is an example of the ongoing battle involved in bringing together a specific economic situation and a particular economic theory, in a public rhetoric in which everything is at issue and the stakes are high: the type of intelligibility that is communicable, its relationship to unfolding events in the world, and the ways in which it can be sustained over time.

Hayek is interestingly and complexly fundamental to posing these questions for modern Nigeria, and eventually far beyond. Structural adjustment policies that downsized the state and opened African economies to more deregulated market forces were a descendant of his theoretical orientation. At the time that structural adjustment policies were implemented in Africa, there were observers from a different theoretical persuasion who saw potential good in this. The African state was beginning to look like a class affair of revolving military and civilian elites who used its infrastructures to establish their own power and consolidate capital accumulation in the midst of economic crisis for the masses. Basil Davidson, for example, supporter of the populist liberation movements throughout the mid-twentieth century, referred to the "curse of the nation state" in the title of one of his last books, *The Black Man's Burden* (1992). Much earlier, Frantz Fanon (1963) had seen the relationship between the African bourgeoisie and the state as ominous for the political future. Hayek had also seen the demands of the German middle class for government favor in the face of economic troubles—in his case the hyperinflation of the Weimar period—as the ground on which the rhetoric and practice of totalitarianism took hold.

From a pragmatic standpoint as well as a theoretical one, Nigeria might be seen as actually quite well situated for greater market freedom and the formation of the kind of spontaneous order that Hayek advocated, if one looks with a positive theoretical eye on its vast "informal sector," already recalcitrant to regulation and taxation. Most people probably already did not "crave" articulated centralized solutions and might well have been positively disposed to a rhetoric that acknowledged a gap of ignorance between the power of human knowledge and the power of the world. Market uncertainty is a well-established expectation. It is much less clear, however, that either the informal sector or the formal sector in Nigeria would accept what Hayek repeatedly refers to as "submission," since local philosophies of life entail active intervention through divination and sacrifice (see Guyer 1993b, 2005a). Hayek writes:

> It is men's submission to the impersonal forces of the market that in the past
> made possible the growth of a civilization. . . . It is by thus submitting that
> we are every day helping to build something that is greater than any one of
> us can fully comprehend. . . . It is infinitely more difficult rationally to com-
> prehend the necessity of submitting to forces whose operation we cannot
> follow in detail than to do so out of the humble awe which religion, or even
> the respect for the doctrines of economics, did inspire. ([1944] 2007, 204–5)

How such submission might work in public life in various political contexts would depend fundamentally on what people can learn to accept
as ignorance and what dispensation they can acquire for "awe" and "respect" for the domains of power that rightly belong beyond full human
comprehension. As it turned out, Nigerian commentators sought "fuller
comprehension" on some issues that are not ignorance but intractable incoherences (or deliberate maskings) in the application of the theory to particular conditions. Their struggles thereby illuminate fault lines in theory
and practice that may be more widely relevant in a world where this same
theory meets experiences of life.

Most current attention in economic debate, both for and against present policies, has been devoted to the dot-connecting concepts that theorists
can claim to have confidence in—freedom, growth, reduced taxation—and
do therefore produce an intelligible policy and informed rhetoric to convey
to citizens. These concepts have been deployed to support novel adven-
tures in visions of the future. But what about the domains of *ignorance* that
are implied in monetarist theory and neoliberal ideology? It is to Hayek's
enormous credit, I think, that he does not sidestep this question. Rather he
expresses steely resolve: "It is the price of democracy that the possibilities
of conscious control are restricted to the fields where true agreement exists
and that in some fields things must be left to chance" (1944 [2007], 69).
His argument is full of warnings about "illusions," "deceiving ourselves,"
and the necessity to "re-learn frankly to face the fact that freedom can only
be had at a price and that as individuals we must be prepared to make
severe material sacrifices to preserve our liberty" ([1944] 2007, 133). Since
The Road to Serfdom reinspires the phase of liberal thought that we now
experience (at least in the United States), its message offers a beacon of
clarity for triangulating the conditions and the rhetoric that we are all im-
mersed in.

The line I explore here, through the lens of Nigeria, is the particular political and rhetorical *burden* of a theoretical position that embraces fluctuation as a necessary condition of the market system but is bereft of concepts

to convey this in positive terms when that fluctuation happens. According to Hayek and followers, market fluctuations are not controllable nor even always understandable, but they are an essential and positive component of the long-term process of growth. In the classical tradition of rhetoric, the utterance extended and transcended truth by taming the zone of ignorance into an encompassing logic. It served the purpose of persuasion in three major arenas—the legal court, the legislative assembly, and the public forum—under conditions where incontrovertible truth could not be ascertained. As Bizzell and Hertzberg write, "In civil disputes, persuasion established claims where no clear truth was available" (1990, 2).[1] Partial truths still provided basic landmarks in the argument. The skill of rhetorical performance extended them to create a coherent and motivating interpretation of a whole that brought the listeners from their various positions of skepticism to a point of convergence. The idea of "persuasion" implies a convergence of interpretation, and thereby of motivation in favor of concerted action. Hayek's theory, however, would imply a converse rhetorical move: a felt collective condition is addressed by actually enlarging rather than contracting the area of shared ignorance and by promoting the felicity of people submitting to conditions in—presumably—their own private and varied ways.

One needs to ask where exactly the burdens of a rhetorical rendition of this theory are likely to fall, because a call to "submission" to "conditions" is not a politically simple one to make. On the one hand, the nearsighted view of *imminent* minute movements in the markets can advocate that actors respond. On the other, there is a farsighted view of *future* growth.[2] But the practical politics of *large* shifts over the *short* run are hard to grasp. Being called on to address painful fluctuation and outright crises when they occur presents the need to contend explicitly with contextual pressures, whereas context falls outside the theory. Explaining crisis under Hayek's theory, either as an elected official or a disciplinary expert, must pose both scientific and political challenges. How can the concepts be made to match the occurrences? How can fluctuation and disorder/reordering be alluded to, as they happen, in terms of a theory that extols them as "creative in the long run"?

The lack of contextual concepts and midrange temporal frames leaves a vacuum of meanings available for rhetorical mobilization. At the high level there are large abstractions such as freedom, chance, sacrifice, democracy, (unspecified) forces one cannot comprehend, "the price" one has to pay, the "humble awe" one has to mobilize, and of course "the market." At the very specific level, there are financial instruments and markets developed in the finest of numerical and conceptual detail. Left out of the terms of this rhetoric are precisely those domains of life and temporal horizons that are most awkward to make a consistently positive claim for, namely the multiplicity of the entailments within any real economy (as understood by its participants) and the near-future temporal frame that "fluctuation" somehow invokes. This, of course, is where people live. When all boats are rising, it might be persuasive to focus on the "now" of demand and the "distant horizon" of our common fate. But finding a consistent monetarist rhetoric in bad or confusing times is surely much more difficult, especially when the "sacrifices" asked of citizens seem "both unbearable and unnecessary," as Hayek ([1944] 2007, 19) noted that they certainly would be.

In his day, Hayek was critiqued on exactly this point, and not from the classic left or the Keynesians. Michael Polanyi wrote that Hayek was "apparently not willing to describe the interplay between the inarticulate and rationalizable aspects of practice, be they in the marketplace or elsewhere, and therefore had effectively reneged on the promise to theorize the role of knowledge in economics. . . . In an era obsessed by the fear of mass unemployment (he turned) an indifferent eye on this problem" (Mirowski 2004, 79). There are two problems of intelligibility that Polanyi is pointing to: "the role of knowledge" in the scientific sense (what does the scientific expertise tell us about the situation?) and the role of communication (what can and should be communicated to a population "obsessed by fear"?). Bad times pose real and unavoidable dilemmas for both scientific knowledge and political rhetoric about the economy. The very idea of "the economy" is based implicitly on an assumption of "nation," that is, a collectivity (see Mitchell 2002). So what options open up, face-to-face with a national population: A rhetoric that preserves theoretical consistency about the ultimate direction of "growth" at the price of public anger and suffering? Or one that addresses the near future in its own terms, at the cost of abandoning in theory or in practice the principle of singularity and direction? Perhaps there are historically specific resolutions rather than a principled one: holding off the great wave of the public's "craving for intelligibility" by stalling for time, or encouraging a onetime historic bailout into the "freedom to choose" (Friedman and Friedman 1980), which eventually entails removing "the economy" from the public forum of debate altogether.

The following alternatives do offer solutions that may be principled as well as pragmatic, although they are certainly fragile. Monetarist public speech does sometimes follow the persuasion and coherence of classic rhetorical form: in this case, however, not by completing present evidence by projecting its logic forward, but by creating a complete model of the future and projecting its terms back onto the present. This "virtualism" draws attention away from present confusion, as experienced, and imposes on it the categories of the coherent model (Carrier and Miller 1998; Baxstrom et al. 2005). Persuasion then amounts to acceptance of the relevance of futuristic categories for recognizing the present. This argument is a brilliant one, but not necessarily easy to sustain in the kind of hard or confusing times that the theory itself predicts because the gap between the categories of the future and those of people's experience in the present may diverge beyond any suspension of disbelief. Radical uncertainty in the world and radical skepticism among the citizenry can recast this rhetorical tactic as "spin" or just plain lies.

The strategy of virtualism is quite different from its alternative: facing the fluctuations of the present head-on, including the extreme detail of the specialist's calculations, and so directly advocating the public's recognition of the limits of knowledge and the importance of submission, as Hayek's position would imply. People must just relearn how to leave things to "chance." The political downsides of this position include offering so much information about the situation of crisis or major fluctuation that an alternative interpretation can emerge. Those who cannot get even into the foothills of an understanding of the financial system are likely to revolt against it, and those who do understand it realize that experts are buffering their own situations, and perhaps even making profits from arbitrage of the spatial and temporal disjunctures entailed in instability. People will demand explanation, and their own worries and suspicions can come to dominate the public debate. Experts then back off into an attitude of "humble awe" (Hayek). Leonhardt (2003) exemplifies a version of this last strategy of emphasizing that "it's beyond us," but with a dash of the allegorical virtualism of the first, seemingly to head off the public from latching on to real accounting (and accountability) with respect to what he calls the "dark side." He argues that "today's economy has escaped definition" and has "flummoxed political strategists" (1); it can best be denoted as a "Goldilocks Economy," with a "dark side" represented by people's concerns not about "the here and now" but about "the big costs down the road" (6). Commentators admit confusion: "Federal Reserve officials, who meet this week, are beginning to suspect that the perplexing decline in long-term interest rates is more than a temporary aberration" (Andrews 2005, C1).

A final possibility for rhetoric leads in a similar direction but to a more radical end. It involves acting strictly on the letter of the theory that government does not manage "the economy," only the money supply, therefore saying as little as possible about anything economic other than money.

Each approach is more or less feasible, so how are political rhetorics managed in an actual crisis event or wide and incoherent fluctuation? In the United States we have not—or had not when this paper was first written—yet confronted extreme friction between monetarist theory and popular experience. But outside the West, there have been places living under monetarist policy whose populations have already seen the kind of unbearable conditions that Hayek alluded to as dangers. Writing of fluctuations in the world currency market, Eichengreen warns that such places and historical periods should be expected: "Large economies, relatively closed, can pursue domestic objectives without suffering intolerable pain from currency swings. For the majority of smaller, open economies, . . . the costs of floating are difficult to bear. . . . Volatile exchange rate swings impose almost unbearable costs" (1996, 196). Several economies experienced major fluctuations in their currency's exchange rates and in consequent conditions of life during the 1980s and 1990s. Africa was among the first, under what was intended to be a controlled process of "structural adjustment" of the place of government in economic life. Nigeria started down this path in 1985. With an ancient commercial culture and a high level of expertise and vibrant economic organizations, Nigerians turned very rapidly to informal and extraformal modes of operation as world markets loosened up. By 1992, a shift had taken place, from expectations placed on government to recognition of the sheer necessity of keeping goods, provisions, employment, and finance moving in spite of economic policy (see Guyer, Denzer, and Agbaje 2002). Yet at the same time, the sheer power and wealth of the federal government constituted both a threat and a resource that would never be ignored. People still made claims and criticisms. Over the twenty years since the particular combination of instability and central power came into focus, the search for a rhetoric of intelligibility has had time to go through several iterations, playing across a repertoire of possibilities as conditions of life and of skepticism shifted. It is to that sequence of iterations that we turn.

Using an archive of newspaper articles collected by LaRay Denzer, students, and me at the University of Ibadan over the 1990s, and with some notable recuperations for the 1980s, we are able to trace out some of the unfolding rhetoric and response as first a populist military president (Ibrahim Babangida, 1985–1993) and then a repressive one (Sani Abacha, 1993–1998) tried to represent some version of a neoliberal national budget to the Nigerian people. Throughout this period the government continued to present an annual budget accompanied by a speech of explanation, which was followed by various published commentaries and critiques. Ultimately the exercise degenerated into enormous confusion. The most common reasons given from the outside are the transparent "greed" of those in power and the pervasive "cynicism" of the powerless. But the debate in the press was not a brawl of symbolic slings and arrows; it was seriously reasoned in economic terms. By tracing out this extreme case, one can point out the extraordinary delicacy of *any* rhetorical claim to uncertainty by those who are closest to the power of both science and the state under monetarist policy, as Hayek predicted. Attention to economic rhetoric allows us to pause longer over the public space and public speech of economic indeterminacy than a dismissive explanation in terms of third world dictatorship would allow.

Nigeria

The Nigerian economy under structural adjustment and military rule (1984–1998) was increasingly presented as unintelligible. Until recently, I—like others—assumed that this was a function of the *military mismanagement* that all observers agreed on. Under autocratic rule, there may be no need for government to bother with persuasive rhetoric from benchmarks in truth, because the public cannot answer back. In any case, the official record—on the trade balance, revenue by source, employment trends, and so on—can be either neglected altogether or kept secret, so there are no "objective" landmarks on which to center the debate. Following Mbembe (2001) and others, Andrew Apter (2005) has made a strong and fascinating argument about the performative—rather than persuasive—nature of Nigerian military rhetoric. I am persuaded by his demonstrations, but no longer to the exclusion of other levels and dynamics of engagement between government and people. The Nigerian government did present the standard economic indicators in the annual budget speech; ministers did comment on economic events and policy directions; and economic journalists did analyze the logic of their statements. My change of mind, to foreground what presents itself as argument over what presents itself as a performance, came from hearing some of the same terminology surfacing in our own public life a decade after it surfaced in Nigeria. The replication seems uncanny. On the side of advocacy, people then and now, there and here, talk about the *very long-run future* and *growth* as benchmark for policy success, the centrality of *control of inflation through the national money supply (inter-*

est rates, control of excess liquidity, savings), and the importance of staying *steadfast, staying the course*, and the wisdom of *individual* leadership. On the critical side, they talk about a "faith-based economy," an economic culture of greed, the resurgence of class warfare, the leaders as "magicians," and the inscrutability of their official pronouncements. In the very last week before the conference for which this paper was written, the *New York Times* ran an op-ed by Paul Krugman (2005b) devoted to the "spin" on the U.S. deficit which shadows almost exactly the debate I discuss below. It would not be difficult to take a newspaper cartoon of the 1991 Nigerian budget, showing popular consternation and confusion, and redraw it about the U.S. budgets—with their deficits, belt-tightening, and massive off-budget expenditures—over ten years later. It is called "The People's View" and includes speech bubbles saying: "Who can help me now?" "I'm not sure I understand," "Now kerosene done cost," and "We need to pray more."[3] I am not taking cheap shots by drawing this parallel but rather opening up a serious question. How do monetarists in fact create an intelligible argument about the near future in bad circumstances?

I do not reject the self-serving, performative and culturally specific interpretation of Nigerian military rhetoric about state and economy, but there was always a recognizable seriously engaged "rational" economic debate in Nigeria as well. The public rhetorical engagement about a monetarist and structural adjustment policy had many years to play out, over what I will describe as three distinct phases: a collective public debate about the meaning of economic terms under rapidly changing conditions (1984–1987), an effort to wrench the nation and the market into a single identity (1987–1993), and a retreat into cacophony and silence (1994–1998). Doubtless it could have worked differently, but the three phases I present here have sequential plausibility to them, as both government and people ran the gamut of available rhetorical strategies about the plausibility of long-term growth one after the other, starting with a struggle over definitional categories for relating actual life in the present and near future to the model, followed by abandonment of claims to intelligibility, and subsequently an interplay of cacophony and silence.

"Deficits," "Contingencies," and "Subsidies": The Debate of 1984–1987

The realistic difficulty for Nigerian economic policy in the structural-adjustment era was that every variable was moving at once. All modern governments are aware of prices, not in "the market" in a generic sense but in the specific market that keeps their particular national economies moving and populations compliant: the price of capital in the financial markets in some, the price of staple foods in the commodity markets in others, or the producer or consumer price of oil and gas in the energy markets in still others. This means using policy instruments to benchmark that price to something fairly stable or amenable to stabilization in people's real lives. For Nigeria, the key market is the world market in crude oil, denominated in dollars, which is markedly unpredictable. The annual budget projection is necessarily based on informed speculation about the dollar price of oil on world markets. If the oil price and the exchange rate for the dollar are changing at once, even contingency calculations are no longer workable.

In the early phase of structural adjustment in Nigeria, the value of the naira was falling against the dollar as the world price of oil also plummeted to $10 in the late 1980s. By the end of the 1980s there was also inflation, in retrospect from large amounts of off-budget government spending. When the budget for 1987 was announced there was a huge debate over whether it was, or was not, a deficit budget, and how one would know. The federal director of the budget, Omowale Kuye, explained that "revenue projections have an element of contingency . . . built in to the tune of N4.513 billion[4] . . . not a set-aside" but an "uncertainty," presumably and justifiably, about the price of oil and other home-produced exports on world commodity and exchange markets that were changing rapidly and not necessarily in any coordinated or predictable fashion. Only this "contingency" of N4.5 billion on the revenue side made the budget appear balanced. This contingency was not an addition to the N17.9 billion total budgeted revenue, but had been included as part of that amount. So journalists argued that the terminology was being used to conceal what was in fact a deficit budget (Omokhodion with Iduwe 1987). There was no way of knowing whether such an amount was realistic or fantastic, and apparently there was no agreement about how it should be conceptualized. The same question—of whether a particular budget was balanced or not when it was presented—continued year after year. In 1988 the plan to reflate the economy involved promising a deficit that would be "modest and reasonable" (*Nigerian Economist* 1988, 13). The year 1989 saw a budget deficit. By 1991, however, the government announced a "surplus budget" (*West Africa* 1991, 12), and at least one newspaper commentator wrote that if one made exact comparisons of the categories included it in fact represented a 70 percent *increase* in spending in comparison with 1990 (Imirhe 1991). By 1991 the critics were also writing of a consistent "overestimation of the price of a barrel of oil" (Adeleye with Olatunde 1991, 52) in the projections on which the budget was calculated, and by 1993 they were writing of a "Budget of Deceit" laced with (to quote a former military governor) "gimmicks" (*Newbreed* 1993, 11). In 1991 the Nigerian government may—or may not—have kept to its budget projections, but at the same time it also "disappeared" the entire $12 billion in windfall revenues from the First Gulf War oil-price hike. The Okigbo Commission was eventually empowered to investigate after the change of government in 1992, but the report was quickly confiscated (Agbese 2005).

By 1996 there was a rising tide of outrage against government manipulation of the budget numbers to produce these elusive qualities—"balanced budget," "low inflation," and so on—as I will come to later. But in the beginning the question of definition was a real one. How *did* one know the referent of the concept of a "deficit" or "surplus" budget when the base price of oil and the exchange rate for the naira, on which all revenue projections crucially depended, could not be known? The budget was a kind of visionary exercise rather than a planning document, although it retained the categories and format of the latter. This sort of ignorance of the market is implied in what Hayek would have us submit to: not only ignorance of the reasons for the movement of conditions and indicators, but also ignorance of the origins and referents of the concepts that classify them. In economic policy, the "craving for intelligibility" can come down to scrutinizing the most banal of concepts and reexamining the most tedious of tables to see how the concepts and the numbers actually work together. Nigerian commentators tried to do this quite persistently.

The definition that aroused by far the most intense popular engagement was the so-called subsidy on domestic petrol prices. In Nigeria, the oil economy was launched under the rubric of national integration, and therefore a certain sense of national ownership, after the Civil War (1966–1970). By the early 1980s, it was already clear that the revenues had been funding massive collective symbolic projects such as the Second World Black and African Festival of Arts and Culture (FESTAC '77; see Apter 2005), the new capital at Abuja (see Elleh 2002), the steel industry at Ajaokuta (see Forrest 1995), the proliferation of states and therefore capitals and administrations, and the spectacular enrichment of the military and upper classes. Behind this front was another revolution: the vast motorization of the artisanal economy and ordinary social life of the Nigerian people (Guyer 1997). Vehicle imports surged; mechanized farming expanded; dealerships and repair shops proliferated; expanding cities were fed from farther and farther away; national trade networks were extended and intensified; and people traveled more and more often to a rising tide of family celebrations, local meetings, chieftaincy installations, courses of study and apprenticeships, and so on and so on. In some quite inexplicit way, an affordable and predictable price of "our" petrol became a populist assumption of the national compact.

The idea that this constituted a "subsidy," and that a government subsidy was a negative thing, was a profound surprise when it was launched under the pressures of structural adjustment starting in 1982. The debate of that era culminated in a standoff about what "subsidy" even meant in the context of an oil-producing economy. A subsequent politicization of the whole issue has recurred with ferocity up to the present. The government was unable or unwilling to make a plausible argument for either knowledge or ignorance, and the population became increasingly unwilling to accept any of its explanations. I recount the first confrontation, in 1985, and briefly some of the rhetorics of others in the twenty-first century, in order to set the stage for subsequently grappling with the claim of ignorance in the face of "markets."

The most fascinating aspect of the interchange about petrol prices at the pump is the attempt to benchmark them morally and practically to various *different* other prices. Monetarism depends on abstractions of abstractions with respect to the management of the money supply and its ramifying effects throughout "the economy." But abstraction seems to be the first quality to fall under attack when prices fail to make sense to people. A price is not just a relationship between supply and demand in people's eyes, but a relationship between one good and another, a person's income and her standard of living, a seller and a buyer, and the state and the people (in the case of certain goods). In fact, one might even define the "craving for intelligibility" as the refusal to accept higher levels of market abstraction in favor of a concept that can be morally, politically, and intellectually pegged to something more or less tangible. And the experts can be drawn into this logic, whether or not it makes sense to them theoretically. For example, in the face of the economic crisis of 1981, the IMF compared the price of Nigerian petrol (pejoratively) to Coca-Cola, implying some just or sensible distance between the two prices. Domestic petrol prices were considered far too low relative to Coke; hence the concept of subsidy, since petrol prices were controlled. But there is no reason internal to market theory that would suggest a cultural or moral ratio between one price and another.

In the 1985 debate the subsidy concept for oil prices was finally accepted by the Nigerian government and announced to be at the exceptionally high level of 80 percent. In line with the reigning theory, the subsidy was removed on January 1, 1986, and petrol prices fixed at a higher, but still controlled, price. Another simultaneous component of structural adjustment, however, was devaluation of the overvalued naira. In 1986 the naira value for trade was allowed to fall against the hard currencies of the world. With a fixed nominal price for petrol at the pump that was set in naira, from an international standpoint the subsidy immediately "reappeared" as soon as the naira fell against the dollar. It was even recalculated, this time at 60 percent. At this point an economist (Ashwe 1987) redefined it as an "implicit subsidy," therefore not a result of deliberate policy; however, that linking of "implicit" and "subsidy" would have to be explained to a population that had only just accepted the notion of subsidy at all. Ashwe tried to redefine the whole situation "starting from first principles . . . when the 'shouting match' started," going through a series of calculations of the price of crude, the cost of refining, the exchange rate and the "cost at the pumps" to arrive at the conclusion (see below) that getting rid of the "subsidy" is highly "dubious," and in any case oil is a Nigerian endowment whose price is set by a world cartel. "Fuel Subsidy: To Be or Not To Be: Government Perches on the Horns of a Dilemma as It Weighs the Economics and Politics of Petroleum Subsidy" (*Newswatch* 1987). Strong voices questioned the subsidy concept altogether. They claimed that since Nigeria was a producing country, the price to consumers should reflect the costs of production and refining, and not the world price at all. Political scientist Claude Ake wrote that the petrol used in Nigeria was never on the international market, "so you cannot translate into dollars. The whole talk about oil subsidy is rubbish" (quoted in Akinrinade 1988, 19).

The battle over the standard for the "right price" was now fully engaged. Then the world price of oil plummeted, and some commentators began to extend the subsidy logic to argue that the Nigerian consumer was actually being *taxed* by having to pay the fixed nominal price that was now *higher* than the world market price. By 1991, when the idea of withdrawing the subsidy came up again, commentators started arguing that "the tape has been rewound. And the drama is starting all over again" (Adedoyin and Dike 1991). This condition of going in circles was immortalized by musician Fela Anikulapo-Kuti under the song title of "Perambulator": "All no progress. . . . If you look de man well, . . . same same place. He no go anywhere. Perambulator!" (Olaniyan 2004, 99–100). But some processes did progress. Since the Communauté Financière Africaine (CFA) franc was stable and Nigeria is surrounded by franc-zone countries, as world oil prices rose again a steadily expanding network of petrol smuggling began. The conditions on the *regional* market now added themselves to those on the domestic and international markets, vying as the benchmark for judging whether indeed the Nigerian consumer was being subsidized or taxed, and by how much. The informal sector money changers quickly developed an acute sense of transborder profits under all kinds of fluctuating conditions, so there were surges and deficiencies in the domestic Nigerian supply. Eventually, those wealthy enough to run arbitrage during supply fluctuations added their own more or less deliberate interference contributing yet another criterion to estimate how much speculative profit was being made from the domestic market.[5] The whole domain became radically incoherent while also being radically essential to the entire flourishing informal economy and social life. The greater the withdrawal of the military government into laissez-faire rhetoric (and self-serving arbitrage on the side), the greater the public's need to count on affordable petrol prices to run its do-it-yourself economy without government at all.

The Nigerian press sources—particularly the tables in *Newswatch* of November 30, 1987, and repeated allusions of the kind quoted in Ashwe above—make arguments for six different ways of grounding the domestic petroleum price in some defensible matrix of intelligibility:

1. By comparison with domestic consumer prices in other oil producing countries: by this standard, Nigeria's price was low, but in part because tax regimes differ. Structural adjustment philosophy was certainly not advocating increasing taxes, so the press did not dwell on this difference. But this difference was large. For example, Britain's price could be indexed at 277 while Nigeria's was 40, where the difference is partly due to much higher taxes in Britain.

2. By comparison with Nigerian incomes: in Nigeria the ratio of petrol prices to incomes is very high: 1:20 whereas in Britain it was 1:30 and in Kuwait 1: 14,480.

3. By comparison with regional consumer prices: the price was much higher in the franc-zone neighboring countries, only Cameroon being an oil producer at the time.

4. By comparison with the costs of production and therefore realistic margins: this was always a nightmare to calculate, since every aspect of production and distribution is managed by contractual terms and government guidelines.

5. In relation to government revenue needs: gaps in the budget could be used as a justification for claiming a subsidy and demanding its abolition. The press caught on to this argument early in the process, since it met media skepticism about the budget.

6. As a simple national right: in an interview in 1992, the president himself vacillated. While complaining about the generally low level of patriotic respect for policy and law, Babangida also noted the Nigerians' conviction of a collective moral claim over "their" oil. "The Nigerian believes that this is his country, God has given him this [petroleum product] and therefore because God gave him, he must use it" (*Nigerian Hand Book Review* 1992). One government strategy of dealing with the whole moral rhetorical issue in the public sphere was eventually (1996) to define a special fund for development financed by oil revenues—the Petroleum Trust Fund (PTF)—to focus attention on at least some sort of gain that members of a suffering population were getting from "their" national oil. This, of course, was off-budget but intervened in the market for everything.

We all remember the rhetoric of "getting the prices right" during structural adjustment, but the Nigerian domestic-oil-subsidy debate (which continues to the present) shows several things about judgments of "rightness": (a) intelligibility *is* demanded by the public, especially of those goods that manifestly and always pass through government hands and that affect the lives of everyone; there is no begging off to "chance" in this crucial case; (b) the options for plausible arguments on the basis of "the market" are, in fact, multiple; there is quite obviously no singular coherent market, and no one standard by which to judge prices, so by concentrating on one argument an analyst reveals quite clearly the priorities he or she accords to key variables and thereby his or her political commitments; (c) it is not possible, then, to prioritize one or other of the plausible arguments (of which we have six here) on supposedly "rational" grounds without revealing an obvious favor for a particular constituency; and (d) by the time that massive arbitrage has set in and been institutionalized, it is almost impossible to make any principled theoretical argument at all because—even under military rule and intermittent intimidation of the press—the basic facts of shortage, gain, smuggling, and so on are totally public knowledge.

Beyond Specific Concepts: The Nation and the Market

In the period between 1987 and the annulment of the elections in 1993, there was a great deal of discussion oriented toward the relationship of market to nation. Debate about terminological issues continued and expanded as various policy instruments were "manipulated." This word is not a judgment; it is Babangida's own: "So what we did was to instruct the Central Bank to keep on manipulating (the naira) without saying so"

(*Nigerian Hand Book Review* 1992). Headlines asked not only "what is a subsidy?" but "what is the Nigerian debt?" (*Newswatch* 1988, 36), "what is profit?" in a "deregulated economy" (*Financial Guardian* 1992, 6), and "is our economy planned?" (*Nigerian Economist* 1987, 10). Public anger boiled over in 1988 and 1989. In 1992 the government itself suggested that the economy was unruly, and in 1993 the World Bank vice president for Africa, Edward Jaycox, was reported in the Nigerian press to have admitted that structural adjustment in Africa had been "a systematic destructive force" (*African Guardian* 1993, 28).

I cover the public rhetoric of this period only briefly. What became clear was that the idea of a *national* economy was coming apart under the conditions of the structural adjustment program (SAP) era. Again, this idea was not necessarily, and from the outset, due to venality on the part of the governing elites. The conditions of monetarist theory departed radically from realities in places like Nigeria. Phillip Cagan writes, "Monetarist theory of aggregate expenditures is based on a demand function for monetary assets that is claimed to be stable in the sense that successive residual errors are generally offsetting and do not accumulate. Given the present inconvertible-money systems, the stock of money is treated as under the control of the government" (1989, 199). These two systemic conditions for monetarism were nowhere close to being fulfilled, so the burden of the idea of a system fell rather on the shifting sands of a rhetoric of economic nationalism. In 1989, in the wake of nationwide riots, the president made a major speech that was reported under the title "SAP is not evil" to explain structural adjustment as a "well-thought-out program that aims at increased production in every sector of the economy in order to create more jobs, more goods and less foreign debts." Its enemies are detractors "bent on destroying the credibility of the military institution," whereas "we have a duty to the nation. . . . We shall do our duty to our country" (*Newswatch* 1989, 20). By 1992 he was reiterating the "unpatriotic" criticism, but to a much broader array of participants and in a much more resigned fashion: "The Nigerian is a very intriguing person. . . . There are at least 100 million opinions on any subject in Nigeria. . . . As long as you run a government in a society that is not docile, just like our own Nigerian society, it is not easy to take decisions. . . . It is a very difficult situation but it makes the Nigerian society tick. I like it" (*Nigerian Hand Book Review* 1992, 119, 120). A certain rhetoric of national character was setting in that now embraced radical multiplicity and radical indeterminacy, with no clear theoretical framework in view at all, just a vacuous prediction that "the naira will rise again," largely because the Nigerian people are who they are.

Cacophony and Silence

By the mid-1990s allusions to nationalism or national character had all but disappeared. Sani Abacha reinstated the neoliberal rhetoric about a national economy and a distant horizon of growth when he came to power in late 1993. Abacha's first budget speech was classic for its emphasis on moral values and implicit sacrifice for the country: "The Federal government . . . reiterated that the success of the 1994 budget was contingent upon the commitment of all Nigerians to the ideals of patriotism and high moral standards" (Edemodu 1996, 18). In keeping with the economic rhetoric of the time, the budget was to be balanced and the Central Bank was mobilized to control inflation. In 1995 the budget was dubbed the "Budget of Renewal," requiring "changes of direction, discipline, and the will to survive . . . patience, hard work and perseverance. Nigerians must not expect miracles overnight in trying to revamp the economy." The goals were set in classic neoliberal terms: reduction of inflation, expansion of the economy's productive base and the level of capacity in the manufacturing sector, creation of jobs, narrowing of the gap between the official and the parallel exchange rates, and reduction of the fiscal deficit by reducing wasteful government expenditure (*Business Times* 1994).

The claim of success came so fast as to be breathtaking. As early as March of the same year, the finance minister, the (eventually) notorious Anthony Ani, announced at a press briefing that these policies were working and that the government budget was now in surplus. He was also working to "articulate [the] debt profile, so as to determine the currencies in which they are denominated" and to help "evolve a viable debt management strategy" (*Daily Times* 1995, 7 and 15). In a replay of the subsidy "debate" of a decade earlier, and evoking the muddle of Babangida's early budgets, Ani was setting up conditions for the furor that eventually broke with a vengeance again in 1996 over what "deficit" meant. The conditions of life had by now utterly deteriorated. In December 1995, the newspaper *Policy* announced "Another Lost Year" (Uzor 1995). The 1996 budget, when it was finally released, was dubbed by the press, "the Budget of Faith" (*Saturday Newspaper* 1996).

Episodes of complete silence now began, interspersed with contradictory claims, even from within the government itself. In 1996 the budget was not published until February 16. On February 15, the *Vanguard* published a cartoon showing a military man labeled GOVERNMENT stirring a giant pot labeled BUDGET while looking over his shoulder at a tiny miserable child labeled NIGERIANS; he is saying "Breakfast will soon be ready—don't worry, be happy." The eventual budget speech was entitled the "Budget of Consolidation," based on the idea that there are external "constraints" and that therefore "economic recovery can only be gradual and must be backed by consistency in policies . . . (which are) allowed to stand the test of time" (Abacha 1996). But behind the scenes, specificity and multiplicity were being fostered without any coverage of theory. Alongside the monetarist talk about certain aspects of the national budget, more and more spending was moved off-budget; reductions in government spending were applied mainly to the federal level, most notably by ceilings on public-sector salaries, while at the state and local level governments expanded enormously. The two official exchange rates—one for debt service and one for all other transactions—were steadily diverging, and fuel, water, and electricity services became intermittent, at best. The new rhetorical option involved maintaining a sliver of the national budget that was intermittently indexed to "keeping a steady course towards a distant future," while off-budget and off-the-air the government was manipulating an expanding range of ad hoc-isms on the side.

After six weeks of anticipating the 1996 budget, the press printed a cacophony of views when it finally appeared, depending on exactly which aspect people most focused on, since the whole idea of an economic *system* had already broken down. In a single article in the *Vanguard* the economist Ibrahim Ayagi proclaimed that the budget had not "addressed the sufferings of the masses," while one Chief Briamoh pronounced it "a masterpiece, for the first time in the past 10 years, our budget is dedicated to the masses" (Iyeke 1996, 1, 2). Ayagi links his interpretation to control of inflation while Briamoh is looking at whether "there might be increase in transportation fares, fuel etc." Both are completely inexplicit on how "their" indicator would work out in any general theory of systemic connections within the Nigerian national economy. Another commentary attacks the rhetorical attributes of the budget speech directly, with no pretense that the terms touch the Nigerian ground anywhere except the self-interest of the rulers. Dele Sobowale calls it "Much Ado about Nothing." Unresponsive repetition of the 1995 budget is at the heart of the critique. The persistence in policy is because "the authors have run out of ideas"; "what the public gets are fig-leaf excuses. That is, when the government cares to explain anything at all"; and "keen observers wonder why it took so long to produce . . . 'Xerox copies' of the 1994 and 1995 budgets." In fact, the government doesn't even *respond* to an IMF proposal for a grant to do one specific useful thing, namely to develop cashew production. In sum, the budget is "mere tropes of words tossed on paper by people who care little about redeeming promises. . . . . Any benefit to the citizenry at large is an unintended by-product of attempts aimed at maximizing the advantages of those in power." Sobowale's final reminder is that the six-week period of silence from January 1 to February 16 "speaks volumes" (Sobowale 1996, 19).

The habit of alternating cacophony and silence intensified over the year, evidenced in "Thrills and Spills of the '96 Budget" (Adewale et al. 1996); "The Budget of Faith" (*Saturday Newspaper* 1996); "Antinomies of a Fiscal Policy" (*Post Express* 1996a); "Storm over Budget Surplus" (*Guardian* 1996c); "Mixed Reactions Trail Budget Performance" (*Guardian* 1996b); and "1996 Budget Still Off-Target" (*Post Express* 1996b). Analytical commentators juxtaposed the inconsistencies from within the government's own pronouncements:

> Nobody knows exactly how much was realized from oil last year. The CBN [Central Bank of Nigeria] put it at $10.35 billion. The 1996 budget says it was $7,957 billion. Nobody knows how much the country spent on oil imports last year. While Prof. Aluko [economic adviser] put it at $800 million, independent sources said it was as high as $1,924 billion. (Gahia 1996, 17)

Into the midst of this confusion, Finance Minister Anthony Ani threw out the news that the budget was now definitely in surplus, only to be contradicted by the Central Bank itself. As one commentator pointed out, one can show a budget surplus just by failing to fulfill budget provisions (*Guardian* 1996a, 17): "[We] need much more information if the budget surplus announced is to make sense." Finally, "Nigerians cannot reconcile a monetary surplus with their present state of penury" (quoting Oma Djebah [1996] in *Guardian*).

The gap between the Finance Ministry and the CBN was never explained. By 1997, when I spent two months in field research, the fuel shortage was deep, chronic, and profoundly damaging. And it was barely explained. Commentators were all over the map trying to make sense of it. Every story had subplots and deviations. For example, the four refineries were out of order, but why? They had not been repaired; the money had not been allocated for repair; the money had been allocated but had gone missing between one ministry and another; the fault was a particular official, to which the reply was no, it wasn't; members of the military government had interests in South American oil so were profiting by importing their own oil to Nigeria to meet the crisis at high prices, and so on and so on. For almost the entire two months I was in Nigeria, in February and March there was no official statement on a crisis that was leaving crops rotting in rural markets, children dying at home for lack of transport to hospitals, industries folding for lack of fuel, and the patchwork efforts to make up for a collapse in electricity and water supply—through tanker delivery of water and home generators for electricity—grinding to a halt. I have never been more aware of the degree to which what we call "modern life" depends on these three commodities—oil, electricity and clean water—of which the sine qua non is oil. Only after about six weeks was there any attention from the top, and then it was simply to promise a personal intervention in the delivery of a certain number of tankers of imports.

Withdrawal into Aso Rock (the fortified presidential palace) in Abuja became one of the distinctive features of Abacha's presidency. Of course we can say that this is a result of incompetence and venality. It is. But the whole syndrome is one outcome of an inability to embrace the reality that "the national economy" cannot be represented consistently as an abstract process on the way to long-term growth. People search for intelligibility. The retreat from it by government rhetoric presents itself to the citizenry less as a humble submission before the awe-inspiring might of the market than as a willful dereliction of attention to what is happening into the collective near future, which in turn inspires close public attention to the various immediate choices of the moment: the public's own but also the choices of those in political and economic power. Everyone searches for points at which any number, thing, word, or concept can be made to attach to any other in a meaningful way.

So what is to be said when there is no sense? It *is* a rhetorical problem. Babangida could be charming and articulate about it. Abacha was personally incapable of populist dissembling. Nigeria became the poster case for a rampant corruption that wove into all the fissures of arbitrage that opened up over this era. But the problem of intelligibility amid turbulence under monetarism is much larger than Nigeria, and even larger than the so-called developing world.

Note Toward a Conclusion

Amid the turbulence, there is one rather surprising persistence. The terms of the rhetoric range rather narrowly across the spectrum I identified through logical derivation from monetarist theory. There is not much innovation. As Adedoyin and Dike wrote in 1991, "the tape has been rewound." The public feels as if reasoning is going in circles, reflected brilliantly in the popular song mentioned earlier: "Perambulator." In Nigeria, the rhetoric of a "national economy," of subsidy and deficit, and the arguments for meaningful reference points for anything from toothpaste prices to "sacrifice" were remarkably recurrent over this period, even though their meaningfulness fluctuated. The occasional referent echoes uncannily from one phase to the next, even in the Western economic press. For example, when the petrol price changes of 2003 caused a national strike, the article about it in the *Economist* contains almost exactly the same terms as the rhetoric of twenty years previously in the same journal: "a litre of petrol cost less than a bottle of mineral water"; " fuel subsidies cost at least $1 billion a year"; "Nigerians suspect the government's motives for taking away cheap petrol and doubt that the money saved will be put to good use" (2003), and so on. Déjà vu all over again (in the famous words of Yogi Berra).

If we put this rhetoric into historical motion, what do we think of its remarkable repetitive perambulation: from debate about terms, to calls for nationalism (of varying kinds), to cacophony and silence, and then back again to the same old terms, that is, the circular argument about form and content? Does neoliberal rhetoric necessarily go through predictable cycles: starting with debate, attempts at imposition of implausible integrating ideas, surly disintegration into meaninglessness and silence, only to be revamped into another round of debate under new political management? Or is it the features of the Nigerian economy and society themselves that are persistent, and people are referring to them in the only stale terms available? Or are we all locked into truly useless myopias about a reality that is shifting so rapidly as to impede us from standing back, catching breath, and actually facing real questions that were posed by Nigerian critics and have gone without answers for decades? What *is* a deficit? What *is* a debt? What *is* a subsidy? Is it really possible to leave whatever they are, or what the "market" turns them into, to the creative power of "chance" and the "necessity of submitting to forces whose operation we cannot follow in detail" (following Hayek)? Possibly each iteration of the same old terms leaves more and more to the private inventiveness of disparate constituencies. The claims of a collective faith in the distant horizon, the singularity of "the market," rational choice rather than reasoning, become increasingly distant and implausible, leaving us gravely disconcerted that the "craving for intelligibility" in the economic lives that people actually live is increasingly generating no concerted answer at all from those charged by the political process and by expertise in the discipline of economics to account for them. If so, lengthening phases of silence—the retreat of the state into the Aso Rock fortresses of the world while the people invent their own analytics and pragmatics—would be one logical form of the "freedom" for whose sake Hayek advocates our sacrifice of intelligibility.

Acknowledgments

The Nigerian journalists responsible for the stories are, as far as possible, named in the text. Without their courageous work no one could reconstruct the history of this period or of these debates.

The collection of the newspaper sources was made possible by a Research and Writing Grant from the John D. and Catherine T. MacArthur Foundation for which we give thanks. We are particularly grateful to Olatunji Ojo, who did much of the clipping (in the days before online newspapers), and Wale Adebanwi, who wrote background histories of all the newspapers for us. Justin Lee excerpted a series of files. William Milberg and Stephen Gudeman offered important suggestions on the paper.

Guyer's study of these sources was supported by a fellowship at the Woodrow Wilson International Center for Scholars in Washington, D.C., in the spring of 2003.

Some items of the material were first presented in an unpublished paper by Guyer and Denzer entitled "The Oil Economy of the Nigerian People," presented to the Program of African Studies, Northwestern University, 1999. The present paper was written in 2005, so well before some of its arguments became directly applicable to the rhetoric of economic crisis in the United States in 2007–2008.

FOUR

Prophecy and the Near Future: Thoughts on Macroeconomic, Evangelical, and Punctuated Time

The thoughts I offer in this article start from personal observation and move toward invitation. As I came of age in postwar Europe, late colonial Britain, the early atomic age, a 1950s–1960s economic boom, and post–*Second Sex*, prefeminist uneasiness, the mood in my public sphere vacillated correspondingly between triumphalism, grief, guilt, fear, complacency ("I'm all right, Jack!"), and a sense of disjuncture between the mystiques and the modes of life. Full of contradictions and emerging lines of struggle, that era's discourse and conviction seem, nevertheless, quite starkly different, in general, from public discourse in the United States today. Far from being experienced as "progression through a homogeneous, empty time" (Benjamin 1968, 261) or even as Fredric Jameson's encompassing modernity, "which entails a sense of temporality that depends on the macro-economic history of the world system" (Irvine 2004, 102), the temporal sensibility of that time was specific and episodic: looking backward and forward. "Before, during, and since the war" mapped the past; struggles and plans projected the future onto near horizons such as the independence of the British colonies, the outcome of the French colonial wars in Indochina and Algeria, and the struggle against apartheid in South Africa, all pervaded by intimations of doom from "the Bomb" (the Cuban missile crisis of 1962) and Rachel Carson's *Silent Spring* (1962). For me, a sense of foreignness in the present has come to revolve around a strange evacuation of the temporal frame of the "near future": the reach of thought and imagination, of planning and hoping, of tracing out mutual influences, of engaging in struggles for specific goals, in short, of the process of implicating oneself in the ongoing life of the social and material world that used to be encompassed under an expansively inclusive concept of "reasoning."[1]

Working in the 1990s in Nigeria under structural adjustment and military rule, I found that neither Nigeria nor the military rule seemed so exotic but, rather, the rhetoric of economic policy did. Vistas of long-term growth were invoked in newspapers that were diligently recycled as market packaging, window coverings, mop-up material, and toilet paper, as people managed the actualities of a desperately disturbed everyday life (see Guyer with Denzer 2009). At the time, this combination of fantasy, futurism, and enforced presentism seemed specific to the lived implications of the economic policies of structural adjustment under military rule in Africa. Years later, the same rhetoric about horizons of long-term economic growth has become far more generalized, powerful, and confident.

Before the end of World War II, economic theorist Friedrich von Hayek had already advocated this orientation, for closely argued reasons. The human capacity to comprehend entire economic processes was far too limited to risk intervention in what would ultimately prove beneficent market forces. Overreaching the claim of reason could be disastrous. Hayek called intrusion into market forces by a near-future kind of reasoning the "craving for intelligibility," which he saw as a contributor to a fascism that could still "lead to the destruction of our civilization" ([1944] 2007, 204). But even with the experience of fascism fresh in people's experience, his theoretical project shared little affinity with the culture of early postwar times. It has far more support now, presumably for a host of reasons, including, I suggest, a greater, and more politically and socially powerful, convergence of temporal emphasis in public forms of representation and argumentation. It is to this perception that I turn in this article, suggesting that anthropology has the means, but not yet the concerted conversation, to develop an ethnography of the near future of the twenty-first century.

From my own vantage point in historical time, the shift in temporal framing has involved a double move, toward both very short and very long sightedness, with a symmetrical evacuation of the near past and the near future. Analysis of the "postmodern condition" has focused almost exclusively on the striking cultural emphasis on the very short temporal focus: time–space compression (Harvey 1990), simultaneity, and a "new nonchronological and nontemporal pattern of immediacies" summarized as a "reduction to the present" (Jameson 2002, 707, 709). Representations of violent eruption in the arts and media, for example, are a "structural effect of the temporality of our economic system . . . [of] late capitalism" (Jameson 2002, 17). Jameson goes so far as to announce "the end of temporality" as people knew it. My own culture shock had focused my mind differently: it seemed that ultimate origins and distant horizons were both reinvigorated, whereas what fell between them was attenuating into airy thinness, on both "sides" (past and future) of the "reduction to the present."

The evaporation of the near future in theory and public representations seemed at least as disturbing as the death of the past. As Jameson also writes, no element of temporal framing can be shifted without affecting the other elements. But for one who takes up this analytical challenge to the ethnography of life-as-lived, and to the ideological and pedagogic texts and media forms that instruct people about living in these times, the many theoretical typifications of "modernism" and of an accompanying "neoliberal–postmodern" rupture that pervade the literature do not help (in my view). What one sees now is not so much a break as a major shift composed of a multitude of small ruptures. The past that included my own mid-twentieth century was not modern in any singular sense (Latour 1993); some minor themes have surged forward, and major concerns leave continuations and reverberations that are configured into themes and images in novel but not necessarily revolutionary ways. For example, the macroeconomic theory of the long run has been in the intellectual and cultural repertoire for over a century, worked out in myriad details and technical innovations over decades, and only in the last twenty years finding certain elective affinities in temporal framing that create the cultural traction with technologies, institutions, and publics that was missing after 1945. To look back at these processes over time is to see them as composites, which then allows analysis to focus on the still-lingering and newly emergent entailments and dissonances that escape their terms of reference and that constitute life in the attenuated temporal spaces in which everyday intelligibilities are forged. The near future may be evacuated as a feature of social or collective doctrines, but it is still—and newly—inhabited. The ethnographic and comparative analytical question is, how?

I thought of using the term "foreseeable future" in this discussion: as a gesture toward a favorite poet (William Matthews [1987]), an engagement with explicit terms in management science (see Allen 2006), and a step toward addressing that most unsatisfactory of sociological concepts, "unintended consequences." I only sideline this phrase, in favor of "near future," because I want here to privilege emergent socialities rather than ideational forms. To ask what becomes "near" when "near" fades from collective consciousness is to ask about social distance and access as well as conceptual horizons. It is to invoke material and political urgencies as well as time–space schema. And out of an enormous potential range of ethnographic and theoretical work relevant to time, I hope this question can identify and highlight a field of practice that may arise in specific ways in the present world across a whole variety of domains, from law to livelihood.

To address "the decline of the near future" in theory and public rhetoric more rigorously than through pursuing a personal hunch, and to strike out beyond the confines of the Nigerian evidence, have turned out to be far more demanding and engaging than I imagined at the outset. Some sources are very densely argued and others are quite thin. Much relevant thinking about time in anthropology is less illuminating about the future than about the past (see Munn 1992).[2] And anthropology's attention to economics is quite limited by comparison with its attention to politics, law, and the state. The "Foucault effect" (Foucault 1991) has resulted in a pervasive attention to politics in all its capillaries of social and personal bodies, but anthropologists are still either avoiding, stereotyping, or walking gingerly around economic theory and rhetoric (although see Maurer 2002 and the critique in Mirowski 2000). For example, in a work that I found inspiring with respect to the seriousness of the analysis of referential texts, Vincent Crapanzano (2000) writes of the recent rise in the influence of doctrinal "literalism," but in religion and the law only. Important analyses of the temporality of lived economies are embedded in an expanding library of ethnographies focused on hope (Miyazaki 2004), despair (Ferguson 1999), disciplined devotion (to market movements; see Zaloom 2005), panic (about debt; Williams 2004), fiscal disobedience (Roitman 2005), and moral unease (Robbins 2004). But relatively less attempt has been made than in the anthropological literatures on power, law, and the state to address economic experience and reasoning in relation to the rhetorics and programs that directly shape that experience and to the theory (or doctrine) that justifies it (although for cases, see Kaplan 2003; Maurer 2002; Mitchell 2002). Modeling by think tanks is crucial here, but our literature is again focused more on the state than the economy (see Baxstrom et al. 2006).

Doubtless there are many more creative allusions to futures in emergent cultures than I can encompass. Hence, the invitation to colleagues to discuss the issue in this forum. To frame the problem tightly at this stage, I look at how temporal evacuation happens within two highly sophisticated and influential bodies of thought, in which the doctrine is explicit and its translation into programs is deliberate. In some sense, these theories privatize the near future while socializing the present and the distant horizon in distinctive ways, and one could think a lot further along this public-private trajectory. But I am less focused here on how phenomena are classified (esp. dualistically) than on teasing out what Pierre Bourdieu ([1984] 1990) called "generative schema" (in the plural) that arise from "experience," in both the recurrent—reproductive and historical—disruptive senses of that concept.[3] One aims to understand how such templates may be created, how framed, how transposed from one practice of life to another. How do they, then, refer to and refine each other across the experiential horizon: from praying to budgeting, from gesturing obedience to making payments, from imagining devotion to providing emotional care and material sustenance? Asking such questions focuses ethnographic attention on the lived futures that emerge in the "gap" in the temporal doxa.

Projection and prophecy in current monetarism and fundamentalist Christianity, especially in their public forms of explication, are the doctrines I explore here. To sharpen a sense of the specificity of the present dispensations, I counterpose each of them with other formulations of the future that coexist within their own intellectual arcs of possibility: neoclassical economics and biblical tradition, respectively. The growth theory of Walt Rostow, for the economics case, and the theory of prophecy of Abraham Joshua Heschel, for the biblical case, serve to highlight specific points of convergence and divergence within and between the two traditions and their variant doctrinal framings. I may risk personal or intellectual nostalgia by making comparisons that inevitably seem to counterpose conditions "then" and "now," "there" and "here": thought in the post–World War II era in Britain and in the post–Cold War era in the United States. But it is neither the particular ways in which the near future used to be addressed nor any necessary ambition to restore them that interests me. Rather, close attention to these cases as examples helps to identify how different temporal philosophies are ideologically marked and made culturally plausible and available.

Because the near future cannot disappear altogether, comparison can refine understanding of the operative time frames, terms, and arenas in which people now crave "intelligibility." One can ask whether the near future has really been "compressed" into the dailiness of postmodern spontaneity; whether, alternatively, care for the near future has become gendered; or whether it is so rigidly programmed into the formal calendrics of financial debt and benefit, self-renewal as a citizen, or insistent work schedules that experientially based intelligibilities have no room to gain any semiautonomous traction in the social imagination at all. Force and neglect create their own spaces and constraints. The final section of this article brings together recent ethnography that fills in some of the temporal gaps. But the necessary preliminary exercise, and the main part of my discussion, explore exactly how the near future has been evacuated in the first place. Looking at the precisely articulated ideologies of time future can make the lived future a more tractable ethnographic project than it has been in an era when memory, and "the past in the present," were the main focus of temporal thinking in anthropology.[4]

Macroeconomic Time and the Decline of the Near Future

It has taken a very long time for the "long run" to become as important a concept as it has in public economic speech at the turn of the twenty-first century, largely through an orientation to "growth" within a monetarist, rather than an institutionalist, theoretical framework. Conventional histories attribute the conceptual division of economic time into the long and the short run to Alfred Marshall, in his *Principles of Economics*, published in 1890. Over a revolutionary career, he defined a shift from theories of value based on land or labor to a mathematical economics based on market demand and supply. The short run became the period of response to demand during which producers could only reallocate existing factors of production, which therefore entailed price fluctuations as ephemeral pressures moved through the market. The long run, by contrast, became the period during which the supply of all factors could be adjusted, resulting in eventual "normal prices," which reflected what Marshall called "persistent causes."

Thus we may conclude that, as a general rule, the shorter the period we are considering, the greater must be the share of our attention given to the influence of demand on value; and the longer the period, the more important will be the influence of cost of production on value. For the influence of changes in cost of production takes as a rule a longer time to work itself out than does the influence of changes in demand. The actual value at any time, the market value as it is often called, is often more influenced by passing events and by causes whose action is fitful and short lived, than by those that work persistently. But in long periods these fitful and irregular causes in large measure efface one another's influence so that in the long run persistent causes dominate value completely (1890, bk. 5, ch. 3, para. 5.3.31).

Marshall was not altogether clear on what these persistent causes are or how they relate to the short run and the intermediate. In one passage, he implies that they are the customary arrangements of political and cultural communities, differing from one country to another (Marshall 1890, bk. 1, ch. 3, para. 1.3.17). He expresses concern about "the intermediate effects [of economic freedom] while its ultimate results are being worked out; and, account being taken of the time over which they will spread, what is the relative importance of these two classes of ultimate and inter-mediate effects?" (Marshall 1890, bk. 1, ch. 4, para. 1.4.10). He also notes that this long run was in some sense hypothetical rather than empirical, because "the tendencies which are being described (often) will not have a sufficiently 'long run' in which to work themselves out fully" (Marshall 1890, bk. 1, ch. 3, para. 1.3.21). The distinction, then, is analytical; empiri-cally, both long- and short-run processes are working together and can be difficult to disentangle. So, for several decades after his publication, the market-based long run took a back place to analysis of the short run and its intermediate forms of governance.

Marshall's student, John Maynard Keynes, famously pointed out that "in the long run we're all dead" and that (perhaps apocryphally) "at Cam-bridge we leave the long run to the undergraduates," perhaps as a simple logical exercise, in light of the successive crises of the interwar years. The economic theory that has shifted the focal length more confidently toward the long run is monetarism: an established theoretical orientation with a very long history that has grown in strength from the 1950s onward and focuses on eradicating institutional and governmental interventions in market prices in the form of taxes, regulations, protections, and redistribu-tive subsidies, to free up market dynamics. Much anthropological writing on "neoliberalism" stops at a simple depiction of the "undermining" of the state and the "freeing" of markets. But there were solid reasons to make a monetarist argument in the era of National Socialism and Stalinism, and alternative techniques were put forward to limit certain sources of price fluctuation. In 1944, Hayek was already advocating monetary policy as a possible instrument for achieving free markets and stable prices at once: "Many economists hope, indeed, that the ultimate remedy (to fluctua-tions) may be found in the field of monetary policy" ([1944] 2007, 121).

Under monetarism, the state assumes the responsibility of regulating the money supply so that the value of money itself—through inflation or deflation—does not run its own separate interference on price determina-tion by consumer demand and supply. This, then, becomes the basis for recuperation of the long run as a viable working horizon: focus on a con-tinuing stable value of money (particularly in capital markets, through the interest rate), faith in freed-up market forces to produce innovation, and calculation by increasingly sophisticated mathematics and model build-ing, all complemented by a whole range of financial instruments that ad-dress (and take advantage of) market risk. If extramarket influences on capital and profit, such as currency inflation and unstable conditions in the world, can be limited by state policy and financial institutions, then conditions for investment can favor the kind of growth and "progress" through markets that Adam Smith predicted and that have been reiterated down through the ages since. For example, "Capitalism helps drive history toward freedom via an algorithm that for all we know is divinely designed and in any case awesomely elegant. Namely: Capitalism's pre-eminence as a wealth generator" (Wright 2005). I should note that Smith was not claiming this progress for capitalism but for markets; he was not claiming it for the use of capital but for the division of labor and the growth of skills (under the labor theory of value). But the temporal framing and indexing to "progress" were famously launched in the first paragraph of *The Wealth of Nations* (Smith [1776] 1927). Paul Krugman (2005a) picked up the temporal theme in a critique of monetarist politics in which he pointed out (in his own quotation marks) the "infinite horizon" in current U.S. political-economic thinking.

I quote Robert Wright for two reasons. He gestures to the religious domain, as does Hayek, and parallels in that domain are the ones I explore below. But more importantly here, he implies that the link of logic between short and long run is quite opaque: "for all we know." If we refer back to Hayek, it is clear that Marshall's discomfort on this question gets replaced under monetarism by a positive embrace of the evacuation of logic from this temporal range. Reasoning from experience can be, as Hayek writes, "an incomplete and therefore erroneous rationalism" ([1944] 2007, 205); "if in the long run we are makers of our own fate, in the short run we are the captives of the ideas we have created" ([1944] 2007, 2). Monitoring movements in very specific indicators and applying financial instruments that discipline very specific temporal zones explicitly preclude linking long and short runs through a humanistically based concept of shared intelligibility. Douglas Holmes and George Marcus (2006) present Alan Greenspan's operative mode of decision making when he was chairman of the Federal Reserve as highly personalistic and intuitive, more like a deeply informed ethnographer (according to their analysis) than a functionary of a system. The *Economist* (2004, 29) refers to Greenspan as a magician, which would be quite consonant with the inhabitation of a space that explicitly does not reduce to the principles that surround it: rational choice in the short run and "makers of our own fate" in the long run.

As logic and model, this combination of rational choice in the very short run, growth in the very long run, and "submission" in the interim needs theoretical elaboration and rhetorical exposition to convey it to the public. Unlike taxes, regulations, and entitlements, this monetary oversight function of economic governance is almost impossible for the ordinary citizen and consumer to see or to relate to, except when it goes seriously wrong. Mainstream historians of economics advocate seeing monetarism as the culmination of capitalist economic governance. *From Mercantilism to Monetarism*—with all stages of pioneering and golden ages in between—is the subtitle of a recent primer in macroeconomics (Vaggi and Groenewegen 2003). The entry on monetarism in *Money*, a book published in the New Palgrave Series, explains briefly why and how monetarism developed, using terms that clearly imply a superiority to this mode of economic governance. The entry defines monetarism thus: "Monetarism is the view that the quantity of money has a major influence on economic activity . . . and that the objectives of monetary policy are best achieved by targeting the rate of growth of the money supply" (Cagan 1989, 195). Because of judicious intervention by the central bank, the "demand function for monetary assets is claimed to be stable in the sense that successive residual errors are generally offsetting and do not accumulate" (Cagan 1989, 199).

With these assumptions about the working of markets, "monetarist thought puts primary emphasis on the long-run consequences of policy actions and procedures. It rejects attempts to reduce short-run fluctuations in interest rates and economic activity . . . as generally inimical to the otherwise achievable goals of long-run price stability and maximum economic growth" (Cagan 1989, 203). This is very similar to Marshall's position a hundred years ago, but the projection of the long run, when prices achieve stability, is possible to model now in a way that Marshall was frustrated to be unable to achieve. With the long-run modeled, market fluctuations can be anchored retrospectively from that futuristic point and thereby seen as instances of the "almost infinite sequence of ripple effects" (Lindsey and Wallich 1989, 235) that make markets work.

So, through the concept of growth and the technologies for management of the money supply, monetarism moves the near future out of the kind of limelight that it once occupied in economic theory and, at the same time, evokes a strange new economic subject: one who can be rational, submissive, ingenious, and infinitely desirous all at the same time. As Benjamin Lee (1997) suggests, there is a profound tension here, unless, of course, there happens to be a division of affective labor, with some deciding, some submitting, others desiring, and yet others managing to be ingenious. Lee sees two forms of public subjectivity: the rational reader-citizen acting on shared information and the spectator–mass media consumerist facing an infinite differentiation of choice. I think the situation is even less coherent than that when transposed into the domain of the everyday. The new indexing of diagnosis of the present to an "infinite horizon" in the future places people in emotional and sociological *terra nova*. The nesting of temporalities and their relative emphasis and mutual entailment for different populations, or for the same population in different affective states, becomes the ethnographic question. Bruno Latour's (1993) point about the modernist production of hybrids is still relevant but with a nuanced addition. Under monetarism, the processes that create difference fall squarely into the undertheorized midtemporal range of "ripple effects," or they fall under theoretical signs—articulation, stages of growth—that have been explicitly rejected. The vagueness of definition about the subjectivities and localities of the midrange and the suspicion of their adherence to "intelligibility" implicitly leave them to emergent horizons of imagination. Advocates call this zone "freedom" (Friedman and Friedman 1980), a strong claim on a concept that carries powerful resonance for so many peoples, from so many historical experiences (Berlin 1958; Patterson 1991).

Just as a reminder of the magnitude of the change, and without nostalgia, one can look at the once-famous theory of economic growth published by Rostow in 1960, which is almost the alternative Rorschach to monetarism. Rostow draws out the shared human values rather than the libertarianism in classical political economy, and he focuses on poor nations, on institutions, and typically on the middle temporal range. In his most famous book, *The Stages of Economic Growth* (subtitled *A Non-Communist Manifesto* and, therefore, not opposing capitalism), he wrote of benchmarked stages, interim processes, and the failing in "wisdom" that would "separate the analysis of the long run and the short run" (Rostow [1960] 1965, 501).[5] This is the language of the five-year plan, of institutional sequencing and the creation of precisely the cumulative effects that monetarism avoids addressing. It may signal planning in ignorance—"planning without facts," as Wolfgang Stolper (1966) puts it—but it was based on understanding vectors and synergies that could be optimized by thought and action over the midrange.

In a democracy, the pressure to understand some kind of near, foreseeable future may be compelling. Some aspect of the theory needs to have traction in the public's mind. To see how "growth" has been reframed for the public, I read almost the whole list of recommended sources on the website of the Washington-based antitax think tank and lobby group called the Club for Growth. It includes *The Wealth of Nations* and other classics of monetarist and libertarian thinking: Hayek's 1944 *The Road to Serfdom* (addressed to "Socialists of All Parties") and Milton Friedman and Rose Friedman's *Free to Choose*, published in 1980. Again, the distant future is the moment of truth. Hayek writes, "Wherever the barriers to the free exercise of human ingenuity were removed," ([1944] 2007, 16) history shows "the gradual increase in wealth which freedom brought about" ([1944] 2007, 19). The Friedmans reiterate this same set of claims about growth in the long run, choice in the short run, and ingenuity in the space between, with monetarist financial management to work the fine tuning.[6] And other popular economics texts on the Club for Growth list make the same point. *Basic Economics: The Citizen's Guide to the Economy* argues, "The crucial requirement for maintaining growth and progress is that successful experiments be continued and unsuccessful experiments be terminated" (Sowell 2000, 73) through market competition.[7] Here is also reiterated the faith in "ingenuity" and "experiment" that enters at many crucial points and justifies the proliferation of financial instruments to allow rapid and flexible investment in newness.

So explanations of freedom in neoliberal thinking appear to concentrate on choice, in the very short run, and the anchoring notions of the distant future ("ways of life"). Although they barely mention failure, it would be a mistake to jump straight to cynicism here. Ingenuity and experimentation about the times of life, including the configuration of a near future, is a crucial topic for the human sciences and for thinking through the ethics of life and professional practice (see Carrithers 2005). Neoliberalism connotes more complex and varied a configuration of ideas and technologies than one term can encompass. It bears careful unpacking rather than mobilization as the kind of epithet one sometimes finds in our literature.

Prophetic Time since the 1970s

The public too is focused on the future, but which future among the many that open up? There may well be other futures that correspond to the monetarist future, but the evangelical concept of prophetic time is striking as a replication and transformation of the near future as a kind of hiatus, whose intelligibility is explicitly in abeyance. Here, the anthropological and other disciplinary literature is far larger and the primary sources more amenable to study than they are for monetarism. They express variant interpretations but also a general conviction that, since some profound changes in branches of Christianity in the 1970s, one is living in a "future unfolding" (Harding 2000, 240), waiting and reading the signs, or living in "the time that remains," a "caesura," an unfinished pause (Agamben 2005, 64), or "living in parentheses" of a prophetic time (Robbins 2004, 159). Again, the near future is evacuated, in a way that is just as disorienting and yet internally logical as its secular counterpart in economics.

At one level, the coincidence would seem surprising. The horizon of one perspective is apocalyptic and the other infinite. Economics is secular, entailing a generally uniformitarian-universalist concept of time, whereas evangelical thought is dispensationalist, in which the entire working of the world changes from age to age according to the nature of God's presence in it. But if one looks into religious analyses of the specific era or dispensation to which humankind now belongs, and at their comparable downplaying or rejection of durational human reasoning, the similarities between the two modes of thinking about time are striking. As in the history of neo-classical economics, alternative temporal emphases coexist within what is generally understood to be the "same" overarching tradition, so the fore-grounding of one over the other must be seen as a history rather than an entailment. So, to suggest historical convergences between the two tempo-ralities—in economics and in religion—is not necessarily far-fetched.

For evangelical Christians, the interim between the first and second comings of the Messiah is the time in which present life is lived. The Book of Revelation of St. John the Divine predicts how the Second Coming will be heralded. Current church leadership works out the implications for life in the present, in an enduring attitude of expectant waiting. Tim LaHaye, of Left Behind fame, and Thomas Ice have published a "Complete Bible Prophecy Chart" with an exegesis in *Charting the End Times* (2001) that lays out in great detail the temporalities of the two eternities and of the time in between, comprising the successive dispensations of prophetic time, each with its own properties and biblical referents. The current age is Dispensa-tion Phase 6, between the Pentecost (when "the Holy Spirit was sent to indwell in all believers") and the Second Coming. The current era is named the Age of Grace or the Age of the Church. It begins with "Law Fulfilled" (Matt. 27:50–51) and ends with "Rapture of the Saved" (1 Tim. 4:16–17) and is depicted as lasting "1970+ years" (LaHaye and Ice 2001, 83).

As the authors lay out all the details of the schema (LaHaye and Ice 2001, 116), it becomes clear that the "plus" in this number is extremely significant. Every dispensational age between the two eternities, before and after time, has a definitive length except the present one.[8] The First Temple lasts 374 years; the exile in Babylon, 70 years; the Second Temple, 586 years; the Third Temple, 7 years; and the Millennial Temple, 1,000 years.[9] In be-tween the Second and the Third Temples is the here and now, the Spiritual Temple: an exceptionally long and unfinished period that has lasted al-most 2,000 years already and has no necessary end in sight. In an alterna-tive figure, based on the Book of Daniel rather than Revelation, LaHaye and Ice literally refer to this period as "the gap," a "parenthetical period" linked to a hiatus between two verses in the prophetic text: between Daniel 9:26—which ends on "desolations" after the Messiah is "cut off"—and Daniel 9:27—which begins "And he shall confirm the covenant with many." What happens during this period, which refers prospectively to the open-time history of the church? How does this "gap" in the logic of the Daniel text work as the referent for its ongoingness? Two processes are at large: "Continual Growth and Increasing Apostasy," that is, "a sowing of the Word throughout the age . . . imitated by a false countersowing . . . doctrinal defection," which is manifested by people "disbelieving God and doing their own thing" (LaHaye and Ice 2001, 48, 34).

The vacillation is constant, unrelenting, and unresolved. "Doing one's own thing" explicitly includes not only crimes of "lust" but also the transgression of reliance on human intellect and experience alone. Examples of apostates include all uniformitarian-universalists: evolutionists and enlightenment thinkers, "particularly in higher education" (LaHaye and Ice 2001, 40). All are grouped together as "scoffers," a term taken from the second epistle of Peter, chapter 3, starting at verse 3: "There shall come in the last days scoffers . . . saying, Where is the promise of his coming? . . . All things continue as they were. For this they willingly are ignorant . . . of this one thing, that one day is with the Lord as a thousand years, and a thousand years as one day" (King James Version). The attempt to render the current moment in time as subject to reason, whether by extrapolation from other times and places or by thinking through logical entailments, is explicitly rejected in favor of faith.

Exploring the richness of this text, its elaborate numerologies, and its implications would require more space than is available here. But these few passages suffice to show how the midrange of personhood, history, and reasoning is profoundly attenuated and seen as morally dangerous. Several recent ethnographic works on Christianity go considerably further in explaining the premises, but they seem to me consonant on this point. The order of salvation "must not be taken chronologically since it is, in a sense, contained in a timeless moment" (Crapanzano 2000, 101). Living in that moment requires a "profound cognitive, emotional and spiritual reorientation" (Crapanzano 2000, 123), involving living in the present with the knowledge that what it means will only become clear in the millennial future (Robbins 2004, 162). The experiential past is no longer relevant; the main cry is "make a complete break with the past" (Meyer 1999, 215), meaning the immediate personal past of family, kinship, and idolatry. To bridge the ultimately impossible process of connecting the pre-Christian biblical text, which of course comes from a previous dispensation, to the practice of a Christian everyday life in this one, the preachers, as Ezekiel 22:30 puts it, "stand in the gap" between God and the people (Harding 2000, 12). The idea of a gap, a space, a rupture in time that cannot and should not be mediated by "scoffing" but endured by waiting, by identifying, by witnessing is the basic approach to time in the near future.

Back to Hayek to bring the almost choral harmonies and rhythms to the fore:

> It is men's submission to the impersonal forces of the market that in the past made possible the growth of a civilization. It is by thus submitting that we are every day helping to build something that is greater than any one of us can fully comprehend. . . . It is infinitely more difficult rationally to comprehend the necessity of submitting to forces whose operation we cannot follow in detail than to do so out of the humble awe which religion, or even the respect for the doctrines of economics, did inspire. ([1944] 2007, 204–5)

Growth is the ultimate value. The "craving for intelligibility" and "rationality" would seem to be direct transformations of the idea of "scoffing."[10]

Again, one can look at an alternative that lies at the center of the Abrahamic traditions. I cannot reflect knowledgeably on Islam, although clearly the idea of prophecy is central in that faith. My example comes from a famous Jewish work. Prophecy refers, in general, to revelation, which can refer to several things: immediate spiritual contact between the (individual) human and the divine (the metaphor of the "spark"); human-divine interactions about the ongoing human life course and community life (the content of biblical prophetic teaching about how to live the covenant); and the merging of divine and human in an ultimate vision of collective being (the "end of days").

Examples of the first two—the inspirational present and the measurable human future—are found in the magisterial work of Heschel (1962; 1996).[11] Heschel begins his two-volume work on the prophets of the Bible solidly and explicitly in the measurable future. These are the opening sentences of the book:

> What manner of man is the prophet? A student of philosophy who turns from the discourses of the great metaphysicians to the orations of the prophets may feel as if he were going from the realm of the sublime to an area of trivialities. Instead of dealing with the timeless issues of being and becom-

ing, of matter and form, of definitions and demonstrations, he is thrown
into orations about widows and orphans, about the corruption of judges
and affairs of the marketplace. . . . The things that horrified the prophets are
even now daily occurrences all over the world. (Heschel 1962, 4)

In Jewish thought and practice, the era of the prophets came to an end, and
the injunctions that they left behind were programmed into the intimate
and collective causalities of daily, seasonal, and life-cyclical time as laid out
by the rabbinical tradition from the first century.

Heschel's mind also moves, however, in this and another work, from
moral time toward the inspirational present and he asks, "What manner
of man is the prophet?"[12] In medieval Jewish thought, he argues, even after the end of the prophetic era, there remained a "thirst for prophetic
inspiration" (Heschel 1996, 24). This concept of prophecy is entirely focused on "divine illumination" (Heschel 1996, 39). Heschel quotes from
The Guide for the Perplexed by Maimonides, the twelfth-century scholar and
sage: "You should not think that these great secrets are fully and completely known among us. They are not. But sometimes truth flashes out"
(1996, 72).[13] So the immediate and the moral intermediate future temporalities of prophecy are solidly established in Judaism, just as they are in
some branches of Christianity.[14] The orientation to a "time that remains"
is lower profile, even within messianic traditions. Benjamin writes that
"the Jews were prohibited from investigating the future" (1968, 264). So
there is nothing inevitable about the derivation of evangelical logic from
biblical sources. As the recent anthropologists of evangelical Christianity point out (e.g., Susan Friend Harding, Joel Robbins, and Amy Johnson Frykholm), the emergence of the phenomenon Crapanzano refers to
as "literalism" has a social history. A present enactment of faith that the
past, present, and future can be fused in meaning and referent by an act
of disciplined thought is not what used to be called, and cultivated as,
"reasoning."

The genre itself is catching. I was struck by how Michael Hardt and Antonio Negri's book *Multitude* follows a similar logic and narrative structure
in its attempt to depict the convergence of a common future toward "the
moment of rupture . . . that can create a new world" (2004, 357). Their
version is, in my reading, as mysterious as the process of "growth" through
the "infinite ripple effects" of monetarism or the prayerful vigilance and
forbearance of evangelical prophecy. No stages to reach for, no synergies
of forces picking up on one another over time: no organization and no
midterm reasoning.[15]

What Next? A Temporality of Dates

The individual and collective near future—thinned out of its complexity as a theory or doctrine embodied in guidelines and benchmarks and indexed to a defined, more distant collective future—still beckons or simply happens. Jameson similarly notes a thinning out ("enfeeblement") of a "modernist" sense of the "past and future within the present" (2002:214). In the search for "alternatives, systemic transformations," he advocates cutting away from the "modern" altogether and learning to identify, in precise and measurable detail, "utopian tendencies" as they develop." Hence, "ontologies of the present" (the name of Jameson's book) that demand "archaeologies of the future, not forecasts of the past" (2002, 215; his final words in that volume).

I like the general direction here but doubt the matrix. The spaces opening up are not alternative or utopian in any holistic sense. They are reconfigurations of elements that are well known already, moved in to colonize particular phases and domains of individual and collective life that have been released from answerability to a more distant past and future. The internal temporal architectures in these spaces become like M. C. Escher drawings: familiar figures, precise, and replicated yet brought together into mind-bending inversions, reversions, and shifting focal points. The spaces opened up offer innovative extrapolation from some vantage points and block any cumulative momentum from others. So temporalities are not "homogeneous" and "heterogeneous," as Partha Chatterjee (2004) suggests, corresponding to civil and political society, respectively. They also have been reconfigured and rearticulated.

In many literatures and in formal and informal daily life, I perceive a similar rising awareness of a time that is punctuated rather than enduring: of fateful moments and turning points, the date as event rather than as position in a sequence or a cycle, dates as qualitatively different rather than quantitatively cumulative. A date has always been unique. Arguably, events of the Ides of March in the year 44 BCE changed Western history. The very familiarity of the idea of unique dates, however, treacherously conceals the importance of its expanded circulation. A date is the day that debt payment is due to avoid a hike in interest payments; it is an end point specified in a statute of limitations on legal claims; it sets a "use-by" threshold on commodities; it marks and evokes a collective trauma; it demands appearance in court on pain of deportation; it inaugurates and terminates contracts, the presence of peacekeeping forces, and the inclusion of nations in pivotal agreements.

Embedded in a matrix of such dates-as-events, people's actions and imaginations pivot around compliance and delay, synchrony and avoidance, and the multiple possibilities for forward looking and backdating. (In case the reader imagines that I am just waxing poetic here, he or she could look up the process called "backwardation" in the commodity futures markets.)[16] In different ways, locations within the global regime are reaching toward control of date regimes. "Seize the day" takes on a whole new meaning, as Ernest Gellner (1965) pointed out forty years ago in his prescient discussion of thought and change. Using Franz Kafka's *Metamorphosis*, he argued that a particular conundrum attaches to the idea that tomorrow is another day, completely other, in which the passing of the date inaugurates new absences as well as new presences. Achille Mbembe argues similarly for Africa that tomorrow lives in a "particular time that is emerging time . . . where different forms of absence become mixed together" (2001, 16). Missed turning points, derailed processes, and dislodged future benchmarks produce an "absence of the presences that are no longer so and that one remembers (the past), and the absence of those that are yet to come and are anticipated (the future)" (Mbembe 2001, 16).

In many contexts, and especially clearly with respect to the formal sector, the points of overlay and interlocking among the presences and absences can be represented by dates on the calendar. As such, they are amenable to representation in old ways as well as new ones: as if they were points in a sequence in empty homogeneous time (a certain brand of modernism) or necessary components of repetitive calendrics (religious traditions) or the time disciplines that E. P. Thompson (1967) famously defined as inaugural to the mechanisms of capitalism (the classic secularity of the formal sector). But they are also now experienced as—and increasingly constructed to be—signal event moments in near-future time at which the whole world could change. One can locate "audit culture" here, in which the date regime of accountability that "has broken loose of its moorings in finance" (Strathern 2000, 2) ripples outward into other domains of social life, subjecting other processual regimes to its punctuations. Indeed, process itself seems downsized as a concept: not necessarily for theoretical reasons but because the world itself falls increasingly into the disciplines of a punctuated time that fills the gap between an instantaneous present and an altogether different distant future.

There are several anthropological literatures on the present in which I see this date-as-event floating very close to the surface of analysis: the burgeoning work on debt in political economy (Han 2004; Obukhova 2002; Roitman 2005; Williams 2004); the temporal projections of hope in the anthropology of religion (Miyazaki 2004) and of second chances in the anthropology of trauma and subjectivity (Das 2006); the manipulations of contractual terms in the anthropology of corruption (Smith 2007); the temporality of the law in the margins of the state (Das and Poole 2004); and, of course, the increasingly sophisticated attention to ideas and practices in finance itself (Maurer 2005b; Miyazaki 2003; Zaloom 2005). It is most obviously implicit in Marilyn Strathern's edited collection on "audit culture," as an intrinsic part of a culture "in the making, . . . recognizable in the most diverse places, . . . evident from the concomitant emergence, and dominance, of what are deemed acceptable forms" (2000, 1). All these literatures include attention to specific date events: relived memories of them. anticipations toward them, disciplines they impose on delinquents, arbitrage spaces they open up for opportunists, ideal minutiae for forgers, lifesaving validation for documents, crucial evidence for supplicants in search of alibis, and one expression of the continuing power of the state over intimate conditions of life.

Another article would be needed to do justice to the richness of the sources and intersections here. One could go one step further here, however, to suggest in what ways and with what implications it helps to tease dates into the direct light of study and to bring all these disparate literatures together. If, indeed, a regime of dated time is filling the near-future temporal frame that has been evacuated by macro-theories of durational social process, then, necessarily, it should be resonating through many social domains and political geographies. Having myself worked primarily on processes—including temporal heterogeneity and contingent articulation (Guyer et al. 2007), all ultimately referring back to questions of historical emergence—the temporal ruptures implicit in the idea of date regimes make new but compelling sense to me. It is as if rupture has been relocated: not at the system level but at the subjective level. To enhance sensitivity to the multiplication of ruptures that such a date regime is creating in the world, analysts have the anthropology and philosophy of the "event" to turn to. The navigation of subjectivity and sociality under a consciousness of events puts process into question and forces inquiry into how events are ever aggregated (or woven) into social synchronies and cultural representations or accumulated over time, and for whom. To be living inside a process may only be experienced as a luxury or a tragedy. In between, are there characteristic or consonant struggles, submissions, and ingenuities of the "gap" in time? Narrative and collective-memory studies provide one set of answers, but they hardly exhaust the possibilities when events that intervene decisively in one life are represented as mundanely repetitive from another's standpoint, or when other accounts are silenced or when language fails altogether. And narrative is retrospective. What kind of "stories" does imagination create when the reference points lie in the future?

In anthropology, the event has been worked out most fully in the study of violence and its lived aftermaths in personal and social time (Das 2006). Reference to events in the sense of ruptures begins to appear under a less catastrophic guise in work in precisely the domains of life most explicitly framed by the monetarism and evangelism I have discussed in this article. Anna L. Tsing's "friction" in global processes, although interpreted mainly through dialogics, is also presented in its "sticky materiality of practical encounters" (2005, 1) as events in time. Clara Han's (2004) account of Chilean experience with the neoliberal policies promoted under monetarist theory profiles the asynchronies of signal events: among the temporal phases and strands of one's own life, between oneself and immediate kin, and between one's intimate sociality and that of neighbors, all enmeshed in a "density of . . . monetary and affective debts" (2004, 177). Han suggests the tragic necessity of abandoning familiar terms of temporal coherence, which once filled the near future with meaning, to take on, instead, a concatenation of shorter- and longer-term borrowing and lending, entailing continual temporal arbitrage to stay afloat.

New converts to evangelism also struggle to create a near future, albeit without the tragic sense of loss of the Santiago poor. Robbins's (2004) account of Christianity in one New Guinea society presents believers' utter conviction about the nature of the immediate present and the ultimate future but a "troubled" consciousness in the face of the near-term creation of a moral synchrony between the quality of social relationships and Christian rhythms and calendrics. A critical event focuses their worry and Robbins uses it to launch a sensitive account. Christmas 1991 was "heavy" and "sinful," even threatening to break up the community and put salvation in danger, because people were unable to resolve disputes about employment in a new mining venture in time to celebrate together. After the crisis, the community council took the unprecedented step of pronouncing a "new extremely harsh law" to ensure "that they never again found themselves facing another heavy Christmas like the one just past" (Robbins 2004, xvii–xxvii, xxiii). Even such apparently minor events as a missed debt repayment or a ruined Christmas or a failed audit review appear in subjective and collective life as ruptures of process, demanding extraordinary effort to counteract and to regain any sense of momentum. One could perhaps reduce all this to an ahistorical "life in uncertain times" or an ancient philosophy of risk "taken on the flood" (to quote Cassius in Shakespeare's *Julius Caesar*). There is, however, a historical specificity to uncertainty now. It is an emerging chronotope (Bakhtin and Morris 1994; see Maurer 2005a), honed into technologies that can deliberately unsettle and create arbitrage opportunities and gridlocks as well as logistical feats of extraordinary precision and power. This particular near future, unhitched ideologically from the present and the distant future, becomes a regime (or series of regimes) in its own right, separated from the "systematic connection of entities in a coherent whole that constituted the flow of modern time" (Latour 1993, 78). Secular time has become effectively dispensational, as intimated by Adam Lutzker and Judy Rosenthal in their review of books on contemporary evangelism, in which they exhort scholars to address the "aporia of modernity" by taking "the next step—an internal critique of secularism—[toward] a better understanding of [its characteristic] unheimlich experience" (2001, 921–22).

As with religion, one needs to look closely at the doctrines, practices, and effects of secularisms. One might suspect that for populations such as Nigerians, their long experience of modernity's aporias in practice has better prepared them for this new regimen than the Euro-American conviction of a coherent modernity has done for its home populations. In any case, people everywhere live with comparable exhortations and rhetorics now, whose terms of reference, such as dates on the calendar, give the impression of us all living in the same world at the same time, although the lived disciplines and ruptures create quite different trajectories.

The shift I describe here remains an ethnographic challenge to think about, so convincing was the mid-twentieth-century persuasion about the power of reasoning, with all its entailments for temporal process and the relationship between thought and action. Empathy with the content of the present economic and religious concepts, which Lutzker and Rosenthal (2001) address, is not necessarily difficult because the ideas, like the elements of an Escher drawing, are all familiar. It is the implications of their new consonance, the "negative space" they open up in the temporal picture, and the date regime they seem to inaugurate that create a sense of novelty. Still unclear to me is whether my perspective is generational or theoretical or gendered or positioned in some other way, perhaps by only a partial knowledge of the richness of the literature or a too-tardy realization that Nigerian realities and the realities of others who had always fallen into the oubliettes and the maroon communities of modernity would become so much more widespread and more visible.

Acknowledgments

This article expands on an address I presented at the annual meetings of the American Ethnological Society, San Diego, April 8, 2005, at the suggestion and with the continuing encouragement of Ida Susser. I greatly benefited from presenting it again at the Johns Hopkins conference "Newness and Tradition" in the same month, and particularly from the suggestions of Naveeda Khan and Sameena Mulla. I was encouraged to think about public speech by Niloofar Haeri and by Stephen Gudeman's and Keith Hart's interesting critiques of an article I wrote for *Economic Persuasions* (Gudeman 2009). In the rewriting for publication I benefited from comments by Keith Hart, Richard Swedberg, Virginia Dominguez, and four anonymous readers for *American Ethnologist*.

FIVE

From Market to Platform: Shifting Analytics for the Study of Current Capitalism

Introduction: The Challenge of Reframing "the (Current) Economy" for Economic Anthropology

"The (Free) Market Economy" was always a depiction that captured just one edge of the dynamics of the substantive (provisioning) function and the formal (allocative) function of "the economy," for contrastive, analytical, and political polemic purposes. All the major theorists posited "the market" as a light (or a coming storm) on the horizon rather than as the ground under our (currently inching forward) feet. It was a vision whose relationship to the "real" had to be worked out. Indeed, the concept of what is real in the economy has been at issue in debates about the estimation of equivalence in value within monetized economies for hundreds of years: from the eighteenth-century labor theory of value, through bullionist realism, to the latest report on the methods of the consumer price index, which is used to depict "real wages" and "real prices" and to inform adjustments in several government disbursement programs (see NAS 2013). "The market" as an abstraction based on "exchange," by contrast with realism based on contemporary depictions of life circumstances in specific historical times and conditions, lends itself to elegant theoretical estimation (neoclassical), to political aspiration (laissez-faire, neoliberal), or to a telos (the logic of capitalism). The emphasis has shifted now—in the economy at large and in our disciplines—toward debt (Peebles 2010; High 2012; Graeber 2011), payments (Maurer 2012b), and the temporal interlocking of transactions in arbitrage (Miyazaki 2013) and over life horizons of economic projection and subjective self- and collective cultivation into whatever is considered to be "the future" (Guyer 2007b; Appadurai 2013).

No one in contemporary studies of exchange doubts the relevance of working on the mundane, long-understood institutional framing of trans-actions in routine life and in finance: the legal framework and the long-term collective practices that permit credit and other temporal engagements to be honored, and the ongoing interrelationship between the nominal and the real. But the political and analytical focus in historical eras where con-trols were being challenged, such as the current postsocialist era, has given attention most fully to "the market" as a self-organizing system. Institu-tionalist theories do mitigate the limitations of focusing analytical atten-tion too largely at the self-organizing ("free") cutting edge of economic life, the locations of rational choice, but most do not try to shift the analytical framing and the terminology. Indeed, the institutions themselves can be defined as an outcome of past rational choice, such as with respect to miti-gating transaction costs. Theories of the commons (Ostrom 1990) and of other heterodoxies are exceptions to this branch of institutionalism, stak-ing out an intermediate position rooted in a historical, rather than time-less, placement of the problematics of analysis. We in anthropology begin to meet some of those positions in the renewed attention we are giving to Polanyi: a deeply historical scholar, analytically committed to the embed-dedness of economy in society, while acknowledging the relevance of both formalist and substantivist analysis (Hann and Hart 2011), and giving very close attention to moments of disorder and transformation, ahead of eras of apparent systemic smooth functioning.

In the light of this staking out of middle ground, with its heterodox theoretical vantage points that combine historical, political-economic, in-stitutional, cultural-linguistic, and "free market" theory, I have started to consider whether we, in economic anthropology, might do well to propose a depiction of the present (twenty-first-century) economic condition that is explicitly historically placed but also opens up to the full range of the analytical toolkit, and faces, straight on, the importance of locally spe-cific entanglements of regulations, practices, rational choice, and future imagination-aspiration under rapidly shifting technological and political conditions in an interconnected world. Our past critical attention to en-tanglements has tended to result in findings, or necessary muddlings, with respect to several conventional systemic models. From the perspective of my own work in Africa, and the view of the West from an African vantage point, it seems necessary to start with an image that could comprise en-tanglement from the outset and place the question of the "real" and what we mean by it closer to the center of attention. This would need to be a framing device first rather than a focus. It should *allow* focus, originating from various theoretical traditions. But it should also *command attention* to the other phenomena that lie within the frame rather than consign them to the "taken for granted." While we might do ceteris paribus kinds of analyses of defined variables, they would need to be explicitly understood as fragments, or moments, or locations, from within moving configurations of more or less durational capacity. Later in the paper, I illustrate the mutual imbrication of "markets," institutions, power, and daily conditions of life through a section on the Nigerian economy of petrol-at-the-pump (see also Guyer and Denzer 2013).

I suggest the concept of "the platform economy" as depicting a combination of architecture, standard applications, and spaces for novel performances. This is the platform of the Greek theater as well as the digital age: a stage that can support the aspirations and tragedies of "all the world" while also being a structure that can be distorted or crashed by overdramatic action (as in "break a leg" . . . of the stage itself, which is the source of the saying). Here I am simply experimenting with such a depiction, and largely to replace the manifestly outdated concept of the "free market economy" and even "neoliberal capitalism" as adequate depictions of the economic world as it is. In its own depiction, the "market economy" has been reduced to two modes: one polemic, which is as empirically vague as it is politically insurgent; and the other analytical, which is as specifically precise as it is limited in the phenomena to which it can apply directly, without undue abstraction. Critical analyses in terms of neoliberal capitalism also, indirectly, invoke the "market economy," although as a structure with its own logics rather than as an ideal to which the real should or could tend. Financialization is a concept of enormous historical importance since the 1980s, brought forward and adapted from the classic distinction between industrial and financial capitalism (Rosa Luxemburg) from nineteenth-century Marxism, more or less in the same way as "neoliberalism" is thought of as a recurrence and adaptation of classic liberalism. The global "money market" that opened up with the demise of Bretton Woods in the 1970s is thought of as a market, while at the same time we know of very large international resource agreements in Africa, to be honored over long periods into the future, that are framed as barter-in-kind, presumably with highly crafted frameworks for prices and exchange rates, all necessarily projected forward into a notional dated future (or perhaps "futures," in a different plural form than the classic commodity futures of the Chicago Board of Trade).

One further shift that permeates the others is the rise of what Maurer refers to as the "payments" industry, where money's function as a mode of payment is taking priority over its function in "exchange." Payment "is orthogonal to exchange: . . . here may be a pyramid of money, but there is scaffolding and infrastructure extending from each level of the pyramid outwards and inwards, holding it up . . . or, as payments professionals put it, the portals, rails and plumbing" (Maurer 2012b, 19). The logic of models based on exchange no longer captures the complex that makes payments possible, for which Maurer and the professionals use material imagery that is completely consonant with—even materializes—the idea of "platform" that I am proposing.

Maurer also points to the current ubiquity of what he calls "money nutters," who are constantly experimenting with what can be done with these portals, rails, and plumbing. He points not only to the spaces they see for inserting novelty but also to the reverse order of thought: the search for novel spaces for an old-established function that begs for preservation. For example, he writes: "An emerging issue, however, is whether mobile money services start and stop at payment and transfer functions, or can be transformed into 'real' means of value storage" (Maurer 2011b, 9).

To summarize, there are—fully acknowledged but not yet drawn together—several historically unique, convergent dynamics in the present that make "the market" an inadequate depiction of the larger economy, even as it might still be applicable to specific arenas and commodity domains. These dynamics include the total abandonment of the gold standard and the rise of the global "money markets" in the 1970s, with their designated reserve currencies (under the IMF special drawing-rights conditions); the global productive and asset economy, post 1989, in which barter and very long-term contracts (so not exactly "exchange") figure prominently; the massive invention of financial instruments in the 1990s, which has led to the expansion of the total money supply and to new market-like arenas; the patchy withdrawal of states from welfare and price-control ambitions (although some supports increasingly being considered in money terms, in the twenty-first century, as "cash transfers"); the proliferation of state-fiat and alternative monies and money-management techniques (see Peebles 2011; Maurer 2012a); the rise of small "civil" wars instead of national wars, often about resources; the increasing awareness of resource limits with respect to fundamental, and formerly "free," basic ("real") needs (clean air, water, mobility); and the proliferation of platforms and apps (applications) in the IT sphere. Focused on the many indeterminacies at the generative centers of these processes, anthropologists of finance, the state, and other domains that are relatively new to us are asking such questions as "Is this still capitalism? And if not, what is it?" (Riles 2012) and suggesting that the state is a "spectral" presence as well as a material force (Das 2004). They meet up with a long history of critical voices drawing attention to mutual imbrications as against logical models.

In this context, my suggestion of developing and combining existing analytics under a new heading that already expects tangles, junctures, and cacophonies, and combinations of the kind of "market devices" proposed by Callon, Millo, and Muniesa (2007), as well as structures with durational qualities and frontiers of innovation, is intended to open up and challenge the empirical agendas for us in economic anthropology. We need deep analyses of documents as well as ethnographies of practice. The "platform economy" has the advantage, in my own view, of designating phenomena that are depicted as such in the world itself, by the participants, while it can also be constructed from empirical evidence, to include all the already-existing, grid-like phenomena considered relevant by the analysts, for which they may see how new apps can be developed. As an image, it draws attention to a solid structure on which, and from which, actions of many kinds can take place.

Simply as imagery, this is very different from "market," whose depiction in the *Wikipedia* entry I have been following over several years and which now (July 12, 2013) has attached many of the old entries that illustrate "actual existing markets made up of persons interacting in a place in diverse ways." They include the Corn Exchange in London in 1809 and Afghan and Czech village produce markets. Whereas a market is depicted as place, people, and commodities, a platform is made up of built components and applications, from which actions are performed outward into a world that is not itself depicted. I will go into this in more detail later. Suffice it here to suggest that the sheer capaciousness and currency of the concept of "platform" offers the anthropologist that breadth of vision, that intellectual permission, to consider at the outset that anything might be relevant to the issues at stake in a particular inquiry, which has always been characteristic of the disciplinary epistemology. We can then describe, debate, and defend the boundaries of inclusion and exclusion from a wide analytical sphere of vision.

The phenomena now grouped under the concept of "platform" are both long existing and entirely novel (proliferating daily, such as the various IT platforms on the World Wide Web, the platforms of the oil industry, the portals and plumbing of the payments industry, and so on). We have to be attentive to phenomena that come forward through centuries of use and become adapted in new ways. According to Gillespie (2010), the *Oxford English Dictionary* lists fifteen different referents for "platform," and the

Wikipedia "disambiguation" page directs us to twenty-two different entries. However, in terms of historical and comparative study, "platform" has the positive advantage of drawing from the current repertoire of "words in circulation" (Guyer 2012d) so is comprehensible in one way or another to almost everyone in the present, while not being so specific to the present that it could not be applied at all to the past. Gillespie (2010) points very well to the ensuing politics of meaning, but this is then a terrain to examine ethnographically. For us in anthropology, the latitude of meaning for "platform" can be an advantage, especially since it allows "the market" to be included as a component rather than either canonized as *the* central focus or vilified and excluded as essentially ideological. Societies have had money and markets for millennia, in all kinds of (what used to be called) "articulations" with other political-economic dynamics. In the "platform economy," "market" could be readdressed as one kind of indigenously defined "app" (application software), with its own variants and translations, each depending for realization on its own part of the "platform" from which it derives its capacities. Hopefully, this would allow at least some of the scholarship to evade the binaries that have plagued our analytics: formalism versus substantivism, political economy versus neoclassical theory; historical analysis versus synchronic modeling; materialist versus ideational focus. We still learn from newer contrasts and their mediation: market/base (Gudeman 2001); capitalism/human economy (Hart 2012); heads/tails of the currency (Hart 1986). It seems to me, however, that we might optimize the eclecticism, by first recognizing that some of our own terms and levels of abstraction cross the median from one theoretical lane to another. The abstraction of time-space compression, near-future evacuation (Guyer 2007b), and the financial imaginary (Miyazaki 2013), along with neoclassical theory itself, all draw attention to powerful abstract formulations relative to current economies, whereas the kind of materialism exemplified by Sidney Mintz's ethnographies of sugar (*Sweetness and Power*, 1985) and money (1964) in Caribbean history draw attention to "how this is actually done," in its own daily arenas, for which see Ho (2009) on Wall Street employees; Peebles on the euro off the Danish coast (2011); Williams (2004) on how to pay consumer debt in Washington; and Povinelli on achieving livability in "abandonment" (2011). In our own lives, we see shifts that catch the generations, cohorts, and subdivisions of national communities very differently in their "real" lives, and thereby evoke the terminology and its affects differently, which then places new dilemmas into intimate relationships. Those who have a certain job security and personal-financial security that was built up on the basis of post–World War II institutions now deal with the intimate needs of the next generations in the family, in neighborhoods and among colleagues, whose life parameters no longer allow the same trajectories because the platform has been reconstructed in some respects and not others. We are asking Mintz's questions about do-ability, while keeping in the picture the valences of power and abstraction.

The oldest issue in the study of monetary economies is still central, namely the generation of money prices and their relationship to each other and to life-as-lived in specific "commonwealths" (as writers put it in earlier centuries). Like the early students of these issues, we need to put far more into the picture than market dynamics. I have been reading archived pamphlets from the British discussions of money and price from several hundred years ago, which was also an era of expanding international trade and of struggle with the legacy of bullion expansion from the wealth of the imperial conquest of the Americas. I find positions such as the following (from 1675): "The Inconveniences which are accident to this Subject of Money are in general but two, Raretie and Confusion. . . . Reason doth convince that there must be a convenient Proportion between their Wages and their Food and Raiment" (Vaughan 1675, 57, 108). Against the bullionists, Thomas Smith argued in 1811 that "in every country, there exists another standard of value, a nominal, or imaginary one" (Smith 1811, 5). Interestingly, he draws on experience in the West African slave trade to support his point. These commentaries grew up alongside, and engaged with, the arguments that became the theoretical canon. As we incorporate price and the "real" into analysis in a way that is broader than neoclassical market analysis and more eclectic than classic Marxism, the anthropological interest in the multiplicity of voices of the kind at play in Britain at turbulent historical moments is better served by a capacious concept such as "platform," which can encourage attentiveness to all components of situations. And also, like Thomas Smith, to see these as varied by place, time, and the sedimentation of past experience. Such historical situations, when the orthodoxy of "money as a veil" was contentiously gaining ground, also correspond better with what Hart (2012) now sees as the current decline of national all-purpose money systems, and with it any pretention of the neutrality of money that undergirded much modern economic theory.

In our own day, we are heirs to the existing grids and infrastructures from the modernist era and to debates about whether they should be privatized, superseded (leapfrogged), repaired, or abandoned, while—in fact and in life—they still exist and are treated as parts of the "platform," taken as "given" most of the time . . . until they break down. Justifiably, "abandonment" is a term that we are increasingly seeing in anthropology, although more with respect to the human domain than the material and conceptual domains (Biehl 2005; Povinelli 2011). That work, however, might well inform a larger project on abandonment considered more broadly, as one of several current dynamics of platforms and their use for current and new applications.

Applications are necessarily predicated on, and designed within, platform structures as they present themselves at a specific time, although they may aim to supersede some of their capacities while undermining, eroding, and abandoning others. So how would we depict and focus on the forms of human intelligence and the styles of reasoning that are brought to bear on the myriad dilemmas and opportunities that arise on the platforms of current economic life? Rational choice is surely too narrow, while improvisation is insufficiently broad to encompass the novelty of the performances created from, and on, platforms. Neither reason nor improvisation come to grips with erosion and abandonment. Sidney Mintz's particular combination of historical political economy and cultural anthropology points us strongly toward the complex of acquisitive interests, cultural values, cognitive knowledge, and embodied skills that human intelligence mobilizes: minute to minute. However, he exemplifies rather than theorizes this combination of qualities (for example, in *Worker in the Cane* [1960] and *Caribbean Transformations* [1974]). His paper on Gresham's Law (1964) as it plays out in the Caribbean comes closest to analysis of both the structure of the situation of currency supply by colonial power and the responses to it. Within an approach to "the platform economy" then, one needs the attention to the performativity that brings platform, app, and price together in life and experience, along with the virtualism (Carrier and Miller 1998; Appadurai 2013) that modeling makes possible and that has feedback effects on the platform itself. It may be that, following Mintz, we should be focusing for the moment on specific generative points as they emerge empirically within particular circumstances and historical junctures.

We are increasingly seeing explicit graphics in our popular consumer culture that draw attention to a platform/app/price nexus. But we might develop greater acuity about where and how particular platform constructs, with their own applications, lend themselves to the novelty that is at the cusp of powerful dynamics with ramifying implications.

In this introduction, I prefigure one other conceptual intervention, before discussing it in more detail later. Our public rhetoric about a destabilized public-private, globalized economic world often includes reference to the emergence of "opportunities" for "innovation." Both of those terms invite examination for the "discursive work" (Gillespie 2010) that they perform (again, on a platform or stage). But they also have a conveniently poetic and analytical resonance with the "platform" imagery: they can merge, as "apportunities." An "opportunity" presents itself at some juncture in the life and structure of the platform, and—given the mode by which it is actualized, through apps—novelty can be inserted in ways that are not reducible either to "rational choice" nor just "improvisation." This term is simply a convenient invention on my part, and it may not work in other languages. But it captures a certain terminological need. The shift from "market economy" to "platform economy" imposes committed attentiveness to very complex phenomena. In conventionalized "normal science," this attentiveness is entirely taken up by training in the techniques of disciplinary traditions. In a mode that is well short of a revolutionary "paradigm shift," but still experimental, phenomena themselves need to be compelling on their own terms. Deep political concern for the future provides that compelling concern, for some, in the present. I want to add here our classic anthropological, disciplinary, "compelling" commitment to the understanding of intricacy: in this case, into the localized "impasses" (see chapter 8) and the systemic collapses and crashes (Tett 2009) that can be created when seizing and inventing apportunities from existing platforms create new entanglements in the real world. The generativity of "small corners" (Tett, as described in the *Economist*, on the financial crisis of 2008) provokes the anthropological imagination across the theoretical spectrum and has been one reason for a renewed recourse to philosophy for a revitalized conceptual repertoire. So working outward from "apportunities" to the platforms from which they draw capacity, and then on downward through the layers of components and flows that hold them in place, can avoid an overmuscular structuralist starting point without rejecting an eventual engagement with structure. It entails addressing what counts as a "platform" *for* specific "applications in practice," at any particular emergent moment. It is utterly traditional as an anthropological approach to focus on a specific instance and work outward: the Gift (Mauss 1990), from the Icelandic Edda and out in space and time; "deep play" from the Indonesian cockfight; color symbolism from Ndembu ritual practice; and so on. The difference here, for use with respect to the global economy, is to see the broader and deeper phenomena as connected with one another, and with the app, creating interactions as well as simple juxtapositions and analogs.

I cannot resist adding a note from the archive here. In 1858 one Hamer Stansfield wrote a pamphlet vilifying the power of the "Money Interest." He noted that a financial crisis was in this group's interest, as distinct from fostering money as a "Mere Instrument of Exchange." On what I would call the "platform" of banking and the novel financial instruments such as dividends on bank shares, he argued that "panics are the harvests of the Money Interest. Dividends are lower in times of cheap money and prosperity and higher in times of dear money and panic" (1858, 10). Whatever the veracity of the facts or the solidity of the argument, he drew attention to sudden advantage of the "apportunity" kind. Close attention to crises and generative moments leads us back to the platform from which they were generated, the performatives that created them, and the implications in "real" terms.

We are already well launched on new anthropologies of the state, finance, the law, and so on from this kind of vantage point. Economic anthropology already has been revitalized. It is just a case of experimenting further. The interaction between platform and apportunity, and the implications for social and economic life, have been downplayed when one or the other is emphasized for polemic oppositional purposes. The next section reviews briefly the oppositional recurrence on which the concept of the market economy has rested, and the final sections use a passage from another of my papers to show how deeply one would need to go, into the platforms of several markets, to make sense of the lifeblood of the Nigerian artisanal economy, which employs and provisions well over 80 percent of the population. By passing through this empirical case, I will suggest that what matters about a platform is its durability and thereby its dependability across whatever temporal rhythms are required by the existing apps and the novel apportunities that different parties perceive and try to act on. The temporalities of the components, connections, and capacities of platforms then become a crucial aspect of understanding how apps are projected and realized over the durational time of infrastructure maintenance and deployment, contractual commitments and forward projections, and with what effects: not only in what they open up (as is particularly emphasized in Joseph Schumpeter's [1960] framing with respect to "creative" entrepreneurial innovation) but also in what they close down, divert, undermine, and so on, for other app searchers and platform attendants (as in Schumpeter's [1960] "destruction," in his overall concept of "creative destruction."

Revisiting the Original Theoretical Contrasts of "The Market Economy"

Each time the "market economy" has been advocated and developed as a concept, it has been in the context of drawing a contrast. For Adam Smith it was the contrast with mercantilism and price control through the mercurial, as practiced in France. Hence the title, *The Wealth of Nations*: the wealth of nations lay in the products of their skilled free labor (largely artisanal labor) and the dynamics of a market economy that operated through participatory dynamics, not in the national "treasure" as a store of wealth. The concept of "free labor" entered the industrial age with a totally new meaning, namely labor shorn of its own asset base in real property. Hence labor as a "commodity" in Marxian theory, and as a "fictional commodity" in Polanyi's formulation, to be contrasted with economies in which anything not created *to be* a commodity is configured and valued differently. "Freedom" then becomes a constructed quality, to be understood in relationship to systemic dynamics. In the context of industrial capitalism, human freedom and the freedom of labor are contrastive, in this formulation. The next moment when "market" and "freedom" were forcefully conjoined was when Hayek recuperated "freedom" in his 1944 warning against the return of "serfdom" in the postwar era, in the context of the experience with totalitarian state regimes that called themselves socialist and imposed managerial models on economic life. Milton Friedman recuperated Adam Smith as the ancestor of modern economics, particularly focused on the importance of unmediated purchase and sale of goods between producers and consumers, again in the context of a contrast with the communist command economies on the other side of the real and ideological wars of the 1960s and 1970s. In each instance there is a reaching back to the idea of the peace that is said to be produced by trade (*doux commerce*, see Hirschman 1977). In our recent political debates over the European versus American ways out of the financial crisis of 2008, many arguments (in the United States in any case) were made in terms of the old binaries: the old world/new world; socialism/free market; austerity/bailout.

The problem with "market economy" is its origin in contrastive categories rather than empirical phenomena, and its capacity to morph in this way. In the application of the two late twentieth-century standard frames of "market" and "nonmarket" economies, terms now regularly cross the median between the two. For example, the *New York Times*, on September 30, 2011, describes the recalibration of mandatory "fee" practices by banks, to preserve their margins in the face of regulatory changes, all under the rubric of making the kind of "profit" that used to be central to the argument for the incentive structures of the "free market." In another article, the "price" of buying out a failed bank CEO from his contract—which is treated as if the salary and conditions were the result of a "labor market"— surpasses his salary, by far. Then there is the theoretical embrace of "risk" and "entrepreneurship," often accompanied by the polemic insistence that what the "markets" really want is "certainty," that is, in the nonmarket structures (taxation, regulations, and so on) that can then be taken out of the market modeling and taken as "given" (I use the concept of "given" advisedly, since we could go more deeply into the concept of "the gift" that is at play here, and the precise assumptions about what takes place outside the market model).

To add confusion, the ubiquitous concept of "innovation" does *not* now necessarily include the full range of activities that Schumpeter (see Swedberg 1991) considered to make up entrepreneurship: invention, creative response, creative destruction, rational decision making, rules of thumb, and perhaps others. For him, innovation was a "new combination" that can lead to the "competitive elimination of the old" through a wavelike, disequilibrating process throughout the social economy (Swedberg 1991, 41, 56). Schumpeter himself explains that entrepreneurship involves "the doing of new things or the doing of things that are already being done in a new way (innovation)" (in Swedberg 1991, 412).

Innovation now appears to refer powerfully to the latter: to adaptation to new situations, such as new markets, rather than invention or even improvement (see *Wikipedia* entry on innovation: "Innovation differs from invention in that innovation refers to the use of a better and, as a result, novel idea or method, whereas invention refers more directly to the creation of the idea or method itself. Innovation differs from improvement in that innovation refers to the notion of doing something different (Lat. innovare: 'to change') rather than doing the same thing better." Other theorists are recuperated to make this shift. Lévi-Strauss pointed out long ago (in *The Savage Mind*) that capitalist economies and scientific knowledge cultures would be particularly hospitable to "games," where the rules are clear and enforced, and where the structure produces unambiguous events, whose results offer definitive winners and losers. If "games" have become a ramifying social form, then "rule making" (as Gillespie points to) becomes a widespread and perhaps unruly process of minutely detailed local specification (see Hibou 2012).

We could take this "rules of the game" image more seriously, since it does offer a framework outside of the classic theoretical divisions. So rather than resting on the one-liner humor that has seemed the only way out of intellectual whiplash (especially during the political season in the United States), maybe critique should lead us toward conceptual "innovation" (i.e., deploying something that already exists into new and more "profitable" ways) in the polemics over "the market." Borrowing this "neoliberal market" technique may be one way past the "wear-by" date of "the market economy," which may simply need to be jettisoned by "creative destruction." It's over two hundred years old: like buggy whips? But then, what do we do with the economies of places that really do have what people call markets (and the approximate equivalents in their own languages of life and commerce)?

Here is where the image of the platform, the apportunity/innovation (as a specific adaptation of what already exists with an element that is new), may be helpful. "Entrepreneur" then regains its etymological meaning: to "take between," "undertake," to work at connecting. The grids, institutions (literally standing in place), parts, forces and flows, and the nexuses through which they operate together, along with entanglements from the past, already exist. The question then reverts to: what does the platform consist of that makes such an apportunity possible? And then: what backward ("destructive" or "constructive") effects on the platform does seizing the apportunity have, accompanying any forward dynamic? It repairs entanglements? Undermines architectural features? Diverts flows? It is worth taking "entrepreneurship" utterly literally. What is "taken" as well as added? The idea of the "platform economy" gives—to me anyway—a compellingly applicable image, for all the places I work, and an intellectual imperative to explore broadly in empirical work.

There follows a short section on the difficulties of studying in Africa with the concept of "the market economy," even though there are vast marketplaces for every commodity.

Disjuncts and Connections: The Markets of Nigeria

At least five large economic platform components create the locations and conditions where all kinds of opportunities (for mundane margin making) and apportunities (for innovation) arise. The "market" for petrol, whose price and accessibility create conditions for all economic actors, consists of (a) the market for crude oil, since Nigeria is a producer; (b) the currency exchange market, since crude oil is denominated in dollars and the local economy in naira; (c) the refined petrol market, since Nigeria has only a small clandestine artisanal refining industry (Ugor 2013) and imports its refined petrol, largely from Venezuela; (d) the state/civil service/union negotiations over the minimum wage, which has recently been politically linked to the petrol price and which relates to the consumer price index; and (e) the vast supply-and-demand market for food, construction materials, clothing, electronics, and all kinds of consumer goods from China, India, and elsewhere.

These market platforms do not move together in any predictable way. The Nigerian exchange rate, the oil price, and the petrol price cut across each other in almost entirely independent ways, creating surges, troughs, and switchbacks that would clearly drive any Euro-American population into panic, as all forward contracts, plans, and fail-safes would have to be revisited if the nominal value of the currency no longer expressed its relative value in a predictable way, especially for a crucial commodity such as oil. Whether, and how, the new petrobarter regimes that China is creating in Africa would give any fixity to the consumer price-access situation is almost entirely unexamined (as far as I have been able to find).

Let us look at refined petrol first. Between 1985 and 2003, the price of petrol at the pump in Nigeria went from 20 kobo per liter to N40 (400K), a nominal multiplication by a factor of twenty. Over the same period, the real wage in dollar terms declined to about 25 percent; and in petrol terms it declined to about 20 percent, while the crude oil price in dollars grew by at least 50 percent. It spiked very high in the early years of the twenty-first century and then settled in. To take just the past six years:

January 2006: $64 per barrel
January 2010: $83 per barrel
January 2011: $88 per barrel
January 2012: $99 and rising per barrel

The national policies have defined the domestic price as "subsidized" for several decades, which makes no sense unless the platform of the currency market is taken into account. The naira has fallen and fluctuated against the dollar in the following way:

1. The naira and the dollar were approximately equivalent until 1985, when structural adjustment measures were put in place, and the naira fell rapidly.
2. By the early 1990s, under military rule, the value of the naira was still falling and by 1995 the margin between the official and the parallel rate for purchasing dollars with naira differed by a factor of four. Those who could access the official rate could almost literally create dollars for themselves.
3. After the return of democratic politics, the official and the parallel markets were allowed to converge again, but the value of the naira has consistently fallen.

Table 5.1   The Nigerian real minimum wage, in dollars and petrol, 1981–2011

Year	Wages	Liters of petrol
1981	N125/month (about $200)	625
2001	N7,500/month (about $75)	187
2011	N7,500/month (about $50)	115

So the wage, the dollar, the petrol price, and other prices are brought together in people's lives in ways that the theory of the "real" cannot do with any plausibility. See table 5.1, for example.

If the dollar value is taken as the "real" value, then the minimum wage fell to 25 percent of its initial value over thirty years. If the petrol purchasing power is taken as the "real" then it fell to 18 percent. A further calculation could be made against a Nigerian consumer price index, which would likely come out with yet another number.

Where do we touch the ground here? There is an impasse in the understanding of the intricacies of economic life if different parties fundamentally disagree about what "real" refers to. In fact, these different parties are best thought of as searching for apportunities on an enormously complex platform of differing structures and flows, all called "markets" by those who operate in them, but fitting together in existential life in ways best captured by the brilliant Nigerian cartoonists as a combination of question mark and exclamation point. A cartoon from 1996 depicts people waiting endlessly in the sun for a bus while commenting on the news that the head of state has promised to reduce the suffering of the masses. One member of the crowd says, "Absolutely true." Then adds, "By the year 2010." Greeted with "!?" (The year refers to the then-ongoing 2010 Commission). A later attempt by the government to impose another vision on all this, and call the difference between the dollar value of crude and the dollar value of retail petrol a "subsidy," which they then planned to "abolish," led to a huge confrontation all over the country in January 2012.

What the imagery of platform offers is an empirical challenge for us to match the cartoonist's impression of orderly confusion, disorders grasped for momentary advantage, and the sense of both certain predictable and improbable durations within almost indecipherable turbulence. The whole platform of life does not collapse. There is still a bus stop, and people still stand in line talking to each other. Petrol still arrives from overseas in tankers, to a port well known for gridlocks in the past, and still gets distributed in tanker trucks, owned and run by what public perception now settles into seeing as a secretive "oil mafia." Nigerian oil is still on the dollar; the naira still fluctuates; the refineries still fail to function. Scholarly attention is then drawn to the rules, the fine print and the *immediate* contexts where the various relevant "markets" meet. It has to embrace the evident entanglements, the coexistence and intricate enmeshment of old and new, the plausibility of differential rates of entropy, predatory dismantlement, retooling, and the continual ferreting around to find the loose ends, spaces, small abandonments, and sudden juxtapositions that can be seen as apportunities. And it *compels* attention to that entanglement: not as anomaly but as "the way it is."

Platforms as an Analytic: The Temporality of Endurance and Connection in the Face of Entropy, Appropriation, and Apportunistic Innovation

My final section is first an appreciation of an article by Gillespie (2010) on "platform" as a ramifying metaphor, and then an extension of the idea into the pragmatics of research.

Gillespie points out the ambiguity that allows "platform" to be both physical and metaphorical; apparently flat and neutral while actually selective—for example, according to "complex economic allegiances" (Gillespie 2010, 359); novel and insurgent while "more like traditional media than they care to admit" (359). For an anthropologist, his misgivings are to be embraced, since they are based on the real situation, as he sees it, with "traditional dilemmas . . . and some substantially new ones" (359). He points to precisely the kind of dynamic that anthropology can address: "[The] shoring up [of] niche positions" (348; see Guyer 1997 on the "niche economy"); "bursts of rule-making that are beginning to establish protections and obligations for . . . intermediaries" (348; see Comaroff and Roberts 1981 on rules and processes); and participants who "must carve out a role and a set of expectations that is acceptable to each and also serves their own . . . interests, while resolving or at least eliding the contradictions between them" (353; see, from long ago, Bohannan on "working misunderstandings" [in Dorward 1974]). And there is a rising volume of studies of negotiations of meaning that have an effect on the popular imagination and the law and business rhetoric that "is partly the result of discursive work" (359; anthropology moved into discursive studies with the linguistic turn). Classic ethnography had made all these observations, and now, beyond them, asks that we focus closely on the originality and generativity of specific instances.

In defining focus, we can benefit enormously from recent work by econ-

omists and economic historians who embrace the complexity and historical specificity of different eras, especially "transitions" of the kind we define ourselves as being in. Laurence Fontaine (2008) describes credit and
confidence in the era preceding the rise of market ideas. Beatrice Hibou's
most recent work, *La bureaucratisation du monde* (2012), points out in detail the proliferation of rule making by many parties, under the neoliberal
rubric. Under neoliberalism, any group can make rules and organizational
protocols: not only states, but corporations and market spaces. "The more
we dismantle regulations, the more we bureaucratize" (2012, 92). I am
indebted to the members of my undergraduate course of spring 2012 for
their studies of "games" in American culture, as a highly varied and extraordinarily extrapolative concept and practice (even *Newsweek* asked, on
its cover after the U.S. presidential election, whether Obama was "a lucky
general or master of the game" [November 19, 2012]). As entanglement
sets in, formal and informal become deeply interwoven and mutually dependent (Hibou 2012), often in ways that are partly hidden, even when
they are not technically criminal.

The ethnographic field opens up. The question of analytics and theorization demands a lot more work. But—in my own view—it needs to be
undertaken on the basis of much more deeply skeptical and searching de-
scriptions, provoked by precisely the sense of the real ambiguity and entanglement of platforms made up of old regulations and structures, insurgent
rule making, and old and new "grids" that permit the rapid grasping of
apportunities. In my current work—on soft currencies in a hard-currency-
mediated world—there are puzzles of practice, like the price at the pump in
an oil-producing economy, surrounded by discourses of "subsidy" and af-
fordability relative to wages, mediated by (perhaps?) complexly organized
"mafias," with national refineries that have never worked, complemented
by other energy sources (artisanally refined stolen crude [see Ugor 2013],
charcoal), and so on. I titled a paper written several years ago "Toward an
Ethnography of Price" (Guyer 2007a, see chapter 10), in which the petrol price figured prominently. Since then, it has seemed essential to aban-
don the term "the market economy," as the main depiction of the whole
economy, so that the ethnographic imperative could *be* an imperative, with
all the complications that would undoubtedly arise. A platform is hugely
complex as it is now constructed. But it is also ambiguous and entangled.
So we may not be trying to describe all of it. But we should be taking key
phenomena, key foci, and following the components and connections as
far as they take us: into the politics of international exchange rates, and the
"deals" in ports (Beuving 2004) and at petrol stations (Guyer 2004).

What is most important, and as my last point, is that the platform as an image demands attention to durability, in the process of constant apportunity building and a new awareness of the possibility of "crisis." Life depends on some durations having predictability, synchrony, longevity. Beatrice Hibou's book (2012) indicates how fragile some bureaucratization might render some forms of life. We work back to the finance of that life: ordinary lives (see Han 2012). And we entertain seriously the likelihood that the kind of "platform" that Gillespie indicates contains a variety of phenomena that the "natives" refer to as "markets." It may be that by moving away from the concept of integrated whole systems, articulations, and "the market economy," we may finally be able to do a fully anthropological comparative and analytical study of what people have called "markets," "commodities," "money," and enterprise/opportunity. Gaps open up in our otherwise inspiring record in comparative and historical economic anthropology, when typological comparisons of the kind that were once seminal to the discipline—from *Ancient Society* (Morgan 1877) to *Trade and Markets in the Early Empires* (Polanyi, Arensberg, and Pearson 1957)—have become less and less plausible framings for the centuries of global and regional interaction, as the world systems and articulation theories of the 1970s and the obvious realities of the 1990s and onward necessarily shifted the parameters. Concepts are required that open up the empirical field and analytical repertoire to examine closely how crucial issues for "real" prices and wages, and other commodities necessary for life, are shaped by the configuration of infrastructures and innovations that produce dynamics as complex and powerful as those at play in the oil economy of the Nigerian people. The "market economy" selectively narrows and distorts the focus, mainly for simple contrastive purposes. "Neoliberalism," and even "late liberalism," borrow terms that depict ideology rather than the full complement of material and economic components that produce the "real" situations of the present and projections of future advantages. And dangers.

Acknowledgments

I am grateful to Bill Maurer for encouraging the amplification of the basic ideas (first written informally in September 2011) into a short presentation (November 2012) and then this worked-out paper (December 2012). Also to the organizers—Alexandre Roig and Ariel Wilkis—and participants in the conference for discussion of this paper in Buenos Aires, and finally to Bruno Théret for his detailed comments on that text, to which I hope to have responded adequately.

PART THREE

Cultures of Calculation

SIX

The Eruption of Tradition?
On Ordinality and Calculation

In completing *Marginal Gains: Monetary Transactions in Atlantic Africa* (Guyer 2004), I became increasingly aware of circumstantial components in my central argument about the operation of ordinal variables. Ordinality emerged, I argued, from the empirical sources themselves as a pervasive principle of society and culture in historical Atlantic Africa, in the era of the great commercial trades in the extractive commodities of slaves, ivory and gold. Many things could be ranked, and counting-number itself stood within the repertoire of ranks, having benchmark or "tropic" thresholds—at 20 or 200 or some other number/icon/concept—at which attachments were created to other ranks across the repertoire such as title society grades in politics and named degradations from "the original" in the commodity market. The attachment of scales to numbers constituted not primarily a one-way reduction of quality to measure but one phase in the creation of equivalence, in a poetic and political play across rankings: price, power, precedence, and access to the spiritual world.

In the present world, increasingly complex "things"—carbon emissions, derivatives, reparations—find their validation and typical expression in mathematical formulae, which then make them susceptible to further calculative and comparative processes, with respect to price, risk, insurance, and so on. The Atlantic African experience makes me pause over moments in this process where rank order emerges. Rank order may be only one form of numerical expression in mathematics but, in various forms, it is a powerful dynamic in social life almost everywhere: as precedence by age, by achievement, by station in a hierarchy. In present-day American cultural life, everything can be put into a competitive mode that yields a rank order. There are veritable factories producing rankings in every domain of life, such as the *Forbes* website, founded in 1996, which ranks and comments on personal wealth, salaries of CEOs, success of companies, and so on, at a rate of "more than 3,500 articles and original videos" every business day (*Wikipedia* entry, May 2008). *U.S News and World Report* is similar for health and education. The Loughborough University's Department of Geography ranks global cities. Professional associations produce ranks for products, expertise, newness (as in "rookie of the year"), etc.[1]

My Africa work encourages an additional "pause for thought" concern: over the middle and bottom of these orders, not just the star figure at the top. Not all rankings seem to do the same thing for the whole range of included instances. What does it mean to be seventh, or eleventh in the title societies in eastern Nigeria in the nineteenth century? Or fourteenth, as my university, Johns Hopkins, is ranked among American undergraduate colleges in *U.S. News and World Report?*[2] What does it mean for my home city of Baltimore that it has 1 point toward a high of 12 points on the scale of global cities, along with Cape Town, Hanoi, and Tehran? And how might any other city—say Nice or Kraków or Paramus, New Jersey—stack up? Does the bottom of an ordinal scale simply disappear into oblivion or is it somehow included, valued, in alternative ways? And again, taken as complete scales, top to bottom, do these Western rankings work ephemerally, as a temporary phase in long calculative processes, or are they more akin to the Atlantic African historical situation, achieving relative stability as powerful "market devices" (Callon et al. 2007)? Perhaps most importantly, do the numerical calculations and the ordinal numerical expressions of them invoke different political philosophies from each other, as Verran (2010) suggests, which are concealed rather than made visible by number itself? If so, are "we the people" invited to participate mathematically in their production, or are we simply consumers of the results of the algorithms of others?

The Puzzle of Orders

So this article arises from two converging sources: On the one hand, challenging questions in the analysis of ranking and equivalence that arose in my West African work; and on the other, questions about what would otherwise be a counterintuitive process under progressivist views of increasing sophistication in number use in the West, namely the rampant "reduction" of complex calculations based on counting-number to ordinal number. Sometimes this is just a phase in a longer process rather than a destination. But its characteristics are puzzling. When examined closely, the imagery of contemporary scales clearly resonates through a rather limited and specific religious and social register before, and beside, their reinsertion into calculative mode. All fields have their own "icons," "legends," "stars," "idols," "MVPs," or "heroes" with "global" reach and "timeless" durability to their reputations. Selective reference to a vaguely feudal past, the epics of King Arthur, Greek and Norse mythology, castles, magical powers, feats of explorers, princesses, and so on in the media and popular culture allude to a "traditional" order that bears no resemblance to laboriously established historians' reconstructions of the real past. Rather it is an imagined configuration, mixing jousts on white horseback[3] with massed armies of strange beings or modern consumers or tele-audience voters on *American Idol*. So the terms become uncannily evocative of an ancient world with "tournaments of value" (Appadurai 1986) upstaging or intertwining with the imagery of neoclassical market competition or the class struggle of the capitalist mode of production. In this "ranking/rating" phase of the calculative process, number can move around, sometimes morphing so rapidly from measure to order to fiction that its authors can forget to make the tables even add up.[4]

The Parabolic Imperative

This would seem like a cheap and superficial "shot" at postindustrial or Madison Avenue semantics if the phenomena were not so vast and so powerful, and in many cases so repetitive in their parabolic scalar form. In very many domains, the "first" is icon or idol, and often at a very wide interval from the second, third, and fourth. In the scale of Global Cities, London, Paris, New York City, and Tokyo (at 12 points) so far outstrip the next that there is literally no city at 11 points.[5] Narrative commentaries often make clear that, at the top, it is, in fact, the intervals along the order scale, and not the absolute amounts, that are at stake in "competition."[6] In many cases, intervals diminish radically going down the scale, both in real terms and in proportion to their next positions. The two charts in figure 6.1 show the distribution of salaries for CEOs and stud fees for racehorses, showing the parabola at work.[7]

A *U.S. News and World Report* ranking of American hospitals would show a similar curve if the popular mathematical imagination were let loose on it to make its own inferences from the points-scale by medical specialty, and the number of rankable medical specialties per center. A total of 5,462 medical centers were ranked; 173 made it into the final list, and of those, 18 displayed "the marked breadth of expertise" that qualified them for the "Honor Roll." We can note what a huge proportion—about 95 percent—

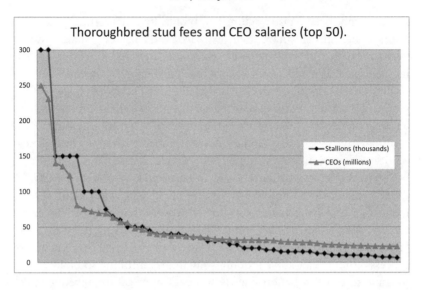

Thoroughbred stud fees and CEO salaries (top 50).

forms the tail of the distribution. Over five thousand are included on equal terms by virtue of category membership, and then individually ranked, but they are ranked by several criteria whose values—once compounded with each other—relegate the distinctions among them to near irrelevance. Such rankings and other honors—as we all know in academia—are further capitalized, in part, simply as "reputation" or "prestige," for backing in the next phase of competitive processes. To understand the plausibility of such ordinal rankings in public life, should we look back in social time, to the symbolism of familiar ladderlike hierarchies, or forward toward some futuristic hierarchical form? In any case, one should pause to see how such scales vary, converge, and gain recognition, resonance, and power.

A Speculative Moment

In the early 1970s, Goux captured the difference between a noble-feudal and a bourgeois-capitalist ethics and symbolism of quantity: "Thus, in opposition to the feudal nobility, which avidly devours more than it possesses, flaunting its luxury as the obligatory *sign* of rank, the bourgeois political economy must preach . . . postponement of *jouissance*" (1990, 203). Hence, with rank as a dominant principle, one has to compete in arenas to sustain relative standing in an ordinal logic, spending up to the hilt to do so. By contrast, the bourgeois logic of saving supports competition in markets, to achieve a niche that is judged by its size rather than by status criteria. There are at least these two, and perhaps another, ordinal dynamics that may add and compound each other's persuasive effects in the present. There is the symbolism of orders from the past, alluded to by Veblen (1899), in his identification of the specific things that can satisfactorily fulfill a role in "conspicuous consumption." Many evoke feudalism: large lands and houses, large dogs, large jewels and large entertainments. We see the invocation of long history in a different form in Bourdieu's (1984) finding that the older and more aristocratic and traditional a thing is— such as furniture, cuisine, fabric—the higher up the consumption scale it stands. Silk brocade still evokes status, in spite of populism and republicanism in the political realm.

Veblen and Bourdieu, however, refer to a fairly simple cultural gradation, built on status and class, symbolized as a structure: a ladder, or a pyramid. So an additional algorithm must account for the specifically parabolic shape of the present curve of value. I explore here the idea that this lies in additional meanings and practices that have been folded into an increasingly ambiguous concept of competition. Arenas and markets are joined by "the ratings": recurrent testing at intervals, by multiple criteria, of the participants in what is—in the meantime—a *continual* interactive process. Between moments when the process stops for the ratings to move in, all participants relate to one another continuously and competitively. The results seem very close to what Bateson ([1936] 1958) called "schizmo-genesis": the continual reproduction, confirmation, and intensification of difference, which is then ritually marked when the process itself is momentarily suspended, as if for collective contemplation and affirmation. In arenas, the lowest category remains there, either eliminated or returning for a next round or "revenge." In the market, rising and falling occur at all times. In ratings, initial advantage offers recurrent opportunities to capitalize on it, and initial disadvantage takes ever- increasing effort, or miraculous intervention, to overcome it. In any ongoing process, then, it is critically important to theorize how, when, and by whose agency snapshot moments are produced, interpreted, and fed back into it.

There is an interesting parallel here with the mathematics of ordinality. The *Wikipedia* entry on ordinals explains that "ordinal arithmetic describes the three usual operations on ordinal numbers: addition, multiplication, and exponentiation." These would pattern closely the social processes alluded to above: the tournament or the games add and subtract status in a "rules of the game," "level playing field" idiom. The market multiplies profit by expanding pools of buyers and sellers. And recursive replication is exponential in the sense depicted above: advantage is recurrently rated, which then folds back into the next stage of the process.[8] In social life, each mode of creating and amplifying ordinality would produce a very different sort of lived social order: all, however, under the same terms of competition and ranking. So do we lay people of the mathematical world ask ourselves whether we recognize these implicit computational variants or whether they are rendered opaque by the use of a common language and a merged set of symbols about—quite simply—"competition"?

A Brief Review of the Great Chain of Being

Several of the images for the peak of the parabolic order come straight from the Great Chain of Being: the encompassing theory of all of life that was developed in Christian Europe under religious intellectual hegemony in the medieval period. It is a vast, inclusive, fixed—that is, *noncompetitive*—hierarchical ordering that seems to be staging a remarkable comeback as a source of imagery, in part in accord with the new evolutionism.[9] In the original version, every class of being was internally ordered and also took its place in the encompassing hierarchy. Each position partakes to some degree of the nature of the next immediate steps above and below, both internal to the class and between the class and its proximate beings in the great scale of things. Narratives and ontologies define the specific places that beings and things occupy. Below the angels and man, the animals are ranked by relative intelligence and independence: the most noble is not possible to domesticate; the next level is domesticated but spirited (horses, dogs); and at the bottom are docile domesticated animals (sheep). Everything in the universe has its place, judged by multiple intersecting criteria. Familiar Shakespearean poetics plays across the categories: the king is like the sun, the lion, the eagle; the heroic leader is "dolphin-like," and so on.

There was also a mathematics of lateral symmetry and internal composition (Tillyard 1942, 51), such as nine hierarchies of bad angels to match the nine hierarchies of good angels. And there were analogs up and down as well as across the registers according to the four ranked elements that exist in all things: earth, water, air, and fire (in ascending order). Within one group—man—the brain has three hierarchical faculties: the sensual; a middle rung consisting of common sense, "fancy," and memory; and the third, the highest, the one shared with God and the angels, "reason" (consisting of two parts: understanding and will) (Tillyard 1942, 71). So the overall hierarchy could be held in abeyance and manipulated for symbolic and instrumental purposes by adding and subtracting the criteria of relevance to specific situations. "It was through their retention of the main points and their flexibility in interpreting the details that the Elizabethans were able to use the great correspondences in their attempt to tame a bursting and pullulating world" (Tillyard 1942, 100).

According to Suber (1997), the Great Chain scheme coexisted with new logics in the work of the foundational early modern mathematicians and philosophers such as Leibniz, Descartes, and Spinoza. So we might also turn to the mathematics of that time, and particularly of emergence of spirals and parabolas, which work ordinality through sequences, giving amplification effects. I am afraid this task lies beyond my level of erudition in the history of mathematics. I tried working with nonlinear series, such as the Fibonacci sequence:[10] developed in the thirteenth century, informing the mathematics of spirals, and remaining important for twentieth-century topics such as fractals (Eglash 1997). Clearly mathematics itself has developed through overlapping and combining theories. The public symbolism of ordinal number may track the same shifting coexistence and therefore not find corrective complaints coming from mathematical experts when important distinctions are not made. The best I can do is to return to the ethnographic question about the ways in which ordinal processes that differ in formal characteristics and social results are expressed. How do "we the people" understand ordinal processes in the arena, the market, and the ratings? Does public culture extrapolate from the arena (through concepts such as "the level playing field" and "the rules of the game") and from the market (through concepts such as "freedom" and "choice") to create a composite vocabulary to guide our own ranking computations? When we concentrate closely, I suggest that we find several such vocabularies together—along with the Great Chain of Being.

A Modern Ranking Scheme, as an Example: Stud Fees for Racehorses

The fact that stud fees can yield more income than racecourse earnings puts the arena, the market, and the ratings in a synergistic recursive relationship. Smarty Jones, winner of the Kentucky Derby in 2004, "stands for $100,000 a mating and has a full book of 110 mares" this year (Joe Drape, "A Pampered Derby Champion's Finicky Taste," *New York Times*, April 28, 2008). The following profile for Point Given, at only $15,000, offers the most complete review of how scalar calculations work alongside symbolic cross-references, to create the upward spiral compound effect of ratings.[11] The numerical ordinals are in bold and the other ordinal scales in italics.

He is the **first** *Thoroughbred* ever to win **four** million-dollar races **in a row**. He is one of just **five** horses since **1900** to win the Preakness-G1, Belmont-G1, and Travers-**G1**. And, for *good measure*, he **added** a victory in the HaskellH.-**G1** in the midst of that **string** of wins. He is a **six-time Grade I** winner, with **five Grade I** victories coast-to-coast in 2001 alone. The **five** are not only a *museum-quality* compilation of races—Preakness, Belmont, Travers, Santa Anita Derby and Haskell—but are the **most** Grade I races won by any horse in the world in 2001. His Timeform **rating of 133 is the highest** for any American racehorse in 2001, and he closed out the year with the *ultimate American honor*—becoming the **11th** 3 year old honored with the *gold Eclipse Award*, as *Horse of the Year*.

Historically, Point Given casts an *even more imposing shadow*. He *annihilated his opponents in the Test of Champions*, the Classic Belmont Stakes, winning by over **12 lengths** in 2:26 2/5, the **fourth fastest** Belmont ever run. This time was faster than the last **two** Triple Crown winners, *immortals* Affirmed and Seattle Slew. And it is nearly **two seconds** faster than 2003 winner Empire Maker. Then, there's the Preakness / Belmont / Travers **"Triple."** In the last **102 years**, *only Hall of Fame* members Man o' War, Whirlaway, Native Dancer and Damascus achieved what Point Given did winning this *trinity* of races.

In his last **four** starts, all **million dollar** races, *record crowds* were drawn to watch the *dominating* horse run, including the **largest ever** in the history of Saratoga and Monmouth Park racetracks for his final **two** starts.

Daily Racing Form *Executive Editor* Joe Hirsch is not prone to *hyperbole*. Upon the announced retirement of Point Given, he wrote: "We were fortunate to have him as long as we did, and we will *treasure* the *rich* memories he left us."[12]

The variables cross the numerical scales: frequency of wins, margin of wins, time at the finish, size of the purse, rank ordering of speed for the history of each race, crowd size and so on; symbolic resonance is conveyed through rank of race, fame, treasure, champion, annihilation, eclipse, gold, museum quality and so on. The price value would seem to be a recursive compound, placing the stud fee on a curve of the kind we see again in CEO salaries and in the ranking of medical centers.

Doing the Calculative Grammar

In public life, the insertion of a math grammar is generally left to the reader (or listener). So what are we invited to do when we witness ordinal sequences, and especially those with an infinite tail? We can apprehend them through the hyperboles of an invented mythical past, shaped by the Great Chain of Being, that convinces us of an upward orientation toward vistas of surpassing worth. Alternatively, we can pause on the specific ordinal mathematics of each case, and the conditions of their creation, circulation, and deployment. As an internally composite complex of number manipulations, where rating and ranking mark ongoing processes, the phenomena of ordinality deserve anthropological attention, as one of the powerful social devices of our moment in history.

Acknowledgments

Thanks to Caroline Bledsoe for advice on figure 6.1, and the conference participants for challenging me to think more deeply about popular calculative cultures than was clear in the first version.[13]

SEVEN

Percentages and Perchance: Archaic Forms in the Twenty-First Century

Introduction: Signposts

This paper is a sequel to a previous one on ordinality and the ever-ramifying application of ranking schemes in the present world (Guyer 2010). In contrast to our conventional political and cultural histories of rupture and revolution, and the scientific histories of paradigm shift, mathematical operations have been historically additive and amplifying, so they come with accrued legacies of borrowing and application, as well as deepening sophistication, both with respect to intervention in the world and to the world's pictorial, poetic, and graphic representations. Rotman (1987) gives an intense example of the constitution of such a legacy, in the cultural florescence around the concept of zero when it was introduced to Europe from Asia in the early Renaissance period. Today, the imperative of states and organizations to coordinate very complex dynamics has come with an expansion of the definition of what is measurable in the world, thereby the domains to which mathematics is applied, and hence, also, the expressive arts of manipulating, conveying, and arguing about numbers with others, in both the specialist world and in the public sphere. The modernist notions of objectivity and transparency in democratic governance and "free markets," now supported by the new technologies of "big data" management, make the present another intense moment in the long history of public cultures of numeracy. Ranking was the particular topic that started me down the path of inquiry into legacy concepts for representing our economies of the present, having worked on questions of number at transactional interfaces in Africa in the past (Guyer 2004). As I discuss below, the provocation derived largely from engagement with Helen Verran (2001), whose work on Yoruba number gave us a different critical manner of thinking and working number logic from the classic cultural relativism of the past. For a conference and collection on number as inventive frontier (Guyer, Khan, and Obarrio 2010), my own paper (Guyer 2010) analyzed how the power-law competitive mode that is insurgent in the present financialized economy works on basic ordinals, which are sequentially equidistant, in a way that results in an exponential curve, where the money-value distance between first and second is greater than between second and third, and the margin diminishes with each successive number until it becomes barely perceptible at the higher-ranking ordinal numbers. The expressive imagery for this numerical mode in social and political life is strikingly allusive to ancient and medieval concepts: icons, legends, myths, epics, and a whole range of apical objects from the Great Chain of Being: roses (the apex of the flowers), lions (apex of the beasts), gold (apex of the minerals), heroes, angels, and so on. I argued that popular expressions for this type of ordinality, quantified in the monetary reward system differently from skill- or market-based competitive ranking, were drawing on this long genealogy of poetic and rhetorical forms for plausibility.

Here, I turn to another simple archaic numerical technique, the percentage, which is also applied widely to and in the public sphere, also basically deeply familiar to the public, and sometimes combined with ranking across new domains. Like ranking, its genealogy of use gives it persuasive as well as instrumental power. The accrued multiplicity of publics, referents, and familiarities of usage may allow situational indeterminacy and flexibility, which may then become an aspect of its plausibility and power, as people come to grips with their own moment in history, in both familiar and novel terms.

Percentage may be even more complex than ranking because it also necessarily contains a philosophical implication of completion, or wholeness of some kind, to the category name—the denominator—that equals the "100." The denominator equates to a category "name" that presumes stability. It seems to me that it is this implicit designation of completion that allows its ever-ramifying inventive applicability. Percentage has moved from being a simple calculation of proportion to demographic depiction, to policy matters with respect to value for fiscal purposes, and in implicit allusion to public justice under liberal principles of formal equality; then to probability, risk, and rates of change; then applied in ever more varied contexts, and combined in sophisticated, combinatory formulations: including in the financial world, as interest rates per unit time and other techniques covered by a section in the *New York Times* entitled "Dealbook."

At one frontier in the present, it seems that the centum—the whole, the benchmark—has accrued aspirational, rather than simply descriptive, qualities. One hundred percent can be a benchmark for identifying how far we fall short, and how much excess is being demanded, with the insinuation that we should work at redressing it. In a graphic in the *New York Times*, on the tax rate, a fierce Uncle Sam is exerting 102 percent at the top end of the income spectrum (*New York Times*, February 4, 2012, graphic for "Think Your Tax Rate Is High?" James B. Stewart, page B1). This graphic can draw our expanded attention to the representational power of these old numerical forms. Beyond the rhetorics and poetics that I drew out for ranking, we find that the percentage lends itself highly appositely to strikingly familiar *graphic* forms, such as columns and pie charts. In a world of "big data," where both the "things" being quantified and the calculative techniques themselves may be unfamiliar to the public, the capacity to represent them visually may be a particular advantage that can be mobilized. I include such striking instances, like the demanding and threatening Uncle Sam (above), from time to time, as illustrations of simultaneous allusions to numerical, rhetorical, visual, and otherwise familiar worlds, throughout the paper. The argument itself suggests ways of tracing out the logics whereby we might see more clearly how such allusions are composed: by acquiring some auras and excising others.

I start the paper with the history of my interchanges with Helen Verran to unpack the process of the multiple applicability of percentages. In Verran's approach to working with number, one returns from the empirical cases to the archive on logic, which offers a variety of views of coherence. And these sources then pose their own puzzles. For example, as I read, it seemed clear that possible worlds theory had to face very difficult questions about whether anything at all—like logic itself, or number itself—can cross from one mode to another. For example, Girle introduces the concept of "semi-relevant logic" (2003, 188) in possible worlds theory. If a question is undecidable, it introduces not just a semiotic or political space but also a formal logical space, into which vagueness—fragmentation?—can seep, along with the pragmatic exigencies that have their place in all such theoretical approaches, to a greater or lesser degree, since all multiplicity implies situational selectivity. These pragmatics now include a growing proliferation of use for the percentage form, the expanding practice of not naming the denominator in clear definitional terms, and visual sophistication for drawing attention to the numerator rather than the denominator. It is the practices of *producing* relevance (Sperber and Wilson 1995) that necessarily become key when we move into a terrain where many dynamics are at play: semiotic multiplicity, historically layered meanings, and authoritative intervention into the multiplicity of allusions in the attachment of the sign to the world, especially as they configure, and motivate, a future.

A widening cultural use of such simple and familiar mathematical formulations perhaps rests on an ever-widening scientific confidence in the cumulative success of, and indeed the need for, measures and calculations, as distinct from other modes of knowledge, which may have lost their systemic power even while retaining the evocative power of their poetics. While Genevieve Lloyd entitles her book *Providence Lost* (2008), and Alasdair MacIntyre *After Virtue* (1981), physicist Mario Livio circles back to entitle his work *Is God a mathematician?* (2009). Since I come at "the new numeracy" as a nonmathematician and a "view from below," I attend to discursive allusions and puzzles as they have come along in an attempt to decode and theorize social and political power, especially in aspirational mode.[1]

I move through some quite varied terrain, all within the public sphere, to illustrate, first, the diversity and plausibility of applications and evocations that the percentage form may have accrued for whole populations. My method works through surprise first, as in this sign, posted on a wall in Baltimore: "Tattoo removal, 40% off." I then move to puzzles and patterns. In that sense, it may seem random, but behind my own ventures in the study of number is a classic anthropological question about whether, and how, people's own accounts of the bundled realities we have called "lifeworlds" (Jackson 2012) and "consciousness" are accommodating to the new possibilities of imaging properties of order and disorder, completion and openness, and, especially with respect to a projected future, in numerical forms. In the final section of the paper, I illustrate this argument with a graphic and a discussion of the combination of ranking and percentage, created for the local public in a free newspaper, to convey the dynamics of economic growth and aspiration in my own city of Baltimore, Maryland. This analysis of percentages in aspirational contexts also complements my earlier paper (Guyer 2007b) on the difficulty of identifying how the "near future" is being configured under present temporal regimes of calendrics and punctuations. Many calendar-based prospective judgments are, in fact, made on percentage measurements, so noting what exactly the denominator refers to, and what it projects as somehow stable in an unstable world, may be a way into the temporal-futurity problem as well.

Does the projection of life, using archaic forms, tend toward logical coherence, experiential systematicity, cosmological consonance, or other "possible worlds" in modular (or virtual) views of life? Or is the social imagination tending to a version of fragmentation, where such consonances do happen, but in a fleeting manner, and over very limited fields? By virtue of their older evocations, both ranking and percentage may now be able to evoke a familiar sense of comprehension and completion—the beginning and endpoints of a ranking scale, and the 100 of the percentage—even when the experience is fleeting and where there is no longer a classic, enduring, encompassing authoritative cultural architecture. Although shorn of part of their mathematical composition and embellished by poetic allusions, these particular, very old, mathematical forms may create a sense of meeting and stabilization, in a world that, taken as a "whole," is no longer experienced as either stable or providential. Both rank and percentage, together and intertwined, were at the center of the Occupy movement's slogan, "we are the 99%" (of October 2011), which mobilized millions across the world to see themselves relationally to each other, although not in any specific, enduring organizational mode. The combination of familiar categories (with their own implicit but optative completions) and permissive vagueness lends particular interest to ranking and percentages in the cultural numerical world of the twenty-first century.

Background: An African Reference Point and Conversations with Helen Verran

"Perchance," or "possibility," is a topic I first addressed in a simple history-of-anthropology sense (Guyer 2009b), only to rediscover in relation to my paper on ordinality that Helen Verran had been prodding me all along in the direction of more rigorous engagement with possible worlds theory and modal logic in philosophy and mathematics. She alludes to this in her book *Science and an African Logic* (Verran 2001) where she raises the question of how the "whole" is implicitly or explicitly configured and finds in African practices an important reference point for thinking imaginatively in this regard. While all number systems relate unity to plurality, the emphasis varies from the one/many form to the whole/part form. It is the latter that Verran could describe in detail from Western Nigeria. "Number, in Yoruba language talk is a degree of dividedness . . . number organizes mode," mode being a collectedness of the "sortal particulars" that designate a particular kind of "matter" in the world (Verran 2001, 198). Matter is sorted, then divided, which then enables number to enter. Situational performances of number then accrue a historical constitution.

In my book, *Marginal Gains: Monetary Transactions in Atlantic Africa* (Guyer 2004), where I argued that multiple principles of ranking order were brought together performatively in situational transactions, I referred in several places to Verran's argument that, in Yoruba practice, a number in social life was never the "dazzling singular purity" of modern Western thinking; numbers in social life were better seen as an order of a kind that she terms "clots," in which "an old series of gestures is still recognizable" (Verran 2001, 11). She suggested that I should explicitly distinguish between, on the one hand, "foundational empiricism" with its "one/many" logics of number based on the spatiotemporal particulars of thingness, cardinal number, and uniformity of practice; and on the other, "modal empiricism," with its "part/whole" logics of number. Of the latter, as she sees them in my book, she writes of "a vague general whole that allows articulation of specifiable parts" (Verran 2007, 181). What matters, what are conserved, are the relational orders of this vaguely delineated whole. By reference to the whole as 100 (of something), percentage may be our main counterpart to a modal empiricism of this kind, within a cardinal number system. One-hundredness is divided into numbered parts, regardless of the cardinal number of the spatiotemporal identities or wholes that make up the denominator. In this case, Verran's perception of the African logics can be a guide to perception of our own, in a rapidly changing world, suggesting that we look closely at the social and historical contexts that cultivate the formation and conservation of continually recomposed definitions of identity, and historically formed "clots" of meaning, implicated in the changing quality-quantity of "hundredness."

For both of us, from our different angles, conservation in West Africa lay in some general notion of scale itself, in a permeating whole/part form of logic. Verran suggested that African economies are built around a concern to conserve multiple local orders (2007). These African "wholes" (in the plural), to which she alludes, may not be amenable to the same kinds of specifically mathematical expression with which we are familiar with percentages, but offer us a broader analytical and comparative horizon for thinking about the mode of whole/part as a philosophical system, and searching selectively for useful analytics that could be extrapolated, if only for exercising imagination and precision on the complexity of percentage statements.

Looking broadly into the ethnographic and artistic sources on Yoruba conceptual frames, one sees evidence for four qualities that suggest that a "whole" might also be thought of, mathematically, as a certain dense center with radiations, rather than as a space or category enclosed by a boundary. First, a quality termed in English as excess or proliferation is a key cultural mode; secondly, fraction is not a common arithmetical function in Yoruba life (Adam 1995); thirdly, scales are elaborated by complicated refinements, additions, and subtractions, so their integrity lies in the central name or principle rather than in any limit conditions of the form of the scale itself; and finally, encompassing judgmental concepts—such as "enough" (ó tó means it's enough (a verb) in Yoruba)—are entirely contingent on the contexts to which they refer at the time they are used. It is not clear then, in West African languages, what exactly a fractional "part" would be, even if we concede a strong sense of integrity, sufficient to justify anticipating a concept of a "whole" of some sort. By explicitly embracing the integral as potentially centripetal, as distinct from bounded, we can also avoid the danger of falling into platitudes about Africa, such as "whole" equals "community" equals "tradition." In the current context, where the "clots" around old concepts have become so dense, an ethnographic approach demands that one keep one's mind correspondingly open to the broad selectivity that becomes possible when "wholes" are at stake but not defined or brought into sharp profile, and possibly with only fleeting integral qualities in the practices of daily life.

Verran draws on the experience of number in the Yoruba whole/part mode to suggest how different modes of number-thought might coexist, and then not be self-contained or stable, in use. "I show how in shape-shifting between the form one/many and whole/parts, and in moving between symbolic/indexical and indexical/iconic modes of semiosis, number works in inventive ways" (Verran 2010, 173). She argues for her own empirical cases that the "conflation" of one with the other in a new "clot" *could* successfully *mask* their fundamental difference (again, in practice): so, in some cases, precisely *not* retaining "an *old* series of gestures" (italics mine) but, in an equally socially powerful process, *shedding* them. The referent for semiotic agency and number rhetoric may then become the future rather than the past, even if the pathways in people's minds toward a sense of participation are opened up by a basic sense of *past* familiarity. By comparing these as modal processes, she—and the participants—may see the deliberate political nature of their mediation and crafting that gets "lost" in the simplified public account.

Here Verran prefigures a more complex set of "clotting processes" in practice than the two logically contrastive models of one/many and part/whole can grasp, very important as these are for clarifying the mind. Now there are penumbras of allusions, overlaps between models, shape-shifting and shedding, and models of "the whole" that differ widely. I see our collective challenge here—as anthropologists, field scholars, and analytical thinkers from various disciplines—as precisely slowing down even further so as to examine the processes of forming the new, and future-oriented, configurations of familiar and novel features to which she refers. Our studies of "complex clots" of value in West Africa, with their conserved histories, may provide some inspiration. Verran (2012) expresses it thus: "The work of the numbers in the report is to mediate the oscillation" between "domains of ordering and valuation." With percentages, I find it compelling to come back even further toward West Africa: from "oscillation" (which implies a two-way pendulum swing from one model to the other) to the more diffused process that Verran implies by the terms "mediation" and "shape-shifting" (the latter is, of course, a concept from West and Central Africa!).

To do this I suggest that one could also draw on Victor Turner's work on what he terms "dominant symbols" (in fact what the Ndembu depict by a term meaning "senior") to examine indigenous processes and logics of "multivocality." He writes that "a single symbol may stand for many things. . . . Each dominant symbol has a 'fan' or 'spectrum' of referents, which are interlinked by what is usually a simple mode of association, its very simplicity enabling it to interconnect a wide variety of *significata*" (Turner 1967, 50). The complexities, and even incongruities, of the juxtapositions of referent that he finds for Ndembu dominant symbols recommend an open ethnographic attentiveness. This is not to claim that numerical forms should be analyzed as if they were symbols, but only to discipline ourselves to notice the way that *all* forms may travel across contexts, picking up meaning and plausibility from one to another. For a disciplinary approach to the narrowing or shedding of meanings, we have the example of the "literalism" suggested by Crapanzano (2000) as the current process of imposition of authority based on insisting on the literal applications of foundational texts such as the American Constitution and the Bible. His example from "sacred" texts offers a possible entry point into the disciplines whereby such fundamental, archaic number conventions are applied and then contained within limits, at least in governance contexts, in a way that would be complementary to the study of processes of proliferation. Turning back to Verran, one can then open up questions about the possible operation of foundationalism in mathematics, especially the official arithmetic of governmentality.

Back to Percentages

Before our very eyes we can see the centum of percentages shape-shift from aggregation to community, from foundational purity to modal referent and to what Verran has called "vague wholes." We have become accustomed, as conventions, to the 30 percent chance of rain; the 10 percent decline in the growth rate of the GDP; the 25 percent rise in obesity. And "40% off tattoo removal"! What seemed, in my ordinality paper, like the straightforward infusion of two totally different modes, numerical and religio-mythological, seems better seen, for percentages, as a continuous and fluid process of reconfiguring multiple modalities and media across a whole continuum of overlapping "possible worlds," to *provoke* as well as *invoke*.

I will suggest that these statements are better seen as performatives, aimed to call forth a judgmental response about "the way things are going": it's getting too much; it's not fair anymore; it's reaching a danger zone. They go beyond the mathematical resolutions—infused with persuasive imagery—of my "ordinal scales" argument that produce a "model of" the world. These percentage statements suggest complexly built platforms for leaping to conclusions about a "model for" a world that is "not yet." This insurgent concept of the percentage seems unmistakably a terrain for Verran's kind of shape-shifting in numbers, applied to public concerns. Thanks to the school curriculum, in percentages the expert meets the people in terms they share, albeit on possibly different grounds.

A Short History

The use of percentages long predates modernity, although it was clearly elaborated for public applicability in the early modern era. The *Wikipedia* entry suggests:

> While the term has been attributed to Latin per centum, this is a pseudo-Latin construction and the term was likely originally adopted from the French pour cent. The concept of considering values as parts of a hundred is originally Greek. The symbol for percent (%) evolved from a symbol abbreviating the Italian per cento. (http://en.wikipedia.org/wiki/Per_cent; accessed December 26, 2011)

The clearest and earliest public record in which we meet the percentage is in the innovations in tax law related to weights and measures. Uniform proportionality of denominations has been built into systems of weights and measures for almost a thousand years in Britain.[2] The commodities enumerated in clause 34 of the Magna Carta (wine, ale, corn, and dyed cloth) are augmented (honey, malt, etc.) over the years and then regularized in one great effort in 1834: "It is necessary for the Security of Commerce and for the Good of the Community that Weights and Measures should be just and uniform" (text of the 1834 law, http://en.wikipedia.org/wiki/Weights_and_Measures_Act; last accessed December 14, 2011). We make note of the "vague whole" concepts of "security," and "community" (capitalized in the original) that give uniformity an ethical cast as "justice." Later in the text of the act, however, the effect on another whole, namely His Majesty's Revenue, is explicitly addressed. In this British legal text, one sees an absolute rather than a proportional logic to the taxes to be paid. For example, the levels of payment on malt production (page 356) are specified by tranches of quantity—0 to 50 standard "quarters," 50 to 100, 100 to 150, and so on by fifties up to 550. Each additional 50 quarters demands the same 7 shillings and sixpence, which then tops out at 550 quarters, and is level from there upward. A percentage calculation was introduced into the revenue system later. The famous Alexander Hamilton law on revenue from import duties for the newly independent United States, passed in 1790,[3] contained both an absolute charge and also a percentage ad valorem duty. I cannot desist from giving an example from the text, to convey the sheer intricacy of the calculations on which the future of new government depended (I italicize to make the "percentum" stand out):

All China ware, looking glasses, window and other glass, and all manufactures of glass (black quart bottles excepted) *twelve and a half per centum ad valorem*; marble, slate, and other stones, bricks, tiles, tables, mortars and other utensils of marble or slate, and generally all stone and earthen ware, blank books, writing paper, and wrapping paper, paper hangings, pasteboards, parchment and vellum, pictures and prints, painter's colors, including lampblack, except those commonly used in dyeing, gold, silver, and plated ware, gold and silver lace, jewellery and paste work, clocks and watches, shoe and knee buckles, grocery, (except the articles before enumerated) namely, cinnamon, cloves, mace, nutmegs, ginger, anniseed, currants, dates, figs, plums, prunes, raisins, sugar candy, oranges, lemons, limes, and generally all fruits and comfits, olives, capers, and pickles of every sort, oil, gun-powder, mustard in flour, *ten per centum ad valorem*.

The list continues; this is about one-third of it. Possibly duties and taxes exacted in absolutes suited systems where prices were predictable and government revenues needed to be so. Ad valorem taxes might suit situations of fluctuating price and revenue, and experimental governance. So even when the denominator of the percentage refers not to a "whole" in any organic sense but to an amount (the price), its selective application in public life may still convey something about the collective properties of a specific system. Ad valorem leaves the aggregate outcome for sovereign revenue to forces emanating from below, that is, from markets. It is perhaps not accidental that the invention of the pie chart comes from the exact same period, and also from a locus of liberal thinking, namely the Scottish Enlightenment. William Playfair is credited with publishing the first pie chart in 1801 to represent the proportion of land in the Turkish Empire located in Asia, Europe, and Africa.

Percentage expressions have grown enormously in the twentieth and twenty-first centuries, through science, income tax law, probability and risk, insurance, price manipulations ("70% reduced sale!"), legal compensation, and political rhetoric. Change brings not only new domains into play, but also the notion that rapid change itself can be expressed in percentages. Complexity deepens. I simply list several domains and variables whose expression as percentages is publicly regular or actually regulated. I then turn to questions and interpretations.

(1) The idea of income tax, as a rate, is as old as tithing. Income tax was introduced into the tax regime in England in 1799 and the United States after the civil war, both expanded and continuously refined throughout the twentieth century. In the United States,

> for 2012, there will be six tax rates of: 10%, 15%, 25%, 28%, 33%, and 35%. The tax rates for 2013 are scheduled to change as follows: the 10% rate will be collapsed into the 15% rate; the 25% rate will become 28%; the 28% rate will become 31%; the 33% rate will become 36%; and the 35% rate will become 39.6%. (IRS website, 2012)

To give precision to these percentages, the annual guide to the tax code in the United States runs to almost a thousand pages of text.

(2) In science: Percentage is selectively retained as a standard scientific expression, as in the eighth edition (2006) of *The International System of Units*, which was founded by the International Office of Weights and Measures in a treaty among seventeen nations in 1875. One section now reads:

> In mathematical expressions, the internationally recognized symbol % (percent) may be used with the SI to represent the number 0.01. Thus, it can be used to express the values of dimensionless quantities. When it is used, a space separates the number and the symbol %. In expressing the values of dimensionless quantities in this way, the symbol % should be used rather than the name "percent." In written text, however, the symbol % generally

takes the meaning of "parts per hundred." . . . Phrases such as "percentage by mass," "percentage by volume," or "percentage by amount of substance" should not be used. (*The International System of Units*, 8th ed., 2006, 134)

Here we see the potential for "vagueness" being defined and removed, presumably because some were, in fact, using these vague expressions in scientific contexts.

(3) In probability: Since probability is expressed along the continuum from zero to one, it also can be expressed in percentage terms. When combined with the magnitude of possible loss to create a risk factor, it becomes a powerful rendition of the imagined future, for several purposes including finance and security. Sophisticated mathematical calculations can be presented in public fora in simple percentages. The following example was quoted on the *Wikipedia* entry for "Risk" in 2007: "There is a 40% chance the proposed oil well will be dry with a loss of $12 million in exploratory drilling costs." Another example given is: "A risk neutral person would consider 20% chance of winning $1 million exactly equal to $200,000 (or a 20% chance of losing $1 million to be exactly equal to losing $200,000)."

(4) In the weather forecast:

On 26 December 2011, for Boston for the coming 10 days the "chance of . . ." was:

Precipitation: 20%
Rain: 20%
Rain: 20%
Precip: 10%
Rain: 10%
Rain: 50%
Precip: 10%
Precip: 40%
Rain: 60%
Snow: 30%

(5) In the popular press on nutrition, weight gain and loss:

When animal subjects drank blood-orange juice daily, they lost up to 13 percent of their body weight in three months—without diet or exercise. . . . Subjects who took 350 mg daily [of African mango] lowered their "bad" LDL cholesterol by 46% and raised their "good" HDL cholesterol by 47% in four weeks and in another study, when patients dosed with 150 mg twice a day, . . . their LDL levels fell by 27 percent and their total cholesterol fell by 26 percent in 10 weeks. (*First for Women*, January 2, 2012, 27, 33)

Heard on the radio: "30 percent of Americans are now in the 95th percentile for weight." The percentile is a standard, not a descriptive, in this case; but the source and date of the standard is rarely clarified to listeners, and I could not (yet) find it on the Web.

(6) The political arena: the rise of numerators. The GAO (General Accountability Office) has published a series of charts, covering 1797 to 2050, on government debt in percentage terms. Several are based on the GDP as denominator, which itself changes vastly over time, although it is calculated in such a way as to be usable as the constant (under the conservation principle):

Federal Debt held by the public as a share of GDP (1797–2010)
The budget balance of state and local government (2000–2050)
Historical events affecting the debt held by the public, as percentage of GDP

To use and then explain GDP as the denominator over the 253 years covered by these graphs, the overview of the *GAO Citizen's Guide to the 2010 Financial Report of the United States Government* (2010) states: "After falling by 2.7 percent during FY 2009, real Gross Domestic Product (GDP) rose at an average annual rate of 3.2 percent over the four quarters of FY 2010" (ii). In a footnote, GDP is defined: "Real GDP measures the value of final goods and services produced in the economy, adjusted for changes in the overall price level (i.e. for inflation)."

The ordinary citizen may know how to compare the 2.7 percent and 3.2 percent against certain standard goals for GDP growth (e.g., to keep up with the population growth rate), but the denominator is probably a black box, especially when projected far back into the past and far forward into the future. Adjustment for price level might seem particularly persuasive— because we remember when a candy bar cost 25 cents—but also mysterious, as we now see the gasoline price fluctuating by 25 percent from one month to the next, and doubling from one year to the next. Any temporal graph uses pictorial representation to shift the imagination toward comparison and inferences based on the numerator. The denominator is presumed constant and so is out of the picture.

We might mention the polemic, as well as graphic, invocation of numerators, although this is not worth dwelling on at length because the shedding of the denominator is so obvious a rhetorical trick. In an emission on November 16, 2011, on National Public Radio, the Republican candidates in the elections outlined their economic claims. Nearly all were expressed in percentages. Governor Rick Perry argued that in Washington we need a 50 percent pay cut for Congress, and federal spending should be fixed at 18 percent of GDP, which he claimed had been the average for the past 50 years. (The commentator demurred that this percentage was, in fact, the average of taxes collected relative to GDP, not spending.) Mitt Romney wanted to cap spending at 20 percent of the "overall economy."[4]

One domain that has interested me is "American small business," as a formal category, whose needs are met by the Small Business Administration, and which is defined by both qualitative and quantitative criteria. As defined, small businesses are entitled by law to 23 percent by value of government procurement, and 3 percent for disabled veterans' small businesses. In some laws, a guideline is set for that specific expenditure, in ethical rather than numerical terms: for example, it was "stipulated that the SBA should ensure a 'fair proportion' of government contracts and sales of surplus property to small business" (www.SBA.gov).

(7) Juxtapositions: For the reader of the daily press, percentage statements about heterogeneous topics pile up on each other. On January 19, 2012, the New York Times ran an editorial on Romney's tax returns titled, "The 1% and That 15%" (page A20), just a few pages after a Saks Fifth Avenue advertisement for fur coats titled, "40% to 60%" off plus an additional 10%." An asterisk refers the reader to very tiny print that stipulates the reference prices to be the "regular and original prices," not any intermediate markdowns. In an op-ed two days later, an article on Newt Gingrich's "southern strategy" is illustrated by a column of six large-type percentage statements from polls (New York Times, A21). On some things, the reader may feel an immediate emotional response to the deviation from 50/50: the numeric that indicates simply "better or worse." On other subjects, it may be the very small proportion that provokes emotional response and ongoing quotability.

However transparent the vagueness of the "100," and the emotive tropic points between 1 and 100,[5] somehow, somewhere, the part/whole logic is implicit in the use of percentages in all these instances in the public sphere, even where it is not identified or measured directly, or where it is produced in tiny print at the bottom of the page. The pie chart is its most obvious explicit representation, and that too seems to be proliferating (as I illustrate below). This part/whole logic, then, invokes and provokes the idea of shares, which in ethics and politics moves into the increasingly invoked domain of "fairness."

Aspiration, Futurity, and the Percentage

What differs in the most interesting ways—it seems to me—between the complexity of the "clots" of numerical meaning in these contexts is that, in the present, the existing complexity is being shaped technically, and deployed rhetorically, as the platform for simplified—perhaps "purified" in Latour's terms (1993)—virtual projections into the future. That future might be weight loss, or it might be the balance of state and local budgets as a proportion of GDP. The "vague whole" is then a *future* state of being, invoked as a provocation to action, whether toward optimal physical health or a healthy "balanced" budget. (I am not "playing" with the concepts of "health" and "balance"; they seem as ubiquitous as the percentage.) "Possible worlds" here refer to a virtual or imagined future rather than—as in my review of anthropology's "possibilities" (Guyer 2009b)—a summary of the range of what we now know, knowing that we do not and cannot ever know everything that is and was.[6]

Michael Silverstein, in his book *Talking Politics* (2003), points to the compounding of information with indexical qualities of language to create a "message" that "projects out from the communicational here-and-now we're experiencing as it is being created" (15). My intuitive move at the outer limits of this range is to explore the term of "fairness," which is also rising in public commentary and implicitly invokes "shares" and a politics of proportions. President Obama's famous speech in Osawatomie, Kansas, puts all these concepts together, under the rubric of shares:

> We're greater together than we are on our own. I believe that this country succeeds when everyone gets a fair shot, when everyone does their fair share, when everyone plays by the same rules. These aren't Democratic values or Republican values. These aren't 1% values or 99% values. They're American values. And we have to reclaim them.[7]

The concept of fairness comes up in Enlightenment thinking about individualism and equivalence, and has been developed in twenty-first-century liberal political philosophy, particularly by John Rawls (2001) in his book *Justice as Fairness*. In fact, "fair" is a term that stretches across the entire range of democratic governance principles, from guarantee of the same weights and measures for everyone, equality before the law, and the formal equality of the vote to "rules of the game" to "equal opportunity" as equal chance to develop "natural ability" and a "fair deal." Doubtless the measure of "opportunity" and "chance" is based on probabilities extrapolated from empirical studies of distributions and trends. So "fair," like the percentage itself, can range seamlessly from the foundational to the modal.

So complex a word is "fair" that the *Merriam-Webster Unabridged Dictionary* (1971) devotes two entire columns of very small print to all its allusions and definitions. Perhaps significantly, the concept derives from the Anglo-Saxon, Indo-European vocabulary of English, so from "the people" rather than the Latinate romance-language, elite-conquest vocabulary, from which "justice" is derived.[8] The following is the etymology offered, to show how the roots of fairness differ from those of justice.

> O.E. fæger "beautiful, lovely, pleasant," from P.Gmc. *fagraz (cf. O.S. fagar, O.N. fagr, O.H.G. fagar "beautiful," Goth. fagrs "fit").[9]

The sense of beauty is basic, deriving etymologically from pleasing proportions, so the meaning can range from beauty to moral rightness to proportions in relation to a whole, which enhances the potential for numerical representation of the constituent parts of wholes as ratios and thereby as percentages. A single concept can be shifted from one mode to another: from beauty to proportion to mathematical expression, bringing its aura of allusions with it. "Earth hath not anything to show more fair" (Wordsworth, *Upon Westminster Bridge*, 1802).

We note immediately in *Justice as Fairness* (2001, 6) that Rawls is focused on "society" rather than government. Without explicitly addressing the political history and etymologies of justice (as the language of conquest) and fairness (as the language of the people), he draws this distinction very clearly. He sees the baseline state of "society as a fair system of cooperation, over time from one generation to the next," characterized by cooperation, guided by rules accepted as appropriate, not by central authority, and fair terms of cooperation, where all parties benefit by a public and agreed standard. He repeatedly refers to the "well-ordered society," characterized by "fair conditions" where "the parties are symmetrically situated in the original position" (18), people have a "fair chance" of success (44), and existential differences fade into irrelevance. "We hope that in a well-ordered society under favorable conditions, with the equal basic liberties and fair equality of opportunity secured, gender and race would not specify relevant points of view" (66).

There is a certain geometry to Rawls's terms. He combines the classic individual equality of liberalism with a dynamic of balance: people are to be "symmetrically situated" (18); there should be "reflective equilibrium" (29), "overlapping consensus" (32), "fair equality of opportunity" (42), and the means of making *formal* equality into *effective* equality, by giving the worst off a "fair deal." One can see how the percentage affords the consonance of one-by-one formal equality, using foundational number applied to both numerator and denominator, and the modal thinking of "fair shares" and right proportions that can predominate once "messages" (plural) move in to prioritize the numerator, leaving the denominator simply understood as 100: a whole and/or a complete inventory, or a quality (rather than a quantity) that vanishes into a fog of compounded complexities.

Modal Logic and Possible Worlds

If 100 can apply in all possible worlds, including virtual worlds, across the range of referents from objects to ethics, then the percentage is a shape-shifter par excellence. It is one mathematical formulation whose mechanics anyone with a basic education can understand, and it carries the potential of conveying transparency in the public domain, persuasive ethical and philosophical allusions, and also moving in only partial form, from one context, and perhaps one mode, to another. As Verran suggests, modal logic and possible worlds theory offer a formal approach to analysis of number constitution to mobilize along with a cultural-historical approach to number application.

Western modal logic theorists wonder how to think about the truth or falsity of statements about worlds whose properties are not strictly specifiable (Girle 2003, 160; see also Jubien 2009). The works I have consulted refer to "explosive growth" (Carnielli and Pizzi 2008, vii), the "enormous variety of systems of modal logics and rather little consensus about which of them capture the logical behaviour of modal terms from ordinary English" (Malmkjaer 2002, 153), and controversies in many domains. At the moment, I can only be concerned about two things: (1) the question of how numbering fits in to modal logic, and (2) the apparent inchoate quality of this field at present. Persistent controversy among logicians within a Western intellectual genealogy may meet up in public consciousness with the invention of parameters in virtual worlds, and the ancient human capacity "perchance to dream" (Shakespeare, *Hamlet*). Dream works and other media in science fiction and gaming are creating (im)possible worlds all the time. Jubien seems to argue that "possible worlds" logic does—at the limit—shade into what we in anthropology would clearly recognize as "the dreamtime," that is, "things as they are" (Jackson 1996) for people living in other cultural, historical, and existential contexts. There is a fascinating approach to the Great Chain of Being (Knuttila 1981) as a precursor, and perhaps foundation, to Western philosophies of modal logic.[10]

Are there any limits at all to the deployment of number and percentages, across modes? One could focus closely on the terms for transactions in Tom Boellstorff's, *Coming of Age in Second Life* (2008), or other virtual worlds. It might be worth returning to physics here, as part of the virtual worlds projection, noting that the logic of derivatives—that is, to splice and dice what were formerly thought of as either organic or classificatory "wholes" into new categories—turns up in the press accounts of more and more domains. On the radio on January 6, 2012, I heard of the tactic of an investment company buying up an "inefficient" company, separating the land (which was valuable because of its location) from the business, then making the business rent the land at a high rate, which then forced the business to cut down on other expenses, like the workforce. On paper, the former business—now diced into two—produced a higher return on capital (expressed in percentage terms of money income per unit time) than the original (expressed as a comparison of percentages). There is much to be said about this kind of maneuver ("vulture capitalism," for example), but here it is simply worth noting that there are real processes of dismantling "wholes" alongside their increasing vagueness in "possible world" logic where perhaps it is only the foundational numerators rather than the propositional-modal denominators that can be envisaged as "constants."

One might turn, at this point, from philosophy and empirical studies of modal logics to the historical processes of such innovative applications. For example, if literalism is extended from constitutional law and the Bible to mathematics, it seems now focused on the numerator, and the measurably caused phenomena in the world. The definition of the denominator, as the "condition of possibility," is more often vague. In ranking, it is the ranking scheme that is mathematized, but the quality of what is being measured in percentages may remain vague, or an artifact of a definitional politics, in the public mind. The inferences for the future are then based on *outcomes*— the realized rank, the stated percentage—without, in both cases but in different ways, clear "conditions of possibility," as developed by Kant ([1788] 1929) and commented on further by Deleuze (1991).

The percentage form remains, however, an artifact, creating a sense of understandability: through historical allusions to historical philosophies of governance, a simplicity of form comprehensible from personal histories, and—by downplaying the denominator—mediating a shift toward the form of plurality with which Verran suggests we are most familiar: the one/many rather than the whole/part. The numerator can then indicate a horizon toward which to orient a view of a vague but, by implication, more complete situation in the future. Broken out, however, into new metrics of newly identified dimensions/components, one can see how the "possible world" to which this form of the percentage refers remains indeterminate.

Example from Baltimore: Proportion and Ranking, Together

Attending closely to everything in the public domain associated with number in the early days of January when I picked up the latest issue of Baltimore's free magazine, the *Urbanite* (January 2012, #91), I found an article titled "C1ty By NuMb3r5: Has a Former Physicist Found a Formula for Growing Better Cities?" (Anft 2012, 28–35).[11] Using the ancient image of the beehive, and "slicing the beehive down the middle and investigating its parts" (29) in massively comprehensive numerical form a "onetime expert on particle physics, began to move away from the field in 1993, when the federal government withdrew money earmarked for a supercollider project in Texas." He proposes to find "common referents of scale" among cities worldwide. He argues that "politicians and planners have only 10 to 15 per cent of the scale of a city to work with"; the rest is determined by size, which offers highly varied economies of scale. Taking "various quality-of-life statistics," he and his team start out by ranking the 366 largest American cities, then analyze relationships to scale and end up with change over time.

The ultimate reference points are overall "growth" and moving up the various rankings. For example: "The rankings show that Baltimore has been making modest strides. Personal income is up (we're at 67 in 2006, up from 123 in 1986), as is the overall rate of innovation, measured by the number of patents issued here. Although the area is still a hornet's nest of crime, its violence ranking improved from 32 in 2002 to 51 four years later." The implicit future is to keep moving up or down the rankings, although there is no specific mechanism identified, such as the possibility that other cities might move up or down by their own dynamics, and not by Baltimore's improvement. The goal is entirely relational, rather than foundational or in some sense qualitative. It is striking that one sees in the website commentary from a member of the public, that, without the definition of the scale itself (or in percentage terms, the denominator), a reader can easily be baffled. Hence the importance of the graphics that accompany the numbers.

One of the graphics (in the paper version of the journal) is a genealogy-like chart, called a dendrogram, of "family resemblance" among cities with respect to wealth, innovation, and crime, with a metric for "decor-relation"—zero to one—along the basic axis. With the aid of a magnifying glass one can make out that Baltimore is a sibling to one city, a cousin to two, and a second cousin to ten others (which include New York and San Francisco). Among the thirty-six others on the graph, Baltimore is most distantly related to Houston and Dallas. The only "take-home" message from this family tree of correlation seems to be support for the overall argument that all cities can be placed on a single metric (of some sort).

Much more clearly conveying a message are the graphics specific to Baltimore's experience, in ranking and percentage terms, using the mathematics of physics (as far as I know; see my previous disclaimer on mathematical ignorance). I am not passing judgment on this article, just trying to see through to its implications, its own aporias, and for the terms of public understanding, as people respond—probably viscerally, or perhaps in different modal logics (in Verran's sense)—to these images of their hometown. It strikes me that it is a similar logic to the one exemplified in the movie *Moneyball* about baseball: making a team by a new logic, choosing particular qualities rather than whole players. Again the question is, what kind of whole does the town, and the baseball team, then become? Are we, collectively, living in two modes simultaneously: a past-present summary and an idealized aspiration, expressed in the same numerical term? Or perhaps we are supposed to have faith in future emergence. Again, the future becomes the horizon of relevance.

Each of five sectors is separately represented in a colored graphic that gives absolute numbers, proportions, and proportional change. The workforce's five categories: "working for the man (the government)" (17.9%); "eds and meds" (19.2%); "making stuff (manufacture)" (4.7%); "you got served" (8.7%); and "moving money" (5.7%). Each sector is then represented as follows:

Title: Name of sector; Number of workers; % of workforce;
Graphics: relevant sector in bright green or red;
Pie chart, showing proportion of total labor force; solid arrow, pointing up or down, showing % change, 2000–2010. Pie charts, proportions, and absolute numbers are combined.

We have the *impression* of this depicting a changing whole, but I want to draw attention to the eventual vagueness of both the denominator and the process by which the future is to be reached. The latitude for either simply "going along," or bafflement, or perhaps misunderstanding, is very wide.

Reading attentively, we note that the percentages of the labor force do not add up to 100, but this fact is not prominently displayed anywhere in the figures or the text. "Making stuff" and "moving money" are the two categories whose absolute numbers and percentage of the workforce declined between 2000 and 2010. But then we are not sure what happened to the absolute numbers in the workforce as a whole between 2000 and 2010. To take the denominator first: The total "workforce" represented in the graphs adds up to 726,300. If we add the percentages together, this comes to 56.2 percent of the workforce. What the other 43.8 percent of "the workforce" is doing remains unspecified, but it seems to disappear from view in the arrows and pie charts that refer implicitly to the "100," the "whole." If this total number made up that percentage of the workforce, then the total would be approximately 1.3 million. The metropolitan population is 2,690,886 (*Wikipedia*, accessed December 28, 2013). So half of that number, as the active workforce, is a plausible proportion. But that still leaves the question of what the rest are doing, especially for an argument that is based on the power of diversity and synergy.

We can go one step further in the logic, to the process of arriving at the future that is indicated by the rise up the scales and the percentage improvements: "The sustainability of cities comes from this opening up, this embracing of diversity. Cities allow homeless and crazy people to walk around the streets. They allow people to do all sorts of creative and strange things," unlike corporations and the large, "paternalistic" industries of the past. Indeed, we are trying to escape from these structures of the past by "analyzing a vast sweep of data, . . . armed with this killer urban-wonk app, . . . to pull off a feat that has eluded generations." The human, social, and intellectual scramble that this diligent numeration—referring to precise enumerators and "vague wholes"—ends up in is too obvious to comment on further. Perhaps the politics are as vaguely shape-shifting and optionally modal, for the future, as the denominator of the percentage form.

The argument does, however, admit its own limits when it ends up with the crucial importance of ongoing growth, promoted by innovation (mainly coming from "eds and meds," which grew the fastest, at 58.7 percent, which is over three times the growth rate of the next category). For rises in the quality indicators, the author is then agnostic about whether this is innovation based on, or promoting, local and small-scale enterprise or "something" else, such as endogenization of external resources, or both, in some combination. In fact, "eds and meds" in Baltimore are mainly accounted for by very large institutions, having the corporate form and assuming some of the social responsibility once assumed by industry.

What mathematics of growth and synergy are available to distinguish between the creative power of the multiplicity of smallness and the creative power of very large "ed and med" organizations that are linked into global networks? Does this work through exponential ranking, through one particular sector? Or through a synergistic process within a "whole"? Or does this entire exercise partake of Verran's shape-shifting, where we sense the pull upward of some sectors and downward of others, by virtue of the numerator, without even sensing the need to specify the future in terms of precise denominators? The author quotes the physicist: "Such stories are manna for those who preach the gospel of economic transformation via innovative urban development." "He can't anticipate exactly what will work, [but] seems optimistic that something will. And whoever comes up with it will probably live in a city." So again we draw on archaic imagery: because the terms are vague, familiar, and aspirational in spirit, scaling and percentage clearly allow futurity to have a hopeful directionality, shorn of the planning familiar from the recent past.

Conclusion

Encouraged by Helen Verran, I have prodded the two rapidly ramifying concepts of ordinality and percentage. Both are built into the political history of democracy, from 1215 onward. Many of the legal provisions expressed in these terms are pragmatically unchangeable, since so much legislation, record keeping, legal precedence, and "audit culture" (Strathern 2000) are built on them. But I wonder how consonant their current versions are with each other: the exponential ranking process and the proliferation of percentage, with a vague denominator, as a descriptive and judgmental referent. I imagine that mathematically they are very simple components of the same world. But out here in society and culture they are running into each other, or compounding, as the one produces a "solution" for the other, in a way that moves beyond the bounds of the *possible* world into the question of a *livable future* world: a world that is not only theoretically possible but humanly inhabitable, ethically and practically, as anthropologists are accustomed to studying from the past.

I have asked Marxist colleagues what the twenty-first-century version of the theory of the "reserve army" is, that is, all those not represented in our graphic of Baltimore's workforce, and thought about the "subjectivities" produced by "irrelevance" as distinct from hegemony, subsumption, or direct domination. Clearly the mathematical expressions that are so persuasive, because they are ancient, precise, scientifically successful, and socially shared as a language, now link into our new literature not only of the science fiction, possible other worlds, kinds, but of the lifeworlds of "abandonment" (Povinelli 2011) and "dispossession" (Butler and Athanasiou 2013), at the bottom of the scale and in the vagueness of the denominator And they can be represented in the persuasive graphics of visual arts, which appear limitless under the new conditions of communication.

In these proliferating and compounding percentage expressions, where the "whole" of the denominator is either vague in its properties or absent altogether in the expression, and where these properties contribute to ranking expressions, the bottom is included (by definition, in foundational logic) but rendered inert, rather like the rocks at the bottom of the Great Chain of Being, whose archaic iconography infuses the "message" of ranking. This is where ethnography takes over: where we work harder on the frontiers of technical invention in number, its public "message," and the domains of the public's own appropriation, which are mobilized to motivate and describe our *own* worlds of the present and future, paying close attention to the zone of "semi-relevance" (Girle 2003, 188) as itself a humanly "possible" or actual condition.

PART FOUR

Platforms

EIGHT

Intricacy and Impasse: Dilemmas of Value in Soft-Currency Economies

The invitation to present this paper offered me two unusual opportunities: First, to link back through large issues that have recurred over years of working on the history of value in Africa. And secondly to give centrality to a very specific issue, of the kind that usually comes up in life only under the designation of official "red tape." I have already worked on the "fine print" in food regulation (Guyer 1993a), taxation (1980, 1992), and commodity transactions (2004) on the interface between Europe and Africa in historical cases. In the process, I have found that addressing the "intricacy" of red-tape creation has shown that it can produce what I call here "impasses." These are not points where straightforward logic can be applied toward a resolution, such as the case with contradiction or even outright conflict, where the "sides" or the "versions" can be clearly defined and thereby mediated. Impasses present as the coexistence of provisions, guidelines, or other conditions that simply do not make enough sense to be clearly mediated by transparent negotiations. What results is often tangled: on the side of authority, political intervention selects its own account of the situation and imposes a solution, which entails, on the side of submission, development of devices to endure frustration and incoherence, evade impossible implications, or otherwise reconfigure life.

These impasses are difficult to describe, since they can evoke a tedium and confusion on the part of the reader that parallels the confusion and anxiety of the participant. And yet a whole series of experiences—in scholarship and in life—persuades me of their power and of the necessity of focusing closely on particularly generative instances of present-day intricacy and impasse: the intricacy of the accumulated definitions and provisions in the formal economic sector, and the impasses when different, but all validated, analytical and practical terms would promote quite different scenarios, interpretations, and points of intervention. Here, I extend the theme of the interface from my earlier historical work, this time focusing less on the evaluative margins at thresholds of conversion than on the margins themselves: Why are they what they are? Are they experienced as points of intricacy and impasse, as well as of the opportunity for mediation that I emphasized in earlier work? As the intricacies of the globalized, turbulent, neoliberal formal sector become more and more complex, we need to focus on the production and location of impasse itself, asking whether and how impasses are "unintended consequences" of a moving and changing world, or whether they reflect certain patterns and institutions of some longevity but changing manifestation.

I focus here on the composition of the current pricing of an essential commodity—petrol at the pump in Nigeria—as the outcome of formal processes, and on popular experience of its mysteries and conundrums, as an ultimate goal of the attention that anthropologists could bring to the study of prices (Guyer 2009a; Guyer and Denzer 2013).

Framework and Focus

The exploration of connections between the general and the particular, or the perception of the large and the small together in a single frame, has been one of the encompassing missions that we have always had for anthropology. And we attempt to do this analytically, eventually going beyond our various troubadours who "see the world in a grain of sand" (William Blake), or "the crack in everything," "that's how the light gets in" (Leonard Cohen). The poets teach us to be attentive enough to locate the generative spaces in the world and in our theoretical architecture, within which originality might arise: out there or in our minds. The *Economist* even quoted Gillian Tett, with respect to her prediction of the 2008 financial crisis, on the capacity of anthropologists to identify a "corner (where) . . . a revolution . . . was happening that had been almost entirely ignored" (*Economist* 2011). We have worked on the "assemblages" (Callon, Yuval and Muniesa 2007) and "clots" (Verran 2001), that is, the novel or ephemeral creations that may arise therein. But I am backing up here to look more closely at the spaces themselves: the corners, margins, gaps, loopholes and "the space at the side of the road" (to quote Kathleen Stewart, 1996) where so many of the people on whom we concentrate find themselves: figuring out which way to turn, watching the traffic go by, and making those extraordinary interrupted conversations that Stewart documents so beautifully.

So "intricacy" first. The concept of "intricacy" implies deep and varied complexities. But it still evokes pattern, so predictable trajectories. I often use artistic imagery and poetic reference in my own thinking, so I will make it explicit here, to counteract the potential tedium of intricate red tape. Clifford Geertz (1963) used this imagery in his famous *Agricultural Involution*, whose title was taken from Alexander Goldenweiser's 1936 paper on "primitive" decorative art. (We could note that Geertz does not explain the title in detail until page 81, which is almost exactly halfway through the book. Hold this thought, that a central point of concentration may lie, literally, at a specific kind of expositional, or geometric, or fulcrum-like center, rather than at the beginning). Goldenweiser wrote that the application of pattern has "the inevitable result (of) progressive complication, a variety within uniformity, virtuosity within monotony." Geertz adds as a footnote that Goldenweiser's own references to late Gothic art demonstrate that there is "nothing particularly 'primitive' about this process" (Geertz 1963, 81). Here the recursivity of fractal processes was found to be deeply regular and apparently almost limitless when closely studied: quantitatively, qualitatively, from within and without. Finding this involutionary pattern in the Indonesian political ecology was the brilliance of Geertz's book.

The concept of impasse, however, implies being stuck somehow.[1] The repetitions turn back on themselves, and intersect with sudden or random interventions, so that the original principle meets impossible conditions for realization of a next step. So we need both concepts—intricacy *and* impasse—in order to differentiate among different results of intricate processes. Do some repetitions and recursive processes, when enacted in social and cultural rather than ecological terms, produce patterned involution "all the way down," while others get stuck in impasses, which may themselves seem to recur, each time in new ways? Can some such impasses become familiar enough that people learn to recognize and endure them, while others produce totally unpredictable and incoherent logjams? Historically, we can ask whether the nexus of ever-complicating modernist and neoliberal administrative techniques classically develops by progressive definition and replication, by involution through regular recursion, or by cumulative splicing, reconfrontation, and reconfiguration that generate impasses.[2]

In spite of a sense of impasse in some places and domains of present social life, one still finds reference to pervasive logical order as a characteristic of modernism. For example, the *Wikipedia* entry on modernity writes of the "large-scale social integration constituting modernity" (accessed March 29, 2012). Max Weber, however, only claimed that the "rational-legal" process of integration was a form of *legitimation* of authority. Deviations in the *actual conduct* of bureaucracy had been questioned before, and alongside, the theoretical movements that opened up the space I move into here. They include neo-Marxist theorization of articulation on a large scale, postmodernist insistence on plurality in general, and a now-twenty-year-old, multiply-inspired, anthropology of thresholds, margins, and disjunctures, wherever they may occur, in all their specificity. In certain domains, in some places, the technical platforms of modern life do, indeed, seem coherent—until they collapse into crisis. So a sense of fragility may also come to the critique of modernity as "large scale integration."

Having written already on thresholds as a *constituent* of the historical monetary culture *within* Atlantic Africa, I want to shift my focus to what I called, in the past, the "interface" *between* the West and the Rest, where a new version of the claim to "modernity" on the one hand and the designation of the *sauvage* (in all its French senses of savage and also wild, untamed, unpredictable, and so on) on the other come together in practice. For my current work, this is the interface—wherever it occurs geographically, institutionally, and in everyday life—between hard and soft currencies: that is, the currencies that have reserve functions on the world money markets and in global financial institutions such as the IMF and the oil economy, and the currencies that are largely media of exchange within national borders and fluctuate unpredictably on international markets.

There, as particularists and ethnographers, we can focus empirical attention on both "sides" and their meeting. And there I have found intricately dense *Gordian knots* of rules and practices, as well as gaps, margins, 'scapes and disjunctures (Appadurai 1990), and overlaps. I note, as I move in this direction, however, the fairly simple *spatio-geometrical* imagery of that earlier work. Here I can draw on the metaphor of "margins," including my own work, while moving into new puzzles raised by what combine here as intricacy and impasse—the logical and experiential incoherences—as they present within the formalized structures themselves.

Just two theoretical points before advancing: First, while we can take some inspiration from the Actor Network Theory of hybrids as inevitable products of modernist rationalization, we also need the much greater caution about the implication that these have a definable "form," which we find in Veena Das's concept of the "illegibility" of the state. For her, the state is present as a "signature," both as a "bearer of rules and regulations and as a spectral presence materialized in documents" (2004, 251). There is "something" in place, then, so not just a gap or a margin. But is it a "form" in any comprehensible sense? And in my own case here, since it falls within *international* formalizations, rather than *sovereign state* formalizations, we need to ask: what are those "point-counterpoints" on which to focus empirical attention? We do have theoretically informed anthropological studies of "privatization" in Africa that point out the *particular* illegibilities of "errant" formal interventions on that interface, such as Beatrice Hibou's (2004) work on the *chemin bouissonier* (literally bushy path, French for errant ways). Sarah Bracking's (2009) tracking of particular state-corporate-banking contractual arrangements in Africa also shows the switchbacks that we could draw from Veena Das's concept: actions moving from rules to spectrality to different rules . . . and on outward. So, we bring forward the concept of "illegibility."

Secondly, the world currency system is a domain in which even the mainstream specialists admit to incoherence. Milton Friedman, who was a great advocate of free markets, wrote in the mid-1980s that international currency "exchange rates have supposedly been free to float and to be determined by private markets. In practice, however, governments still intervene in an attempt to affect the exchange rates of their currencies" (1987, 19). Kurt Schuler (2006)—an economist at the U.S. Department of the Treasury—has pointed out that "at present no coherent, comprehensive, generally accepted scheme for classifying exchange rate arrangements exists." In a different theoretical mode, but still macro in ambition, Tim Mitchell (2011, 5), in his new book on the global energy system over a century, refers to political and economic domains being "tied intricately together," and travels through that image to the bypasses, sabotage, delusion, and other practices that have been created *within* the formalized systems themselves. My work is in sympathy with this move, although focused farther out to the dendritic logics and capillary circulations to the level of "the people": in this case, the customers.

So onward: from the dubious claims of modernity to the sites where the people face intricacy and experience impasse in the world of money, prices, and value. I will come to the oil economy toward the end, but start with my own trajectory on this question, which begins with the food economy.

Intricacy, Impasses, and the "People": Introduction to My Own Trajectory

So what strategies can we pursue to connect the claims of modernity to rational coherence and the conditions of the *sauvage* in hard and soft currency dynamics, and to see this particular world perhaps *not* in anything so "formed" as a pile of "grains of sand" but rather as a set of analogous experiences of illegibility? How to think clearly about "confusion" is not self-evident, even with theoretical guidelines. One may need images and touch-stones. So in my own domain of study, I often bring to mind, alongside the literal "patterns," a particular piece of work on a modernist project that I read for a paper about twenty years ago, and which is about eighty-five years old, on a venture that is a hundred years old: namely Lord Beveridge's (1928) history of World War I food rationing in Britain. On the one hand, he invokes great principles, such as the "love of justice" at a time of unprec-edented national threat. And then later he refers to the "toiling ingenuity" of the administrators of the rationing system who actually delivered food "justice" through thousands of "forms and circulars," marked with destina-tions like "chocolate for bakers." The forms and circulars were massively intricate, but apparently they largely worked—at least, adequately for the purpose of the time.

> The philosophy: "of the two master passions of democracy, the love of lib-erty and the love of justice, the latter is with the British people deeper and stronger" (1928, 234).
>
> The practice: "forms and circulars, reports and instructions, schemes and counterschemes, all so many monuments of toiling ingenuity" (1928, 344).

So these are my touchstones for the concept of intricacy in my title: the decorative arts (as in Goldenweiser and Geertz), where complexity is im-pressively internally coherent, since it works from pattern; and a wartime bureaucracy, like the British rationing system, where the impulse coming from the rationalizations of modernity is that "complication" *has to* pro-duce coherence, but acknowledges the difficulty of doing so. Too much is at stake to let it drift into impasses, and "toiling ingenuity" keeps the logis-tics from moving in that direction. A decentralized, nonpurposive, open-ended neoliberal endeavor, such as global currency markets, focuses the "toiling ingenuity" differently. It is not a question of bridging one large and consistent interface, between general principle and minute details. Rather there are many different daily—even minute-by-minute—interfaces, analo-gous to what Beveridge called the "coral islands" of formalities, accounting for the conditions of coexistence of over 180 sovereign currencies in the present world.[3] Only a very few currencies are expected to maintain value over time and thereby to function as international reserves, so this vari-ability in function over time carries enormous potential for moments of in-coherence as they all fluctuate against one another on the markets. We are accustomed in anthropology to analyzing "value" *within* specific systems,

Table 8.1   Five-year fluctuations in value, per dollar, 2007–2012

Country	Value
Ghana	1.1 to 1.5 to 1.9
Nigeria	125 to 150 to 157
Mozambique	25 to 37 to 31
Uganda	163 to 222 to 243*
Congo	430 to 910 to 900

*Amounts reduced to ratios for ease of comparison.
Source: OANDA.com, accessed July 22, 2012.

whether designated theoretically—capitalist, neoliberal, and so forth—or ethno-linguistically. Money is then a measure only. But in a multiple currency, globalized commodity world, the money itself is a commodity with a relative value that emerges from complicated processes, including the specific capacities, or classic functions, that each currency comprises. And much is changing, much of the time, in spite of the fixity of contracts and treaties.

The vast majority of the world's peoples live in these soft currency economies. Table 8.1 shows you fluctuation over five years in more detail, so that you see what I am talking about.

(The longer pattern, especially including the devaluation due to structural adjustment policies in the 1980s and 1990s, is much more dramatic).

Clearly, it is complex, governed by thousands of "forms and circulars," in all the official languages of the sovereign states that issue their own currencies. But we cannot just depict general "complexity" and enormity when so much is at stake: the simple livability of life in a globalized economy. My own favorite geometric for imagining the phenomenon itself with its amplifying processes of creation, and the process of our empirical exploration and argument, is a spiral: so nonlinear (in the straight line sense), moving out and then in again around the central object of ethnographic enquiry, in what is intended to be principled ways. Particular moneys do not just "circulate" in the same way as images or discourses in mediascapes or in discretely differentiated and buffered spheres, levels, or circuits. Indeed, a spiral imagery helps us to see these cross-level continuities, like a Möbius strip but also to see where it is that the spiral-in-the-world loses coherence. Monies interact as well as coexist. They intrinsically amplify or diminish in their capacities and value at each small transaction along the way, as we see from the exchange rate charts. But then they run back into each other at further iterations, as I will illustrate later. Although we may have dual categories like "hard" and "soft," actual transactions and objects move through phases of invoking and mediating one or the other (Appadurai 1986).

My journey here is itself spiral, starting with the very big issue of price incoherence in African history, then finding small puzzles within specific transactions, and then pursuing a spiral track of empirical research and analytical artisanship between them. Here, in two sequential examples, are my own first provocations about international exchange rates and local prices in Africa: from a theoretical puzzle to an empirical puzzle, vice versa, and then back again.

I give these short examples from my past published work to show the problem, and then I look at one current example from a paper written last year. I am asking: if impasses in fact *recur, like a pattern,* should they be seen then as part of the political dynamics and technical algorithms of the intricacy itself? What then follows: for theory and for people?

Monetary Value and Impasses
of Modernity: Two Past Examples

In the 1980s I started working on African currencies in museums because I was nonplussed by the apparently contradictory nature of economists' judgments from the 1970s about markets in Africa. These economists argued that food prices were "too high" (for the consumers) but then also "too low" to provide incentives to producers. How could that be if markets were supposed to intersect supply and demand? Hence the theoretical puzzle. But at that point I decided to take an empirical route onward. It was the happenstance of having the Peabody Museum at Harvard University literally "down the corridor" from my office in the early 1980s, and the fact that it housed a large collection of objects, photographs, and documents from Southern Cameroon (where I had carried out field research), that gave me the idea of just returning from market theory to my own discipline, with its tangible archives and collections, to ask about media of exchange in the African past.

In that process, I visited the Museum of Mankind in London and the Pitt Rivers Museum in Oxford for a geographically broader view. And I came away deeply puzzled by an odd *empirical* fact this time. Manillas had been (in those days . . . I'm not sure about now) classified and displayed in museums as "primitive money." The Museum of Mankind had a vast collection, stored off-site, and itemized one by one in a huge file folder of dot matrix printouts. I sat there thinking: well, if the storage is a few miles north

of here it will be almost in the same place where these items were originally manufactured, in the foundries of Birmingham, under early modernist industrial conditions. Manillas were produced in Europe for the slave
trade, just as cowries were transported halfway around the world for the
same purpose. In fact, cowries were even more convenient for merchants—
although not for manufacturers—since they could be classified as ballast
in ships, so not subject to any taxes or duties of the kind that were increasingly standing as backing to sovereign debt developed through the Bank of
England from 1694: the model for all subsequent central banking.

I keep the material image of the manilla collection in mind, while join-
ing the cycle of historical logic, to show that the most advanced industry
of its day, at the frontier of the development of capitalism with its famous
"freedom" of labor, was producing primitive money for the development
of forms of plantation slavery that had never existed before, except perhaps, in the Roman and Greek empires, from which we were also recuper-
ating concepts of democracy, secular (read non-Christian) ideals of beauty
and proportion, and scientific ideals of principled knowledge, all alongside, and integrated with, the novel invention of the financial powers of the
modern nation-state.

I have written this long sentence on purpose, because one needs to see
the whole arc of logic and then pause over one part or another, to concret-
ize the central question of how some parts of this complex, or phases in
the amplifying spiral of growth, were designated as "primitive" and some
"modern." This is a question that critics of modernity have addressed in
general categorical terms. But the intricacies are also specific, powerful, embodied in "forms and circulars" at many stages of the spirals of derivation,
and some are enduring, reshaped in novel ways.

As a second example, and again in a long sentence, I'm going to add
here—for dramatic effect—another apparently odd cycle of historical
logic that emerged during my studies of money in Africa. This one is already published in my book *Marginal Gains* (2004), but it bears repeat-
ing, in sketch form (the whole story is tortuous!). When Pierre Savorgnan
de Brazza was sent to Central Africa from France in 1883, he refused the
military arms that the government wanted to send with him, for barter purposes, on the grounds that the Central Africans would not accept them and
preferred a different, outdated model. The only way to get this model was
from an arms dealer in Belgium, so through an international trade that
proved highly contentious. (Get ready for another improbably long sentence that depicts a spiral process!) It took "three ministries, a national assembly, several instruments of public finance, an international convention"

(Guyer 2004, 43–44), and the very considerable imagination of—and I am not inventing this—the minister of public instruction and fine arts, to convert a stash of 1822 vintage rifles into assets for De Brazza to take to Africa in 1883. The minister justified it to pass through his own auspices on the grounds that "the mission . . . is peaceful in character" (2004, 44).

Is this the rise of rationalism? Yes, in its own way, but mainly by the technicality that everything was recorded on paper and made accessible through government archives, eventually to people like me. Otherwise, what kind of "rational" is this? We are clearly closer to Veena Das's concept of "the spectral/magical" at the heart of the state than to derivational linear logics.

I may have confused you again by these two puzzling cases, and these long sentences. But by placing them on a spiral geometry of argument rather than a derivational logic from theory, I have tried to exemplify, for my own topic here, the necessity of continuing the critique of Weberian "modernity"—as rationalization, secularization, and disenchantment—right into its own quintessential instruments of "forms and circulars" and "magical modes" (Das 2004, 231) in amplification mode rather than in stable dualistic or overlapping modes that depict levels of articulation. The critique "from the South," as Jean and John Comaroff (2011) recently put it, draws attention to "margins" and enchantments. On money, we can go even deeper than that, into the very heart of it: to specific locations of incongruence and incoherence *within* "modernity" *everywhere*. I mentioned, in my book *Marginal Gains*, and citing back through Hammond and Beveridge, the "coral reef of formalities" (Guyer 2004, 163) that has grown up piecemeal in Africa. But one can see from my two examples that the illegibility of formality starts well upstream, in the ministries, customs offices, banking institutions, and factories at the heart of modern economic governance.

Incoherence: Another Version of "We Have Never Been Modern"?

It has taken me several further research efforts to bring those intricacies and impasses, those "cracks in the edifice," those barriers to logic, to the very forefront: not as "failures" of modernity, punted into the future for eventual resolution "in the long run," but as constitutive, maintained and cultivated, sites of "toiling ingenuity." My own past difficulty with how to address intricacy and impasse is evident in the single sentence of *Marginal*

Gains that I would change if I could, by one phrase. In the last paragraph of the conclusion, which is entitled "Bewilderment Revisited," I wrote this: "African monetary practices present a challenge to theories that attempt to 'reduce entropy' in standard ways that depend precisely on the institutional forms Locke [that is John Locke] promoted—unambiguous law, a purist approach to money, and a central bank—but only succeeded in implementing at home" (Guyer 2004, 176). Without further research, I have no idea whether Locke even considered a purist money destined for use in, for example, the slave trade. It seems very unlikely. The modern state's capacity to sanction idiosyncratic innovations with the currency at home was hard-won, and hard suffered by transgressors (by capital punishment, for example). Trying to police the British merchants on the high seas would be utterly implausible and unnecessary . . . if you can call manillas a commodity and their exchange for slaves "barter." Probably no one ever tried, and it is quite clear where the interests would lie. But I do not know for sure that no thought was ever devoted to the question of regulating merchant monies. So I should have simply left out that last phrase. Between the universal claims and aspirations of the economic theory of the time and the very specific domains of its practical implementation "falls the shadow" (to quote T. S. Eliot in "The Hollow Men"): the shadow of the cracks people fall through, the shadow of the spaces and loopholes they exploit, the shadow of crafted zones of ignorance, the shadow of illegibility into which the near future may sink when all eyes are turned on the bright lights of the theoretical horizon.

A point that complements the Comaroffs' (2011) "Theory from the South: Or How Euro-America Is Evolving Towards Africa" is that it may be Africa's intrinsically more incoherent experience of the intricacies of modernity that makes it a source of inspiration about impasses that may be emerging and proliferating elsewhere. The drive toward coherence of narrative and institutional platform in the Euro-West kept covering up its own "muddle," especially as national wars have required the creation of a much shorter causal chain from act to result than is often the case in civilian life. My argument here would follow Latour (1993) in one sense: we *have* never been "modern," in the sense of coherent, except perhaps in wartime. But not only because of hybrids. Incoherence and incongruity are built in, in some locations, and then they amplify and accrue new powers as they spiral out and find their places within a world containing internal and also adjacent, fractal, modal, and linear logical processes, all changing, often at different rates.

A Current Example: The People's Petrol Price in Nigeria: The Dollar, the Naira, and the Oil Complex.

My present-day exemplary case is not so much an illustration as a telling focus for more empirical study, where the topic is crucial on a world scale and where the local evidence across the entire spiral arc is fairly profuse: the price of gasoline at the pump in Nigeria.[4] In December 2011 and January 2012, there were intense popular and political demonstrations and confrontations about a price hike. But this was not the first time. Ever since "first oil" production in Nigeria in the 1970s, the price to the people has been a huge bone of contention. I could drive you to distraction—or sleep—by delving into the intricacies of (for example) the part of the spiral where the refineries have failed to be successfully repaired for decades, but I won't. Let me look first at the outermost ring of the spiral and then inward to actualities of the people: waiting in line for hours, siphoning oil from spills, waiting at bus stops, and reflecting vociferously on their situations.

First, in that outermost circle: the international markets for money and for oil. The Nigerian exchange rate, the oil price, and the petrol price cut across each other in almost entirely independent ways, creating surges, troughs, and switchbacks that would clearly drive any Euro-American population into panic, as all forward contracts, plans, and fail-safes would have to be revisited if the nominal value of the currency no longer expressed its relative value in a predictable way. Especially for a crucial commodity such as oil.

Let us look at petrol in Nigeria (see table 8.2). Between 1985 and 2003, the price of petrol at the pump went from 20 kobo per liter to N40 (400K), a nominal multiplication by a factor of twenty. Over the same period, the real wage in dollar terms declined to about 25 percent; and in petrol terms it declined to about 20 percent, while the crude oil price grew by at least 50 percent. And yet the national and international politics defined the domestic price as "subsidized" (see appendix on prices for details).

Table 8.2 The Nigerian real minimum wage, in dollars and petrol, 1981–2011

Year	Wages	Liters of petrol
1981	N125/month (about $200)	625
2001	N7,500/month (about $75)	187
2011	N7,500/month (about $50)	115

Note: For sources, see appendix to this chapter.

Table 8.3   Price of crude oil per barrel, 2006–2012

Month/year	Price
January 2006	$64
January 2010	$83
January 2011	$88
January 2012	$99 and rising

If the dollar value is taken as the "real" value, then the minimum wage fell to 25 percent of its initial value over thirty years. If the petrol purchasing power is taken as the "real" then it fell to 18 percent. A further calculation could be made against a Nigerian consumer price index, which would likely come out with yet another number. But perception of intersections is important here. Nigeria is seen by its people as a producer as well as a consumer in the oil economy. The dollar value of the wage fell while the price of crude oil—as export, paid for in dollars, therefore entering Nigeria as national income—rose (see table 8.3).

Where do we "touch the ground here"? What does "real" mean, as in "the real price," or "real wages": relative to what, when the value of the soft currency, the price of the crude product (export value in dollars), and the price of the refined retail commodity (imported and valued in naira) are all moving in their own directions, and some of the nominal prices that are definitively anchored in soft currency, such as wages, are static?

There is an impasse in the understanding of the intricacies of economic life if different parties fundamentally disagree about what "real" refers to. Local petrol prices adjusted to international prices? Local wages adjusted according to the retail petrol price (which is a crucial component of the cost of living for everyone in a largely artisanal economy and where the formal sector workers have to hire transport to get to work)? Local wages in dollars, according to the exchange rate, and thereby benchmarked to the crude price on the world market? I hope you are confused, because certainly the people are confused, and an attempt by the government to call the difference between the dollar value of crude and the dollar value of retail petrol a "subsidy," which they then planned to "abolish," led to a huge confrontation, all over the country, in January 2012.

So in our spiral exploratory logic on exchange rates and key prices in the lives of the people in a globalized economy, we are led to spiral back down to a concept that we can surely make progress on, with our anthropological combination of macro-philosophical theory and ethnographic attentiveness: namely the idea of the "real."

We can learn how "real" might be seen by the people from the Nigerian cartoonists. The exclamation point and the question mark, together, over the heads of the hapless citizens, become ubiquitous: in bus queues, and many public spaces. Is this the particular form of illegibility in Nigerian political culture? Does it stop here, with either an imposition of a resolution by power or the puzzled endurance of a cultivated and unresolved incoherence, by a people apparently increasingly seeing themselves as functioning in a "do-it-yourself" economy?

Impasse and Resolution about What Is "Real"

To retrace our steps: We moved back from immediate crisis, out into the spiral, to the recent history of prices and exchange rates. And in a full development we would move yet farther out, to take in the whole question of hard and soft currencies, and their interfaces, in the present world. And then we focus in again on the "particular" generative practices and images of impasse that lie at the center of this spiral logic: as expressed by the people.

Here the ethnography should begin, again: in my book (2004, chapter 6), I described an incident of petrol shortage and the mediation of what I treated as a local "real price" by a very skilled seller who happened to have secured a supply: so, someone who knew how to create a "real" price, in local terms. What was real—that is, recurrent, legible, and legitimate to the people, a recognizable "res," a thing—in her management of the sale of a tanker of petrol, in a time of shortage, under the watch of the army as well as the people? I analyzed the day and came up with a conclusion. The seller enacted a series of congruences of local scales of value: money, people, amounts, time spent waiting . . . all backed by the "spectral" presence, not of the state, but of notions of fairness and potential suspicion of greed or witchcraft. The process of sale was orderly; the logic was understood by all; endurance was only demanded for a finite time period; and the authoritative breach of the impasse had been achieved by a certain charismatic performance of collectively understood values rather than the imposition of an unfair or dangerous resolution.

Conclusion

The Nigerian people's petrol price is not a hybrid, nor an assemblage, nor an emergent contingency. It is a regularly recurring quantitative expression of impasse within the intricacy of pricing and exchange rates, so perhaps best seen as a product of that intricacy. "Red tape" all the way down to the last "form and circular," marked at every stage with the current equivalent of "chocolate for bakers" but without a transparent driving logic. It is perhaps appropriate to end this chapter with a sincere gesture of respect for linguistic, archeological, and biological anthropological methods. No tooth is too isolated from the jaw, no shard is too broken, no plain is too apparently featureless, no textual fragment or lexical element is too torn, to give up hope of training one's imagination, applying one's own experience, listening and searching relentlessly through perhaps unpromising territory, to plumb deeply into the places that are generative of the future. It is perhaps the combination of artistic images, people's experience, and the commitment to persevere in "reading" the *recurrent* illegibilities of our ramifying formal sector that can result in an apprehension of futures, as projected from the "now": futures where, as Achille Mbembe writes in his appreciation of the Comaroffs' *Theory from the South*: "global capitalism today seems to be moving in many directions at once" (Mbembe 2011). That seems to me the place where all of anthropology—with our acute attention to the particular and our encompassing attention to ever-wider "wholes"— becomes the key discipline for discernment. "More anthropologists"—as *the* Economist put it—are needed in many places other than Wall Street, within the intricacies of life in the growing "coral reef of formalities" in the twenty-first-century world.

By way of history and geography, I conclude as I began: with art and the spiral logic of exploration and understanding. This is a spiral by Escher, where a tiny figure at the center, carrying a heavy load, struggles to walk straight up a wall, passing a closed door at a ninety-degree angle, between the light and the dark, between the gravitational pull of an abyss and the attraction of a bright horizon. Hardly could one come closer to an image of modernist intricacy that leads into impasse.

If I searched harder, I am sure I could find an African equivalent to Escher's famous depiction of the spiral staircase. Until then, I have loved Fela's song title "Perambulation" and its lyrics. That song too expresses a version of turning around in circulating modes, returning over and over to the "same place." In Fela's representation of Nigerian political life, that place is a space of impasses. In our own work on the conditions of the world, that same inner point of perambulation can be the fulcrum for attention and inspiration.

Appendix on Prices

The exchange rate for the naira, over the period from 1985 to 2003 went from 1.7 to the dollar to 140 (multiplication by a factor of about eighty).

Relative to the dollar, the domestic price of petrol went from 34c per liter to 35c; and the international crude price was also pretty much the same at the end as at the beginning of this period. *But* how are the numbers read—and lived—relative to what else? In 1981, the first legislated minimum wage was N125 per month (so 625 liters of petrol). In 2001 it was revised up again to 7,500 naira and 6,500 naira for federal and state government workers respectively (Folawewo 2007). So in 2003, with a federal minimum wage you could buy about 187 liters per month. By 2011, the price of crude oil had more than tripled to over $100, the exchange rate was N150, the petrol price was N65, and the minimum wage was the same at N7,500 (then 115 liters). So, as the dollar earnings of those working in dollars rose (because of the rise in the price of crude and the fall in the value of the naira), the real value of the minimum wage in naira, valued against petrol, fell steadily.

NINE

Indexing People to Money:
The Fate of "Shelter"

The consumer price index is an enormously powerful instrument of national and international economic governance, reaching its one hundredth anniversary in 2013. For a hundred years, it has been subject to multiple refashionings. A particular technical paper on the revision of the American CPI, written in 1980, sharply exemplifies the *ongoing* nature of the process—defined by Marx and taken up by Polanyi—whereby qualities that had been mutually embedded have been extricated, renamed, and separately submitted to monetary measure. The CPI then reorders them, according to its own logic, in a definition consonant with those of "constructs." It is

> a statistical estimate constructed using the prices of a sample of representative items whose prices are collected periodically. Sub-indexes and sub-subindexes are computed for different categories and sub-categories of goods and services, being combined to produce the overall index with weights reflecting their shares in the total of the consumer expenditures covered by the index. . . . A CPI can be used to index (i.e., adjust for the effect of inflation) the real value of wages, salaries, pensions . . . for regulating prices and for deflating monetary magnitudes. (*Wikipedia*, accessed August 7, 2014)

The CPI was never "emergent," in the sense proposed for assemblages, and is certainly too vast to qualify as a "device." So it is by studying particular moments of revision that one can bring into profile elements and equivalences as they were scrutinized, revised, and changed, thus revealing their auras, logics, and conundrums. Thomas Stapleford's (2009) history, *The Cost of Living in America: A Political History of Economic Statistics, 1880–2000,* looks closely at the larger and ongoing questions of the relationship between economic statistics and the theory and practice of governance. He explores this as a highly contingent history of Weberian rationalization, in changing times.

Indexing, and reindexing, the "human" to money has changed over several centuries, through several phases, each involving reconceptualizations that unbundled and rebundled its different components, to profile the "real" value of money income in relation to an acceptable "standard of living." This paper tracks a concept that has been there from the beginning, but has been redefined and repositioned in a way that shifts its referent without shifting its name, namely "shelter," or housing (*logement* in the French version, to be brought up later), although new composite terms such as "rental equivalence" are brought in to indicate the actual basis for calculation.

There have been at least three "modern" benchmarks for an index of human value in money terms, beyond—of course—the outright sale of slaves, who are not technically legally "persons," and other conveyances of rights in personam. We are perhaps now living the inception of a fourth. These can be seen as a status equation, a labor-reproductive value equation, a citizenship-value equation, and an asset-value equation. Each one has been sequentially upstaged as the central anchor of a philosophy of value, while certain elements endure from one to the next. In "premodern" systems, property ownership was only valued in money for tax or tribute assessment, commanding loyalty and services in kind toward those from whom the grant had originated. In that classic system, only the free could be so valued. In the ancient Greek political theory outlined by Aristotle (bk. 1, pt. 3), those with property gained magnificence by donating to public projects, as an expression of honor.

In early modern political economic theory the equation of human labor with value lasted several hundred years. That labor time had a money-equivalent value is implicit in labor-tribute systems, going back into the ancient world. From at least the sixteenth century (and in some sense going back to the Bible), the wage and the cost of the laborer's reproduction had to be proportional, a measurement judged in Britain by the justices of the peace, until the "reforms" of the nineteenth century. The concept of consumption was intrinsically related to reproduction over several different time horizons, of which the "daily bread" of the Lord's Prayer was only one. Seasonal and intermittent life-course deprivations were mediated in Britain by local government (in kind) and by the friendly societies (in cash). The cost of generational reproduction, including the cost of the protection provided by a roof over one's head, was built into the Poor Law, which was also aimed at preventing vagabondage and training the future labor force by requiring apprenticeship for children of the lower social classes. As I indicate in the paper on "the real economy," the necessity of an equation between viable prices, viable lives, and a strong labor force, in a national market economy, infused the labor theory of value and underlay the CPI when it was instituted in 1913 to turn the equation into an index to be tracked over time. It became the formal measure of inflation, that is, the purchasing power of the currency.

After World War II, the CPI came forward as the basis for implementing the commitment of states toward their citizens in a democratic welfare state model: to fill in where markets were failing them (unemployment, disability, minority, and old age, and falling below the "poverty line" even though employed) and to prepare the population for possible mobilization in new competitive international endeavors of various kinds (from war to trade to sports and entertainment). In this era, there was an expansion of consumption and rising standards of living, and it was democratic citizenship, political order, and consumption that gave the terms for the equivalence between wages and an ever-expanding frontier of what could be considered a "need." Novelty in the consumer's "basket of goods" became an issue to be explicitly faced in the composition of the CPI. Cameras. Vacations. Eventually, computers. The categories and subcategories expanded, although the main divisions have remained: Food, Clothing, Rent, Fuel, House Furnishings, Miscellaneous.

The most recent, and perhaps fourth, phase of governance and market combination has involved taking these equations in some new directions. After the 1971 shifts in the function of the IMF, with floating exchange rates and money markets, the national CPI became more important as a general index of inflation for comparative purposes, and thereby a criterion for IMF surveillance of the global financial order. The CPI is now defined first and foremost in those terms: as the official measure of inflation in consumer prices. The international guides, published and regularly revised by the United Nations and the International Labor Office, run to several hundred pages. The last edition was published in 2009. The current version of the U.S. CPI was instituted in 1972–1973 (NAS report, 2012), but has been revised in at least two major efforts: in 1983 and 1996. In this capacity, it now becomes a component of the judgment of the profitability of capital investment, since the interest rate is generally crafted to exceed inflation: otherwise capital goes elsewhere, unless the projected, very long-term values would outweigh the losses, and unless the whole deal can be denominated in international reserve currencies or barter-in-kind. A paper published in 1980 (Gillingham, to be discussed later), about 1980s interventions, outlines how the CPI explicitly created differentiation between durables (as investment) and consumables (as consumed in the year of the measure) as the financial investment economy began to take off. Another revision was made in 1996. This too has now been brought under criticism and examination by the authorizing body itself (see Poole, Ptacek, and Verbrugge 2005). By looking at how housing figured in those revisions, we get a glimpse into the redefinition process.

First, here is a summary of how increasingly important a place housing has occupied in the cost of living over the past century: it was weighted at 13.4 percent (1917–1919), then 18.1 percent (1934–1936) (Stapleford 2009, 162). By 2006 it was reported at 32.76 percent,[1] and for 2012, 41 percent. The proportion of the consumption accounted for by food has fallen steadily by comparison. Rents have recently risen faster and higher than the price of housing purchase, and media reports suggest that a very high proportion of renters now spend much more than the 30 percent that was envisaged as total housing costs in the 1950s, when the American Dream of home ownership was laid out, so a deeper examination would demand entering into the distributions, as distinct from averages or weights. For the present purpose, it is the terms under which concepts have been unbundled and rebundled—relative to legacy concepts, the creation of models, and the challenge of logistics in life—that is the focus of this paper.

Phases in the Place of Housing

Housing has been central to this shift in the criteria for indexing people to money, in each phase. In the first phase, a house was mainly an attribute of status. In the second, it needed to be consonant with the reproduction of labor—daily, seasonally, across the life cycle, and intergenerationally. In the third, it was a location for comfort and consumption: a place for intimate processes of reproduction of social orders. Then, as housing and land prices rose after the late 1970s, owner-occupiers became investors, which also separated the financial dynamics around collateral in debt economics in a new way.

In some sense the feudal/classic status aspect of human value never entirely dissipates. Centrality, as a point of reference for value, however, shifts over the three "modern" official designations of the "human"—as laborer, as consumer/citizen, and now emerging as asset bundle or owner-manager thereof—and the components of a "cost of living" have shifted accordingly, but in very specific ways that do not completely dislodge the categories of the past. The theme that interests me most here is how, exactly, the "standard basket of goods" on which basic human value and the CPI have always been based seems to refer backward and forward in time across *all* these human valuation frameworks, potentially including income and expenditure from property and labor, then relating to the necessities and aspirations for citizens' consumption (and thereby social peace, welfare, and mobilizability in collective effort), and then implicitly projecting life courses into a future which is now in the process of reframing and turbulence under a philosophy of investment in assets, such as "the ownership society" advocated by President George W. Bush and the Cato Institute since the first years of the twenty-first century. Here the source of everything that can be defined and marketed as a "durable" source of "consumable" commodities may become a vehicle for investment, realized as an asset through "ownership." It is no longer entirely for protection and consumption. This cascading of historical legacies with respect to human value in formal monetary indices, and their rebundling as times change and contexts vary, is my theme here (as far as I can go with it).

In my work for the chapter on price composition (chapter 10), what struck me, beyond the itemization itself, was the *absence* of certain items that must certainly have been components of the final payable charge to the buyer. Most striking, and discussed in that paper, were the absence of "profit" in the oil industry's explanation of the components of the petrol price and the costs of financialization, particularly risk, risk mitigation measures, and other financial instruments that had become reconfigured as commodities and folded into the price of goods. The financialization of durable objects or conditions (such as uncertainty) since the 1970s figures within other already-existing human-value practices, in explicit and/ or concealed ways. The apposite "red thread" to trace out in the present paper is housing. Once a matter of a "holding" (as in "household") in a property-status system, it then became a "habitation" or "shelter" (as a necessity for the reproduction of life and labor), then a matter of welfare and citizenship (the Charles Booth generation on overcrowding and unsanitary conditions), finally moving into the era of a house as a private asset that underlies the expansion of mortgage-backed securities and the whole postwar financial projection of the life course, using such long-term assets as collateral in the loan structure. These changes have posed serious conceptual problems for an index based on annual "consumption." Shelter was brought back as "shelter services" to distinguish the asset aspect from the consumption aspect.

Our current phase in housing and finance seems novel again. In a tur-

bulent world, residential structures in certain places with some stable durational attributes—cities designated as global, especially in stable hard-
currency systems, and picturesque and coastal locations—have risen in
value as a kind of parking space for international capital. In the old industrial belt of the northern United States, Robert Putnam (2013) reports
on multimillion-dollar lakeside gated communities in an area where small
middle-class housing, only a few hundred yards away, is becoming de-
crepit; and this is not very far from the city of Detroit, where—in 2013—a
house could be bought for $10,000 or less and the city was bankrupt. The
macro-dynamics are vast, and again their study demands more empirical
grasp than I can mobilize at the moment. This paper stays with the meaning of "living," as in "cost of living," so it moves toward the measurement
and representation of household budgets in the CPI in the United States.
How do housing and finance figure in the "basket of goods" on which the
CPI is based? How are they "present" in the itemization: as a cost in relation to need for shelter? As an asset? As a commitment/liability? Discussion of how to parse and unbundle the attributes of housing have recurred.
A recent paper by experts in the CPI, at the Bureau of Labor Statistics, ends
with one of its key questions being "Is there a perception that the changes
in rent have been different than the changes in the cost of shelter services for owners, and how can we at BLS address this perception?" (Poole,
Ptacek, and Verbrugge 2005, 45).

After a brief indication of the equations under the old dispensations,
since certain terms do recur in recent shifts, I turn to two moments of redefinition as the asset economy takes off.

Terms of Reference in the Early Phases of Indexing

The English law on wages, as enacted from the Statute of Labourers, passed
in 1349, and in force until the repeal of the wage clauses of the Statute of
Artificers in 1813, has been described by the famous historian R. H. Tawney
(1913, 307). He pointed out that this whole system, which also included
measures against enclosure of land and eviction, was instituted in an era
of "grave practical evils" as all prices rose together, probably as a result of
the massive import of bullion into Europe by Spain. He wrote, "People
had been accustomed from time immemorial to ascribe a rise in prices to
the covetousness of brewers and bakers and the uncharitableness of artificers and merchants. Now they saw all prices rising together. . . . The whole
economic environment had been revolutionised by the fall in the value of
money" (1913, 319, 326). Food prices fluctuated violently, whereas: "the

practice with regard not only to wages but to prices and the rate of interest was based on the idea that values were objective realities" (1913, 336) and could therefore be fixed by local authorities.

The struggle to define how wages and prices could be brought into consonance, to create not only a growing economy (which became an increasingly important criterion from the eighteenth century) but also a livable human life, continued for several centuries. Provoked to research *The State of the Poor* (1797) by "the difficulties, which the laboring classes experienced, from the high price of grain, and of provisions in general, as well as of cloathing [*sic*] and fuel, during the years of 1794 and 1795" (i), Frederick Morton Eden affiliated his more-or-less Smithian approach to remedies to the theory that "the price of every commodity is the labour which is paid for it," "estimated by money" (vii). This payment had to be consonant with the reproduction of life. Wages and prices should move together: a goal that E. P. Thompson (1971) shows became intermittently impossible to achieve under the growing market conditions of the eighteenth century and which was seen to be hardly legitimate to expect, at all, for the "crowd" who had been educated in the fixing of just prices and wages by justices of the peace.

In the 1790s, Eden (1797) collected budgets, labor conditions, and Poor Law institutions all over the country. One very interesting aspect of his equations is how little housing figures into them at that time because the cottages of the laboring class were generally attached to the job, as they had been under feudal conditions of employment. Rents were variable and low, although the structures themselves might be "hovels." He writes of a man earning £50 a year, paying £4.4s in rent, so less than 10 percent. In other cases (569–74): in Enfield, near Oxford, "cottages are mostly rent-free." In a neighborhood of Mount Sorel, Leicestershire: "the Poor have 4 or 5 acres each assigned to them for a garden, at a very moderate rent." In Lincolnshire "many labourers have their rents paid by the parish." And in Yorkshire "the rents of cottages vary according to the quantity of land annexed; and are from £1. to £1.10s. Many of the cottages on this coast are miserable hovels; built of mud and straw. Such habitations are sometimes granted by the parish to poor families." And so on.

While Eden never doubts the importance of documenting "habitation" as one of the "necessaries" of life, one can perhaps see how it could fall in importance for detailed monetary study, relative to food, whose price fluctuated more widely. This makes sense of the classic review of real wage rates in England over seven centuries, where Phelps-Brown and Hopkins (1956) focus entirely on "consumables" to the exclusion of shelter. They also note that the archival sources on rent were very limited, and indeed much rent was paid in kind. By the time of new budget studies in the nineteenth century, reviewed by Stigler (1954), housing makes an appearance but is very low profile by comparison with food (cf. the statement of Engel's Law that the proportion of income spent on food declines as income rises). The Belgian worker's budget included by Stigler devoted only 8.7 percent to housing by comparison with 70.9 percent to food (1954, 98), and as income rose, the proportion spent on housing also fell, like food. But we have no political economy of housing to work with here. Were most workers' houses attached to the job, or paid for in kind, or perhaps inherited, so owned outright?

We also see that housing could be *explicitly* excluded from official definitions when it came to poverty. For example, Gillie (1996) quotes a charitable board in London defining eligibility for relief in terms of "exceptional distress (where) The weekly scale (for food and fuel, excluding rent) was 3s. 6d. for an adult living alone, 2s. 6d. each for two adults living together, 6d. each for children under 4, 1s. each for those aged from 4 to 12." They look at "income after rent" and Gillie adds that "the use of after-rent incomes per head to assess the ability of families to pay school fees may have been quite common" (Gillie 1996, 719). On the other hand, a source from 1884 notes how significant rent had become by then, as urban life expanded. We see a similar bracketing of housing as a consumable necessity. Williams (1884) (quoted in Gillie 1996) calculated that "46 per cent pay from one fourth to one half of the wages earned as rent; 42 per cent pay from one fourth to one fifth; and the remaining 12 per cent pay less than one fifth" (722). He regretted that this "allows for each day no cheering luxuries, but only the bare amount of nitrogenous and carbonaceous foods which are absolutely necessary for the maintenance of the body . . . oatmeal . . . meat . . . cocoa and bread. . . . Rent for two small rooms . . . 5s. Schooling for four children. . . . Washing. . . . Firing and light" (724).

In the late nineteenth century, Charles Booth was concerned less with the cost of housing than with its quality for health and welfare. In a separate comment (a pamphlet, n.d.), in an era of rapidly rising property values, he argued in favor of a change in the tax system for housing, since, when food—"for the advantage of the consumer, and in the interest of towns and of trade"—had been made exempt from taxes, it had not been foreseen that houses would then become taxed more heavily. He proposed separating the site value from the house value, which he argued would benefit the tenant in several respects (through the incentive to the owner to build and maintain houses) without penalizing the owner.[2] We realize here how the decomposition of rent into site, house, services of the owner to the tenant, and the tax policy was obfuscated in the reporting of "shelter" as a simple "cost of living." Reform, as Booth saw it, would depend on unbundling the qualities and repricing them to promote the quality of human life for the rent payer.

I think what we see here is that "shelter" was always more difficult to measure than food, since access and pricing inherited old and new, local and general attributes and could never be reduced to what a later technician called simply "shelter services." Indeed, I discovered an official Norwegian source on the CPI that pointed out how "some products within the established consumption groups are missing. One such important product is housing. Nevertheless, arguable prices on wood give an indication on the long-term development of rental prices as it mirrors prices on material for building and construction. And in fact, some sources do not necessarily split between wood for building and construction and wood for fuel" (Grytten 2004).

The struggle to define housing continued, and continues. Even the words confound us. The word "starving" generally applies to food alone these days. But the dictionary and the occasional usage remind us that in British English it can also refer to perishing from cold. Hence our reading of old sources needs to be attentive to possible referents: both food and warmth being considered essential from the outset. There is no doubt, however, that in the era of a labor theory of value, the price of food was considered by far the most important item of consumption, the most vulnerable to rapid change, the most obviously linked to capacity to work, and—in fact—high in the proportion of the wage that it took up. We can keep in mind that the latest American CPI figures attribute a mean of 15.2 percent of expenditure to food and beverages, by comparison with the 70.9 percent for the Belgian worker of the nineteenth century reported by Stigler. Housing now accounts for over 40 percent whereas for that Belgian worker it was under 10 percent. It emerged as a value, beyond its "taken for grantedness," under feudal and early modern conditions, as it was separated from status into a market item, mainly in the nineteenth century, and then the financial market which demanded further definition and commensuration.

The CPI and Housing in the "Basket of Goods"

The American CPI is based on surveys and budget diaries with respect to over eight hundred items, expressed as 211 budget shares (NAS 2012, 18). As mentioned earlier, I have been unable to do the necessary digging into the history of the categories, except to note the oft-referred-to debates on how to include novel items as they appeared in consumer life. There is, throughout, a certain underlying attention to the idea of "necessities" which comes forward from the labor theory and finds its way into the citizen-consumer theory. Is entertainment a necessity? As mentioned above, among the nineteenth-century reformers there was already concern for including in the household budget some of the joys of life and the opportunity for self-education. The items of expenditure now include a wide variety of consumables that enhance the lives of people as citizens and participants in a growing market economy. The NAS (2013) report on methods notes "consumer spending has changed dramatically over the past 30 years through such things as online shopping, electronic banking, payroll deductions, and greater use of debit and credit cards" (5). This assimilation of novel items has been complex and has had to face the "owner-investor" emphasis that has emerged in recent years. Can all money spent by households be understood as acquiring commodities for consumption, still less as a "necessity"?

The CPI as an Index of the Cost of Living in the Postwar Era, and the Policy-Philosophy Changes after 1980

Under state-run welfare provisions, the CPI becomes a crucial source for indexing payments, since its sequence over time measures inflation.

> The Consumer Price Index (CPI) is one of the most widely used statistics in the United States. As a measure of inflation it is a key economic indicator. It serves as a guide for the Federal Reserve Board's monetary policy and is an essential tool in calculating changes in the nation's output and living standards. It is used to determine annual cost-of-living allowances for social security retirees and other recipients of federal payments, to index the federal income tax system for inflation, and as the yardstick for U.S. Treasury inflation-indexed bonds. (National Research Council, 2002, quoted in NAS 2012, 21)

Inflation has been quite considerable over the past decades. The average CPI for the United States for 1970 was 38.8, for 1980 it was 82.4, and for 2011, 224.9.[3] So rising well above the 3 percent per annum that used to be the standard goal to 4.3 percent and then 4.9 percent. During the twenty-first century it has fallen considerably, to 2 percent in 2014.[4] I understand that there is a generally agreed proxy figure written into long-term contracts (but this too remains a topic to explore further).

The 1980s

In the welfare-person era, housing appears to have been unproblematic as a category in the CPI, in part since certain aspects were controlled or deeply influenced by state policy with respect to public housing, subsidy, tax breaks, mortgage rate control, and so on. Decent housing was thought to be in a sense a right, especially of those returning from war. This would apply particularly starkly in Europe, where whole urban neighborhoods were bombed out. Unbundling all the components of the citizen-consumer model was not faced until the 1980s. It is fascinating that, in his recent analysis of the impact of the monetarists on economic policy, especially since 1980, Daniel Stedman Jones (2012) devotes the entire culminating chapter to redefinitions of housing policy in Britain and the United States. He concentrates mainly on the aim of setting people loose from "dependency" on the state. The escalating financialization of housing, through the expansion of mortgages, was not entirely envisaged at the time, but it cannot help but be one of the factors accounting for the rise in housing as a component of national capital from this time onward.

For the CPI, the difficulty that eventually arose was that of defining *which* component of housing costs was "consumption" (for a *consumer* index), as we moved into an asset-based theory of value and the price of housing started to rise rapidly. Just to give a personal example of house price inflation, a house that we know (in the United States) was bought in 1977 for $67,000. It went on the market thirty years later for almost $1 million, so very much more than the CPI index would account for as the effects of inflation (which could account for at most 20 percent of the rise). As far as one could tell from the outside of the house, there had been little or no "improvements" made over that period. Location was a key factor, with possible consumer advantages of good schools and transport. But the remaining rise in price? Clearly the equation of this house with increasing *consumer* utility could not cover the whole rise. By then, such a house, in such a location, was an investment.

Gillingham (1980) has analyzed discussions about how to deal with this situation within the CPI administration, where it was proposed that "the housing component of the CPI—for both renters and homeowners—should measure the cost of consuming the flow of shelter services" (31) over the single year that is the temporal unit of measurement for all consumer items. Shelter services were defined as comprising "interest costs, taxes, maintenance, etc.," judged to be "extremely complex," but separable from the investment component. As a general principle of consumer theory, "the consumer's welfare is determined by the flow of consumption services received. . . . Satisfaction is derived from the act of consumption, ownership of a source of consumption services—a durable good—produces no additional satisfaction. In other words, the purchase of a durable good is an "investment," designed to provide consumption services over a future time span" (1980, 31). Finding it "impossible" to construct a valid user-cost model for all the many "services" that "shelter" provides, the CPI administration turned to a rental equivalent estimate instead. The consumption quotient for owner-occupiers, paying mortgage rates on houses bought much earlier, was to be the imputed opportunity cost of not renting the same house. A concept from early modern and nineteenth-century practice—namely "rent"—is brought forward into the financial era without disaggregation, even where "interest costs," as well as insurance, security, and other enhanced accouterments of asset-holding, are folded in under the ancient legacy concept of "shelter."

There is a further challenge to explore, with respect to the "human": rent may be a proxy for "shelter services," but its level can hardly be summarized by any of the proxy definitions. Shelter as a money value has moved beyond the scope of need, collective membership in a community, and even market consumption to reflect the investment aspect much more broadly, and the place of a dependable durable "reality" of the house itself in a financial architecture. We hear these days of the financial interests now buying up residential housing, especially in stable and desirable places, and securitizing them for financial interests to invest in the income stream from the expansion of rentals, which must necessarily result as owner-occupiers are competed out of the market. At present, this happens by the rapidity with which financial interests buy up properties at or above the asking price, for "cash": a term that now applies to immediate payment by bank transfer of the whole price, in one transaction. So rent in any one place reflects the conditions of competition for capital in the capital markets, and for investment in other housing markets elsewhere. This particular unbundling of the 1983 changes, then, set shelter quite largely within an asset market logic, but represented it as a function of the rental "market." The financial component is rendered invisible. Perhaps the elements of the labor theory of human value—"shelter services"—are slowly disappearing altogether as a literal allusion and now survive as a convenient concept for covering what is now rent, including interest and taxes, in a very old, but still current, vernacular concept.

Rent, of course, is its own composition, to which I turn. But first note that it is surprising how successful this redefinition of rent as payment for "shelter services" has been, even in relation to critical scholarship. In his book on capitalism in the twenty-first century, Thomas Piketty (2014) shows clearly how enormously housing grew as a component of national capital in all Western countries over the twentieth century, but he repeats the French, and international, CPI definition in terms of "shelter."

> In all civilizations, capital fulfills two economic functions: first, it provides housing (more precisely, capital produces "housing services," whose value is measured by the equivalent rental value of dwellings, defined as the increment of well-being due to sleeping and living under a roof rather than outside), and second, as a factor of production. . . . Historically . . . increasingly sophisticated forms . . . came later, as did constantly improved forms of housing. (213)

This is simply phrased as the advantage of a roof over one's head, although it necessarily now includes—though unmentioned—the generated returns to asset ownership, interest payment, and taxes. The French CPI goes on to define "rent" (*loyer*) as "the sum given by an occupant [that] is counterpart for the enjoyment of a housing unit," that is, a separate and independent habitation. The definition then rules out certain components of "enjoyment," presumably because they will be separately measured, but then attributed to, and paid by, whom? For example, rent does not include "costs of occupation, which are destined to cover a certain number of expenses for the renter and linked to the consumption of water and energy, the use of the elevator, the collective heating of a building, part of the expenses of upkeep or repair of the collective facilities, taxes for the removal of household garbage, etc." Some costs to owners can be considered "imputed" or "fictional" when they revert to them, as distinct from being passed on to the renters. Of course, this simply means that all these components are itemized and priced, and then there is the question of to whom they are attributed. Again, are the financialized components passed on as part of "rent" or assimilated to something else? More murky than this question is the one about ownership by "foreign investors," who enjoy tax credits or other increments to the whole financial Gordian knot that housing has become.[5]

If we look at urban housing rents in our major cities, it would be deeply obtuse to define their benefits in terms that revert us to the hovels of the status economy and the basic protection from "starvation" of the labor theory of value. Unless, or course, we define as "consumption" the safety of the capital invested, the iconic value of location (even when only rarely actually "enjoyed," as a consumer), and other utterly intangible benefits. So precisely not a "roof over your head," except perhaps metaphorically: shelter protection for long-term capital assets held in money, and tax shelters (in certain cases). Surely, current housing-as-capital, as Piketty himself points out that it is, should be examined with the same acute attention as anthropology has devoted to "wealth" and "valuables" in the whole range of present and historical cultures. So, is the fate of "shelter" in the CPI a harbinger of things to come in other as-yet unbundled concepts that have been moved from one framing to another? Here I move to the American CPI revision published in 1996, and then simply sketch what the people seem to be saying, as an example of the kind of decomposition that we need to do, analytically, and its enormous importance in the analysis of personhood in markets.

The 1998 Revision: Ptacek and Baskin

A CPI revision described by Ptacek and Baskin in 1996, for implementation in 1998, addressed the concepts of rent and rental equivalence, along with other aspects, such as sampling. Since 1987, the rental equivalence of an owner-occupied habitation was estimated by the owner and excluded certain costs, such as utilities. This was to be continued, with certain size, quality, and location features made explicit. For the category of "rent," the value was the "contract rent": that is, whatever was written into the contract between owner and renter: "The 'rent' estimator is based on the change in the 'economic rent,' which is basically the 'contract rent,' adjusted for any changes in the quality of the housing unit." There seems to be no recognition of other components that might be driving the "economic rent." Indeed, the document's details are all concerned with the techniques of collecting usable interannual data, and—understandably—not with disaggregating the price on a market, which makes rent "economic."

All the "basic" terms for housing—such as "shelter services"—permit, and even encourage, a certain myopia. Recent economics journalism about the variation in housing costs in American cities defers largely to the markets: the job market and the supply-and-demand measures in the housing markets. The social journalism, meanwhile, is documenting the broad transfer of ownership in major cities to wealthy foreigners, and the development of devices for rendering rental insecure enough to keep it moving within the shifting market conditions. Even the idea of a house as a commitment to a neighborhood or community is coming into question as a disincentive to the mobility of the labor force in response to markets. Shelter, at least, is ephemeral, substitutable.

View from Afar (or Farther Away)

The U.S. Housing Act of 1949 benchmarked the cost of housing to 30 percent of income. This was already considerably higher than historical prices, which were about 10 percent for the poor in England, and—in Stigler's vast compilation on historical standards of living for Europe—lower than that for Belgian workers. Of course, the quality of the house was expected to be much higher, under a philosophy of "the American dream." A Harvard study in 2013 showed that "nearly 50% of renters" now pay more than 30 percent of their income for rent.[6] And rent is now rising faster than purchase price. What accounts for this? The research suggests market forces in both housing and the labor/wage markets. But I also want to look at the place of the financial returns in the price composition. Gillingham reports that in choosing rent as a proxy for the consumption aspect of housing, those responsible for revising the CPI methods decided to acknowledge that using rent included "building up the user cost of shelter services from its components—interest costs, taxes, maintenance, etc." (1980, 31). But we see that these are not broken out into "elements" when they are reported, even by Piketty. The word "shelter" does its work to blend the elements, each generated in its own locus, into a single entity.

Then a model can be created and manipulated, Gilllingham continues, "by defining user cost in the simplest case, in a world of certainty without taxes and with perfectly competitive markets" (1980, 32), proceeding with the concept of "in a perfect world": perfect, doubtless understood in model terms. But by representing it as a function of rent as a "market" price, this component is rendered invisible in the official conceptualization. Perhaps all the elements of the labor theory of human value are slowly disappearing altogether, and "shelter" has become a simple euphemism to make a new bundle of valuations seem so familiar that only patient scholarship is able and willing to focus in, minutely, on what makes up the compositions with which we now live. So, is the fate of "shelter" a harbinger of things to come in other domains that are unbundled and then rebundled?

There is a new discussion of exactly this problem with respect to housing, undertaken by economists who focus on the CPI (see, for example, Verbrugge 2008). My chapter here simply points to these discussions for future attention, since they do not yet seem to have made their way into shaping changes in the international comparative exercise, relative to the "real economy" issues raised in chapter 12.

Conclusion: Engel's Law, or the Financialization of "Durables" and Their Reclamation

It is worth returning to our own classics for inspiration, and to detect silences and gaps, on our topic of the "human" beyond the "consumption" assumed necessary under the labor theory of value, and desirable under the citizen-consumer theory. As far as I know, Engel's Law largely puts aside the changes in economic structures that might help explain the food/nonfood substitution process in budgets as incomes rise and fall over major changes since Engel himself first proposed this observation in a world where food took up a much larger proportion of the budget than it does now, in part because housing was so low profile in the beginning. If food falls in its proportional contribution to expenditure, that could also be due to the rise in the price of assets, as well as their simple availability. It seems clear in our own era that all our most durable qualities are now being spliced out in a different fashion from simple "reproduction," and amplified and financialized—as timeless masterpieces in art, world heritage sites, global cities, extractable resources for the mining industry, DNA, gender attributes, etc.—to be dependable sources of consumable "services" into the future, through financial mediation. What is this configuration producing as a "human economy," and are there ways into its logics?

For us in anthropology, the question can best be turned into the ethnographic mode to ask how the CPI is actually created and applied, here in the West and elsewhere. And how the people are valuing themselves and others under the composite regimes under which they live. Moments of recrafting of powerful devices such as the CPI offer a window into how constructs and assemblages are taken apart, remade, and represented, in the light of new discriminations. We can see that there are conceptual recuperations that reach back far into history, even in works such as Piketty's, devoted to inferences about the present moment in capitalist history. The proliferation of instruments, devices, assemblages, and "provoked realization" with which we live, all the time, may well be partially concealed by these portfolio concepts from the past, as their components are grouped and regrouped, allocated, estimated and reported, under headings and categories whose collective import is enormous. Housing as a category became 41 percent of the CPI. Since this will include utilities, do the effects of the derivatives markets for congestion contracts—discussed in the final paper—raise the level?

PART FIVE

Toward Ethnography and the People's Economies

TEN

Composites, Fictions, and Risk: Toward an Ethnography of Price

Introduction: Fictions and Prices

The topic of this paper—popular understandings and social processes of commodity price formation—has engaged me for a long time and weaves its way through much of my work, from urban food supply to bridewealth to secondhand automobile spare parts. It has seemed, however, too vast to take on directly and there will never be enough time to address the economists systematically on an issue that they have owned for a hundred years. Only on an occasion such as presented here, an invitation to review aspects of economic anthropology in light of a rereading of Karl Polanyi's *The Great Transformation*, has it seemed worth placing some thoughts into circulation. Those thoughts focus on how price is produced, presented, revealed, and concealed *as a composite* as distinct from a *singular* amount.

In all but catastrophic inflationary conditions, market participants are describing and judging absolute and relative prices all the time. Allusion to the composition of prices, through distinct but converging processes, has recently become one of the regular reference points in popular and even corporate justificatory discourse. This is a departure from concepts that take price "as a whole," such as "worth" in a religious register, and the intersection of supply and demand (scarcity and desire) in the marginalist neoclassical register. Although the use of a composite idiom seems on the rise at present, the component categories in circulation actually refer back to classical theory: to returns to land, labor, capital, and the state. So although the price instabilities of recent years have provoked a more explicit compositional idiom, its terms diffuse the evidence of the very innovations whose broader influences have made composition so compelling an idea to invoke. Novelties in financial, futures, and insurance technologies, and possibly the effects of intellectual property rights and contractual engagements, are all embedded in other terms by the time that price enters public discourse. I concentrate on these popular terms, trying—when I can—to identify places where direct evidence or circumstantial argument can show both the increasingly explicit reference to classical elements and the existence of other elements that are concealed by them.

Anthropological theories of price have always been implicitly composite, in order to encompass and to recognize sociocultural components. Marx argued that the commodity and its price are a fetish that conceals the social relationships on which they are based and confuses the analytical components of use and exchange value. Polanyi refers to the component costs of land and labor as "fictions," since there are no market relations at all behind their production. The concealment of composition would then be one of the main functions of price ideologies, since it dampens reasonable doubt about worth and circumvents the moral and political commentary that might ensue from close analysis. Indeed, throughout history, many authorities have aimed to maintain "customary" or "just" prices so as to avert negative commentary, at least in certain domains that are crucial to political purposes. As E. P. Thompson (1971) argued and illustrated so forcefully, the questioning of simple equations between things and their prices is a sure sign of fundamental unrest. In Thompson's case of the price of bread in the eighteenth century, it was the miller's margin that came under violent selective scrutiny when price was questioned. Restoring a meaning to the price-livelihood equation can restore and buttress the legitimacy of government. For example, during my childhood, living on postwar rationing in Britain, people knew that prices were artificially stabilized and subsidized, although no one knew by how much and everyone was thereby coaxed into a permanent position of collective gratitude (even when tempered by grumbling). Conversely, under antitax ideologies, public attention is deliberately drawn to sales and value-added taxes, in part to keep their levels clearly in the public eye in time for the next election.

In the twenty-first century, however, an interesting phenomenon has begun to emerge, namely an increasingly open recognition that prices are composites, across the board. People are actually reminded that all prices are fictions—literally the results of narratives of creation, addition, and subtraction—in ways that go far beyond Polanyi's discussion of "fictional commodities" in the mid-twentieth century or Marx's theory of commodity fetishism in the mid-nineteenth. Consumers are now trained by discount outlets to notice retail markup rates; by the *Lou Dobbs* show to know about differential global wage rates; by foreign travel to pay attention to currency exchange; by many prices—from airline tickets to retail commodities—to know about added taxes, fees, and payments, which are often now itemized; by eBay and the automobile market to know about depreciation; and by their own experience with financial institutions to read the bills for compulsorily itemized charges and fees. Since the 1980s, we are aware of a premium for celebrity on an expanding range of goods, for the brand image as glamour rather than guarantor of quality. Each of these additions is a quite familiar concept in itself; consumers themselves have just not focused on isolating and measuring each one so self-consciously until recently.[1] The experience of doing so probably persuades all of us that there must be other components we don't yet know about and still others we don't understand.

The result is a moral economy of transparently composite prices, which nevertheless retain the mystery of their components. My exploration here is far from exhaustive and the ethnographic examples come from domains of which I already have particular knowledge rather than from full-scale research. But I can point to where it is going, in anticipation of the kind of revitalized debate, apposite to our own moment in history, that Hann and Hart (2009) launched, and for which the original of this paper was written. The question is, now that prices are popularly recognized and vigorously engaged with as fictional, fetishistic, and composite, what can and should analysis focus on, and about what is analysis revelatory? I will argue, following the logic if not the substance of Polanyi's argument, that we pay attention to elements of price that are hidden in plain sight among the multiple traditional price elements by the very diffuseness of their presence.

Price Composites, Historical Moments, and the Moral Economy of Prices

Prices have always been understood as fictions and composites at some historical moments and have been naturalized and moralized at others. My own orientation comes partly from living up to the age of about ten in the moral and political economy of administered market prices. I passed my whole childhood taking regular trips to the shops with money in one hand and a ration book in the other, knowing the official rhetoric of justice behind a wartime rationing system and participating on the local calibrations of shortage and access. For the money price to be stable and unitary, ancillary prestations were made but not considered a part of the price. To be assured of items during peak periods of seasonal demand—chocolates for holidays, fruit for jam making in summer—we needed friendly relations with the local retailers. As errand runners for the family, children bore a pretty serious responsibility to be deferent and cheerful to the shopkeepers at all times. And then some things came free: MoF (Ministry of Food) orange juice, the compulsory one-third pint of milk a day during midmorning break at school, and—if my memory serves me right—cod liver oil. We also received food parcels from Australia, with luxuries like sugared almonds. The morality and civility of the gift thereby entered the commodity distribution system, alongside government redistribution, with all the implications for personal status cultivation within an egalitarian ideology. A decade later at university, our generation needed the textbook training of Economics 101 to get the hang of equilibrium prices in self-regulating markets, in part because it implied a different nexus of citizenship, different local transactions, and a shifted responsibility for managing personal budgets. The one thing we all knew deeply from our own pre-rationing past "by heart" was that there were severe sanctions backing our ability to adjust to the relative prices that would be produced by the market. They should fit into a budget. The Dickensian saying of Mr. Micawber, from *David Copperfield*, was often quoted: "Annual income twenty pounds, annual expenditure nineteen pounds nineteen and six, result happiness. Annual income twenty pounds, annual expenditure twenty pounds nought and six, result misery." The latter could easily lead to debtors' prison. Personal debt was culturally imbued with danger and horror; the unique price and selective availability nexus of rationing had offered protection.

My familiarity with one regime of administered prices fostered my interest in how others had been created under other political regimes. It was price formation in the urban food supply system of colonial Cameroon that took me into studies of money in the first place, over twenty years ago. The price of food in the urban markets of colonial Africa (see Guyer 1987) seemed arbitrary: not the currency itself, which was by definition an arbitrary symbol of value and imposed from above, but the amounts, the numerical aspect of commensuration. Labor was not paid for in Southern Cameroon. Neither was land. The French mandate state set price ceilings, still known in administered systems as the *mercurial*. But clearly officials worried about food supply. In the early colonial system food was a "fictitious commodity" in Polanyi's specific sense of that concept (1944, 72): not initially produced for the market nor through market relations. Economic commentaries on African urban food prices have referred to prices as "high" or "low," with no obvious theoretical or practical referent except civil service salaries, which were also set by administrative fiat. "Getting the prices right" (as a much later policy called it)—that is getting all relevant prices to work in synergy—proved an elusive process. The continuing colonial and postcolonial impasse about bringing the price/wage/tax nexus into a dynamic and plausible systemic relationship lies at the heart of today's "fiscal disobedience," according to Roitman's (2005) trenchant analysis. So price fictions can also fail. They can be incoherent in themselves and become vulnerable to other and competing narratives and moralities of entailment, consequence, and avoidance under changing historical conditions.

Rapid fluctuations, however, probably always test the systemic tolerance, even in otherwise plausible price configurations. Price movements in Nigeria in the 1990s rose and fell in ways that can only be explained, if at all, in rather distant retrospect (see Guyer, Denzer, and Agbaje 2002). In the longer run we are all living through price shifts that have been difficult to comprehend in terms of a simple version of demand and supply. A house we bought in 1977 went on the market twenty-five years later at about fifteen times our purchase price. On the other hand, many consumer goods go on sale for up to 80 percent off. And yet again, in the summer of 2006, the Baltimore public turned intensely inquisitive about the sale, deregulation, and merger of the domestic energy company, which was projected to result in a 72 percent rate hike, just at the same time as an unprecedented rise in the price of gasoline. For many goods, there is a vast vista for hunting-and-gathering forays on the Internet, where comparative pricing constitutes a big part of the excitement of the chase on eBay and Craigslist. For many things, people's acceptance of customary price explanations has been shaken loose of its moorings. For services and insurance, we are increasingly aware of getting stuck in mazes of mini monopolies, trick clauses, qualifying conditions, and other channeling devices that are almost as profoundly sanctioned by a revised bankruptcy law as in Dickensian Britain. Warranties, service contracts, membership dues, and so on tie the buyer to the seller to specific dates over time, and when conditions alter, unforeseen clauses swing into view. The aftermath of Hurricane Katrina in the insurance and real estate sectors, and the explosion of Enron in the energy sector, have opened up to public view many profit-making maneuvers and components of prices of which they had been unaware.

There are several ways to study the moral economy of composite prices; the most important at this stage would be through ethnography. This preliminary foray is written from secondary sources. The next section takes a key commodity, oil, and looks at representations of its price-as-composite in several contexts. It ends by showing how the place of finance and financial institutions remains fairly hidden even after various decompositional exercises.[2] This matters enormously, and especially for comparisons between price regimes in financial institutional settings that are quite different from each other: Euro-America and West Africa, for example. So the next part of the paper asks whether there is a gain in dropping back in time to Polanyi (and Marx) for the concept of "fictitious commodity" to apply to the risk and risk-mitigation instruments that are now incorporated into price, and then work forward from there. Like land, labor, and capital in their own times, risk now figures pervasively in price composition and capital accumulation, as both an addition and a subtraction. But it is far more diffuse and difficult to identify than the classical factors.

A note first on oil as an example. One might argue that it is not a very good example of principles of price composition because of its uniquely political dimensions. I would argue, however, that this actually helps to throw some general processes into relief and especially the processes of self-representation to the consumer public. Because we know that finance is a hugely important and growing component of the petroleum sector at every level, its diffusion throughout the pricing process makes it possible to trace at least some of the price implications.

Custom and Composition in Oil Prices

The following three small junctures in the massive edifice of oil pricing illustrate parts of price creation and representation to which we, the public and scholars, can have access and they open up vistas beyond which the processes and devices are far more opaque.

Representations of Custom: The United States, Summer 2006

The retail price of gasoline in America rose from around $2 per gallon to over $3 per gallon over the first half of 2006. This is still a low price by European standards, but the rapidity of change had a large economic and psychological impact. It instills fear that all projections are now suspect: domestic budgets for owning this or that kind of car out to ticket prices in an airline industry already in deep financial trouble. In the face of public outrage, the petroleum industry had to explain the forces shaping the market. And since the "majors" cover the entire commodity chain from exploration to the pump, there was no evading the question or passing it on to another party. The price of crude is said to be difficult for corporations to influence. Even the major private companies hold direct control of a very small proportion of world reserves because of the prominence of national companies in most of the producer countries. And certainly it seemed plausible that increased demand from China and India would put uncontrollable pressure on world energy prices. The striking thing about the companies' explanations for my purposes here was not the possibility of self-serving reporting or an equally possible avoidance of mentioning all the smaller points at which price advantage can be gained (the judgment of quality, the criteria for setting royalty payments, and so on). It was their reliance on the notion of a *customary level* to proportional shares in the price received by the traditional market participants: producers, the government; the processors (refineries) and the retailers. A bar graph that was widely published in newspaper advertisements and explanatory literature showed that despite a large rise in the *nominal* price, there had been a fairly steady *proportion* of returns over several years amongst (a) the crude product (53 percent in 2005), (b) taxes (19.7 percent), (c) refining costs and profits (18.1 percent), and (d) distribution and marketing (9.0 percent) (Lexecon 2006). Profit on capital is not included, although one newspaper version did give a profit rate of "8.5 cents on every dollar of sales," but external to the graphic, so implicitly accruing to all parties.[3]

Finance is a component of all capitalist enterprise, but "profit" was not presented in the historical sequence, thereby implying that it does not change much. One result of the status and undeveloped nature of this category is that any new aspects of the extremely complex set of costs of finance are then indiscernible: capital investment, insurance, participation in futures and derivatives markets, and doubtless many other financial instruments, including speculation on the markets. Indeed, Rex Tillerson, CEO of ExxonMobil, expressed doubt that it would be possible for the public to understand the price composition of oil, although he committed himself to trying to explain "the fundamentals" during the maelstrom of confusion on Capitol Hill in May 2006. This was cited in an article in which it was claimed that "last year alone the top 10 oil companies spent more than $30 million on their lobbying battalions" (Phillips and Bosman 2006). The costs of finance are in fact diffused across actions and actors at every stage. I know from involvement in the Chad-Cameroon Pipeline project that financial instruments are inserted in several places, sometimes under nonobvious names, possibly in relation to categories in the tax code. For example, what is referred to as the "transport tariff" includes two financial elements, beyond the material and labor costs of maintaining the pipeline itself: an amount ensuring debt service (at an agreed rate, not pegged to the market price of crude) to the lenders, shareholders, and affiliates with respect to the immediate project, and a contribution per barrel to permit recovery and remuneration of company shareholders' investments. Since these rates are fixed in the contracts, for the duration of the agreements they are the "price of doing business" and also a nonproportional obligatory payment, irrespective of the price of the product. So large and so numerous are the total payments in the early years of production in a new field that the varied kinds added together—from royalty rights and customs duties to insurance against oil spills—can add up to the entire price of the crude oil under certain world price scenarios. Below that level, a company would suspend production since finance payments take priority over income. Some payments are mandatory only as long as production continues, so suspension offers temporary relief. Price is presented to the general public, however, in a different way: as proportions of the retail price, based on *actors* ("producers," government, refiners, retailers), and crafted to appear customary.

One sensed that the China-India demand explanation of the oil price in the spring and summer of 2006 could not be sufficient, so rapid was the rise. I had written these paragraphs of the draft paper before reporters started indicating a whole new element. The concept of contango entered the discussion, and then was referred to routinely, although never fully assimilated into the public explanations of price movements. National Public Radio reported:

> Chief among (the factors) is "contango," a market term for the situation in which a commodity—like oil—has a higher future value than its current price. Oil companies and others like to buy futures contracts to make sure they've got oil coming to them well into the future. But lately, people who have nothing to do with the oil industry are buying oil futures, holding them as can't-lose investments that can return well over 10 percent. Investment banks from Morgan Stanley to Goldman Sachs are making so much money from oil futures that they've become a hot investment for all sorts of big-money players. Some of the biggest players are U.S. pension funds, which have put billions of dollars into oil futures. At least one analyst thinks that pension funds have become part of the machinery driving higher gas prices. "I think if you saw all the pension funds walk away," says Ben Dell, an oil analyst at Sanford Bernstein, "you'd probably see a $20 drop in the crude price." (Davidson 2006)

The final interpretation was that investment in futures was driving up the oil price, which then combined with rising consumer demand which in turn intensified an incentive to invest in the oil markets (although not necessarily in oil exploration and production). Twenty dollars per barrel would be about 28 percent of the price at the time. A contango condition indicates riskless profit, and indeed Goldman Sachs earned the highest profit it had ever registered in 2006. When we return to the artisanal diagram, this profit can only figure as part of the market price of crude. But why then do the proportions of the price break down so similarly in 2006 as they did in the past? The naive consumer becomes a probing skeptic, increasingly demanding breakdowns into new components that seem buried in antique reporting customs in which whole new industries of risk management and consulting disappear.

Consumer Petrol Prices in Nigeria

Since the early 1980s, the Nigerian consumer public has been in intermittent insurrection over the price of petrol at the pump. There have been strikes, demonstrations, shortages, government pronouncements, and a great deal of consequent suffering. It became clear that people were certainly willing to pay money for petrol but that everyone, in one way or another, thought that citizenship in an oil-producing country entitled the buyer to a price that bore a stronger relationship to the cost of living than to anything else. In other words, the payment—if any—should go in the opposite direction as a right of birth. In another paper (Guyer with Denzer 2009), we showed how Nigerian commentators resisted referring to such an implicit payment as a "subsidy" and tabulated at least six different arguments from the press about how the petrol price *should* be composed. Twenty years before the American Petroleum Institute tried a "shares metric" for public education, the Nigerian government tried a similar tactic. In the face of critique and continuing price fluctuation, the government eventually got totally lost in the layers of actual and imputed costs of the commodity chain. Several newspaper articles tried to break it all down and add it up again: production, refining, transport, retail, global markets with changing exchange rates, and so forth. It never made any sense. But neither did other arguments. The reading public clearly thought that the price ought to be intelligible, which meant being able to trace out a logic of composition as a narrative connecting the oil field to the petrol pump. In the absence of other logical explanations, one growing theme in the popular accounts became the cumulative margins skimmed off by the military leadership, the civilian leadership, the companies, and increasingly the illegal activities of bunkering. In the popular mind, insisting that there should be, in fact, identifiable components of the national petroleum price gave rhetorical traction on the political reality of a price that could not be explained in technical or economic terms.

At the Petrol Pump

One chapter of *Marginal Gains* (Guyer 2004) was devoted to the negotiation of the "real" price in a single buying event at a rural station in Nigeria in 1997, at the height of a profound petrol drought and under mandated prices The unemployed youth who made a living from motorcycle taxi services were destitute; the farmers' and transporters' goods were rotting before they could reach the great urban markets; the professionals could not get to work or circulate around their networks; and the officials could not officiate. The arrival of one tanker truck in a somewhat remote area would provoke an enactment of price composition that was charismatic in its skill on the part of the station owner. There was a mandated money price from the government. Everyone on that day knew that rationing by a self-regulating price mechanism of allowing a bidding war would have brought social chaos, even if it had been possible, under and around the perspicacity of the police and the army. As it turns out, the station owner worked the customary named components of a market price, in a manner that was similar in structure, even though different in content, to the company advertising described above. After standard Yoruba marketing practice, there are add-ons and subtractions, measurement adjustments and social recognition factors, indices of relative suffering (exposure to sun, need, etc.), which translated into longer and shorter waiting times, more or less of the amount one wanted, "dashes" to the helpers and the soldiers, and so on. No one expected the station owner to operate at anything less than a profit. But she herself had to be careful that her practices kept within the limits of the discernible and recognizable, against the sanction of being accused of extortion at best and witchcraft at worst. This was not the same composite as the American Petroleum Institute, but still profoundly framed in familiar customary terms.

Inferences

The relationship between customary price, old and novel compositional logics, and popular political culture is a crucial one, and one to which theory itself contributes. Breaking out the components has been seen as a method of intellectual and political insurgency, even though its referent points may be "traditional" or perhaps visionary. Faced as we are now by price skepticism, economic anthropologists could try to sort through the empirical situations and rhetorical and theoretical dynamics. E. P. Thompson (1971) argued that a moral economy imbued the stability of prices in precapitalist England. People were enraged and selectively punitive when they moved out of customary equivalences. The impression is given by scholars in the Polanyi tradition that certain precapitalist commitments survived enough to deeply influence how the fictitious commodities were treated. It is unclear, however, what he thought about a moral economy of the "genuine" commodities and markets in general, particularly with respect to inevitable price fluctuations. What these junctures in oil markets suggest is that "custom" emerges at many points as a stabilizing representation, but that its own techniques of identifying actors and defining categories of cost eventually invite further skepticism when realities break out of the framework: from contango effects to disappearing subsidies to the works of witchcraft. One can clearly imagine that the classic "functions of money"—as equivalent exchange, as hierarchical payment, as fixed standard unit of account—each comes with its own moral compass and its own justifiable version of custom, and therefore that "multipurpose" money and price must always carry the potential for falling apart into conflicting moralities. But each instance of challenge is not necessarily a generic reiteration of this predictable "falling apart." The "modernist" effect of the kind that Latour (1993) theorized, where definitions inevitably breed hybrids, must sometimes generate novelties that fail to fall into any obvious conceptual or moral categories. So do customary accounts, even those drawing on old and familiar nonmarket moral terms, come to conceal as well as reveal, to stand in the way rather than point the way (as Polanyi hoped)?

Where Is Finance? And Is Risk a New Fictitious Commodity?

I am not making a "for or against" argument with respect to risk technologies. This would be futile and presumptuous (since I do not know this field other than through the anthropological and popular literature and personal experience). I am simply moving back and forth from "risk" to the classic work on "fictitious commodities" to clarify each in light of the other, and to pose anthropological questions about the public's changing culture of composite prices.

The extraction of risk from its commonsense matrix—designated variously as "danger," "the wild," "hazard" (Beck [1986] 1992), "rigid long-term commercial arrangements," (Lexecon 2006) or most broadly, a human condition that combines too much exposure with too much commitment—is claimed to be as pervasively important a shift as any that has taken place in the past fifty years. Writers from within the financial sector (e.g,. Gleason 2000; Bernstein 1996) seem in agreement with Beck (1999) and Latour (2005) that the measurement and mitigation of risk/uncertainty have moved us into a new era of market practice, sociality, and social theorizing. Those who operate within the new financial markets describe ever-expanding frontiers of innovation.[4] So important do they consider these interventions that Bernstein rewrites the history of modernity as the history of "the mastery of risk . . . rooted in the Hindu-Arabic numbering system that reached the West seven to eight hundred years ago" (1996, 1, 3). "The past twenty-five years have seen more changes in capital markets than were introduced in the entire prior history, which spans centuries" (Gleason 2000, 3). Niall Ferguson even attributes the final crisis of Russian communism to the "substantial risk premium" (2001, 409) Gorbachev had to pay to borrow on international capital markets that had become more and more precise about profile and reputation.

The rise of risk and its mitigation was not predictable when Polanyi wrote *The Great Transformation*, even though it had precursors in the credit and insurance sector. But according to its practitioners, new financial instruments based on risk calculation have become a fundamental means of global market integration (see Lee and LiPuma 2004) by allowing the vicissitudes in a range of commodity, stock, exchange rate, futures, and new financial instruments' markets to be estimated and mitigated. These vicissitudes can include almost anything: shifts in the geography and timing of demand, political conditions in producing countries, climate shifts and other longer-term changes that fall outside the parameters of "rational choice." We used to assimilate some of this kind of risk management to the many functions of government, valuing it by paying taxes to cover it, and holding officials accountable for its application to any and all "problems arising." But over the past twenty-five years risk management has become more and more independent of government control, extricated from institutions for collective deliberation, and located in the private corporate sphere.[5]

This much is well known (in outline), but what does it mean for our analysis of "popular" or "peopled" (Löfving 2005) economies in the present and future? In my review of our social science literatures, I find that risk turns up with varied referents: as the human condition, as modern sociological principle (Beck 1992), as moral challenge (Douglas 1992), and as various other not-quite-consonant ideas. We have not fully assimilated what risk has actually become as a *gainful commodity*. Beck's seminal book of 1986 looked at "the hazardous side effects to the growth of wealth" (1992, 20) but grasps only at a conceptual level that mitigation will become a commodity with a price. In a later book, Beck (1999) reviews the "eight major points" of his sociological concept of risk and the risk society, none of which grapples with the burgeoning growth of risk management for sale in markets. Neither does the wider social science literature (as judged by the entries in the *International Encyclopedia of the Social Sciences*; Thrift 2001; Yearley 2001) pay much attention to risk instruments as commodities with prices. Latour's (2005) new introduction to Actor Network Theory is organized around "uncertainty" but neither the index nor the chapter titles include either finance or risk or markets or profit or prices. Zaloom (2004, 2005) and Maurer (2006) stand out as taking the profit of risk management in stride as they move into the specific cultures that make the price of risk mitigation plausible and livable.

In the professional finance literature, by contrast, risk instruments are, indeed, noted to be sources of new *profit* as well as enormous intellectual satisfaction and perhaps (even) increased general welfare. In his history of the mastery of risk, Bernstein concludes that "all of them [famous forebears in probability theory] have transformed the perception of risk from chance of loss into opportunity for gain" (1996, 337). But Bernstein himself leaves ambiguous whether he means collective "gain" through the eventual mitigation of shared or generalized risk or something more immediate and individual. Surely he includes the more immediate meaning: gain from the market sale of information about risk and of the control mechanisms to mitigate the projected scenarios. Within the financial world, the profitability of novel risk-management instruments is surely utterly taken for granted. This is one way in which money is made.[6] But the public has yet to catch up in this case. The newspapers try to inform us: "The company [Enron] came to symbolize the transition to a world where practically anything can be traded, from weather predictions to broadband Internet connections to forecasts involving the housing market. . . . Enron pioneered . . . the trading of commodities that had never been traded before." To his credit, the journalist keeps returning to one chorus: "At their best, new markets can provide efficient new forms of insurance, enabling people or businesses to transfer risks they cannot control—for a fee, of course" or "at a price" (Berenson 2006, 1, 4).

I like this passage for two implications. First, like the sociologists, it recognizes that "risk" is "transferred" not eliminated, so we can ask some classic anthropological questions that are rooted in social and semiotic thinking: what is "risk" as a "thing" transacted? From whom and to whom is it transferred? Since mitigation can only ever be partial, where is the excess located in relation to a theory of "ownership" (see Maurer 1999)? But secondly, there are two intellectual icebergs partially hidden in the above passage. The first is the implication that the original object—risk—is already "out there" to be disembedded from a shared social matrix, transformed into a definition, and linked to an insurance strategy, in order to be revalued for sale on the market. Secondly, and probably relatedly, there is a conflation of "fee" and "price" that is very intriguing, given our classic concepts for "the functions of money." Fees and prices are considered by Polanyi and a long list of writers on money as analytically separate: fees as "payment" and price as "exchange" (see Polanyi 1977 for extended discussion). Money as exchange is for "the acquisition . . . of desired goods" (1977, 104) whereas money given in payment "is the discharge of an obligation by handing over quantified units" (1977, 105). The former reflects market forces; the latter social relations. To claim that neither category is stable, and that their relationship is reflexive, is certainly to move beyond the analytical categories that derive from "the first modernity" (Beck 1999). But moving too fast over the process itself of mutual imbrication misses the price moment, when *both* may be explicitly at play at the same time and where both bring specific conditions and consequences into "reality." We do buy a commodity (an insured product) at a price but we cannot choose what modes of insurance it accrues nor whether to buy it (the insurance component), hence the concept of "fee."

Given the ambiguities and perhaps blind spots in new social theory, would it help to apply Polanyi's concept of "fictitious commodity" to lend to risk mitigation some qualities commensurate with its stated importance? Polanyi's entire argument for the world historic disembedding of the self-regulating market from the social matrix in the nineteenth century and its subsequent restructuring centers on the fate of what he calls the "fictitious commodities" of land, labor, and money, which he differentiates from simple commodities.

> None of them is produced for sale. The commodity description of labor, land, and money is entirely fictitious. Nevertheless it is with the help of this fiction that the actual markets for labor, land and money are organized; their demand and supply are real magnitudes. . . . But no society could stand the effects of such crude fictions . . . unless its human and natural substance as well as its business organization was protected against the ravages of this satanic mill. (1944, 72–73)

Social history in the nineteenth century was thus the result of a double movement: the extension of the market organization in respect to genuine commodities was accompanied by its restriction in respect to fictitious ones. (1944, 76)

Polanyi is making three different arguments here, each of which may be relevant. First, he endorses the classical categories of the factors of capitalist production—land, labor, and capital—and their establishment as commodities as the defining characteristic of the historical event of capitalist transition. Second, he refers fictitiousness to the *ongoing* historical battle between society and the disembedded economy. Fictitious commodities *remain* recognizably fictitious because of the continuing inability of the "genuine" commodity form to contain all their attributes. Labor is irretrievably embedded in people and thereby in hunger, anger, mockery, and collective capacities for all kinds of sociality. Land may degrade, subside, and flood. And money is never fully instrumentalized (see Maurer 2006). De Angelis (1999) picks up the *continuing* quality of fictitiousness in Polanyi's terms to argue that Marxian "primitive accumulation" is a continuing process rather than a historical event.

Another way to put it would be through Karl Polanyi's concept of "double movement" (Polanyi 1944). In Polanyi's terms, the continuous element of Marx's primitive accumulation could be identified in those social processes or sets of strategies aimed at dismantling those institutions that protect society from the market. The crucial element of continuity in the reformulation of Marx's theory of primitive accumulation arises therefore once we acknowledge the *other* movement of society. . . . Therefore, the current neoliberal project, which in various ways targets the social commons created in the post war period, set itself as a modern form of enclosure, dubbed by some as "new enclosures." (1999, online, no pagination)

We could argue that it is precisely collective insurance, from the state to localized socialities, that currently constitutes the most important and most lucrative commons that is being privatized and commoditized, but this takes me further than the present paper.

Third, there is another implication of fictitiousness that is particularly important for an anthropology of prices, and perhaps better indicated by Marx under the concept of fetishism than by anything Polanyi developed theoretically. As means of production, the "fictitious commodities" are those that are a condition of *all subsequent actions and transactions.* At the same time as being "means of production," land, labor, and capital are also the selected framing devices to define returns in a conventionalized manner as rent, wages, and profits.[7] As many have pointed out, including Leslie White in anthropology, there are other options for calculating efficiency than reducing it to the use of land, labor, and capital, including energy and information. Beck argues that "we must conceive of *relations of definition* (with respect to risk) analogous to Karl Marx's *relations of production*" (1999, 149; emphasis in the original).

The configuration of risk has not yet been shaken down into a public culture or set of narratives in any of these senses, although the accounts given by its advocates suggest that it certainly deserves to be. The uneven advance of financial instruments in the world (see Thrift 2001) poses familiar political disjunctures and consequent moral ambiguities with respect to those defined outside them altogether. For example, one passing CNN comment after the tsunami of 2004 was that "fortunately most of these people do not have insurance; otherwise the whole industry would collapse." Of course, those who lack private insurance are also those for whom their states have limited capacity for collective insurance, as well. Hence philanthropy. For those living within a developed risk/price regime, the implications of the mode of insurance for day-to-day living are more obscure. Industry advocacy of risk instruments is phrased entirely in terms of the benefits for everyone. For example, for the oil industry, "Consumers benefit because holding down producers' risks encourages investment in future supplies (Lexecon 2006, 16). Beck, however, sees the identification of dangers and their parsing into "risk" and other cognates such as "hazard" as creating "a *bottomless barrel of demands, unsatisfiable, infinite, self-reproducible*"; they are "the insatiable demands long sought by economists" (1992, 23, emphasis in the original). That is, particular markets are so permeated by risk technologies that we would not even know how to unearth exactly what they cost as an added element to the components of the "cost of living" in a risky world or as producing remnants that are "defined out" and thereby fall to our aggregated philanthropic effort. The breakdowns in price and cost-of-living figures, however, come from a different era of stable definitions, and—in this case—definitions that have always rendered aspects of financial costs and benefits particularly difficult to discern. In household budget studies, for example (see below), the interest on a mortgage appears under "housing," not "finance." The difficulty of "seeing" finance and risk mitigation is due largely to the traditional-customary nature of our categories of price composition, even while the exposure of the

compositional process itself seems like a radical shift in public accountability for price levels.

Finance in Comparative Perspective

Does it matter that we can't see the price implications of changing financial instruments? We can detect the insertion of payments into prices when
they directly affect us, or the public at large, when they become issues in
the press. We can look at the phone bill, the insurance bill, and other itemized accounts that do a conventional breakdown for us. Or we can read
the cost-of-living statistics and wonder where certain costs are counted (interest on college loans? fees and rates on credit card debt?). And we can
continue to study markets and prices in Africa in which formal financial
instruments figure only intermittently to offer comparative and analytical
insights. One of the analytical paradoxes we may face is that the places
Bohannan and Dalton (1965) characterized as "peripheral markets" may
well be more competitive and self-regulated than the payment-permeated
systems now growing up in the West. But we are almost certainly grossly
naive about the full range of components that a new ethnography of price
composition could reveal, in all the varied market matrices of the twenty-
first-century world. What people sense without knowing, or simply do not
know but are connected to: these are all elements of consciousness and
consequence, and they must be analyzed.

Polanyi, following Marx (see Halperin 1984), set up categories for
comparative analysis between capitalism and other economic forms. He
lived long enough to see some varied forms arise *within* capitalism, largely
around the economy-society relationship. The expansion of risk instruments as commodities seems to be creating yet other possibilities in the relationship between monetary valuation in price regimes and forms of sociality. Before figuring out how powerful they might be and making sweeping
claims, one needs to first locate the actual ways in which risk instruments
intervene in the world and the terms under which they are understood,
exploited, circumvented, analogized, and so on. I am not yet able to think
forward in time, as Marx and Polanyi did, because it would take the kind of
knowledge of the financial sector that they built up about labor, wages, and
political dynamics over a lifetime of empirical study. Theirs were studies of
practice and not only of principle. What I can do is to think back to how
finance has figured in studies of issues that have been important to us in
anthropology in the past, and ask about the implications of concepts that

conceal it. In a reanalysis of budget studies, I started along the critical track with respect to financial costs by examining the conventional categories of data gathering and analysis (Guyer 2004; Udry and Woo 2007).

There are two implications of this work. One is the implication for a comparative understanding of diffused financial costs as their own component of the price of things in economies in which financial instruments are available versus those where they are not (like the middle and working classes in England in the 1930s; in Africa and other "soft currency" economies in the present). We cannot expect prices to be composed similarly across this spectrum: either in people's consciousness or in the consequences. The other implication is temporal. As financial commitments play out, the purchasers who thought of themselves as "buying a policy" on a human actuarial time frame, may become fee payers living according to strict entailments, for a price, and on pain of monetary sanction. Indeed, the idea of "making payments" as distinct from "paying prices" is far more widespread than it used to be: the service contract, the cable TV, the consumer debt, the penalty for early repayment, transfer costs for bank transactions, and so on. One senses that these small fees based on limitations and cornerings are proliferating in some contexts, appearing in many forms in what are otherwise referred to as "markets."[8] And they may be less and less recognizable, either in the record or in the popular conscience as the price of "something" that is recognizable.

Final Thoughts

There does seem to be widespread tacit acceptance of the idea of the self-regulating market, with price as a mediator of supply and demand in some impersonal sense, and of the idea that this harmonizes with customary configurations that are livable. But with greater emphasis on price and markets, as at present, payments creep in as ever more crucial components of the price of staying in the business of living. Making these price components explicit would constitute a new kind of pragmatic and moral economy. On closer inspection, however, the traditional character of price may conceal its most novel components. So has the moral focus of this new economy taken shape yet? People are being weaned of any "redistributive" expectation. Philanthropy may revive and reshape a morality of "community" and "reciprocity." But is there some other emergent social form or process on which the moral compass and the analytical lens is, or should be, focused?

An anthropology of value that fails to address prices is unsatisfactory, and so are studies of risk and reflexive categories that don't take on the composition, levels, conditions, and consequences of price. Price is a major cultural as well as political-economic phenomenon. I have tried to illustrate key features of this phenomenon that ethnography, and an adaptation of classic theory, could open up much further, in order to realize the potential of new theory for economic anthropological analysis. I agree with Beck (1999) and Latour (1993) that we may be in the foothills of a brave new world, for which past social theory is a limited guide. One of its features, however, is clearly monetization and the components of price: water in drought-prone areas of Africa, insurance against a downturn in housing prices in the United States, a trick with a trafficked Colombian prostitute in Tokyo, a nugget of cobalt dug up by a child laborer in Congo, a portfolio of financial assets, a hedge against exchange rate fluctuation, and the cost of environmental protections. Everything costs. But customary components or a model of "supply and demand plus tax" can no longer constitute a satisfactory popular explanation, nor should they for categories of anthropological analysis. There is a space here to look closely at the categories and their implications for revelation, concealment, and moral commentary in the twenty-first century. Thompson exemplified this for the eighteenth century and Polanyi argued the same when he looked back at the nineteenth and forward to the second half of the twentieth.

ELEVEN

Soft Currencies, Cash Economies, New Monies: Past and Present

Multiple Currencies of the Present

Before we turn to an anthropological perspective on popular monetary practices, the most recent phase of differentiation among national currencies and forms needs a brief review in terms of borders, thresholds, and shifts. After World War II, gold was gradually moved out of its role as the primary reserve, and the great empires were broken up into separate nation states, each with its own currency. In 1969, the system of Special Drawing Rights of the International Monetary Fund was instituted as a component of the world reserve system. Soon after, in 1971, gold backing of fiat money was finally abandoned. The Special Drawing Rights, initially valued against the dollar, eventually became valued in terms of four reserve currencies: the dollar, the pound sterling, the euro, and the yen.

In a brilliantly illuminating review of the dynamics of the fiat money markets in the decade since 1971, Milton Friedman noted the rise in "the demand for money as an aspect of wealth/asset theory" rather than exchange theory (1987, 23). He wrote that "exchange rates have supposedly been free to float and to be determined by private markets. In practice, however, governments still intervene in an attempt to affect the exchange rates of their currencies" (19). What he called "high-powered" money (10), having international reserve functions, became distinguished from moneys with primarily exchange functions over short time frames in relatively unstable political contexts. The dollar was already the world's safe haven, a store of value currency, and it also fulfilled certain key accounting functions. For example, the interest rate on U.S. treasury bills is the standard risk-free rate against which others are measured in portfolio management; derivatives are valued in dollars, and the global oil economy is accounted in dollars. The centrality of the dollar since the 1970s has also offered economists a common denominator comparison—as Collins et al. (2009) show in *Portfolios of the Poor: How the World's Poor Live on $2 a Day*—although a deeper analysis of poverty also attends to purchasing power parity (PPP). The work by Collins et al. discusses the importance but also the difficulty of making and applying PPP calculations (5–7). In many places, however, holding dollars and holding the equivalent soft currency at either the going exchange rate or PPP offer their holders different time horizons for conserving value in money form, which must then affect their projection of futures.

The current multiple currency system of hard (reserve) and soft (exchange) currencies that Friedman (1987) indicated is only about forty years old. It went through additional changes after the revolutions of 1989 in the socialist world, which also gave momentum to the creation of new financial instruments in the 1990s. The wars in the aftermath of the Cold War have siphoned cash dollars into other regions; illegal extraction in the accelerated global search for resources has created clandestine monetary practices; labor migration has expanded the remittance economy; and international online transactions have surged. Therefore, the difficulties of empirical research and theory building with respect to the use of money by the billions of people now living largely in soft currencies and cash emanate, in part, from the brevity, turbulence, magnitude, and apparent irreversibility of these shifts. At the same time, academic theories of decision making have so closely focused on the technical innovations and financial margins to be made on the assumption of the solid platform provided by the dollar, the strong state, financial institutions, information technologies, and precision modeling that theoretical attention to the ongoing composition and erosion of the highly varied platforms for decision making in monetary terms in the rest of the world, as complex sites of human agency, has lagged behind.

Bringing explicit theoretical attention to the soft end of the monetary range, economist Pan Yotopoulos (2006) notes that countries "bear an additional risk of devaluation of their currencies by the positional-good nature of reputational asymmetry" (15). A positional good is one with value as a function of ranking (Hirsch 1976). According to Yotopoulos (2006), a low political reputation can become a self-fulfilling prophecy, because exchange rate shifts, perceptions, and actual political conditions influence one another in feedback loops that can produce unpredictable lurches. Soft currencies' limitation to exchange functions can ensure the restriction of their zones of use and make sudden shifts in purchasing power more likely, in turn ensuring their restriction to those people with little or no choice (that is, the national citizenry at the poor end of the wealth hierarchy).

Within this syndrome of coexisting and interconnected hard and soft currencies, chronic uncertainty can be generated by the money system itself. Take an example of concurrent soft-currency dynamics in the lives of the people. The price of petrol in Nigeria is a complex function of the price of crude oil (the major Nigerian export that brings national earnings in dollars), the price of refined petroleum products on the world market (denominated in dollars and imported back into Nigeria for domestic purchase in naira), and the exchange rate of the naira against the dollar. These variables move against each other in indeterminate ways, whereas the whole artisanal economy and urban food supply depend crucially on the steady supply of gasoline, kerosene, diesel oil, and natural gas for vehicles, generators, home cooking stoves, and light. Under structural adjustment, price subsidy was viewed negatively; however, public debate could never settle on an acceptable definition of subsidy, because exchange rate fluctuations produced their own deviations between world and domestic prices, sometimes referred to as implicit subsidies. As a result, the domestic petrol supply and the terms for understanding it have been a major theme in social and political unrest for thirty years from military to civilian government and into the second decade of the twenty-first century.

Study of domestic prices and markets, therefore, has to take in all of the relevant thresholds between hard- and soft-currency domains: from international commodity and currency dynamics to people's own remittances, small-scale trade across national borders, and global trade diasporas. Additionally, we have to examine how the soft-currency economy manages functional analogs to reserves and futures. We recuperate and take further the classic article by anthropologist Sidney Mintz (1964) on Gresham's Law in Jamaica in the eighteenth century, where he advocates "cross-cultural comparison of dissimilar economies . . . [in the] many contemporary situations [that] afford better testing grounds" of how bad and good moneys coexist and interact (262). British policies in Jamaica were negligent of the people's need for usable cash. The work by Mintz (1964) suggests that "more can be revealed by the specification of the loci of exchange, and the equivalences between media as well as anything which is known about how the equivalences were put in force" (262). Key features across the "dissimilar economies" of "contemporary situations" as well as historical cases may emerge through the configurational logic by which theory, concepts, cases, and comparison are brought together in anthropology (Mintz 1964).

Theory and Logic of Inquiry

The topics and findings in my own fieldwork, museum and archival studies, and library research in Africa (which are taken up later) have led to a central focus on a kind of transaction that a classic anthropological source (Bohannan 1955) referred to as "conversion," a transaction in which a fundamental incommensurability is recognized and preserved. Bohannan (1955) took the conventional definition of conversion—as a transaction translating one national currency into another—and applied it to certain transactions internal to a single society. Drawing on the work of Franz Steiner (1999) in the early 1950s, Bohannan (1955) applied the concept of morally and politically ranked spheres of exchange to the Tiv economy of central Nigeria. Each sphere had its own measure of value and medium of exchange. Exchange within a sphere was termed conveyance and exchange across spheres was termed conversion. It was difficult, and even morally suspect, to convert up from mundane short-term goods to prestige goods and from prestige goods to the rights in people that alone embodied dependable value in the present, mediated the extent of alliances in space, and generated the potential to reach forward in time. West and Central African systems have been termed a wealth in people model, in which the enduring values were embodied: people's skills, their capacity to forge alliances, and their power to reproduce across the generations (reviews in Guyer and Eno Belinga 1995; Guyer 1996). The work by Parker Shipton (2007) on East Africa inserts the concept of entrustment for long-term asset building for economies in which land and livestock also represent and enable the endurance of value and social identity through time. By now, there are several decades of ethnographic study of comparable economies.

The much larger multiple currency economies of world history have left written records for both money practices and moral philosophies of wealth. The pioneering work on multiple currencies by economic historian Akinobu Kuroda (2008a, 2008b) extends the comparative base through detailed archival studies of China, Japan, Central Asia, and parts of Europe. In this approach, which is now widely shared, the classic four functions are disaggregated, and any evolutionary implications of the special to all-purpose trajectory are abandoned in favor of empirical attention to specific practices of legal framing, asset holding, accounting, and transacting across currencies. Where records allow, historical change can also be traced, such as the movement of silver across Asia in the thirteenth and fourteenth centuries (Kuroda 2009). In this comparative context, Friedman (1987) can be seen as reflecting a historical reprofiling of Aristotle's four functions when he focused on the reserve function of money as the most high powered. Aristotle considered the medium of exchange function to be the most important, and wealth was appropriately held in intangibles such as honor and virtue. Therefore, the continuing rise of the reserve function, placing liquidity rather than exchange at the center, would be a historic innovation.

Modernity liberated whole sections of populations from exclusion from one or another kind or function of money, while opening up money itself to having wealth/capital as its primary function: in private and corporate accumulation, the public financial nexus, and the relationship between the two areas. According to the work by Ferguson (2001), it was the invention of the public debt, based on modern sovereign capacities to raise money through taxation and bond issue, that provided the deep pockets from which the state could invest in public goods at home and use military force for wider purposes abroad. In our own era, the work by Ferguson (2001) defines these purposes as "making the world safe for capitalism and democracy" (418). (We make note of the long temporal reach of the key qualities offered by this kind of wealth: safety, capitalism, and democracy.)

In another recent history of the qualities and functions of money in the West over almost five centuries, the work by Amato and Fantacci (2011) shows in detail how this growing primacy of the store-of-wealth function was instituted and theorized and how it has been recurrently elaborated and preserved by central banking, the national debt, and corporate law. The backing of the strongly institutionalized state allowed some debt to join the store-of-wealth nexus, amenable to deferral and accumulation and stretching indefinitely beyond the moral frames of personal life cycle debt under the primacy of the medium of exchange function. The work by Amato and Fantacci reminds us that the term "finance" derives from the Latin *finis*, meaning end. Making endpoints more varied in length, calculation, and management is an advancing technology with intricacies that are partly hidden by the simplicity of the customary terminologies that are enshrined in long-existing law and precedent: "the very concepts of credit and money become hazy" (24).

Amato, Fantacci, and other historians also bring attention to how the cash and markets of the ordinary people's exchange, accounting, and payment functions have been related to the state and wealth function: "Blocked in its function as a store of value, money can no longer function properly as a way of paying off debt" (Amato and Fantacci 2011, 24). The practical conditions of life lived in all-purpose money—that is money that combines the classic purposes of medium of exchange, means of payment, unit of account, and store of value—have been contested in various ways.

The English people in the sixteenth and seventeenth centuries were short on sufficient money to mediate new trades (Poovey 2008, 57) as was the fledgling American colony in its early centuries (Baker 2005; Mihm 2007). People, and even local governments, invented and adopted other things (such as wampum) for a monetary function. Illegal practices included clipping coins and counterfeiting bills, and informal practices included proliferating personal promissory notes and also developing a shared political currency of rhetoric to contest the mercantilist colonial policy of enforced penury in the money supply for the exchange economy. Even under modern conditions, the people have created ear-marking practices and alternative monetary institutions (Zelizer 1995; Maurer 2005c), and within reserve money policy-making circles, there have been debates about how money should function as a unit of account. During the formative 1970s and 1980s, Friedman (1987) envisaged "a still more radical series of proposals . . . that the unit of account be separated from the medium of exchange function, in the belief that financial innovation will establish an efficient payment system dispensing entirely with the use of cash" (36). Keynes had unsuccessfully suggested such a unit of account, the bancor, at the Bretton Woods Conference in 1944.

The prediction by Friedman (1987) of financial innovation in the hard-currency economies has indeed come about, although focused particularly on the elaboration of the wealth/reserve functional nexus and developed on the tracks of the payment nexus in an expanded world of credit and insurance applied to private assets and the expansion of public asset backing in bond markets. The consequent growth of the U.S. national money supply through the financial sector has been, as one set of experts put it, "vertiginous" (Homer and Sylla 1991) since around 1990. Among the kinds of money recognized by the Federal Reserve, a small and declining proportion of the total money supply is in the categories defined as currency (issued by government) and M1 (demand deposits backed by government-regulated liquidity ratios). Currency and M1 are the monies directly manipulable by the people. It is still unclear how mobile moneys will be tracked, regulated, and accounted, and the more inventive online monies can have rules of their own, because they are not (yet) official moneys (Boellstorf 2008; Maurer 2011a, 2011b). The gain in money supply since 1990 has been predominantly in M2 and M3 (that is, financial instruments).

All these histories show processes of mediation within a world of increasing multiplicity. The focus on conversion can be extended then from the old conventional meaning as currency exchange on national borders to transactions between spheres of exchange in small societies on trade routes out into world historical studies of aspects of Western (Ferguson 2001) and global (Hart 1999; Graeber 2011) monetary history and back to mediations in present economies with their newly fractionated rankings, functions, spheres, and communities of money use in a hard- and soft-currencies world. Concern with the experience and sociocultural creativity of the people within the nexus of institutions returns us to empirical research on conversions and their associated ideas and practices through fieldwork.

The next section of the paper moves back to monetary conversions in the vast region of Atlantic Africa: first, for properties forged during the era of the slave and primary commodity trades and second, for the management of soft currency in the present global economy. As a guide through the following ethnography and to prefigure topics that call for additional analytical attention, I list five inferences briefly here.

First, conversionary transactions take place across many relatively nuanced positional differences and not only at major borders and thresholds.

Second, this finding draws us into the study of coexisting positional ranking principles and their intersections: from qualitative difference on nominal variables to simple stepwise ordinal scales to quantified interval scales with arithmetical practices implicated in conversion to iconic ordinality on an exponential logic, where value concentrates at the top of a parabolic curve (a form that seems characteristic of certain ranking principles of the global present) (Guyer 2010).

Third, fictional units of account have served to mediate both the recording of transactions across differently ranked goods and their nature as conversions rather than strict equivalents.

Fourth, the temporal reach of whatever qualifies as wealth is particularly important, especially with respect to horizons along the life span versus spans that are intergenerational, such as legal perpetuity (as with corporations) or reaching even farther into a sovereign future (as with the financial obligations of states) and the life everlasting (in religious terms).

Fifth, the concept of niche serves as an apposite metaphor for the social nexus, where combinations of conversionary concepts, valuation practices, operative time horizons, ethical qualities, and moral-legal commitments are generated (Guyer 1997).

Moneys of Atlantic Africa

I return to the Equatorial African history where I started my work on money in the early 1980s. Until then, the other main strand of my research had been the productive economies of Africa. In the context of studying the growth of the urban food supply (Guyer 1978, 1987), I found a gap between the historians' studies of political economies of regional and international trade and the development economists' analysis of urban provisioning in terms of price-setting markets. The institutions and pervasive practices of valuation and exchange, within and across differently organized societies, were hardly in evidence in the studies of the present. Because markets long predate colonial rule, I turned to the archives and museum collections of indigenous currencies to renew anthropological attention to market value creation in Africa and the localized use of currencies as media of exchange.

I started on an ethnographic history of African currencies and exchange through studies of the varied miniature spear-shaped iron bikie of precolonial Equatorial Africa collected in the nineteenth and early twentieth centuries and deposited in large numbers in ethnographic museums (such as the Peabody Museum at Harvard University). I had run across references to bikie in field research on the history of food production in Southern Cameroon. Made locally from iron ore by iron smelters and blacksmiths, they were said to be used primarily for marriage payments but also for regional trade in other items. In the wider equatorial region, European manufactured currency items had entered through trade over several centuries: copper mitakos, wire, and other idiosyncratic metal forms such as out-of-date French rifles, which in some places, became standards of value in payment systems (Guyer 2004, 43–44). Thirty years ago, I was still able to show museum photographs to old people in Cameroon who could remember how the currency items had been manufactured, controlled, and transacted (Guyer 1985, 1986). Taking advantage of anthropology's multidisciplinarity, I could then follow up with metallurgical analysis of individual museum objects and linguistic attention to the numerical and calculation systems to bring into profile the social experience, technical expertise, and cultural imagination of the whole currency complex. For example, metallurgical analysis from the collections allowed us to estimate the quality and quantity of the iron that was being devoted to moneys and tools. We could then infer the relatively high importance of the exchange and payment economies by comparing the quality and amounts of the iron used for currency in transactions with the iron used for the metal toolkit.

Photographs from several collections allowed the different shapes and their geographical and ethnic distributions to be mapped out (fig. 11.1) to allow for identification of borders in the multiple currency regional system. Additional geographical, ethnographic, and museum analysis (including

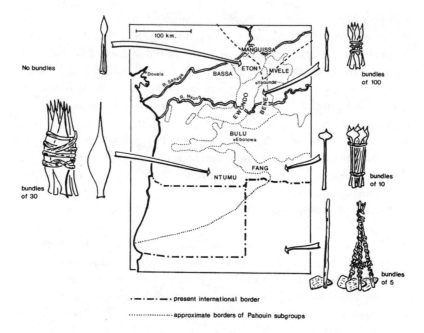

```
·—·—·— present international border
················· approximate borders of Pahouin subgroups
```

collections and acquisitions data from the Royal Museum for Central Africa in Tervuren, Belgium) allowed for the definition of other zones, where differently shaped and bundled currencies circulated. Therefore, two areas could be compared: the forest regions of Southern Cameroon and the vast riverine network of the Ngiri River, a tributary of the Congo. From there, I could reposition the Tiv spheres in regional trade through new historical works (Dorward 1976), then apply these insights to a reconsideration of less fully described systems, and, finally, work out to commonalities and variations in the whole multiple currency economic zone of historical Atlantic Africa as it grew and changed in the context of the slave and commodities trades (Guyer 2004). The basic finding was that, after the mercantilist logic of retaining one's own reserve treasure, the European traders paid at the coast in inconvertible items such as cowries (from the Maldive Islands), brass manillas (manufactured in Birmingham and Nantes), and other items made expressly for the Africa trade. These currency goods made their way inland into regional trade networks, crossing many borders between societies and thresholds within them as they traveled. An intricate multiple currency system of borders, thresholds, and conversions was created.

It became clear that the internal conversions across the thresholds between spheres that Bohannan (1955) saw within the Tiv system could also be made by working conveyances stepwise, in smaller increments by exchanging across the borders into the regional economy and then back again. For example, one could purchase cattle and brass rods from the Northwest with domestically produced tugudu cloth. All of these goods could be exchanged as conveyances within the prestige sphere. Cattle could then be converted up into wealth in people, such as bridewealth in marriages to the Northeast, whereas brass rods could be used to purchase firearms from the South. Tiv tugudu cloth was in demand as one of the currencies of trade throughout the wider region, and therefore, it could be used to acquire a variety of trade goods. Small transactions in the lowest sphere could support the cloth production. Therefore, converting up could be worked stepwise through the labor regime and trade networks. Similarly, in the Equatorial region, there were small shifts in currency use and value as items moved incrementally upriver: each novelty item carried a premium at the interface on the inland border. Cultural terms reflected the shifts in conditions. In Western Nigeria, money was a stranger, coming and going at will (Falola and Adebayo 2000). After I could bring more systems, currencies, and kinds of transaction into view, this kind of small-step conversion became clearly more generalized than equivalence in conveyances.

This preservation of distinction differs in kind from the formally legalized and mathematized modern reduction to common denominators. On classification, I was first instructed by the saying *mekyae, mekyae* in the Beti language: "there are many kinds" of everything. Number itself contained benchmarks and tropic concepts for the operation of ordinal as distinct from simple counting functions. Numbers such as twenty and two hundred had evocative collective qualities, and some large numbers had memorable musical form through the tonality of the language. These tropic points acted as connectors between the rankings that had to be brought together to make a transaction. They allowed unequal equations to be made through matching the same word in different languages rather than matching the exact amounts indicated by that word within its own language. For example, the combination of textual, photographic, and object collections from Cameroon suddenly solved a puzzle of numeration, namely the strange reference to many different bundled amounts of bikie (fig. 11.2) by a term now meaning one hundred (*ntet*). Bundles of as few as five (as referred to in archives) and as variable in number (when counted in the museum) as sixty-five were all *mintet* (plural). Then, an archival photograph and a dictionary both designated *ntet* as a kind of basket (fig. 11.3) and, therefore, perhaps a term for the style of raffia binding around the bundle rather than the number of items that it contained.

These small accounting techniques—names for sortings of diverse goods, formulaic numbers, and types of exchange—retained the transactional history of exchange as conversion. The work by Verran (2001) provides a deeper analysis of the scientific logic here.

The African sources indicate ordinal scales for all goods, with this kind of tropic numbering mediating among them. Criteria for the distinction and ranking in currency-mediated exchange include the kind of good; within one kind, a variety of criteria, including in recent times, a benchmark quality marker (as the original) with named deviations from it; the geographical direction of the trade and the distance of the transaction to or away from the coast; and conventionalized ways of applying numbers to different transactions (cardinal, ordinal, linguistic, and poetic/musical). Precision in the time factor seems to not have been strongly institutionalized, even for delayed transactions. Time itself was managed largely in rhythmic terms rather than on calendars. It was counted in market weeks and seasons, with patterns of auspicious days on their own sequence. Some terms may themselves have stabilized temporal understandings, although such terms are hard to reconstruct empirically. The attachments between scales and the margins gained there did become conventionalized and stabilized in named practices, large and small, within widespread trade and markets without, however, people losing the sense of a marginal gain (Guyer 2004) and an embedded history. For example, in the Southern Cameroonian ceremonial exchange called *bilaba*, trade goods were exchanged between neighboring leaders in a way that performed the non-equivalence of the goods relative to their trajectory to or away from the coast and between the parties to the transaction relative to their prominence as *minkukuma* (usually translated as "headman" but more literally, "owner of wealth," or *akuma*).

History and ethnography both suggest that, more broadly, naming was one of the conceptual tools for market response, change, and innovation. A novel good, practice, crop variety, or currency type was brought into scalar and exchange dynamics by giving it a new identity that both differentiated it from existing goods and also grouped it into an existing class. The users then selectively applied existing knowledge and social templates to the question of how that good or currency would enter into regional and local circulation. In the poetic, oratorical, and musical cultures of Africa, where people performed great feats of memory, naming is particularly powerful for establishing conditions for action in the world.

Formalized fictional units of account are found in the historical record on the coastal trade of West Africa in the era of the slave trade. Fiction means that a currency of account has no material referent or counterpart. The most famous is the trade ounce, which once reflected the value of an ounce of gold. By the height of the trade, it indicated varied sortings of goods according to preferences in the regions (Polanyi 1964; Johnson 1966). Economic historians find that such fictional units of account have been a widespread practice in other areas (Kuroda 2008a, 2008b). There is still much work to be theoretically assimilated here, especially from studies of accounting in the historical practices of Asia, India, the Near East, and Mediterranean worlds, which are the source of mathematical abstractions such as the zero (cipher) and other practices that were brought into Europe by Leonardo Fibonacci in the thirteenth century and credited with supplying the basis for the modern numerical and monetary systems. Indeed, West Africa's integration into Muslim trade through the Sahel and trans-Sahara caravans may well be an important influence on their own number practices, including fictional units of account.

There is one systemic factor of which we can be fairly sure: the preservation of currency items as stores of wealth was indeed framed by the moral ranking to which Bohannan (1955) referred to preclude heritability beyond the personal life cycle. In Ashanti, even masterpieces of gold artisanship were melted down and made over between owners (Garrard 1980). There is an adequate historical record for drawing inferences about money as wealth in Atlantic Africa only (so far) for the manilla economy of Eastern Nigeria (summary in Guyer 2004). Manillas endured for trade in export crops into industrial Europe until the British withdrew them from circulation in 1948. Within the societies of that area, manillas figured in a formalized political ranking process through title societies. Successful people, both men and women, were encouraged to achieve, save, and then convert their manilla currency into the prestige of a stepwise rise in ranked title holding. Their celebrations of advance up the hierarchical ladder then periodically returned the currency to circulation to pay the large numbers of craftspeople, musicians, religious functionaries, and so on who created the arts and architectures of social prominence. Savings and credit were strongly developed but on cycles of years between titles: therefore, beyond the punctual microcredit kind of response to crisis, utilitarian income smoothing over the annual cycle, and small investment but also far short of the in-perpetuity asset building of the modern reserve function.

To summarize, during the era when new currency goods flooded in from Europe, the moneys of Atlantic Africa were largely contained within the medium of exchange and mode of payment functions. They existed in multiple forms and were managed through practices that cultivated elaborate naming and ranking techniques that preserved gain in each transaction. For theoretical and comparative purposes, it is important not to conflate gain with profit in the standard capitalist sense, because it does not arise from production-sale dynamics or the accounting techniques of the state, although the actual amounts transacted in conversions may still fluctuate in response to regional market and trade conditions (Guyer 2005b). These media of exchange currencies flowed at a high velocity of circulation and were indexed to a clearing logic with respect to wealth. They were converted up into the long-term wealth of generational succession and political reach. This was a system of Africa-generated scales and conversions that grew up in light of the inconvertibility tactics of Europe in the interface with Africa and became deeply embedded over centuries. Whether and in what sense there may be continuing dynamics of transformation in these practices, in the context of soft currencies, and in the logics of new economic situations, are questions for localized empirical research. Meanwhile, the case offers comparative insight into systems with variable convertibility. First, however, is the larger question of the nature of present-day soft currencies as a category.

Soft Currencies in Present Day Life

What determines the kind and quantity of money for exchange and payment in the soft-currency economies of the present? Units of account can be fictional. Reserves can be qualitative and even abstract. However, media of exchange generally have some tangibility and some framework for determining the total mass in circulation. Hence, I included cash, even in hard currency, in the comparative study. For people largely limited to currency, M1, and life cycle wealth, having one's ordinary life functions subject to the dynamics of the store of wealth function may have unforeseeable implications, especially when an increasing proportion is in private hands and, therefore, not accessible through the democratic political process and the concept of the public purse. If the store of wealth is not used as a classic capitalist investment fund, which generates production and employment in the human economy, then people may ask what it is doing locked into inaccessible circuits. The alternative money movements have so far tended to be founded on a moral-political general objection to capitalist profit (Mihm 2007). One cannot necessarily assimilate all such oppositions to a general objection to capitalism. The oldest complaint of the ordinary populations in monetized economies is that the controllers of the money supply are not issuing enough into circulation to meet their exchange needs and demands. From plantation Jamaica to colonial America to present-day Nigeria, popular rhetoric has focused explicitly on enemies of the money supply.

I have argued that the Western Nigerian growth trajectory in the popular economy during the latter half of the twentieth century has followed a niche logic (Guyer 1997, 2005). A niche economy grows by developing more and more specialist occupations and crop varieties in greater and greater synergies of collaboration, exchange, and competition with each other across proliferating conveyance and conversion thresholds in response to market growth and improvements in transport, energy supply, and other crucial infrastructures. These niche processes make major contributions to feeding Lagos, one of the most rapidly growing cities in the world. Models based on a frictionless price dynamic cannot show how people move into the opportunities that a growing urban market opens up, because their responses depend on social templates, life careers, and constant circulation of the means of exchange. Whereas the concept of liquidity refers to the capacity of stores of wealth to cross the threshold between functions, the people have to be concerned with their propensity to do so. I have started to think of niche practices, taken together, as platforms, to compare with the hard/reserve currency platforms.

The responsiveness and growth of such a niche economy is deeply dependent on the exchange function of money. A situation of monetary penury for exchange purposes forces people to reexamine all their expectations across all of the lines of synergy and competition. The conventional quantity theory of money in economics concentrates most on the problem of too much money as a source of inflation and, thereby, devaluation of long-term reserve wealth in real terms. In an economy focused on money as a medium of exchange, the real threat is too little money as a stress on the exchange function, the productive economy, and the potential for conversion into the longer-term values in which reserves can be held. The following ethnographic case shows how negatively the failure to convert up by hanging on to money as a reserve can be judged in the kind of moral economy of exchange and niche creation that developed in Atlantic Africa over several centuries.

In ongoing field research in Nigeria, I have been examining two topics that are inaccessible for the past. First is a quantity theory and practice of the money supply for soft currencies, with attention to all of the associated practices and institutions that account for the penury or surfeit in supply, including the velocity of circulation. In the area of Western Nigeria where I currently work, there have been episodes of penury in the money supply because of strikes when government workers were not being paid and—as seen from the people's perspective—deprivation as a result of straight hoarding by the rich and those people in power. The niche economy institutions that maintain the velocity of circulation of the cash currency come under pressure, adapting and eroding in ways that also depend on the second process, namely manipulations of temporal horizons. Following in part from the velocity issue, the temporal horizons in the uses of cash money management come to the fore: the form of accounting and the timing of promissory notes, the deadlines for debt clearance, the moral judgment that shifts keeping or saving into hoarding, and the life paths of intergenerational expectations. Yoruba terms for debt make a clear distinction between delayed payment (*awin*), usually fixed on the market cycle, and debt (*gbese*), which is dated, incurs a fee, and is usually backed by a guarantor. Very long-term obligations fade into other categories. The terms that we might translate as "saving" distinguish between taking care of (*toju*), storing (*pamo*), and locking away from others (*hawo*). The first term is morally fine, the second term is tolerable but questionable, and the last term is reprehensible. People with money are under pressure to lend it out. Charging interest or fees is acceptable; locking money away, effectively reducing the stock of currency in circulation, is not acceptable. The reserve function returns as a topic for research, particularly in relation to the study of time horizons.

In the West, it was the theorization and institutionalization of the phases of a standard life cycle in the 1950s and 1960s that laid the basis for a new phase of Western financialization and securitization processes (Modigliani 1986): student loans, thirty-year mortgages, health insurance, and so on. How life—its arc, cycle, or pathway of many intermediate and cumulative or disrupted steps—is then lived in relation to reserve money instruments in the soft-currency economies and cash-based niches of common practice is a topic that invites new attention. The coordination of the temporal multiplicities that make up life as sequences of entailments in between the short-run impulse of choice and the long run of an eventual deferred and abstract future is the theme of my paper on theoretical evacuation of the near future (Guyer 2007b, here chapter 4) in Western economic culture before the crisis of 2008. One key gain that upward conversions in this near-future range can achieve is to buy time: not as quantity alone but as reach to future horizons of varying distance. Conversely, converting down foreshortens time. For anthropologists, the space of the near future and the operation of media of exchange and units of account in that space open up to additional empirical inquiry.

Conclusion

By this logic, then, we must necessarily examine the novelties of present monetary systems in a broad and ever-widening historical and comparative perspective. Although some anthropologists do address the financialized segment of world monies—what the economics textbooks refer to as M2, M3, and now (sometimes included in the macroeconomic analyses) derivatives—there is also within anthropology an expanding attention to the monies of the people (that is, the currency and M1 [demand deposits] of money supply theory). Maurer (2005b, 2011a, 2011b) comes to this domain through his increasing empirical focus on e-money and the poor, asking what this e-money is in the long history of money and how it is being domesticated by people in practices of their own, which may or may not come forward from the past. The work by Hart (1999) reviews the long history of money and considerably sharpens our conceptual repertoire with his heads-or-tails-of-the-coin distinction (Hart 1986). The work by Graeber (2011) examines debt over the first five thousand years. I have continued to work at the day-to-day level of life-as-lived in Nigeria, with modern polymer bank notes, including paying attention to people's own concepts of value, means of numeration and calculation, management of the functions of money, and their moral economy of cash transactions and future promises under conditions that they recurrently define as *kòs'ówó* (Yoruba term for "there's no money," see Guyer with Salami and Akinlade 2011). Others work on the management of remittances and cash in both hard and soft versions and their conversion of value from one moral domain to another. East Asia is particularly interesting in this regard (China is discussed in Chu 2010, and Vietnam is discussed in Kwon 2008). These are the mundane and legal practices of the people. The larger topic would include currencies in war zones (Nordstrom 2008) and among illegal mafia networks.

Hard-currency systems do store and protect wealth in money. Their conditions of existence, however, are historically recent, particular, and rapidly changing, and therefore, they are not amenable to an assumption of normality across time and space. They can affect the functioning of currencies that are restricted to being media of exchange, and their real and symbolic power may also preclude new innovations in the kind of monies of account that historians have found in many past systems, Keynes envisaged for post–World War II, and Friedman (1987) mentioned as a frontier for the world post-1971. When the monetary world is examined from the standpoint of those people who depend crucially on its medium of exchange function, the five topics prefigured earlier and illustrated here loom large: the many frontiers on which conversions take place (including but not limited to international exchange rates), the value scales that structure transactions as conversions among positional goods, the units of account that record transactions, the temporal horizons that different monies and financial instruments offer to their holders, and the niche-like communities of ethics and practice that conventionalize all of these factors into transactional regimes. Because so many of the world currencies are soft to some degree and so many people live within soft-currency systems and largely within the cash nexus of hard-currency systems, these topics coming out of the historical and anthropological archive become compelling frontiers for empirical study and analytical development.

Acknowledgments

Fieldwork support in Nigeria by Kabiru Salami; collaboration on the study of the Nigerian petroleum economy by LaRay Denzer; and comments on this paper by Bill Maurer, William Milberg, and Akinobu Kuroda are gratefully acknowledged. LaRay Denzer edited the manuscript.

TWELVE

Is the "Real Economy" Disaggregating, Disappearing, or Deviating?

This paper is a new reflection on the concept of the "real" as we find it in economic life, in economic anthropology, and in more general questions of method that I raised in order to introduce this collection of past papers. It arose, as a discrete topic, from the work for the CPI paper, and from discussions with colleagues in Latin America, for whom the "real" (as indices) and "real life" (in some vernacular sense) have been lived in enormous tension with each other (Neiburg 2010). Then there are ways in which economic anthropology has taken "reality" and "realization" in new directions. And, behind this, there are broader and deeper theoretical shifts that do implicate, I now think, the puzzlingly low attention to the elements that make up assemblages, and their manner of expressing, or pertaining to, framings that are otherwise being placed under a deeply skeptical scrutiny, such as objectivity, materiality, and nature, as part of the culture of "the moderns." Some of the skepticism is due to what is seen as the moderns' intellectual custom of binarism in which each of these terms is implicated: real/imaginary, objective/subjective, material/abstract, nature/culture (or construct), actual/virtual. We could add tradition/modernity and many other similar binary analytics that anthropology has drawn on in the past. Linked to this is the avoidance of allowing any implications of essentialism to creep in. In addition, though, the apparent skirting around "elements" in the ANT-Economics work seems due to entailments of the emphasis on performativity, so on the forward-looking projective processes in the immediate situations in which assemblages are framed and activated rather than on the preceding modes of existence that might account for their presence on the scene, in some condition that allows them to be "found" (as in the artistic framing, as "found objects").

In economic life, however, the "real" has been too crucially important a concept to try to contain so vigorously, without analysis of its past and present technical uses, and its vernacular applications. Its referents and meanings have changed over hundreds of years, and the term is still applied in governmental and analytical contexts. So I think that our ethnographic philosophies and epistemologies are challenged to take on its active presence. With the proliferation, and also dispersal, of the use of the concept of the "real" in economic scholarship and in commentary in the public sphere, and given the very long-term struggle in anthropological research with a touchstone for the "real" when both empiricism and constructivism have been intertwined, the economic concept of the "real economy" and its various vernacular uses make sense as a topic to open up here, as a way of closing this collection.

The "real economy" is a topic that has animated several of my recent interchanges with international colleagues. These conversations, and engagements with the new anthropology of finance, sharpened my interest in the concept of "the real" and hence provoked a journey back into the philosophy and theory of "realism." This has led me directly to the discovery of a philosopher who was unknown to me until now, a Scottish contemporary of David Hume—Thomas Reid—whose work on the "philosophy of common sense" helps clarify certain relevant conceptual and epistemological issues on which he argued with Hume and offers a different pathway into the pragmatism from which the ANT theorists also draw. Charles Sanders Peirce depicted his own philosophy as "critical common sensism," drawing directly on Reid's work. My reading of Thomas Reid also offers a guide to a terrain I recently explored in a paper on anthropological method in general, entitled "The Quickening of the Unknown: Epistemologies of Surprise in Anthropology" (Guyer 2013b). An advance reader of this collection remarked that there is a pervasive sense of "puzzle" in these papers. In that recent paper on the intellectual importance of surprise, I referred back to Hume's empiricism, where I followed a particularly puzzling space within its logic. Hume famously wrote: "Reason is, and ought only to be, the slave of the passions," which was a position appreciated and developed further by Deleuze (1991) in his analysis of empiricism and subjectivity. Passion impresses, at the beginning of the creation of knowledge, and settles, at the end. Reason traces the pathways between the two. They meet, obviously, in the two transitional pauses in which the shift is made from one to the other. So, my question became, what are the first and last steps in that arc of thought that starts and ends in passion (impression), the transition in which reason picks up and rests its trajectory? Deleuze adopts the principle of habit and association, and the endurance of passion *within* imagination.

In my own case, I drew on sources on African divination to suggest that "it is not *my own* curious mind but my receptive attentiveness to phenomena that declare *their own* existence that comes forward" (Guyer 2013b, 289).

Circling through Reid, Hume (and their mutual influence, in person), Deleuze, Peirce, the ANT theorists, the anthropological sensibility, the historical imperative, political economy and current experiences, in places outside of "the West," to address "the real" would require yet another book, but the connections seem compelling to me with respect to my own question here, namely, is there a space for "the real" in economic anthropological work on the present, in some mode that is recuperable from the complex nexus of philosophical debate about constructs, from the shifting uses of the concept of the "real" in economic life, and from the daily turbulence of "real life" in so many places? So, finding a provisional harbor-for-thought between the otherwise separate journeys along which "the real" comes into play—in economics, in the relevant anthropological literature, with respect to more general philosophical questions, and in life—can make for an anchoring place for what were always exploratory papers, whose own trajectories will continue.

The Real Economy: Some Historical Landmarks

Outline

"Real," as in real money, may sometimes have referred to the intrinsic value of bullion, as a material commodity, on the precious metals market. The gold standard, as the backing for banknotes, lasted almost two hundred years (de Cecco 1984). This, however, was not the meaning of "real" as applied to the economy at large. In fact, in the sixteenth century, it was the wave of bullion from the Americas passing into Europe that provoked the defense of "real" as a value. The "real economy" has been the subject of major theoretical engagements and has generated some of the most powerful concepts in national and international financial governance. In the past, the concept of the "real economy" used to denote the value attributed by a particular population to the conditions for transactions of goods and services alongside, but independently of, their nominal price in money. As if the market exchange could be barter. For Adam Smith, money was a convenience created by reason, as a means of exchange. For the quantity theorists of money, money was supposed to be neutral with respect to value, and nominal prices a veil for real value, which emerged from the lives and preferences of the people. In the twentieth century, Keynes opposed the implications of the "real economy" theories because they failed to deal with the *active* role played by money, liquidity, interest rates, and all the particular attributes of *capital*, as distinct from the *market*. The economic theoretical concept of the "real economy" was downsized into an indicator of the inflation rate: the *changes* in the purchasing power of money, year to year, as a central, and internationally reportable, component of national economic dynamics. "Real value" remains with us in the vernacular world, where we still use the concept of "worth" to indicate a vague implicit value, as in "getting your money's worth" in the market. With the recent expansion of the financial sector, the concept of the real economy has returned in public discourse and economic journalism, as a contrast with the paper economy, although its referents are vague and varied.

The one attribute that the "real" appears to retain through the changes is its literal etymological implication of a thing, *res* in Latin, and therefore something that endures through time. The materiality of thingness, however, has also varied over time. As Luigi Einaudi (1953, to be discussed later) pointed out with respect to medieval and early modern valuation, the material world was seen as a passing world. Reality lay with God, therefore the possibility arose for being "scrupulous in preserving the identity of the *word* pound in *sound* rather than in *value*" (Einaudi 233; italics added). In the current world, where versions of essentialism, constructivism, and more radical indeterminacy have coexisted across philosophies, within different constituencies of interest, and through the changing situations in the world, a basic and powerful historical word such as "real" can morph and shift in deeply evocative ways.

A Brief Review of Origins and Development

As far in the past as the early sixteenth century, Copernicus, writing for the new Poland in the context of a history of wars and struggles, expressed concern about how the quantity of money in circulation would affect prices and values. This was the period when bullion from the New World began to move through European economies, bringing inflation, and normative political-economic communities were being undergirded by mercantilism, predicated on the preservation of a treasury of national wealth. Although I have not been able to trace the first uses of the term "real" back this far, there was clearly an assumption that the preservation of values, and value in general, against fluctuations, erosion, and outright military and political attack lay at the heart of governance.

The first version of the quantity theory of money is attributed to

Copernicus (1473–1543). He was the child of a merchant from Danzig, the major Hanseatic port of the eastern Baltic, and advised the government of Royal Prussia on monetary policy as the area realigned with the king of Poland in the face of attack by the Teutonic League, and following years of sporadic warfare. His theory was therefore a state-building enterprise. He points out that an oversupply of money can threaten a communal sense of value. Monetary exchange ought to reflect and express culture: "La monnaie est donc en quelque sorte une mesure commune d'estimation des valeurs" (Money is therefore in some manner a shared measure for the estimation of values).[1]

The question then arose of whether "real value" could be indexed and measured in terms of something tangible. One of the metaphors for the goals of monetary policy was to produce a situation in which money is a veil, leaving the actual price relationships within a system to be a function of something of more stable value, which would not be susceptible to surges and retreats in quantities of the medium of exchange. These could be the supply/demand configuration within a single economic system, which was taken to reflect the population's values in the normative sense, and/or the abstract measure of a key input into a commodity, which would be most basically—for over a hundred years and through several different political convictions—a measure of labor. The labor theory of value was a convention and conviction shared by the classical theorists, including Adam Smith, David Ricardo, and Karl Marx.

There is a fascinating, but not very well-known, literature on another historical artifact that anchored value in times of political turbulence and monetary experimentation. Copernicus would surely have known of this from his family history in the Hanseatic League: the convention of "imaginary monies," for which there was no material form at all and which mediated exchange rates and functioned in trade as units of account. It was the terms themselves that defined "entities" to be quantified, such as pounds, and *livres*. Einaudi (1953) wrote on multiple currencies and imaginary moneys in European history, where particular monetary concepts were used in trade and accounting, when the actual transactions were taking place in other currencies. A money of account was "an instrument of extraordinary flexibility which had been slowly developed in the ten centuries after the reign of Charlemagne" (241). Many gold and silver coins circulated. The market price of bullion fluctuated. Einaudi argues that a sense that value could be unstable was inimical to medieval orientations in life: He quotes Galiani (1750) in arguing that prices should reflect "the consensus of the public," in a culture where "the longing of medieval men for the eternal, the immutable, the universal, [is] accompanied by an abhorrence of the transitory, the mutable, and the particular" (246). Confidence then depended on the unit of account, and its stability through time for all parties to transactions and predictions. In terms that would seem familiar to us now, he argues that "imaginary money," created from below, was "a mere instrument or technical device used to perform some monetary functions" (237). In this configuration of the cosmos, it was the imaginary that was more real, in the sense of enduring. Substance was subject to fluctuation, dissipation, and deterioration.

The practice of devising devices that stabilized, or gave the impression of gravitas to, money exchanges over time under highly unpredictable conditions was brought forward into the merchant practices of the slave trade. It is remarkable that in the merchants' accounts, where more than one fictional unit was being deployed, the units' purchasing power hardly fluctuated at all *against each other*, over time, even where the tangible goods shifted in their money prices and there were several different currencies in circulation. Table 12.1 on the relative values of the bar, the trade ounce, and the rigsdaler has been reconstituted from several empirical sources (especially Johnson 1966). The stability is remarkable, over a century of shifting currency prices and volumes of trade.

At the same time, Einaudi suggests that this was largely a culture where the relevant range of confidence was created among the traders. He writes that the ordinary people often saw the system as "surrounded by a thick mist of strange terminology, repellent to the layman and conducive to deceitful practices. . . . The public was befuddled as to what was actually going on" (1953, 247–48). His implicit distinction between the real (the stability in the exchange rates among imaginary monies of account) and the actual (the logistics of life on the ground) might be useful to keep in mind. It is also useful to remember the etymology of the term "barter," which includes the notion of trickery and cheating, as well as exchange of ideas. So barter's assumed equation with the emergence of "real" value, according to a population's collective values, need to be reentangled with the contents of historical cultures of confidence. This moves it away from

Table 12.1 Correspondences among imaginary units, Atlantic Africa in the eighteenth century

Bars to ounces	Rigsdaler to ounces
1723: 15	1749: 18
1790: 14	1784: 16

a seamless equivalence with "truth." As barter, it can only refer to the concepts and orientations within a collectivity with market-relevant values and engagements, other than simply desire and "demand" in some objective, quantitative sense. "Real" emerges from European economic history as an aspirational concept, within communities of practice.

In certain historical and cultural contexts, therefore, what is fictitious, as with Polanyi's fictitious commodities, may well represent something that has been seen as *more* real than the material, in the sense of enduring: an endurance that is ensured by committed and skilled constituencies, applying their craftsmanship to the situations of their times. The history of trade and markets shows how Platonic-type essentialism, as a point of reference in an inconstant monetary world, has taken different forms: a substance such as gold, a concept such as a fictional unit of account, an authority such as God (and His representatives on earth), or perhaps the emperor's imprimatur, in long-lasting imperial systems. Several of the crucial innovations in the creation of European monetary practices were made under the auspices of monasteries: double-entry bookkeeping in the fifteenth century, with its aura of "purity" (Carruthers and Espeland 1991), and the calculation of time and money underlying modern interest-rate-making, by the School of Salamanca in Spain in the sixteenth century.

The eighteenth century is always considered a seminal era in the development of modernity, including the theory and practice of national market economies. It is also a strangely inventive and challenging century to make sense of. The theory of a national economy with its own "representative money" and shared values in a "real exchange economy" was established alongside a practice—by the same people—of exporting currencies as commodities in one of the most lucrative trades in world history: the Atlantic slave trade (Inikori 2002). John Locke theorized liberty, ran the Royal Mint (so punished counterfeiters and coin clippers, doing their own "inventions"), and invested in the Royal African Company, one of the main British companies in the Atlantic slave trade, which profited from commodity currencies. The fact that both national economy and international trade were intrinsic to the development of the early modern economy and economics creates an instigation to dig further into practices on the ground, and into how concepts gravitated back and forth, from the practices in the margins to the concepts at the center. In a pamphleteer's comments in 1811 criticizing monetary policy in England, we can already see the paucity of nuanced concepts for money and value, and the convenience of importing concepts already in circulation elsewhere. The author, one Joseph Smith, expresses himself in terms very close to those quoted by Einaudi for previous centuries. The following passage (Guyer 2013a) picks out the terms he uses.

> "Had they only examined a little farther, they must have discovered that, in every country there exists another standard of value, a nominal or imaginary, one, of which the coins, passing in circulation, are only symbols or tokens; and which standard is perfectly invariable" (5). He then uses "barter" in its most inclusive sense: for all exchange, including the barter of ideas which "leads to growth and accumulation of knowledge" (10). Against a labor theory of value, he argues that "labour may be the real measure of value, but not the value by which it is commonly estimated. . . . [Rather, there is] a rough equity which, though not exact, is sufficient for varying on the business of common life" (20). "Value is not a quality inherent in any thing" (23); indeed, "value in exchange is . . . entirely fictitious" (30). Here he uses the "bar" in the slave trade as an example. "The African when he valued his slave at 100 or 150 bars of iron did not expect really to receive that quantity of iron in return, he only looked for a quantity of rum, tobacco, cloth, &c equivalent thereto" (32). It was Whites who fixed 1 bar at 2 shillings (presumably at a particular moment in time), so a slave whose price in L15 "is said to be worth 150 bars." He then extends this line of reasoning to the pound sterling at home, where there remains a cultural concept of the value of the pound, even when completely released from its content as "sterling." "All that was required was a fixed point of comparison" (35), which he then advocates for England in the early nineteenth century. The real, in this case, is the "worth": the value of a fictional unit, the pound, released from "sterling" but continuing as a "fixed point of comparison."

There is surely a deeper and longer history to all these practices with respect to value, endurance through time, and money than I have been able to configure here, especially of their applicability in Europe and its trades outside Africa, in the wider world. Akinobu Kuroda (2013) has found fictional units of account in Chinese history. Such a history would greatly inform an exploration of the range of what has been considered to fall within the realm of the "real," its relationship to the "fictitious," the related naturalist concept of "normal" or normative, the meaning of the "actual," and the place of money in the whole mix. The potential for slippage, or for insistent precision, across the range of terms to which "real" belongs is profound. Doubtless some of these philosophies and practices from the past inform and legitimize the category of element that I have termed "legacies."

One classic divide within the very long history of economic thought is implicated in certain trajectories: Aristotle's (*Politics*, bk. 1, pt. 2)[2] division between economics (based on *oikos*, the household economy), which was natural, for provisioning; and chrematistics (the accumulation of wealth in money), which he saw as unnatural. The more that economic activity moved into money making, the less "real" it would be. Brought forward into the twentieth century, and into market economics, the "real exchange economy" was a concept used by Keynes to identify how classical economic theory brought the "real" in as a misrepresentation, as itself a fiction, in order to maintain a general theory of value and to control the place of money and finance in their analyses. He writes ([1936] 1964, 30): "It may well be that the classical theory represents the way in which we should like our Economy to behave. But to assume that it actually does so is to assume our difficulties away." In fact, Keynes writes of the "real economy" assumption: "this procedure deprives our analysis of all reality" (60). With his focus on employment conditions, he argues that the supply of labor is not solely a function of real wages, and that we need a different framework in order to examine "the actual employment" (8). Fantacci (2013) argues that Keynes's writings on money were aimed at escaping from this relegation of money to only the question of quantity, consigning it to being a "veil," in order to address money as it actually operates, which he saw as a kind of capital that redistributes income toward rents, which then pulls it out of the kind of investment that generates employment. Hence a theory of value, which used to undergird all reference to the "real" in economics, went into cold storage, often replaced by "actual," for reference to economic activity. In technical terms, it survived only as an index of inflation rates.

The extraction of real wages and prices from a nexus in any strong, or even strongly *implicit*, theory of "the real economy" as a whole system was instituted in the early twentieth century with the consumer price index. A standard basket of goods was defined, after the concept developed by Arthur Pigou, of "wage goods": "goods upon the price of which the utility of the money wage depends" (Keynes [1936] 1964, 7). The money price of the basket of standardized goods, from year to year, is assumed to reflect the money mass and its circulation, as well as market conditions of supply and demand, so the comparison is calculated to make an index of inflation. This generates "real wages," "real prices," "real interest rates," and inflation adjustment for any monetary quantity written into commitments over time frames longer than the one year on which each study is based. This then became the device through which the money-economy prices were normalized for national and international comparisons and for calibrating social payments, some commercial instruments, and economic projections that are indexed to inflation. Inflation indices are crucial to the international economic governance from the International Monetary Fund and to assessment of macroeconomic summary statistics such as gross domestic product. The IMF model for creating a CPI is generally applicable to all member countries, and the calculation, and power, of GDP in specific cases (Jerven 2013 on Africa), and in general (Fioramonti 2013), has come under critical scrutiny. The GDP system has been accused of encouraging countries to "cook the books" in one way or another to manipulate the projection of economic growth. Most recently, several European countries have included gambling, sexual services, and some illegal activities such as the drug trade in the calculation of GDP (Alderman 2014) in order to reflect monetary transactions with greater accuracy, although how this refers back to the composition of the CPI remains to be seen.

Although it is not entirely uncontroversial, this particular use of the concept of "real" as an index of inflation is not yet under totally adversarial critique, in a way comparable to Keynes's dismissal of the "real economy" as a misleading representation of the capitalist system in the 1930s, which included a broader critique of a purist approach to the commodity market alone as driving economic dynamics under capitalism. We may be entering yet a new era of the formal documentation of "the market," to comprise the so-called sharing economy and the "second machine age" (Brynjolfsson and McAfee 2014). Given the deeply institutionalized importance of indicators of inflation, economics has retained the concept of the "real" by migrating it largely into specific instruments in the macroeconomic policy domain. Cochrane's (2005) article, written for the National Bureau of Economic Research, entitled "Financial Markets and the Real Economy," is particularly devoted to how monetary policy affects financial markets. Here, the "real economy" is seen essentially as a source of instability, of possible "bad times," whereas assets are projected to maintain and grow their monetary value. Model building focuses on how projected "real economy" fluctuations will affect the demand for high returns on assets in the shorter-run conditions that affect markets. In an economic world of expanding categories of assets, submitted to their own market pricing, this shift of the "real" into government policy is perhaps partially due to its effects on inflation-adjusted financial products and the overall projections needed for asset valuation.

The shifting meaning of the real here is possibly linked, conceptually, to the rise of assets as distinct from capital in the broader sense. A massively broader range of "things" can now be priced in money and can carry *varying* implications of holding value over time frames that are long enough to generate a regular income stream, through financialization. In the era when the real economy was invented, most of what we now call assets, such as land, rarely went onto the market at all. The market was mainly "goods and services." Piketty's graphs (2014, 116–17) of the shift in the composition of national capital show a rapid decline in agricultural land as capital over the twentieth century and a rapid rise in housing. Both land and houses would have changed hands largely through inheritance in the past. They now change hands in marketplaces, and the price value of housing has been deeply imbued with financial instrumentalization (mortgages, for example), through which it has shown remarkable conceptual and legal-contractual stability and very significant quantitative growth in money value, and thereby can promise future income. Aristotle's *oikos* is moved into the realm of chrematistics, and in an age of rapid change in the units depicted as "households," even the term *oikos* itself is becoming anachronistic. As the CPI revision paper of 1996 shows, the housing category now accounts for 41 percent of the value in the "basket of goods," and, as I recount in the next section, energy—one of the most basic of basic needs supplied by "shelter services"—has also moved into financial markets in novel ways.

Assets, as whatever can be sustained in value over time, have expanded and moved more deeply into the financial sector. Aspects of the human body and its somatics can be turned into assets: body parts, surrogate parenthood, DNA, and so on. Even though many enduring aspects of human and social existence are at the basis of the inventive processes by which they are converted into assets, each conceptual step in the formalized sector seems to back farther away from any broad substantive meaning of the term "real," as meaning enduring "things" and values. The shift moves *instability* out into the realm of macroeconomic indices and policy, now referred to as the "real economy." The real is the indices referred to by the word "real," thus resonating with Einaudi's depiction of imaginary units of account where the word "pound" endured, whatever it actually valued, in whatever amounts. In the context of expanding asset markets, the public sphere discussion has sharpened its own allusion to the actual, tangible, material aspects of life, and to the content of the wage-good basket rather than to the index it generates. Thus are the referents of the "real" diffused across a range that now comprises inconsistency, especially with respect to the locations of unpredictability. The search for conceptual grounding has the qualities of a scramble.

Economic Culture in Journalism and the Public Sphere

Although the CPI gives the "real" a very specific referent, in the economic journalism there remain certain vague general purposes for which "real" is mobilized, such as to designate the manufacturing sector of the economy, which produces "real" things, in the tangible sense, for "people," sometimes with the designation of "natural," and reflecting societal "norms." For example, in an article entitled "Get Ready: Here Comes the Real Economy," the author writes of his

> demographic study comparing lifetime investment and spending patterns derived from societal norms and compared to economic cycles since 1900. . . . It is the lifelong natural investment cycles that we experience throughout our lives that govern long-term economic cycles. . . . Unless society changes significantly, people today will continue to live their lives similarly to the way our parents did, and our children will do the same, all technological changes aside. That means we will grow up, go to school, buy a house, raise a family, send our children to college, retire, and by that time our children will start the cycle all over again. This is a societal normality, and the findings of the Investment Rate are predicated on these societal norms, . . . [so investors should be attentive to] the real underlying economy and the almost certain reversion to the natural growth rates. (Kee 2013)

One can see how "the life cycle as a rational proposition" is proposed again, as being external to finance, also "natural" and "normal": an objectively knowable and predictable life, and hence a particular kind of calculable opportunity for financial investors. Of course, the census and the rates of house rental show that these conditions and aspirations no longer prevail in the same way as they could be constructed in the postwar period, at the time of the institutionalization of "the American Dream" (actually, a generally Western Dream, as Piketty shows through his graphic parallels). So "real" and "true," and even "aspirationally normative," can part company from each other, and yet also be forcefully merged back together by retaining old terminologies and administrative practices, as I suggest in a review of the "household" in relation to methods such as the CPI (Guyer 2014). The "real" here becomes something more like "the familiar," what is generally understandable to large segments of the ordinary population, or what moves forward as an institutionalized legacy. Or even what inspires confidence enough to support implausible assumptions. Gregory (1997) gives a sharp example of this last assumption. To encourage the wealthy to find "escape hatches" to store their wealth, an adviser suggests that "only gold and silver remain widely available . . . *real money*" (286; emphasis in the original). Each participant and situation brings out its own vernacular meaning of "real" for inclusion in the mix. Such an old concept in economic life has much to bring.

A broadly inclusive meaning is exemplified by Gillian Tett, of the *Financial Times*, when she referred to Janet Yellen, as she came in as the new chairman of the Federal Reserve Bank, as a Keynesian who would be more focused on the human economy, the whole economy, the real economy (PBS *Newshour*, January 7, 2014). This is a different meaning from the term than Keynes would have used, but then Gillian Tett is an anthropologist by training, and what was being indicated here would be Keynes's emphasis on employment, and thereby on the lives of the people, as distinct from the investors.

A recent newspaper article (Creswell and Gebeloff 2014) brings the financial and the "real" together, in this public-culture sense, with respect to a very specific financial instrument. The overworking of the American power grid, in times of peak energy demand, in a deregulated and private-sector market structure, has provoked the development of localized "congestion contracts"—"complex financial instruments that gain value when the grid becomes overburdened"—that mediate and hedge the resulting sudden price rises. They were intended to generate funds, and provide incentives, for private investment in infrastructural improvement. Derivatives of this market have now been devised and traded. Some financial organizations hold thousands of congestion contracts and make large profits, which come out of the higher prices paid by consumers during these times. In terms very similar to the financial-sector ethnography, the operators use the terms "formula," "algorithm," and "computer-driven trading models." The authors of the article then describe market "manipulation" undertaken to convey the impression of impending or actual congestion conditions, in order to mediate them financially, to increase profit. They refer to this as "non-real congestion" and mention the importance of monitoring bodies getting data in "real time" to identify and combat it. Fictional is straight fabrication in this case. To nail the point about abstraction from daily life, the article points out the origins of these algorithms in the specialist mathematics of Ivy League PhDs and a particular Harvard professor who invented the basic concept of the congestion contract. It then counterposes these personages with comments from the mayor of a small affected town, who invokes the "ratepayers" as the rightful recipients of any benefits from the congestion contracts, which were supposed to make markets more efficient. The concept of the "real" returns to its grounding in the familiar, the local, the immediately accessible, and their political-ethical frames of reference. But as enduring assets, the congestion contracts are real, and energy cost itself figures in the CPI, so informing some part of the 41 percent of the index that derives from "housing" costs and then recirculates into economic analysis as a component of the "real economy," understood as the macroeconomic world that produces inflation rates. The financial component of the energy price to the consumers and communities remains disguised, as I suggest in the paper on price composition.

For any ethnographic style of inquiry, these shifts in the concept of the "real"—from value in general, to money-inflation measure, to tangible goods and services, to natural norms of the human life cycle, and to whatever is familiar—command attention, in the manner I suggest in several of the papers. The price system is an enormously complex platform, from rationing in wartime to congestion contracts in the financial markets of the twenty-first century. Both mediate scarcity under duress, have distributional implications, and reach into ethical-political domains where the use of "real" crosses the whole spectrum, in an inconsistent and punctual fashion, or may be sidelined altogether by reference to efficiency as the touchstone. Under the current market philosophy, monetary transactions of all kinds are no longer considered as conceptually, ethically, or pragmatically challenging as our early forebears considered them to be.

We can then examine whether, how, and by whom the "real" and its varied possible contextual antonyms are created and conserved as an archive to be deployed; also how, and where, "real" is equated with material and nature. Which is ephemeral: substance, because it erodes, or fiction because it can evaporate without trace? What is enduring: substance because it stands, as a thing, or fiction because it has shown how tenaciously ideas can endure, and travel, and return, as what scholars in literature and the arts call reprise? And where, then, is turbulence located? It seems to me too limited an understanding of the "real" conditions of life, for large portions of the human population, to depict their lives in terms of risk, uncertainty, and indeterminacy as these terms are now used in finance, as if their circumstance in life could be submitted to the same kind of calculative prediction as is used by operators in the financial markets. Hence my use of "turbulence" instead of uncertainty, when it refers to actual life, my affinity for Lord Beveridge's concept of "toiling ingenuity" in the face of conditions in the world, and my stretching of Hayek's "craving for intelligibility" to include everyone.

During the financial crisis of 2008, American economic culture invented a new binary distinction, between Main Street and Wall Street, that evaded the "real economy" confusions. The concept of "the real economy," however, is itself "real," in the sense that that it has endured as a large umbrella concept for centuries, adaptable in many contexts, a source of precise devices as well as vague allusions, but always indexing, in some direct or indirect way, as a counterpoint to, or mode of dealing with, turbulence and its mitigation. Some of the most inventive and profitable, and probably also deceptive, elements in economic assemblages have derived from the play of the correspondences and antimonies of the "real" in relation to money, fluctuation, predictability, foreignness, and the many other instigations to "drop anchor" where it may hold ground: theoretically, in enlightenment aspirations, or pragmatically, in the harbors of trades that have shaped the world.

This review can become a foil and a context for the renewed attention to the "real" in the work of the ANT-Economy group, in relation to theories of performativity, particularly in the financial world, and to the real as it comes forward from philosophical groundings. I turn next to the recent book by Muniesa (2014), as he studies the financial markets as a "provoked economy," with a subtitle referring to "economic reality."

Reality in New Theory

Reality figures prominently in the performative turn in ANT-Economics studies. There seem to be two different ways in which this is done, and one in which it is not yet done. Let me indicate these, briefly, from a new text by Muniesa (2014), entitled *The Provoked Economy: Economic Reality and the Performative Turn*. Muniesa quotes Latour as arguing that "constructivism becomes realism" (11) in that, in science, where "objects turn objective . . . in the laboratory" (11), constructivism makes a "realistic account of science." So an account of the process of producing results, whether a scientific outcome or another kind of assemblage, can itself be realistic in that the account tracks that process, presumably in its own terms of relationship with the world (that is, anthropologically). The second application is to the world itself, where the "effects" of objects are provoked. He quotes Deleuze that "effect—that is effectuation—is the name of reality" (21) and gives his own version that "reality is really real when it is provoked, and hence realized" (17).

To be internally consistent, "effects" are not to be described objectively, just as the preexisting entities are also not to be described in objective terms, except through very brief allusion to the vernacular terms deployed by the actants. Both entities and effects remain imbued with their processes of creation, or articulation, through "events." Muniesa quotes Latour on the experiment as an "event in the sense that it provokes a new articulation," which in turn allows "competence" to be "acquired" (2014, 23). Here one sees at work the focus on process, rather than elements, to which I drew attention in the introduction. And also the migration of the locus of study from the laboratory to an equally experimental and formalized locus, the financial world, where actors are self-consciously producing "products," many of which are intended to be "new articulations" of existing elements, and where concepts as important as "truth" and "value" are at stake (Ortiz 2014). Muniesa writes, "Financial markets can also provide a fertile test bed for the concept of simulacrum" (2014, 22). That is, this is an arena in which a test can be deliberately undertaken. Clearly, those of us working outside the formal experimental arenas may eventually be able to apply the conceptual armature learned from these processes of realization to the arenas in which others in the world—often under conditions that produce turbulence for which they have no buffers and very few lifelines at all—have to do their own experiments, "in real time," without ceteris paribus model-building possibilities or very significant powers to manipulate the terms. They can only create their own processes of prioritization and exclusion, undertake their own social and logistical bricolage, with all its attendant interrogations of what appears to be intelligible and possible for them. There is perhaps a horizon of mutual cultivation here within economic anthropological scholarship: bringing together the diverging, but also, conjoining, logics of bricolage, assemblage, model building and realization, with respect to situations where livelihood and wealth are at stake, as well as political and ethical valences.

I return, however, to a different and eventually more formal-philosophical question: that of the "elements." There are two aspects here. The use of the concept of "real," as in any of the "real economy" senses *within* economics and in the instruments and practices of financial operators, is more or less absent from sustained consideration in the ANT-Economy work. Cochrane's article clearly indicates that there is tension and irascibility in the investment world with respect to the "real economy" indices and the inflation rate, which can actively interfere with the kinds of calculations and projections that Muniesa's specialists would be trying to manage in order to "realize" future money earnings, in some cases precisely to profit from the interstices of unpredictability out there in the "real world." Perhaps there are sources I have not yet seen, but it is unclear whether and how the financial operators face and deploy the formal concept of the "real," as in wages, prices, interest rates, inflation-indexed products, and any other way in which this particular "real" actually exists in their world. There may well be a tension, then, about the definitions at play in the process termed theoretically as "realization," and about what elements are screened out, neutralized, and actively combatted, in addition to the consideration of inclusion and invention. The concept of the "real economy" does not arise, as such, except to refer negatively to any implication that finance is "less real than the objects of what has come to be referred to, strangely enough in [Muniesa's] view, as the real economy" (2014, 20).

It is possible that these financial operators have so routinized the effects of inflation, through embedded adjustment techniques, that the indicators can be ignored as long as they remain within conventionalized limits. In my undergraduate era, inflation had been conceptually normalized to 3 percent per annum, to remain lower than the interest rate, so that it did not obliterate all incentive to invest. And certain payments were routinely adjusted for "standard of living" reasons. There does remain, however, a compelling question about how this particular, and very powerful, meaning of the "real" figures in, as Muniesa puts it, "the constitution of economic realities—economization, abstraction, valuation, and capitalization" (38).

The second way in which the sense of the "real" is quite particular in this work is that it orients prospectively toward effectuation rather than toward a world that has already been realized. The tense of the verbs is present and future: "The emphasis is not on things just as things, but on things happening. A fact is an act: the act taking place" (16). "Reality is really real when it is provoked (and hence realized)" (17). Again, what is already there—what I have called the legacies, logics, and logistics—takes a backseat to the forward-looking process of effectuation. I pick this point up, in the philosophical terms that it claims, in the final section, but also note that a similar point has been made by Bessire and Bond: "the ontological turn replaces an ethnography of the actual with a sociology of the possible" (2014, 449).

Interlude: Tying the Threads of the Argument

The historical mobility and motility of the concept of the "real economy" within economics and economic policy are so striking as to demand excavation. Its undoubtedly most powerful current form is in the creation of precise time series for incomes, prices, and interest rates: for national policy, international comparison, and doubtless foreign investment. The manual for constructing a CPI, which is published by the IMF, runs to almost 400 pages (English version of 2009). Its application is monitored, and any "constructions," in the sense of fabrications, are censured. "Realization," as application, is kept within strict limits. The vague allusion to materiality, the natural life cycle, and actual goods and services seems to remain just that: a vague allusion, sometimes used in deeply anachronistic senses that may be validated simply by the breadth of its past reach. For example, in his vast historical study of capital, Thomas Piketty (2014, 337) equates "rent" of housing with "the value of the well-being brought by the fact of sleeping under a roof rather than outside." The financial columnist Thomas Kee, quoted earlier, equates "real" with the aspirations of the "natural life cycle." Between poetic fabrications and narrow precisions may lie a range of "realizations" of phenomena depicted as somehow "real" in economic life, but differently by different participants in different locations.

The varying and shifting referents for the "real" economy, over the centuries and in the present, could be an important frontier for deeper research. In the meantime, it is the work on the small analytical frontiers, which are embedded in method, to push in that direction, in all arenas where the term "real" is used at all, by anyone. As for this type of concept, to address the question of "elements," Muniesa refers to the "habits, idioms and apparatuses that constitute a significant part of the reality of business" (2014, 127). This resonates with my own orientation toward components, but I would give heightened attention to two domains that take the "real" into more empirically searching directions. The first is the need to take the questions of intelligibility, experiment, assemblage, and articulation more deeply into study of the historical dynamics and particular current challenges in the logistics of economic life for *all* parties who occupy the infrastructures of the platform economy. Highly placed policy personnel discuss and revise definitions and practices that lie at the heart of the articulation points of macro-micro dynamics. While perhaps assembled in "assemblage" fashion, from various inputs or "elements," the combinations they create are also infused with enormous power to affect many of the domains that overlap in that locus. At the receiving end of the effects of, for example, congestion contracts, are the mayors and citizens of towns, trying to fit the costs of energy shortage into budgets and daily life. Beyond centers of economic power and laboratory-like invention, a vast range of others are also articulating intelligibility and putting it into realization in their own ways.

There is a second direction that I would push our work, which then gives me the opportunity to take on a deeper theoretical issue. I would emphasize the importance of taking up the *craftsmanship* of the past that puts elements into availability, along with entailments (as models), auras (as memories) and practicability (as local knowledge and logistics). Giving an analytical designation to the "elements," which assemblage presumes, pushes the research directions. Legacy elements have been made, archived, and imbued with particular powers (of various kinds, including ranking and iconicity). Then there is the relative necessity of the entailments already built into what Muniesa refers to as a "model" that is "an abstractive machine" (11), which clearly works on the world in a way that requires the *continuing* entailments of its parts. It is striking, then, that these "habits, idioms and apparatuses" are not key conceptual landmarks in Muniesa's text; they appear in neither section titles nor the index. This may be because they are already too familiar in ANT theory to require explicit mobilization. But then the elements become very heterogeneous again, and undesignated, as he writes that "business realities consist of nothing more and nothing less than the piling up of a public display of layers of documents, presentations, diagrams and formulas that designate business objects and, in so doing, grant them with agency" (127).

This sentence is uncannily close to Lord Beveridge's (1928) depiction of the remains of the World War I food control measures in Britain. In his final sentences, quoted earlier, Beveridge wrote of his own 429-page effort, with dozens of tables on such topics as seasonal milk supply and consumption of bread and flour: "The account . . . of these particular experiments, long as it may seem, is no more than a surface gleaning of the archives. These forms and circulars, reports and instructions, schemes and counter-schemes and plans for another war, all so many monuments of toiling ingenuity, lie mouldering gently into dust and oblivion" (1928, 344). Except, of course, he feared that they would *not* disappear into oblivion. He indicates that they contained both experience of a recent past and also projections of a possible future. Eventually, they informed the food control measures of the next war, which then informed the policies of the Food and Agriculture Organization of the United Nations (FAO) and postwar international food policy. As I completed this paper, my colleague Michael Hanchard showed me an article (Nixon 2014) about a comparable process: how a specific legal solution for mediating the current huge debt overloads in Europe is being picked up from the British legal system's "piles and layers" from colonial rule in India, which ended in 1947, almost seventy years ago and half the world away from Europe. It can remind us of Michael Ralph's (2015) and Jonathan Levy's (2012) tracing of certain key instruments in modern insurance to the slave trade.

The processes of assemblage are one crucial part of the intellectual challenge. But so also are these elements, lying moldering, or carefully archived, in those "piles" and "layers," which become deeply relevant to what I am inclined to see as the "really real," namely the historically crafted forms within which people find resources to come to "terms"—literally, create intelligibilities and possible realizations—with life as they see it, in relation to other parties, with their own *agencements*. To do so would allow the work on *agencements* to meet up with the situations depicted by other anthropologists: "savage money" (Gregory 1997); late capitalism in Australia and other places (Povinelli 2011); development "frontiers," as seen in Africa; capitalism in the twenty-first century (Piketty 2014), recurrent warfare and all the turbulent conditions in which monetary transactions figure prominently, and the new work on money and debt (Hart and Ortiz 2014; Maurer 2006; Yuran 2014; Peebles 2010; Graeber 2011; James 2014; and many others).

There are crucial *agencements* in all these situations. It remains to identify them sufficiently forensically to move into archeological-excavation mode for the elements; ethnographic mode for the compositional processes; and engaged-projective mode for the events that they, in turn, can provoke in arenas outside of those in which they have been newly framed. Above all, forensic analysis could be applied to historical situations in the political economy where vastly differential stakes for the logistics of life are at issue. In African studies, we have detailed examination of the concept and practice of customary law and its highly selective mobilization, as land comes under pressure aimed at the dispossession of the customary tenure holders (see Peters 2013). In an explicit critique of limiting economy and money to the study of markets, and particularly with respect to financial markets, Maurer (2007) writes of the legal and political device of the Grey Money tax amnesty (2003–2004) through which capital in offshore accounts could be legally repatriated to South Africa. He infers "the importance of payments, not exchanges, in finance" (Maurer 2007, 134). This matches, at the macro-level, my own plea for the analytical decomposition of prices. Certainly this contributes to the "making of markets" but to other powerful monetary flows as well, and not solely by "economization." In fact, to extrapolate the dynamics of the operators in the financial economy to the economy more broadly buys into—by default—precisely the ideological shaping of markets that has been studied in political economy theoretical mode for at least a hundred years. The power to make and impose "devices," in this case new forms of contract that create dispossession, is crucial to the components of the process. Indeed, there will undoubtedly be invocation of the concept of "real" prices, the CPI, and the impact on GDP in order to project "growth" and lend an imperative to the legal formulae created for the purpose. To make these ANT-Economics analytics powerful in the wider world, then, they have to be taken beyond the laboratory-like instances, and even there, the "elements" need to be examined more closely.

Another disciplinary problem with maintaining the laboratory approach is the downplaying of the power of the distinction to be maintained between the vernacular and the analytical. In some contexts it seems hardly to matter, on first reading. For example, Muniesa returns seemingly unreflectively to the moderns' own terms, such as "piles of paper." One's "real doubt" (a concept to return to) asks, piles: really? In the computer age? And then skeptical doubt sets in. Even if they are in paper form, are they not arranged in a way that enables rapid and selective mobilization, through imaginative foresight? Attention to indigenous terminology is crucial, but it is also an analytical frontier into which to delve more deeply through looking closely at the legacies, logics, and logistics of precisely these elements: material, linguistic, or whatever form they take at the moment when they are taken up into a new composition.

As a transverse orientation to all of this, I would develop attention to preceding and subsequent crafting: a broader version of "toiling ingenuity," in that it would allow for deeply learned skills to be mobilized without, and alongside, very strong self-conscious reasoning or struggle in rationally purposeful mode, by bringing forward the domain of familiarity, which I take to be more than simply routinization or habit. The familiar is persuasive, and it works. The craft skill of queuing that I brought into the introduction would be an example. It can be composed with complex, and perhaps multiple, orientations simultaneously at work. I take some comparative guidance here from Karen and Barbara Fields' book on "racecraft" in America (2012). Here, the term "nature" has been applied to "the sense of inevitability that gradually becomes attached to a predictable, repetitive social routine" (27). There is an "inborn feature of what we encounter" that would be excised if we tried to turn it into just a "fact" (181). The familiar social world contains "invisible ontologies" (200), crafted seamlessly into "real worlds" (212). They offer the example of provoking laughter in an interracial exchange, quoting Toni Morrison who noted that "every black writer who heard those words understood" that a laugh was "a gesture of accommodation and obedience" (Fields 2012, 92). It is the capacity for doubt, about the familiar—"something that is (in) the very texture of any insider's thought" (223)—that can open up the craft through which "an idiom of thought is protected by secondary elaboration, . . . is acquired as obvious and uncontroversial, and so on" (223). But some corpus of familiarity needs to exist already; otherwise ethnographic doubt and surprise, and critical reasoning, could not identify the points on which to focus. Obviously, actors with different familiarities, from different life experience, are likely to act differently from each other. Ferguson (2009) makes a similar point when he examines how formalization creates new bridges between "formal" and "informal" economies in South Africa.

Moving On: A "Pragmatic" Theoretical Issue

If the "real" is a vast and old conceptual confusion and conflation, and "objects" come back into a disciplinary language otherwise focused on *agencements*, we would seem to have only two, complementary, possibilities for ethnography and analysis: to be deeply attentive to the indigenous terminology and its mobilization, however contradictory it may be among those using it; and to supplement the theoretical approach. I have already emphasized the importance of a historical and political economic contextualization of the foci of analytical attention (see also Hart and Ortiz 2014). I think it can be further augmented by turning to an aspect of Thomas Reid's philosophy of common sense in the eighteenth century, when so many of the questions about "real value" were raised in our Western intellectual traditions, and to the extensions of the theory by Charles Sanders Peirce, as the ANT theorists draw most explicitly on the philosophy of the pragmatists. It can be extended still further when certain other philosophical bridges between semiotics and political economy are created (Kockelman 2006).

Reid distinguished between the judgments of our perception and the products of reason (in the sense of rationality). The former are "indubitable" truths, such as that the world exists, the floor is under my feet, the person I saw yesterday is the same person as I see today, and so on. These judgments are common sense, in the sense of being so repeatedly confirmed by experience that they are not immediately subjected to skeptical reasoning, and also in the sense of being shared with others within the same context. Without common sense, Reid argued, reasoning itself would not be possible. The latter are subject to Hume's kind of self-conscious skepticism, an intrinsic part of empiricist reasoning. In his dedication of his major work in 1785, and referring implicitly to Hume and Descartes, Reid expressed appreciation for "the skeptical writers" who are attending to the "holes in the fabric of knowledge wherever it is weak and faulty," while also rejecting their assumption that "nothing is perceived but what is in the mind which perceives it; That we do not really perceive things that are external, but only certain images and pictures of them imprinted on the mind, which are called *impressions* and *ideas*" (4). According to Reid, skepticism and reason can only enter after, and within the context of, "indubitable truths." He even teases a proponent of what he calls "the ideal system" that the latter necessarily "wrote it in the belief that it should be read and regarded" and hopes that "he wrote it in the belief also, that it would be useful to mankind" (4). That is, he presumed a particular world to receive his writings, even though the logic of his theory was throwing exactly this assumption into question. The most basic proposition here is simply that the "real world" impresses itself as real, through processes that may be seen as "self-evident." Clearly, an overextensive theory of "common sense" may risk treating *anything* that impresses people through familiarity as if it were actually "true" in the same sense as the "sun rises" is true. The Fields' work notes (2014, 129), for example, that a concept we know Thomas Jefferson took from Reid, that of "truths (we hold) to be self-evident"—in this case, that all men are created equal and endowed by their Creator, and so on—was extended by him in contradictory and erratic fashion into a world infused with racecraft. Familiarization through life experience and culture then demands excavation through different forensic methods than familiarization through the body. But we do still need the framework of "craft" to refer to familiarization with how the world we inhabit is apprehended to work. Even Reid, in the eighteenth century, perceived that individual and cultural variation are still based on what he called the "principles" or "seeds" of a *common* human nature, which "either by their native vigour, or by force of culture, will thrive and grow to great perfection" (14). He argued that philosophers were reluctant to find words for the idea that reasoning might vary and were developing a scheme of rationality that was "so adapted to the prevailing system, that it cannot fit any other" (14).

Here are the seeds to the critical common sensism of the pragmatists, and for an ethnographic focus on person, history, experience, situation, context, and so on. Reid's concern about the inflexibility of general theory, built on rationalism with little place for common sense, is almost uncannily close to Gudeman's argument about economics' "supposed realism . . . presumed to apply to all situations" which masks "the necessary presence of local, substantive conversations" (2009, 79).

Peirce and the pragmatists take up the philosophical challenge here, by parsing out kinds of doubt rather than by rejecting common sense itself, and by depicting their own school as "critical common sensism." As Ni

(2002) writes, alluding to Peirce's positive, though critical, appreciation of what he called the Scotch school of common sense,

> There are indubitable, though contingent, truths such as the judgments of our perception. Those truths are the basic premises of our reasoning. They can be doubted in a broader sense of the word "doubt," but not in a narrower sense which Peirce calls "real doubt." Real doubts are those that cannot be induced deliberately, just as one cannot give oneself a surprise. In that sense, neither Descartes not Hume ever really doubted the existence of the external world, though they did doubt those kinds of belief in a broader sense of the word "doubt." (79)

As Peirce himself stated it:

> It is important that the reader satisfy himself that genuine doubt always has an external origin, usually from surprise. And that it is impossible for a man to create in himself a genuine doubt by such an act of will as would suffice to imagine the condition of a mathematical theorem as it would be for him to give himself a genuine surprise by a simple act of will. (1905, 484)

Here, "real," as in "real doubt," refers precisely back to the perceptions of common sense. Objects do not disappear. As Kockelman (2006) points out, Peirce's semiotic triangle consists of object, sign, and interpretant. At the moment of perception, all are at play and in interaction, as is implicit in common sensism. Those perceptions can be gathered into an eventual critical examination and subjected to skeptical doubt, but could not be so unless they had already passed into consciousness as "self-evident truths," those truths perceived and accepted as real with respect to an external world, at the moment of "impression" (in Hume's terms). For my own earlier concerns with how Hume would transport the mind from passion to reason and back, we can find some components here: the recognition (through experience) of indubitable properties of an external world, and the framing of the self-evident terms under which the impression it makes is ordered (by common sense, in both the material and cultural senses), and then submitted, at will, to the processes of skeptical reason.

Reid's approach was also, and perhaps necessarily at that time, built on a certain providential philosophy about what he refers to as the "divine Architect" of "the curious and wonderful" ([1785] 1997, 11) human mind, and on the assumption that all the arts of life, from statesmanship to poetry, "touch . . . the strings of the human frame (and cannot) rise to the

dignity of science, until they are built on the principles of the human constitution" (11). It is effectively these religious and cultural underpinnings
and implications of the philosophy of common sense that are picked out
for critical attention and selective appropriation by the pragmatists. Peirce
retains the distinction between "reasonable, deliberate, self-controlled"
reasoning and "immediate consciousness" (1905, 482), giving both their
place in the theory, but also strongly advocating the possibility of linking
the two, by "sufficiently energetic effort" to "bring out" "whatever hides in
the depths of our nature" (483).

The ANT school gives most emphasis to the process aspects of pragmatic philosophy: "The emphasis is not on things just as things, but on
things happening. A fact is an act: the act taking place" (Muniesa 2014,
16). But this does not take in sufficiently the other component one can see
as presumed within "critical common sensism": that the "found objects"
that go into assemblages would first impress human consciousness as
products of a world that impresses itself on common sense. That is, a sense
built up by exposure to repeated perceptions that obviate "real doubt" as
to their existence in forms that we recognize powerfully enough to find
them in the first place. And that it is only from this perception that they
can then be submitted to the "energetic effort" of deep reasoning. We may
here be struggling with the language itself: a *fait* (fact), in French, somehow
preserves the verb *faire* (to make) from which it derives, as distinct from
donnée (also fact, or truth) that derives from *donner* (to give) and thereby
implies "givens." Maintaining both aspects of reasoning—common sense
and skeptical doubt—seems a helpful position from which to take on the
ethnographic "reality" of economic life, as well as other works of intellectual craftsmanship.

Rather than banishing the "real" altogether from theoretical and ethnographic realms, it seems ripe for greater ethnographic attention and situated
analytical precision, in use. Since it has become such a "mishmash"—to
use a term of Ernest Gellner's (1965)—of referents and meanings, its sheer
availability within a platform-performative infrastructure and process can
make for the wider conversations from which I have always benefited. The
"real" appears to be a concept that can apply within common sense, in
reasoning and in the creation of events, whether those events are created
through "realization" or straight ideological and political power. And it can
apply to both the elements and effects of assemblages, because it has gar-
nered such profound familiarity and diffuse applicability over so long. The
"real" in economic life is itself a legacy. It can invoke whichever philosophical logic suits the moment, and is deeply implicated in the figuring out

of logistics. It can be a serious concept of governance, a claim in practice, and a vernacular rhetorical device that can imply the possibility of challenge. In American English, "real" is far more widely in use than "actual" (which also translates inaccurately into French). People have to "get real" in order to move to the very next phase of impression by the world, and onward to skeptical thought about its foundations. At this point, British English offers many different intonations, with totally different meanings, with which to exclaim "Really!!??" Rhetorical flourish, deploying concepts such as "real" that have become highly diffused, is part of the assembling and dismissal of possibilities for intelligibility, for living and acting with it. And with each other.

The "real" can be the recurrent turbulence of experience under macroeconomic policy shifts. It can be the recurrent violence of dispossession. It can be a measure of inflation. A term for any particular kind of recurrent event: "realization." It is a portfolio word that has been deployed analytically, so is not only subject to vernacular shifts. It may have been binary in its basic meaning in forms of rigorous thought, from religious doctrine to economic theory, as—real/imaginary, real/monetary, real/quantified—but it has now gone in contradictory directions, diffusing over many vernacular and technical domains. Its ancestral binarism deviates, as the whole meaning of "realism" comes under examination. But then "real" returns as a polarizing rhetorical device in its politics, expressing the right to name what is "real," to draw attention to a topic that has been sidelined, and by strong implication, it also indicates what it is not. The binarism of the "real economy" can be easily recuperated in another guise: Wall Street and Main Street. An ethnographic and historical focus on the political economy could bring into view the play of the current multiplicity of meanings, as subject matter, while also maintaining a grip on what is known by the "commonsense" experience of peoples differentially situated on, within, and at the very margins of, the intricate platform economies of life.

CHAPTER ONE

1. *Economist*, November 15–21, 2008.
2. Money in the Making of World Society (MITMOWS) network, based at the University of Pretoria, South Africa.
3. Etymology dictionary, www.etymonline.com, August 6, 2014.

CHAPTER TWO

1. Also see the special issue of *Theory, Culture and Society*, devoted to global processes (Featherstone 1990).
2. The sheer vastness of the modern regulatory process is often referred to in ideologically negative terms these days; and, in fact, it can be difficult even for a social scientist with a doctorate to comprehend the "how" and the "why" of the process. To cite a few recent personal examples: an explanation of the law with respect to building a deck on a house is found to take up five single-spaced pages; the officials doing a property-tax reassessment on a home improvement admitted that it is unexplainable; the legal contract for a major public works construction can be as large as a telephone directory; expediters need their own expediters to maneuver building plans through the permit process in New York City; it can take seventeen different steps to discharge a body from the hospital; and a photograph for the immigration service has to show the subject's right ear. The issue for the scholar as distinct from the political partisan is the nature, not the necessity, of this process in its varied contexts. In a densely populated, mobile, multivocal, imaginative, disease-prone, and waste-producing world, our very lives clearly depend on the nature of government regulation. As a process from which it is utterly impossible to imagine oneself aloof, regulation should lend itself to study in the increasingly reflexive mode advocated by recent anthropological theory.
3. Other detailed works on ideology take a similar basic stance on the structures of multiplicity in the modern era. Comaroff (1989) describes differences as "moral refractions" of the ideology of a class that is subject to "internal fragmentation" (674, 664). Eagleton (1991) writes that ideology "is neither a set of diffuse discourses nor a seamless whole. . . . It is . . . scarred and disarticulated . . . by conflicting interests" (222).
4. Anthropology, of course, has addressed this issue in non-Western cultures (see Bloch 1977). As Trouillot (1989) points out of anthropology's own vocabulary, many ter-

minologies both emanate from and indicate particular historical phases while at the same time they are being used analytically to define reality in the present.

5. While I agree with Appadurai (1990, 21) on the importance of the dynamics of local interfaces ("links between flows," in his own terms), I am more inclined, as I argue throughout, to leave space for great power in specific loci and at specific moments. Hence I underscore the importance of keeping purposes and effects clearly to the fore.

6. Stieb (1966) has remarked on "the rather peculiar British system of amending and incorporating without repealing existing statutes" (131).

7. "Success" has two senses here: that projects actually achieved their own goals to a substantial degree and that people also believed they had done so. New concepts, measures, and personnel became legitimate parts of the public debate.

8. Glasser's (1982) definition of iterative time, taken broadly, could apply to many of the processes through which Western thinking has engaged with the rest of the world: "the renewing or initiating of periods in conjunction with other periods in order to produce a two- or more-fold social time" (668).

9. See Foucault, Donzelot, and others in Burchell, Gordon, and Miller (1991).

10. Moore (1986) insists that the institutions, rules, and practices that compose a structure do not follow its key ideas in a determinate fashion.

11. See, for example, Comaroff (1982) and Comaroff and Comaroff (1992).

12. Where the present argument could be enriched by knowledge not available in those media, I indicate it in the notes. State processes that government representatives are less open about than they are about food policies may be so recalcitrant to study from publicly available sources (see Abrams 1988) that a refined ethnographic method, using all kinds of "unobtrusive measures," is the only way of studying them at all. I have in mind such critical processes as financial regulation. A substantial literature is burgeoning on such specific technical endeavors as colonial agricultural research (Richards 1985), conservation (Beinart 1989), public health (Packard 1989), family law and policy (Chanock 1985; Cooper 1989), and taxation (Guyer 1992), but strikingly most of it is historical rather than contemporary, possibly owing to problems of accessibility.

13. Witness almost any discussion of the nutrition supplement programs in the United States, such as the famous Reagan-era debate over whether ketchup was a vegetable. Writing of Nigeria's apparent food crisis of 1988, one editorial claimed that people were experiencing shortages and blamed drought and inadequate government buffer stocks of routine staples (*Daily Times* 1988), whereas the agriculture minister blamed people's tastes for foreign foods—such as eggs, rice, caviar, and smoked salmon—that no government felt compelled to deliver (quoted in Ikeano 1989).

14. Stieb points out that every step of achievement in food regulation was a struggle; the nineteenth-century metropolitan state, and later the colonial state, did not embrace regulatory functions, let alone initiate them. In fact, food standards appear to have been consistently developed by the lobbies of "civil society" and only taken up by the state once they were developed "packages." Again, food regulation may have its own history in this regard.

15. Kula (1986) notes the link between the standardization of measures and state power, and he indicates the conceptual link to "perfection," as with the metric system in France: "The post-1830 Bourbon monarchy restored the metric system in its 'purity.' . . . The struggle between the state and society was now concluded" (263). In the United States, the food control measures of 1906 are known as the Pure Food

Laws (see Young 1989 for a comprehensive history). The late nineteenth and early twentieth centuries were the critical era during which governments slowly achieved standardization in many economic areas (see Born 1984 on currencies and banking). The extent to which the ideology of pre–World War I state legitimation was linked to concepts of purity and perfection would be a fruitful line of enquiry.

16. Stieb (1966) reprints an 1855 *Punch* cartoon in which a small child asks the grocer for "a quarter of a pound of your best tea to kill the rats with" (214).

17. I do not want to imply that ideology alone drove the measures put in place. Certainly, a definition of caloric adequacy met bureaucratic needs for simplicity as well as for expressing the legitimating rubrics of justice and equality. Neither was the need for functioning laborers and foot soldiers irrelevant. But I am concerned here with the shape of a model rather than with the full dynamics of its formulation.

18. I have been unable to find a detailed discussion of how the food control system dealt with "self-provisioning," from the landed gentry's hunting of grouse and venison to the small Irish farmer's cultivation of potatoes and the urban Victory Gardener's cultivation of vegetables. The rationing system was deliberately based on the individual rather than on the family. Radical individualism is consonant with the science of caloric needs and the ideology of equality and justice, but it cannot easily cope with the existence of social groups and networks. The definitions of some types of distribution along social networks as acceptable and others as favoritism must express the official ideology of social relations. The court records of rationing violations might reveal how the individualism of the model was interpreted during implementation.

19. The paragraph continues with a profession of hope that the "monuments of toiling ingenuity, [will] lie mouldering gently into dust and oblivion—lie buried, please God, for ever" (Beveridge 1928, 344).

20. Orr and Lubbock argued, for example, that bread was "probably the most essential food" and that bacon, by contrast, could not "be considered an essential food." They advocated the composition of "a list of food regarded as essential and, therefore, to be subsidised" (1940, 63, 70).

21. After the war, Orr served as the first director-general of the United Nations Food and Agriculture Organization, where he used figures similar to those from his 1936 report to animate concerns about nutrition in the rest of the world (Ellen Messer, personal communication, 1992).

22. Field (1990) discusses the determined efforts that the government also made during World War II to alter the entire style of living of the poor, including family organization and sexuality.

23. Scholars and politicians rarely refer to the depths of nutritional deprivation of metropolitan working-class populations before World War II when implicit comparisons are made with the third world. In the urban north of England where I grew up, a whole generation of the working class had stunted growth, possibly as a result of Depression conditions during their childhood. What we referred to as "bandy legs" and "knock-knees" from poor bone development were common enough to have their own popular terminologies.

24. The purity of milk was an exception, but it is worth noting that the policy was referred to as the "safe milk" policy, not the "pure milk" policy, stressing the welfare of the consumer over the intrinsic quality of the milk (Hammond 1956).

25. "When the larger measures of food control should come to an end, the Ministry's reforms in the field of standards and labeling would stand out as a solid gain, unobtrusively snatched from the years of austerity" (Hammond 1951, 321).

26. The history of the key terms should lend itself to anthropological analysis. Reading the sources on World War II, one is struck by the juxtaposition of the concepts of "warfare" and "welfare." The idea of the "commonweal" dates back to the sixteenth century, but "welfare" may have been forged in the crucible of war. The associated concept of a "democracy of consumers" predates the war; it was introduced by Sydney and Beatrice Webb in the 1920s (1963, 134) with respect to changes in local government during the nineteenth century. Thinking of the citizenry as consumers therefore has a three-stage history: new practices adopted locally in the nineteenth century were analytically defined by prominent political thinkers in the early twentieth century and became explicit government policy during and after World War II. The present article concentrates on the ways in which past models remain accessible in the present, because this is most relevant to policies in the world ordinarily defined as underdeveloped. But there is a parallel project in the study of multiplicity, namely the analysis of ways in which future possibilities are prefigured in the present.

27. As Hammond (1954) wrote: "Would it, after ten years of government imports of wheat, be possible to restore the competitive structure of the grain trade, that had already been losing ground in the face of the great flour-milling combines? Would it be desirable, even if it were possible, to restore the 16,000 slaughterhouses reduced to some 800 under the Meat and Livestock Control Scheme?" (223).

28. In 1926 the United States rejected several shipments of Gold Coast cocoa because they failed to meet the standards of the Pure Food Laws (Leubuscher 1939, 166, 169).

29. There is another history worth exploring here because prominent anthropologists such as Raymond Firth, Audrey Richards, and Margaret Mead were directly involved. Early in the development of the nutrition movement they were exploring direct parallels between the impoverished of the metropole and those of the colonies with a view to intervention and regulation with respect to both populations. As early as 1934, Raymond Firth was concerned that although provisioning hospital patients and workers was "a comparatively simple matter," it was "more difficult to regulate the food situation of a free-living native tribe" (1934, 401). Labouret (1938) reviewed the history of scientific concern about the colonial diet from the 1931 League of Nations conference on rural diets in Europe for a major international publication of 1937. Some of Britain's key nutrition experts, including Orr, published on the colonies *before* publishing on Britain. Debates about the colonies at this stage, however, pursued the issues of knowledge and interpretation rather than policy formulation and implementation. For example, Bascom's (1951) description of the intricacy of the Yoruba diet implicitly countered the established supposition that the African diet was necessarily deficient.

30. The interventions that were implemented in West Africa, such as slaughterhouse inspection, were for the control of food-borne infectious diseases.

31. As a consumer item, cassava starch was used in the production of sweets. For a complete history of Nigerian cassava in World War II, see Falola (1989).

32. The interventions with respect to the quality of cassava products were reactive rather than regulatory. During a major scare about poisonous *gari* in the markets in 1988, one method of government intervention was to televise advice given by the Ministry of Health on how to recognize bad *gari* (by the stickiness and a certain sheen).

33. An episodic approach obviously backgrounds a series of other dynamics. One of those is the development during the 1950s of a Nigerian public health civil service that took on activities relevant to consumer welfare, such as market inspection.

In the 1950s, this process followed the rubrics of contemporary parallelism rather than the combination of evolutionism and complementarity that framed the debate over the cassava starch scheme. Which measures define government policy in the public imagination and which do not is an interesting and largely empirical question. Does the ubiquitous *wole-wole*—the Yoruba term meaning "come in, come in" that is applied to inspectors of all kinds—more closely define the government presence than the meteoric schemes, or does this change over time? The implications of development "projects" and campaigns versus institutional development for government legitimacy depend on judgments about this probably volatile process.

34. Textiles, clothing, cement, beer, soft drinks, salt, and motor vehicles are mentioned by Oyewole (1987, 284).

35. I am not aware of any official source that explains either the NNSC's origin or its persistence through one civilian and three military governments. A detailed institutional history of such organizations would add enormously to our knowledge of postcolonial governance. It is not yet clear, for example, whether the NNSC was included in the recommendations of the committee on the state marketing boards of 1976 and how particular commodities came to be designated as "essential." By the Shagari regime of 1979–1983, "essential commodities" had become a current term: for example, Umaru Dikko became "Chairman of the Presidential Task Force for the importation of essential commodities like rice" (Oyewole 1987, 107).

36. See, for example, the list of goods named in the *Concord Weekly* (1984c). Wheat seems to have had its own "story," one unconnected to the NNSC (see Andrae and Beckman 1985).

37. Salt shortage, however, does have profound symbolic importance in southern Nigeria; people can date events according to the two past periods of shortage, the last in 1942.

38. Whether and where overt corporatism is acceptable to the public *and* in the interests of business is a fascinating issue. I sense that corporate influence is extremely powerful but almost entirely politically covert in the postcolonial world.

39. I am trying to suggest not that "blame" should be shifted from person to system, but that we can hardly know how the "system" was constructed unless a comparative and processual analysis is undertaken.

40. A remembered version of the Anglican confession contains the clauses "We have left undone those things which we ought to have done and we have done those things which we ought not to have done, and there is no health in us. But thou, 0 Lord, have mercy upon us, miserable offenders."

41. For fine examples of the matching between metropolitan and non-Western populations, see Comaroff and Comaroff (1992) and Robertson (1984).

42. This vision of global welfare may well find some of its inspiration as well as some of its conceptual challenges in works such as Margaret Mead's eloquent statement about food policy that comes from the welfare era at the end of World War II, in which she already stressed the importance of acknowledging "people's common humanity without robbing them of their special humanity" (1944, 264).

43. I have addressed this scrambling of sequences and selective replication with respect to taxation and democracy in Nigeria, in Guyer (1992).

CHAPTER THREE

1. My limited critical knowledge of the vast literature on rhetoric means that I take the "student's" route of accessing compendia and textbooks for issues that seem pertinent to my own concerns.

2. The entry on monetarism in *Money*, published in the New Palgrave Series, states this succinctly: "Monetarist thought puts primary emphasis on the long-run consequences of policy actions and procedures. It rejects attempts to reduce short-run fluctuations" (Cagan 1989, 203).

3. The convergence becomes stronger with each passing day. As I discuss in more detail below, President Babangida implied that he did not know how the Nigerian economy worked, largely because international investors had not responded as predicted to his policies. In spring and summer of 2005 the U.S. Federal Reserve was puzzling over the persistent decline in long-term interest rates, "a new reality," "clearly international in origin," on which "Wall St. economists are as divided as Fed officials about the proper interpretation." Later in the summer, the press started to talk about excess liquidity: too much capital in the world in search of too few investment opportunities, which—however—is "good for growth—but risks are mounting" (Miller 2005, 49, and cover story). (Nigeria undertook a series of mop-up campaigns for excess liquidity in the 1990s.) Alan Greenspan offered that when balance would be restored "people would know it when they saw it" (Andrews 2005, C1 and C9). The business pages of the *New York Times* redound with "culture," "charisma," "vision," "superstars," "brand names," and the idea that Greenspan's pronouncements are now considered "a strong fundamental for the stock market" (Associated Press 2005). Also, see Kaplan (2003) for a discussion of Greenspan's rhetorics.

4. Nigerian currency is in naira (N); billions are British billions of 1 thousand million. The naira was originally at parity with the British pound sterling, but fell over this period to fifty or more to the pound.

5. The following rumor circulated in 1997: Because members of the governing elite owned rights in oil in Venezuela, they deliberately ran shortages in Nigeria in order to make the economic and political rent on imports to meet the clamorous unmet demand at elevated prices. The veracity of the story is less important for my purposes than the popular vision.

CHAPTER FOUR

1. My first concerns with reasoning in this sense were inspired by Philip Mirowski's minisymposium on economic anthropology, which raised the question of the difference between rationality, rational choice, and reason (Guyer 2000). Ben Fine (1998) has also written on this distinction.

2. Over 20 years ago by now, Nancy Munn warned that in neglecting the future, in general, anthropologists were neglecting a crucial topic: "Futurity is poorly tended as a specifically temporal problem. . . . Anthropologists have viewed the future in 'shreds and patches,' in contrast to the close attention given to 'the past in the present'" (1992, 116).

3. My own reading of Bourdieu is that he is inexplicit about any potential difference between experience in the sedimented, cumulative sense and experience in the punctuated sense. Attention to both is needed and to where and how they might be differentiated in subjective and collective dynamics.

4. It is striking how the anthropology of time settles so quickly into the "past in the present" and memory. This area of research is of the utmost importance, and I have made my own contributions to it. But the following consecutive sentences can illustrate a wonderfully promising statement followed by certain short-circuiting of the future. "The plain minimalist approach to time . . . fails to recognize the collusion

of people in the making of material life and events through significant timing. There is still a need to rescue an 'anthropology of time' which can engage with history and the work of historians" (James and Mills 2005, 14). Wallman (1992) stands as an early attempt to examine the future in classically framed ethnographic case studies.

5. Worth noting is how little attention Rostow devotes to the "Austrian School": Hayek, Milton Friedman, and so on. He ends his short review of their contributions (in a seven-hundred-page book) with the conclusion that they came up with "some moderately useful tools for both short- and long-run analysis of the investment process" (Rostow 1990, 225). Friedman is extremely critical of such "liberal" economists as John Kenneth Galbraith. See "From Galbraith to Economic Freedom," in Friedman (1991).

6. Friedman advocated, and contributed enormously to, a microeconomics that would embed the midterm—in this case, the life cycle—in specific financial instruments. He designed means for instilling economic discipline in individual financial management such as stock ownership, savings, and individual pension investment, rather than in either wages or tax payment and entitlements. The internal consistency of his approach and the vastness of his empirical and policy works are sometimes underestimated by those who see mainly the ideological impetus behind them.

7. All these works excoriate the fallacies of basing thought on emotional or moral responses to specificity, hence, to the mid- and short-term: "Nine-tenths of the economic fallacies that are working such dreadful harm in the world today . . . stem from two central fallacies, or both: that of looking only at the immediate consequences of an act or proposal, and that of looking at the consequences only for a particular group to the neglect of other groups" (Hazlitt [1946] 1979, 17).

8. These two "eternities" have their own names and atemporal properties: "Alpha" and "Omega," "Past" and "Future," and the presence of Shekinah characterizes both (La-Haye and Ice 2001, 116). This last attribute, however, is not as clear in the early phase as in the final one. Shekinah in Hebrew and in Judaism refers to "the indwelling presence of God in this world" and, in kabbalistic thinking, as in some sense a feminine dimension of the divine (Green 1999, 33–34). Here, as elsewhere, and perhaps in deference to the enormous importance placed on the Jews in evangelical religious history, LaHaye uses concepts from Hebrew and Judaism that have not been taken up in other Christian traditions, which largely depend on the Greek language and Hellenic thought. For example, LaHaye and Ice refer to the judgment seat of Christ as the "Bema," the Hebrew word for the elevated place from which the Torah is read in a synagogue.

9. The movement into the Millennial Age can be broken down into much shorter segments and sequences, of which the Tribulation—after which LaHaye and Ice's Pre-Trib Research Center is named—is one. It is preceded by the Rapture, from which LaHaye's Left Behind series begins.

10. Some present-day U.S. evangelicals, however, explicitly inhabit the more classic Hebrew prophetic tradition, in differentiation from others, and they do focus on "the widow and the orphan." See Wallis (2005). The entire prophetic spectrum remains a labile field.

11. Heschel finds correspondences in some medieval Muslim—especially Sufi—thought, and one can juxtapose key Christian thinking, so this is not exclusively a Jewish view. Because of the enormous complexity of the crisscrossing of ideas and derivations within and across the Abrahamic traditions, the current popular concept

of the "Judeo-Christian tradition" seems inaccurate and limiting, although I am my-self limited in addressing only Jewish and Christian sources here.

12. And from his preface, "the totality of impressions, thought and feeling which make up the prophet's being . . . [his] awareness of his confrontation with facts not de-rived from his own mind" (Heschel 1962, vii).

13. The relevant future is the spiritual journey of perfecting the soul, in the belief that every man "has the power to be as righteous as Moses our Teacher" (Heschel 1996, 98). The conditional moral future is enfolded and presumed, rather than elaborated, through the notion that preparation for prophetic flashes of inspira-tion required perfection of the intellect, the imagination, and the character, doubt-less avoiding at all costs the multitudinous infractions against which the ancient prophets railed. There is, however, a version of messianism in some Jewish tradi-tions whose temporal framing is more similar to the evangelical view. A recent and public example is seen in the full-page advertisement taken out in the *New York Times* by the Lubavitcher community after the invasion of Iraq in April 2003. It announced that the by-then deceased Rebbe Moses Menachem Schneerson had uttered "prophetic words" about the event during the previous Desert Storm mili-tary campaign. "With the gift of prophetic vision, the Rebbe was able to correctly interpret events as they unfolded then" and to urge every person—man, woman, and child—to study, observe, and act with righteousness to "tip the scales in favor of humankind and bring redemption to the entire world." The statement goes on, "Our entire generation is living on the threshold of the Messianic era. . . . All of us can work to . . . provide a more fitting reception to Moshiach and Redemption" (Springer 2003, A9).

14. Although I cannot hazard interpretations of Islamic thought on these questions of temporality and prophecy, I understand that there are apocalyptic claims within Shi'a Islam that have some popularity in present-day Iran. Attention to varieties of Muslim approaches to the near future would greatly enrich this discussion.

15. One might note, however, that anarchists expressly avoid developing a "vanguard" plan of action as one road toward hierarchy. See Graeber (2004).

16. From the *Wikipedia* entry on "contango," the condition in which the futures price is higher than the spot price because of the cost of holding the good in the meantime:

> But if there is a near-term shortage, the price comparison breaks down and the contango may be reduced or disappear [because demand drives the price up towards the futures price before the due date]. Near prices become higher than far prices because for consumers future delivery does not suffice, and be-cause there are few holders who can make an arbitrage profit by selling the spot and buying back the future. This is called backwardation. (Wikimedia Foundation n.d.)

CHAPTER SIX

1. For example, Mallard (2007, 165) notes for product testing by consumer advocates: "The most usual device is the ranking of products and the attribution of grades to them, for instance on a scale from 0 to 20."

2. In case of interest: Princeton, Harvard, Yale, Stanford, Caltech, Penn, MIT, Duke, Columbia, Chicago, Dartmouth, Wash. St. Louis, Cornell . . . then Brown, North-western and Johns Hopkins together.

3. Cf. Annie Leibovitz's photo of soccer star David Beckham as a knight on a white horse.

4. See a case included in the original paper about the scientific ranking of Canadian university research (Gagnon, Macnab, and Gagnon 2000).
5. It is odd that Dubai does not seem to figure at all up to 2004 (http://en.wikipedia .org/wiki/Global_Cities), but its symbolic strategies for moving up are classic: to build the tallest buildings, host a world-class golf tournament, become a center for horseracing and golf, attract sports icons to live there (David Beckham, for one).
6. For example, on a salary case for a "Wall Street legend": in "the me-too meritocracy [he must earn] at least as much as the average of his high-paid peers. The compensation package is expected to vault him ahead of the $22.5 million pay package of his predecessor" (Dash 2005).
7. For another example, of many, a website on ecotourism notes the enhanced value of "icon species": "In Guam, 'icon species' that are valued by divers include sharks, turtles, manta rays (Manta birostris), and the Napoleon wrasse (Cheilinus undulatus)" (Tupper and Rudd n.d.).
8. See Hart (2010) for reference to the phenomenon he refers to as the power law.
9. Many modern uses, from *Mad* magazine to *Nature*, can be found by entering "Great Chain of Being" into the Internet.
10. In the Fibonacci sequence of numbers, each number after the first two is the sum of the previous two numbers. Thus the sequence is 1, 1, 2, 3, 5, 8, 13, 21, 34, 55, 89, 144, 233, etc.
11. Ideally, this account would include an analysis of the odds in specific races, but I am not sure how to include it.
12. See Horse Hats, www.horsehats/stallions.html.
13. I am indebted to several of the papers in the *African Studies Review* (ed. Geschiere, Goheen and Piot 2007), special issue on the book (Guyer 2004) for highlighting further the problems with implicit temporal progressivism. Bill Maurer (2007) and Helen Verran (2007) made particularly strong cases. Discussions with Naveeda Khan and Juan Obarrio have always been a spur to go further, often in several directions. Some of the results find their place here, and the rest remain a challenge. I am aware that there is French scholarship on classic ranks, such as the Michelin guides, but have not had a chance to study them.

CHAPTER SEVEN

1. In comments on my paper, Verran saw a connection between my tackling of an old, small but powerful numerical technique; my interest in multiplicity, modes, and shifts; and my eventual focus on political economy. She quotes Foucault (Verran 2001, 16) to bring out a possible necessary vagueness, as a "permanent correlative" that is part of the exercise of governmentality.
2. Measures and their standardized denominations may have a much longer history elsewhere, and certainly we should leave a space in our minds to discover standardized proportionality in ancient Asian systems and their modern descendants. Many ancient systems of Western Asia were not based on 10.
3. The metric system was invented and institutionalized in the same period too: the year 1792 was the measurement phase; in 1800 it was "declared to be the sole measurement system for the entire nation [of France]" (Alder 2002, 261).
4. "Perry Plan Would Make Big Changes to Washington," *Morning Edition*, National Public Radio, November 16, 2011, http://www.npr.org/player/v2/mediaPlayer.html ?action=1&t=1&islist=false&id=142385401&m=142385424.
5. Tropic points are a concept I used for the attachment points between numerically

expressed scales for the purposes of transactability in Atlantic Africa (Guyer 2004). I think we may find it useful as we examine the emergent modal geometries internal to the "100" of the percentage, in our own usage.

6. There is a fascinating difference here, which may be captured by the difference between the religious metaphors used in mathematics (God the Mathematician, the God particle, etc.) and logic (the "Holy Grail") for "the proof of completeness" (Girle 2003, 192), and anthropology's certainty that completeness is impossible, since the human past and present are far vaster than our knowledge of them can ever be. The first works from the confident projection of a, so-far unspecifiable, coherence; the other works from an acceptance of limitlessness. See Lloyd (2008) on providence and science.

7. Quoted in "Full Text of Barack Obama's Speech is Osawatomie, Kansas," *Guardian*, December 6, 2011, http://www.theguardian.com/world/2011/dec/07/full-text-barack-obama-speech.

8. Since "it's not fair" is *ce n'est pas juste* in French, I was puzzled as to how Rawls's title might be translated into that language. I asked a translator, who suggested "Justice comme justesse." But the juxtaposition hardly works the same way. Since then, I have been advised that the actual French translation of Rawls's book uses *equité* for "fairness."

9. Online Etymology Dictionary http://www.etymonline.com/index.php?1 =f&p=1& allowed_in_frame=0, accessed January 6, 2012.

10. I was struck by the convergence of this book, unbeknownst to me at the time, with my own use of the Great Chain (Guyer 2010) as the source of most of our metaphors for iconic ordinality. I think most of us in anthropology would be inclined to see the Great Chain as both familiar and foreign at the same time, but then orient our minds toward analysis as "foreign."

11. The contributors to the *Urbanite* are independent writers and artists, so their modes of collaboration are not directly accessible. The authors of the research, the article, the illustrations, and the charts are different people. My appreciation and critique are thereby focused only on the overall thrust for the reader, particularly through the visuals. The journal aims to present alternative approaches to urban life, so I assume that it was in that spirit that the article was contributed: presumably to escape old vested interests and stereotypes, and to make a stronger gesture toward a new future. Control of the metrics and the modes of their application, however, are not directly addressed.

CHAPTER EIGHT

1. Marc Sommers's (2012) new book on the position of youth in Rwanda is appositely entitled *Stuck*.

2. My paper on food regulation in Britain and Nigeria (Guyer 1993a), discussed later, suggests that democratic and imperialist processes, together, may produce so much interested, partial, and cumulative tinkering as to result inevitably in impasses.

3. See Hammond (1954, 227) citing coral islands with respect to World War II rationing.

4. This section is taken from the collaborative paper written by me and LaRay Denzer (2013) in a volume edited by Wale Adebanwi and Ebenezer Obadare.

CHAPTER NINE

1. United States Department of Labor, Bureau of Labor Statistics, *Computer Price Indexes for Rent and Rental Equivalence*, http://www.bls.gov/cpi/cpifact6.htm.

2. There seems to be no date on this short publication, put out by the English League for the Taxation of Land Values. Probably 1890s.

3. US Inflation Calculator, http://www.usinflationcalculator.com/frequently-asked -questions-faqs/, accessed August 5, 2013.

4. US Inflation Calculator, http://www.usinflationcalculator.com/inflation/current -inflation-rates/, accessed August 19, 2014.

5. I am indebted to Alexandre Mallard for references to the French CPI and the Piketty text in French, and to the Interdisciplinary Market Studies Workshop, June 2014, for information from other countries.

6. "Study: Half of US Renters Pay More Than 30 Percent of Income for Housing," CBS DC, December 9, 2013, http://washington.cbslocal.com/2013/12/09/study-half-of -us-renters-pay-more-than-30-percent-of-income-for-housing/.

CHAPTER TEN

1. For example, the British Airways online booking service gives a flight price and then adds, explicitly itemized: an online booking fee; a share of all taxes and fees demanded by governments, authorities, or airport owners; an insurance and security surcharge (since 9/11); and a fuel surcharge.

2. Here I would agree with Maurer that there can be convergences of analytical and vernacular terms. But there is one aspect that I think has not been discussed enough: namely that there is bound to be a *range* of vernaculars within any "society." For the layperson, all may seem mysterious, whereas for the specialist it's hidden in plain sight ("*Of course* we are looking for loopholes!" as one American accountant said to me as I was working on a paper of that name, mainly about Nigeria). Money, insurance, statistical economics, and so on, as entire domains of expertise, are bound to use different terminologies and forms of argument from the "public." The question is how closely they track each other.

3. This advertisement does not reproduce well. It consists of a dollar bill cut into three pieces: 55 percent crude oil, 26 percent refining distribution and service stations, 19 percent taxes, with the 8.5 percent profit as a footnote (see *New York Times*, April 28, 2006, A5 and article May 3, 2006, C1). If one were studying the sources, one would immediately notice that these proportions differ from those in other publications of the API, including those reproduced with this paper: possibly the newspaper figures are more recent.

4. In fact, the journals devoted to risk date largely from the 1990s:

   1964 *The Journal of Risk and Insurance*
   1981 *Risk Analysis: An Official Publication of the Society for Risk Analysis*
   1997 *Risk Management and Insurance Review*
   1998 *Journal of Risk Research*
   1999 *The Journal of Risk Finance*

5. A publication of the American Petroleum Institute that explains crude oil markets points out the recency of the institution of futures markets in oil (Lexecon 2006).

6. See, for example, the history of Standard and Poor's Depositary Receipts (pronounced "spiders") invented in the late 1990s: "Typical volume for the SPDR is over 42 million shares per day" (*Wikipedia*). If one puts SPDRs into Google over 28,000 entries appear. These are not small phenomena.

7. There is an interesting commentary by Joan Robinson that profit has never been adequately theorized or measured. However, it is reported, thanks to the corporate tax provisions. I remember a social conversation with a business school professor

who related the two conditions: the tax law determines how profits are measured, which results in murkily inaccurate representation of the profitability of American business as seen from an economics perspective.

8. The line between extortion and earnings is necessarily blurred here; criminal actions are fairly easy and common, like the one penny that a colleague said was being taken from his Barclays bank account as some kind of fee that ended up being a fraud.

CHAPTER TWELVE

1. The available translations of Copernicus's *Treatise on Money*, from Latin to Polish, French, and English, differ in quality as grammatical texts. The texts are also not paginated. However, the treatise is short enough, and the argument is clear enough in its major points, that one can have confidence in these quotations, taken from the online French and English versions.

2. All references to Aristotle are from his *Politics*, bk. 1, pt. 3. Page references are not given due to the variety of editions.

REFERENCES

Abacha, Sani. 1996. "Budget of Consolidation: Full Text of the 1996 Budget Address." *Guardian*, February 16, 18, and 24.

Abrams, Philip. 1988. "Notes on the Difficulty of Studying the State (1977)." *Journal of Historical Sociology* 1 (no. 1): 58–89.

Adam, Susanna. 1995. *Competence Utilization and Transfer in Informal Sector Production and Service Trades in Ibadan, Nigeria*. Bremen, Germany: Bremen Afrika-Studien.

Adedoyin, Ademola, and Isodi Dike. 1991. "The Oil Subsidy Debate Again." *Sunday Magazine*, November 3.

Adeleye, Deji, with Femi Olatunde. 1991. "Combating the Deficit Scourge." *Times Week*, December 23, pp. 51–53.

Adewale, Terry, Lanre Alabi, Aisu Owens, and Olusola Bello. 1996. "Thrills and Spills of the '96 Budget." *Vanguard*, February 19, pp. 12–13.

African Guardian. 1993. August 2, p. 28.

Agamben, Giorgio. 2005. *The Time that Remains: A Commentary on the Letter to the Romans*. Redwood City, Calif.: Stanford University Press.

Agbese, Pita. 2005. "The 'Stolen' Okigbo Panel Report: Of Malfeasance and Public Accountability in Nigeria." In *Vision and Policy in Nigerian Economics: The Legacy of Pius Okigbo*, ed. L. Denzer and J. I. Guyer, 55–75. Ibadan, Nigeria: Ibadan University Press.

Akinrinade, Sola. 1988. "Fiery Welcome to Hikes." *Newswatch*, May 2, 14–19.

Alder, Ken. 2002. *The Measure of All Things: The Seven-Year Odyssey and Hidden Error That Transformed the World*. New York: Free Press.

Alderman, Liz. 2014. "Black Markets, Red Light Districts and Measuring GDP in Europe." *New York Times*, July 10, pp. B1 and B8.

Allen, Dwight. 2006. "The Fallacy of the Foreseeable Future." *Management Quarterly* 47 (no. 1): 1–11.

Amato, M., and L. Fantacci. 2011. *The End of Finance*. Oxford: Polity.

Amin, Samir. 2011. *Ending the Crisis of Capitalism or Ending Capitalism?* Dakar, Senegal: CODESRIA.

Andrae, Gunilla, and Bjorn Beckman. 1985. *The Wheat Trap*. London: Zed.

Andrews, Edmund L. 2005. "Low Rates Could Be around for Long Term." *New York Times*, June 27, pp. C1 and C9. http://www.nytimes.com/2005/06/27/business/27fed.html.

Anft, Michael. 2011. "C1ty By NuMb3r5 Has a Former Physicist Found a Formula for Growing Better Cities?" *Urbanite Baltimore Magazine*, December 30.

Appadurai, Arjun. 1986. "Introduction: Commodities and the Politics of Value." In *The Social Life of Things: Commodities in Cultural Perspective*, ed. Arjun Appadurai, 3–63. Cambridge, UK: Cambridge University Press.

———. 1990. "Disjuncture and Difference in the Global Cultural Economy." *Public Culture* 2 (no. 2): 1–24.

———. 2013. *The Future as Cultural Fact: Essays on the Global Condition*. London: Verso.

Apter, Andrew. 2005. *The Pan African Nation: Oil and the Spectacle of Culture in Nigeria*. Chicago: University of Chicago Press.

Aristotle. *Politics*. Book 1, part 3.

Ashwe, Chichi. 1987. "The Petroleum Subsidy Bogey: No Deal." *Nigerian Economist*, October 14–27, p. 51.

Associated Press. 2005. "Upbeat Talk by Greenspan Gives Share Prices a Lift." *New York Times*, June 10. http://www.nytimes.com/2005/06/10/business/10stox.html?_r=1& oref=slogin.

Baker, J. 2005. *Securing the Commonwealth: Debt, Speculation, and Writing in the Making of Early America*. Baltimore, Md.: Johns Hopkins University Press.

Bakhtin, M., and Pam Morris, eds. 1994. *The Bakhtin Reader*. New York: EdwinArnold.

Barrett-Gaines, Kathryn. 2004. "Introduction: A Keener Look at the Evidence." *African Economic History* 32:1–13.

Barry, Sandrine. 2007. "Struggling to Be Displayed at the Point of Purchase: The Emergence of Merchandising in French Supermarkets." In *Market Devices*, ed. Michel Callon, Yuval Millo, and Fabian Muniesa, 92–108. Oxford: Blackwell Publishing/The Sociological Review.

Bascom, William R. 1951. "Yoruba Food." *Africa* 20 (no. 1): 41–53.

Bastide, Roger. 1970. "Mémoire collective et sociologie du bricolage." *L'Année Sociologique* 21:65–108.

Bateson, Gregory. (1936) 1958. *Naven: A Survey of the Problems Suggested by a Composite Picture of the Culture of a New Guinea Tribe Drawn from Three Points of View*. Stanford, Calif.: Stanford University Press.

Baxstrom, Richard, Naveeda Khan, Bhrigupati Singh, and Deborah Poole. 2006. "Networks Actual and Potential: Think-Tanks, War Games and the Creation of Contemporary American Politics." *Theory and Event* 8 (no. 4).

Beck, Ulrich. (1986). 1992. *Risk Society: Towards a New Modernity*. London: Sage.

———. 1999. *World Risk Society*. Cambridge, UK: Polity.

Beinart, William. 1989. "Introduction: The Politics of Colonial Conservation." *Journal of Southern African Studies* 15 (no. 2): 143–62.

Benjamin, Walter. 1968. *Illuminations*. New York: Schocken.

Berenson, Alex. 2006. "The Other Legacy of Enron." *New York Times*, May 28.

Berlin, Isaiah. 1958. *Two Concepts of Liberty: An Inaugural Lecture Delivered before the University of Oxford*. Oxford: Clarendon.

Bernstein, Peter L. 1996. *Against the Gods: The Remarkable Story of Risk*. New York: John Wiley.

Bessire, Lucas, and David Bond. 2014. "Ontological Anthropology and the Deferral of Critique." *American Ethnologist* 41 (no. 3): 440–56.

Beunza, Daniel, and Raghu Garud. 2007. "Calculators, Lemmings or Frame-Makers? The Intermediary Role of Securities Analysts." In *Market Devices*, ed. Michel Callon, Yuval Millo, and Fabian Muniesa, 13–39. Malden, Mass.: Wiley-Blackwell.

Beuving, J. J. 2004. "Cotonou's Klondike: African Traders and Second-Hand Car Markets in Bénin." *Journal of Modern African Studies* 42 (no. 4): 511–37.

Beveridge, William H. 1928. *British Food Control*. London: Humphrey Milford.

Biehl, Joao. 2005. *Vita: Life in a Zone of Social Abandonment*. Berkeley: University of California Press.

Bizzell, Patricia, and Bruce Hertzberg. 1990. *The Rhetorical Tradition: Readings from Classical Times to the Present*. Boston: St. Martin's.

Bloch, Maurice. 1977. "The Past and the Present in the Present." *Man*, n.s., 12 (no. 2): 278–92.

Boellstorff, Tom. 2008. *Coming of Age in Second Life: An Anthropologist Explores the Virtually Human*. Princeton, N.J.: Princeton University Press.

Bohannan, P. 1955. "Some Principles of Exchange and Investment among the Tiv." *American Anthropologist* 57:60–70.

Bohannan, Paul, and George Dalton, eds. 1965. *Markets in Africa: Eight Subsistence Economies in Transition*. Garden City, N.Y.: Anchor.

Booth, Charles, n.d. *1890s. Rates and the Housing Question in London. An Argument for the Rating of Site Values*, 11 pages. London: English League for the Taxation of Land Values.

Born, Karl Erich. 1984. *International Banking in the 19th and 20th Centuries*. New York: St. Martin's.

Bourdieu, Pierre. 1984. *Distinction. A Social Critique of the Judgement of Taste*. Cambridge, Mass.: Harvard University Press.

———. (1984) 1990. *The Logic of Practice*. Redwood City, Calif.: Stanford University Press.

Bracking, Sarah. 2009. *Money and Power: Great Predators in the Political Economy of Development*. London: Pluto.

Bryceson, Deborah F. 1987. "A Century of Food Supply in Dar es Salaam." In *Feeding African Cities*, ed. J. I. Guyer, 154–202. Manchester, UK: Manchester University Press for the International African Institute.

Brynjolfsson, Erik, and Andrew McAfee. 2014. *The Second Machine Age: Work, Progress, and Prosperity in a Time of Brilliant Technologies*. New York: W. W. Norton.

Burchell, Graham, Colin Gordon, and Peter Miller, eds. 1991. *The Foucault Effect: Studies in Governmentality*. London: Harvester-Wheatsheaf.

Burgin, Angus. 2012. *The Great Persuasion: Reinventing Free Markets since the Depression*. Cambridge, Mass.: Harvard University Press.

Business Times. 1994. "Budget of Renewal," February 6, p. 21.

Butler, Judith, and Athena Athanasiou. 2013. *Dispossession: The Performative in the Political*. Oxford: Wiley.

Cagan, Phillip. 1989. "Monetarism." In *Money* (New Palgrave Series), ed. John Eatwell, Murray Milgate, and Peter Newman, 195–205. New York: W. W. Norton.

Çalişkan, Koray, and Michel Callon. 2009. "Economization, Part 1: A Research Programme for the Study of Markets." *Economy and Society* 38 (no. 3): 369–98.

———. 2010. "Economization, Part 2: A Research Program for the Study of Markets." *Economy and Society* 39 (no. 1): 1–32.

Callon, Michel. 1998a. "Introduction: The Embeddedness of Economic Markets in Economics." In *The Laws of the Markets*, ed. Michel Callon, 1–57. Oxford: Blackwell.

———. 1998b. "An Essay on Framing and Overflowing: Economic Externalities Revisited by Sociology." In *The Laws of the Markets*, ed. Michel Callon, 244–69. Oxford: Blackwell.

Callon, Michel. 2008. "Il n'y a d'économie qu'aux marges" A propos du livre de Jane Guyer" (Marginal Gains: Monetary Transactions in Atlantic Africa). Chicago: University of Chicago Press, 2004. *Le Libellio d'Aegis* (2008) 4 (no. 2): 1–18.

Callon, Michel, Pierre Lascoumes, and Yannick Barthes. 2009. *Acting in an Uncertain World: An Essay on Technical Democracy*. Translated by Graham Burchell. Cambridge, Mass.: MIT Press.

Callon, Michel, Cécile Méadel, and Vololona Rabeharisoa. 2002. "The Economy of Qualities." *Economy and Society* 31 (no. 2): 194–217.

Callon, Michel, Yuval Millo, and Fabian Muniesa, eds. 2007. *Market Devices*. Malden, Mass.: Blackwell.

Carnielli, Walter, and Claudio Pizzi. 2008. *Modalities and Multimodalities*. Dordrecht, Netherlands: Springer.

Carrier, James G. 1992. "Occidentalism: The World Turned Upside Down." *American Ethnologist* 19: 195–212.

Carrier, James G., and Daniel Miller. 1998. *Virtualism: A New Political Economy*. Oxford: Berg.

Carrithers, Michael. 2005. "Anthropology as a Moral Science of Possibilities." *Current Anthropology* 46 (no. 3): 433–56.

Carruthers, Bruce G., and Wendy Nelson Espeland. 1991. "Accounting for Rationality: Double Entry Bookkeeping and the Rhetoric of Economic Rationality." *American Journal of Sociology* 97 (no. 1): 31–69.

Carson, Rachel. 1962. *Silent Spring*. Boston: Houghton Mifflin.

Cawson, Alan. 1986. *Corporatism and Political Theory*. Oxford: Basil Blackwell.

Chanock, Martin. 1985. *Law, Custom and Social Order: The Colonial Experience in Malawi and Zambia*. Cambridge, UK: Cambridge University Press.

Chatterjee, Partha. 2004. *The Politics of the Governed: Reflections on Popular Politics in Most of the World*. New York: Columbia University Press.

Chayanov, A.V. 1966. *The Theory of Peasant Economy*. Homewood, Ill.: R.D. Irwin.

Chu, J. 2010. *Cosmologies of Credit: Transnational Mobility and the Politics of Destination in China*. Durham, N.C.: Duke University Press.

Cochrane, John H. 2005. "Financial Markets and the Real Economy." Working Paper 11193. Cambridge, Mass.: National Bureau of Economic Research.

Cohn, Bernard S., and Nicholas B. Dirks. 1988. "Beyond the Fringe: The Nation State, Colonialism, and the Technologies of Power." *Journal of Historical Sociology* 1 (no. 2): 224–29.

Collins D., J. Morduch, S. Rutherford, and O. Ruthven. 2009. *Portfolios of the Poor: How the World's Poor Live on $2 a Day*. Princeton, N.J.: Princeton University Press.

Comaroff, Jean, and John L. Comaroff. 1992. "Home-Made Hegemony: Modernity, Domesticity, and Colonialism in South Africa." In *African Encounters with Domesticity*, ed. K. Hansen, 37–74. New Brunswick, N.J.: Rutgers University Press.

———. 2011. *Theory from the South: Or How Euro-America Is Evolving Towards Africa*. Boulder, Colo.: Paradigm.

Comaroff, John L. 1982. "Dialectical Systems, History and Anthropology: Units of Study and Questions of Theory." *Journal of Southern African Studies* 8 (no. 2): 143–72.

———. 1989 "Images of Empire, Contests of Conscience: Models of Colonial Domination in South Africa." *American Ethnologist* 16: 661–85.

Comaroff, John, and Simon Roberts. 1981. *Rules and Processes: The Cultural Context of Dispute in an African Context*. Chicago: University of Chicago.

Concord Weekly. 1984a. "Dikko: Kidnapped, Drugged and Found." July (pilot issue), p. 5.

———. 1984b. "Economic Outlook: Recovery Still a Long Way Off." September 14, p. 37.

———. 1984c. "Essential Goods Still Costly." August 24, p. 17.

———. 1984d. "Food Locked in Warehouses." September 14, p. 37.

———. 1984e. "The Military: Leadership by Example?" August 24, p. 13.

Connolly, William E. 2013. *The Fragility of Things: Self-Organizing Processes, Neoliberal Fantasies, and Democratic Activism.* Durham, N.C.: Duke University Press.

Cooper, Frederick. 1989. "From Free Labor to Family Allowances: Labor and African Society in Colonial Discourse." *American Ethnologist* 16: 745–65.

Cooper, Frederick, and Ann L. Stoler. 1989. "Tensions of Empire: Colonial Control and Visions of Rule." *American Ethnologist* 16: 609–21.

Copernicus. 1526. *Treatise on Money.* http://translate.google.com/translate?hl=en& langpair=la%7Cen&u=http://www.taieb.net/auteurs/Copernic/monete.html.

Crapanzano, Vincent. 2000. *Serving the Word: Literalism in America from the Pulpit to the Bench.* New York: New Press.

Creasey, Gerald. 1947. Letter to Sir Arthur Richards, Office of the West African Council. February 19. (IbMinAgric 18584 Vol. I). National Archives, Ibadan, Nigeria.

Creswell, Julie, and Robert Gebeloff. 2014. Traders Profit as Power Grid Is Overworked. *New York Times*, August 14.

Culwick, G. M. 1943. "Nutrition Work in British African Colonies since 1939." *Africa* 14 (no. 1): 24–26.

Daily Service (Lagos). 1942. Gari Contract to U.A.C. July 19. (C.S.0.26:37909/6–18). National Archives, Ibadan, Nigeria.

Daily Times. 1995. "Budget '95: Three Months After." April 22, pp. 7 and 15.

Daily Times (Lagos). 1988. "Daily Times Opinion: Imminent Food Crisis." January 20, p. 10.

Das, Veena. 2004. "The Signature of the State: The Paradox of Illegibility." In *Anthropology in the Margins of the State*, ed. V. Das and D. Poole, 225–52. Oxford: Oxford University Press.

———. 2006. *Life and Words: Violence and the Descent into the Ordinary.* Berkeley: University of California Press.

Das, Veena, and Deborah Poole. 2004. *Anthropology in the Margins of the State.* Santa Fe, N.M.: School for Advanced Research Press.

Dash, Eric. 2005. "Where 25 Million Is Merely Average." *New York Times*, July 6.

Davidson, Adam. 2006. "Analyst: Blame Investors for High Gas Prices." National Public Radio, Business Section, August 24.

Davidson, Basil. 1992. *The Black Man's Burden: The Myth of African Tribalism and the Curse of the Nation State.* New York: Times Books.

de Angelis, Massimo. 1999. "Marx's Theory of Primitive Accumulation: A Suggested Reinterpretation." Personal Home Pages, University of East London, UK, http:// homepages.uel.ac.uk/M.DeAngelis/PRIMACCA.htm.

de Cecco, Marcello. 1984. "The International Gold Standard: Money and Empire." London: F. Pinter.

DeLanda, Manuel. 2006. *A New Philosophy of Society: Assemblage Theory and Social Complexity.* London: Continuum.

Deleuze, Gilles. 1991. *Empiricism and Subjectivity: An Essay on Hume's Theory of Human Nature.* New York: Columbia University Press.

Derluguian, Georgi, and Timothy Earle. 2010. "Strong Chieftaincies out of Weak States, or Elemental Power Unbound." In *Troubled Regions and Failing States: The Clustering and Contagion of Armed Conflicts*, ed. Kristian Berg Harpviken, 51–76. Bradford UK: Emerald Group.

Director of Commerce and Industries. 1948. Letter to the Chief Secretary to the Government. September 2 (C.S.O 26, 36895 Vol. Ill). National Archives, Ibadan, Nigeria.

District Agent, John Holt and Co. 1941. Letter to Captain Mackie, Director of Agriculture, Moor Plantation, Ibadan. August 26 (C.S.0.36895/S.4). National Archives, Ibadan, Nigeria.

Djebah, Oma. 1996. "Storm over Budget Surplus." *Guardian*, September 17.

Dodd, George. 1856. *The Food of London: A Sketch of the Chief Varieties, Sources of Supply, Probable Quantities, Modes of Arrival, Processes of Manufacture, Suspected Adulteration and Machinery of Distribution of the Food for a Community of Two Millions and a Half.* London: Longman, Brown, Green, and Longman.

Donzelot, Jacques. 1988. "The Promotion of the Social." *Economy and Society* 17 (no. 3): 395–426.

———. 1991. "The Mobilization of Society." In *The Foucault Effect: Studies in Governmentality*, ed. G. Burchell, C. Gordon, and P. Miller, 169–80. London: Harvester-Wheatsheaf.

Dorward, D. C. 1974. "Ethnography and Administration: A Study of Anglo-Tiv 'Working Misunderstanding.'" *Journal of African History* 15 (no. 3): 457–77.

———. 1976. "Precolonial Tiv Trade and Cloth Currency." *International Journal of African Historical Studies* 9: 576–91.

Douglas, Mary. 1992. *Risk and Blame: Essays in Culture Theory.* London: Routledge.

Eagleton, Terry. 1991. *Ideology: An Introduction.* New York: Verso.

Economist. 2004. "And for My Next Trick." *Economist*, April 24, p. 29.

———. 2011. "More Anthropologists on Wall Street Please." *Economist*, October 24. http://www.economist.com/blogs/democracyinamerica/2011/10/education-policy (accessed March 21, 2012).

Edemodu, Austin. 1996. *Guardian*, January 5, p. 18.

Eden, Frederic Morton. 1797. *The State of the Poor.* London, printed by J. Davis.

Eglash, Ron. 1997. "When Math Worlds Collide: Intention and Invention in Ethnomathematics." *Science, Technology and Human Values* 22 (no. 1): 79–97.

———. 1999. *African Fractals: Modern Computing and Indigenous Design.* New Brunswick, N.J.: Rutgers University Press.

Eichengreen, Barry. 1996. *Globalizing Capital: A History of the International Monetary System.* Princeton, N.J.: Princeton University Press.

Einaudi, Luigi 1953. "The Theory of Imaginary Money from Charlemagne to the French Revolution." In *Enterprise and Secular Change: Readings in Economic History*, ed. Frederic C. Lane and Jelle C. Riemersma, 229–61. Homewood, Ill.: Richard D. Unwin.

Elleh, Nnamdi. 2002. *Architecture and Power in Africa.* Westport, Conn.: Praeger.

Ernie, Rowland. 1961. *English Farming Past and Present*, 6th ed. Chicago: Quadrangle.

Ezekiel, May Ellen, with George Otiono. 1985. "Consumers Still Hard Hit: As Supply Company and Distributors Pass Buck, Prices Continue to Soar." *Newswatch*, August 12, pp. 22–23.

Falola, Toyin. 1989. "Cassava Starch for Export in Nigeria during the Second World War." *African Economic History* 18: 73–98.

Falola, Toyin, and Akanmu Adebayo. 2000. *Culture, Politics and Money among the Yoruba.* New Brunswick, N.J.: Transaction.

Fanon, Frantz. 1963. *The Wretched of the Earth.* New York: Grove Weidenfeld.

Fantacci, Luca. 2013. "Why Not Bancor? Keynes's Currency Plan as aSolution to Global Imbalances." In *Keynesian Reflections: Effective Deman, Money, Finance, and Policies in Crisis*, ed. Hirai,Toshiaki Maria Cristina Marcuzzo, and Perry Mehrling, 172–96. Oxford: Oxford University Press.

Featherstone, Mike. 1990. "Global Culture: An Introduction." *Theory, Culture and Society* (special issue) 7 (nos. 2–3): 1–14.

Ferguson, James. 1999. *Expectations of Modernity: Myths and Meanings of Urban Life on the Zambian Copperbelt.* Berkeley: University of California Press.

———. 2009. "The Uses of Neoliberalism." *Antipode* 41 (no. S1): 166–84.

Ferguson, Niall. 2001. *The Cash Nexus: Money and Power in the Modern World, 1700–2000.* New York: Basic Books.

Field, Geoffrey. 1990. "Perspectives on the Working-Class Family in Wartime Britain, 1939–1945." *International Labor and Working Class History* 38: 3–28.

Fields, Karen E., and Barbara J. Fields. 2014. *Racecraft: The Soul of Inequality in American Life.* London: Verso.

Financial Guardian. 1992. August 10, p. 6.

Fine, Ben. 1998. "The Triumph of Economics: Or 'Rationality' Can Be Dangerous to Your Reasoning." In *Virtualism: The New Political Economy*, ed. James Carrier and Daniel Miller, 49–73. Oxford: Berg.

———. 2003. "Callonistics: A Disentanglement." *Economy and Society* 32 (no. 3): 478–83.

Fioramonti, Lorenzo. 2013. *Gross Domestic Problem: The Politics behind the World's Most Powerful Number.* London: Zed.

Firth, Raymond. 1934. "The Sociological Study of the Native Diet." *Africa* 7 (no. 4): 401–14.

Folawewo, A. O. 2007. "Macroeconomic Effects of Minimum Wage in Nigeria: A General Equilibrium Analysis." Paper for CSEA Conference 2007: "Economic Development in Africa," Oxford, UK, March 19–20. http://www.csae.ox.ac.uk/conferences/2007-EDiA-LaWBiDC/papers/042-Folawewo.pdf.

Fontaine, Laurence. 2008. *L'économie morale, pauvreté, crédit et confiance dans l'Europe préindustrielle.* Paris: Gallimard.

———. 2014. *Le marché: Histoire et usages d'une conquête sociale.* Paris: Gallimard.

Forrest, Tom. 1995. *Politics and Economic Development in Nigeria.* Boulder, Colo.: Westview.

Foster-Carter, Aiden. 1978. "Can We Articulate 'Articulation'?" In *The New Economic Anthropology*, ed. John Clammer. New York: St. Martin's.

Foucault, Michel. 1991. "Governmentality." In *The Foucault Effect: Studies in Governmentality*, ed. Graham Burchell, Colin Gordon, and Peter Miller, 87–104. London: Harvester-Wheatsheaf.

Friedman, Milton. 1957. *A Theory of the Consumption Function.* Princeton, N.J.: Princeton University Press.

———. 1987. "Quantity Theory of Money." In *Money* (New Palgrave Series), ed. John Eatwell, Murray Milgate, and Peter Newman, 1–40. New York: W. W. Norton.

———. 1991. *Monetarist Economics.* Cambridge, Mass.: Basil Blackwell.

Friedman, Milton, and Rose Friedman. 1980. *Free to Choose: A Personal Statement.* New York: Harcourt Brace.

Gagnon, R. E., A. J. Macnab, and F. A. Gagnon. 2000. "A Quantitative Ranking of Canada's Research Output of Original Human Studies for the Decade 1989 to 1998." *Canadian Medical Association Journal* 162 (no. 1): 37–40.

Gahia, Chukwuemeka. 1996. "Antinomies of a Fiscal Policy." *Post Express*, August 15, p. 17.

Garrard, T. 1980. *Akan Weights and the Gold Trade.* London: Longman.

Geertz, Clifford. 1963. *Agricultural Involution.* Berkeley: University of California Press.

Gellner, Ernest. 1965. *Thought and Change.* Chicago: University of Chicago Press.

Geschiere, Peter, M. Goheen, and C. Piot, eds. 2007. Special section, Jane Guyer's "Marginal Gains: Monetary Transactions in Atlantic Africa." *African Studies Review* 50 (no. 2): 37–202.

Gillespie, Tarleton. 2010. "The Politics of 'Platforms.' " *New Media and Society* 12 (no. 3): 347–64.

Gillie, Alan. 1996. "The Origin of the Poverty Line." *Economic History Review*, n.s., 49 (no. 4): 715–30.

Gillingham, Robert. 1980. "Estimating the Use Cost of Owner-Occupied Housing." *Monthly Labor Review* (February): 31–34.

Girle, Rod. 2003. *Possible Worlds*. Montreal: Queens-McGill Press.

Glasser, Barry. 1982. "An Essay on Iterative Social Time." *Sociological Review* 30 (no. 4): 668–81.

Gleason, James T. 2000. *Risk: The New Management Imperative in Finance*. Princeton N.J.: Bloomberg.

Gluckman, Max, ed. 1964. "Closed Systems and Open Minds: The Limits of Naivety in Social Anthropology." Edinburgh: Oliver and Boyd.

Goldenweiser, Alexander. 1936. "Loose Ends of a Theory on the Individual Pattern and Involution in Primitive Society." In *Essays in Anthropology Presented to A. L. Kroeber*, ed. R. Lowie, 99–103. Berkeley: University of California Press.

Goody, Jack. 1962. *The Developmental Cycle in Domestic Groups*. Cambridge, UK: Cambridge University Press.

Goux, Jean-Joseph. 1990. *Symbolic Economies*. Ithaca, N.Y.: Cornell University Press.

Governor of Nigeria. 1940. Governor's Broadcast (15). Extract of the West African Pilot, November 25. (IbMinAgric 18584 Vol. I). National Archives, Ibadan, Nigeria.

Graeber, David. 2004. *The Twilight of the Vanguard*. Chicago: Prickly Paradigm.

———. 2011. *Debt: The First Five Thousand Years*. Brooklyn, N.Y.: Melville House.

Green, Arthur. 1999. *These Are the Words: A Vocabulary of Jewish Spiritual Life*. Woodstock Vt.: Jewish Lights.

Gregory, C. A. 1997. *Savage Money: The Anthropology and Politics of Commodity Exchange*. Amsterdam: Overseas Publishers Association.

Grytten, Ola H. 2004. "A Consumer Price Index for Norway." In *Historical Monetary Statistics for Norway 1819–2003*, ed. Øyvind Eitrheim, Jan T. Klovland, and Jan F. Qvigstad, 47–98. Norges Bank, Occasional Paper No. 35.

Guardian. 1996a. August 21, p. 17.

———. 1996b. "Mixed Reactions Trail Budget Performance." September 18.

———. 1996c. "Storm over Budget Surplus." September 17.

Gudeman, Stephen. 2001. *The Anthropology of Economy: Community, Market, and Culture*. Oxford: Blackwell.

———. 2009. "The Persuasions of Economics." In *Economic Persuasions*, ed. Stephen Gudeman, 63–96. New York: Berghan.

Guyer, Jane I. 1978. "The Food Economy and French Colonial Rule in Central Cameroun." *Journal of African History* 19 (no. 4): 577–97.

———. 1980. "Head Tax, Social Structure, and Rural Incomes in Cameroun, 1922–37." *Cahiers d'Etudes Africaines* 20 (no. 3): 305–29.

———. 1985. "The Iron Currencies of Southern Cameroon." *Symbols*, December, pp. 2–5, 15–16.

———. 1986. "Indigenous Currencies and the History of Marriage Payments: A Case Study from Cameroon." *Cahier d'Etudes Africaines* 104: 577–610.

———, ed. 1987. *Feeding African Cities: Studies in Regional Social History*. Manchester, UK: Manchester University Press.

———. 1992. "Representation without Taxation: An Essay on Democracy in Rural Nigeria, 1952–1990." *African Studies Review* 35 (no. 1): 41–79.

———. 1993a. " 'Toiling Ingenuity': Food Regulation in Britain and Nigeria." *American Ethnologist* 20 (no. 4): 797–817.

———. 1993b. "Wealth in People and Self-Realisation in Equatorial Africa." *Man*, n.s., 28 (no. 2): 243–65.

———. 1994. "The Spatial Dimensions of 'Civil Society' in Africa (with Particular Reference to Nigeria): An Ethnographic Approach." In *Civil Society and the State in Africa*, ed. John Harbeson, Donald Rothchild, and Naomi Chazan, 215–29. Boulder, Colo.: Lynne Rienner.

———. 1996. "Traditions of Invention in Equatorial Africa." *African Studies Review* 39: 1–28.

———. 1997. *An African Niche Economy: Farming to Feed Ibadan, 1968–88*. Edinburgh: Edinburgh University Press.

———. 2000. "Rationality or Reasoning? Comment on Heath Pearson's '*HomoEconomicus* Goes Native, 1859–1945'." *History of Political Economy* 32 (no. 4): 1011–15.

———. 2001. "The Life Cycle as a Rational Proposition, or 'The Arc of Intermediate Links' (Simmel, *The Philosophy of Money*, 208)." Unpublished paper for a panel at the American Anthropological Association meetings on Temporalities of Rationality.

———. 2004. *Marginal Gains: Monetary Transactions in Atlantic Africa*. Chicago: University of Chicago Press.

———. 2005a. "Confusion and Empiricism: Several Connected Thoughts." In *Christianity in Africa: Essays in Honor of J. D. Y. Peel*, ed. Toyin Falola, 83–97. Rochester, N.Y.: University of Rochester Press.

———. 2005b. "Niches, Margins and Profits: Persisting with Heterogeneity." *African Economic History* 32: 173–91.

———. 2007a. "'Africa Has Never Been 'Traditional': So Can We Make a General Case? A Response to the Articles." *African Studies Review* 50 (no. 2): 183–202.

———. 2007b. "Prophecy and the Near Future: Thoughts on Macroeconomic, Evangelical and Punctuated Time." *American Ethnologist* 34 (no. 3): 409–21.

———. 2009a. "Composites, Fictions and Risk: Toward an Ethnography of Price." In *Market and Society: The Great Transformation Today*, ed. Chris Hann and Keith Hart, 203–20. Cambridge UK: Cambridge University Press.

———. 2009b. "On Possibility: A Response to How Is Anthropology Going?" *Anthropological Theory* 9 (no. 4): 355–70.

———. 2010. "The Eruption of Tradition? On Ordinality and Calculation." *Anthropological Theory* 10 (nos. 1–2): 123–31.

———. 2012a. "The Burden of Wealth and the Lightness of Life: The Body in Body-Decoration in Southern Cameroon." In *Lives in Motion, Indeed. Interdisciplinary Perspectives on Social Change in Honour of Danielle de Lame*, ed. Cristiana Panella, 351–68. Royal Museum for Central Africa, Tervuren, Belgium.

———. 2012b. "Life in Financial Calendrics." *Fieldsights—Theorizing the Contemporary, Cultural Anthropology*, May 14. http://www.culanth.org/fieldsights/338-life-in -financial-calendrics.

———. 2012c. "Obligation, Binding, Debt and Responsibility: Provocations about Temporality from Two New Sources," in special issue on debt, ed. Holly High. *Social Anthropology/Anthropologie Sociale* 20 (no. 4): 491–501.

———. 2012d. "Terms of Debate versus Words in Circulation: Some Rhetorics of the Crisis." In *Handbook of Economic Anthropology*, ed. James Carrier, 612–25. Cheltenham, UK: Edward Elgar.

———. 2013a. "Quantities in Multiple Currency Systems: Preliminary Thoughts from

African History." Paper presented at the Meeting of the Group La monnaie entre uni-cité et pluralité, Paris.

———. 2013b. "The Quickening of the Unknown: Epistemologies of Surprise in Anthro-pology." *HAU: Journal of Ethnographic Theory* 3 (no. 3): 283–307.

———. 2014. "Gross Domestic Person?" *Anthropology Today* 30 (no. 2): 11–15.

Guyer, Jane I., with LaRay Denzer. 2009. " 'The Craving for Intelligibility': Speech and Silence on the Economy under Structural Adjustment and Military Rule in Nigeria." In *Economic Persuasions: Studies in Rhetoric and Culture*, vol. 4, ed. Stephen Gudeman, 97–117. Oxford: Berghahn.

Guyer, Jane I., and LaRay Denzer. 2013. "Prebendalism and the People: The Price of Petrol at the Pump." In *Democracy and Prebendal Politics in Nigeria: Critical Reinterpretations*, ed. Wale Adebanwi and Ebenezer Obadare, 53–77. New York: Palgrave-Macmillan.

Guyer, Jane I., LaRay Denzer, and Adigun Agbaje, eds. 2002. *Money Struggles and City Life: Devaluation in Ibadan and Other Urban Centers in Southern Nigeria, 1986–1996.* Ports-mouth, N.H.: Heinemann.

Guyer, Jane I., and S. M. Eno Belinga. 1995."Wealth in People as Wealth in Knowledge: Accumulation and Composition in Equatorial Africa." *Journal of African History* 36: 91–120.

Guyer, Jane I., Naveeda Khan, and Juan Obarrio, eds. 2010. "Number as Inventive Fron-tier." Special section, *Anthropological Theory*, 10 (no. 1): 36–197.

Guyer, Jane I., et al. 2007. "Temporal Heterogeneity in the Study of African Land Use." *Human Ecology* 35 (no. 1): 3–17.

Guyer, Jane I, with Kabiru Salami and Olusanya Akinlade 2011. " 'Kò s'ówó': il n'y a pas d'argent!" *Politique africaine* 124 (December 2011): 43–65.

Halperin , Rhoda. 1984. "Polanyi, Marx, and the Institutional Paradigm in Economic Anthropology." *Research in Economic Anthropology* 6: 245–72.

Hammar, Amanda, ed. 2014. *Displacement Economies in Africa: Paradoxes of Crisis and Cre-ativity.* London: Zed.

Hammond, Richard. J. 1951. *Food*, vol. 1: *The Growth of Policy* (History of the Second World War). London: His Majesty's Stationery Office.

———. 1954. *Food and Agriculture in Britain 1939–45: Aspects of Wartime Control.* Stanford, Calif.: Stanford University Press.

———. 1956. *Food*, vol. 2: *Studies in Administration and Control* (History of the Second World War). London: Her Majesty's Stationery Office.

Han, Clara. 2004. "The Work of Indebtedness: The Traumatic Present of Late Capitalist Chile." *Culture, Medicine and Psychiatry* 28: 169–87.

———. 2012. *Life in Debt: Times of Care and Violence in Neoliberal Chile.* Berkeley: Univer-sity of California Press.

Hann, Chris, and Keith Hart. 2009. *Market and Society: The Great Transformation Today.* Cambridge, UK: Cambridge University Press.

———. 2011. *Economic Anthropology: History, Ethnography, Critique.* Cambridge, UK: Polity.

Harbeson, John, Don Rothchild, and Naomi Chazan, eds. 1994. *Civil Society and the State in Africa.* Boulder, Colo.: Lynne Reiner.

Hardin, Gary. 1968. "The Tragedy of the Commons." *Science* 162 (no. 3859): 1243–48.

Harding, Susan Friend. 2000. *The Book of Jerry Falwell: Fundamentalist Language and Poli-tics.* Princeton, N.J.: Princeton University Press.

Hardt, Michael, and Antonio Negri. 2004. *Multitude: War and Democracy in the Age of Empire.* New York: Penguin Press.

Hart, Keith. 1986. "Heads or Tails? Two Sides of the Coin." *Man*, n.s., 21 (no. 4): 637–56.

————. 1999. *The Memory Bank: Money in an Unequal World*. London: Profile.

————. 2010 Models of Statistical Distribution: A Window on Social History. *Anthropological Theory* 10 (nos. 1–2): 67–74.

————. 2012. "The Roots of the Global Economic Crisis." *Anthropology Today* 28 (no. 2): 1–3.

Hart, Keith, Jean-Louis Laville, and Antonio David Cattani. 2010. *The Human Economy: A Citizen's Guide*. Cambridge, UK: Polity.

Hart, Keith, and Horacio Ortiz. 2014. "The Anthropology of Money and Finance: Between Ethnography and World History." *Annual Review of Anthropology* 43: 465–82.

Harvey, David. 1990. *The Condition of Postmodernity: An Enquiry into the Origins of Cultural Change*. Cambridge, Mass.: Blackwell.

————. 2014. *Seventeen Contradictions and the End of Capitalism*. Oxford: Oxford University Press.

Hayek, Friedrich von. (1944) 2007. *The Road to Serfdom*. Chicago: University of Chicago Press.

Hazlitt, Henry. (1946) 1979. *Economics in One Lesson: The Shortest and Surest Way to Understand Basic Economics*. New York: Random House.

Heschel, Abraham Joshua. 1962. *The Prophets*. New York: Harper and Row.

————. 1996. *Prophetic Inspiration after the Prophets: Maimonides and Other Medieval Authorities*. Hoboken N.J.: Ktav.

Hibou, Beatrice. 2004. *Privatizing the State*. New York: Columbia University Press.

————. 2012. *La bureaucratization du monde à l'ère néolibérale*. Paris: La Découverte. [*The Bureaucratization of the World in the Neoliberal Era*. Translated by Andrew Brown. New York: Palgrave Macmillan, 2015.]

High, Holly, ed. 2012. Special issue on debt, *Social Anthropology* 20 (no. 4): 363–508.

Hirsch, F. 1976. *The Social Limits to Growth*. London: Routledge and Kegan Paul.

Hirschman, Albert O. 1977. *The Passions and the Interests: Political Arguments for Capitalism before Its Triumph*. Princeton, N.J.: Princeton University Press.

Ho, Karen. 2009. *Liquidated. An Ethnography of Wall St*. Durham, N.C.: Duke University Press.

Hobsbawm, Eric, and Terence Ranger, eds. 1983. *The Invention of Tradition*. Cambridge: Cambridge University Press.

Holmes, Douglas, and George E. Marcus. 2006 Fast-Capitalism: Paraethnography and the Rise of the Symbolic Analyst. In *Frontiers of Capital: Ethnographic Perspectives on the New Economy*, ed. Melissa Fisher and Greg Downey, 33–57. Durham, N.C.: Duke University Press.

Homer, S., and R. Sylla. 1991. *A History of Interest Rates*. New Brunswick, N.J.: Rutgers University Press.

Hyland, Richard. 2009. *Gifts: A Study in Comparative Law*. New York: Oxford University Press.

Ikeano, Ngozi. 1989. "Nigeria Is Self-Sufficient in Staple Food: Nasko." *Daily Times*, March 3, p. 14.

Imirhe, Toma. 1991. "Short of the Magic Wand." *African Guardian*, January 14, pp. 29–30.

Inikori, Joseph. 2002. *Africans and the Industrial Revolution in England: A Study in International Trade and Economic Development*. Cambridge: Cambridge University Press.

International Bureau of Weights and Measures (BIPM: Bureau International des Poids et Mesures). 2006. *The International System of Units*, 8th ed. Paris. http://www.bipm.org/en/publications/si-brochure/.

Irvine, Judith. 2004. "Say When: Temporalities in Language Ideologies." *Journal of Linguistic Anthropology* 14 (no. 1): 99–109.

Iyeke, Peter. 1996. *Vanguard*, February 19, pp. 1 and 2.

Jackson, Michael, ed. 1996. *Things as They Are: New Directions in Phenomenological Anthropology*. Bloomington: Indiana University Press.

———. 2012. *Lifeworlds: Essays in Existential Anthropology*. Chicago: University of Chicago Press.

James, Deborah. 2014. *Money from Nothing: Indebtedness and Aspiration in South Africa*. Stanford, Calif.: Stanford University Press.

James, Wendy, and David Mills. 2005. "Introduction: From Representation to Action in the Flow of Time." In *The Qualities of Time: Anthropological Approaches*, ed. Wendy James and David Mills, 1–15. Oxford: Berg.

Jameson, Fredric. 2002. *A Singular Modernity: Essay on the Ontology of the Present*. London: Verso.

Jerven, Morten. 2013. *Poor Numbers: How We Are Misled by African Development Statistics and What to Do about It*. Ithaca, N.Y.: Cornell University Press.

Johnson, Marion. 1966. "The Ounce in Eighteenth-Century West African Trade." *Journal of African History* 7 (no. 2): 197–214.

Joseph, Richard. 1987. *Democracy and Prebendal Politics in Nigeria: The Rise and Fall of the Second Republic*. Cambridge, UK: Cambridge University Press.

Jubien, Michael. 2009. *Possibility*. Oxford: Oxford University Press.

Kaplan, Michael. 2003. "Iconomics: The Rhetoric of Speculation." *Public Culture* 15 (no. 3): 477–93.

Kee, Thomas H. Jr. 2013. "Get Ready: Here Comes the Real Economy." CNBC, December 10. http://www.cnbc.com/id/101259050, accessed August 18, 2014.

Kant, Immanuel. (1788) 1929. *Critique of Pure Reason*. Translated by Norman Kemp Smith. New York: St. Martin's Press.

Keynes, John Maynard. (1936) 1964. *The General Theory of Employment, Interest and Money*. New York: Harcourt Brace.

Kjellberg, Hans. 2007. "The Death of a Salesman? Reconfiguring Economic Exchange in Swedish Post-War Food Distribution." In *Market Devices*, ed. Michel Callon, Yuval Millo, and Fabian Muniesa, 65–91. Oxford: Blackwell Publishing/The Sociological Review.

Knuttila, Simo, ed. 1981. *Reforging the Great Chain of Being: Studies of the History of Modal Theories*. Dordrecht, Netherlands: D. Reidel.

Kockelman, Paul. 2006. "A Semiotic Ontology of the Commodity." *Journal of Linguistic Anthropology* 16: 6–102.

Krugman, Paul. 2005a. "The $600 Billion Man." *New York Times*, March 15, p. A27.

———. 2005b. "Un-Spin the Budget." *New York Times*, July 11. http://www.nytimes.com/2005/07/11/opinion/11krugman.html.

Kuhn, Thomas. 1962. *The Structure of Scientific Revolutions*. Chicago: University of Chicago Press.

Kula, Witold. 1986. *Measures and Men*. Princeton, N.J.: Princeton University Press.

Kuroda, Akinobu. 2008a. "Concurrent but Nonintegrable Currency Circuits: Complementary Relationships among Monies in Modern China and Other Regions." *Financial History Review* 15: 17–36.

———. 2008b. "What Is the Complementarity among Monies? An Introductory Note." *Financial History Review* 15: 7–15.

———. 2009. "The Eurasian Silver Century, 1276–1359: Commensurability and Multiplicity." *Journal of Global History* 4: 245–69.

———. 2013. "What was Silver Tael System? A Mistake of China as Silver 'Standard' Country." *Moneta* (Belgium) 56: 391–97.

Kwon, H. 2008. *Ghosts of War in Vietnam*. Cambridge: Cambridge University Press.

Labouret, Henri. 1938. "L'alimentation des autochtones dans les possessions tropicales." *Africa* 11 (no. 2):160–73.

LaHaye, Tim, and Thomas Ice. 2001. *Charting the End Times*. Eugene, Ore.: Harvest House.

Latour, Bruno, 1993. *We Have Never Been Modern*. London: Harvester-Wheatsheaf.

———. 1999. "Recalling ANT." *Sociological Review* 47 (no. S1): 15–25.

———. 2005. *Reassembling the Social*. Oxford: Oxford University Press.

———. 2012 *Enquête sur les modes d'existence: Une anthropologie des modernes*. Paris: La Decouverte.

———. 2014a. "Another Way to Compose the Common World." *HAU Journal of Ethnographic Theory* 4 (no. 1): 301–7.

———. 2014b. "Technical Does Not Mean Material." *HAU Journal of Ethnographic Theory* 4 (no. 1): 507–10.

Law, John. 2009. "Actor Network Theory and Material Semiotics." In *New Blackwell Companion to Social Theory*, ed. Bryan S. Turner, 142–57. Oxford: Blackwell.

Lee, Benjamin. 1997. *Talking Heads: Language, Metalanguage, and the Semiotics of Subjectivity*. Durham, N.C.: Duke University Press.

Lee, Benjamin, and Edward LiPuma. 2004. *Financial Derivatives and the Globalization of Risk*. Durham, N.C.: Duke University Press.

Leonhardt, David. 2003. " 'Egalitarian Recession' Keeps Anger At Bay." *New York Times*, June 15, Week in Review. http://query.nytimes.com/gst/fullpage.html?res=9B0CEFD81738F936A25755C0A9659C8B63.

Lepinay, Vincent-Antonin. 2007. "Parasitic formulae: The Case of Capital Guarantee Products." *Sociological Review* 55, Issue Supplement S2: 261–83.

———. 2011. *Codes of Finance: Engineering Derivatives in a Global Bank*. Princeton N.J.: Princeton University Press.

Lessig, Lawrence. 2008. *Remix: Making Art and Commerce Thrive in the Hybrid Economy*. New York: Penguin.

Leubuscher, Charlotte. 1939. "Marketing Schemes for Native-Grown Produce in African Territories." Africa 12 (no. 2): 163–88.

Levi-Strauss, Claude. 1966. *The Savage Mind*. Chicago: University of Chicago Press.

Levy, Jonathan. 2012. *Freaks of Fortune: The Emerging World of Capitalism and Risk in America*. Cambridge Mass.: Harvard University Press.

Lexecon. (Kenneth Grant, David Ownby, and Steven R. Peterson, eds.). 2006. *Understanding Today's Crude Oil and Product Markets*. Policy Analysis Study. American Petroleum Institute.

Lindsey, David E., and Henry C. Wallich. 1989. "Monetary Policy." In *Money* (New Palgrave Series), ed. John Eatwell, Murray Milgate, and Peter Newman, 229–43. New York: W. W. Norton.

Livio, Mario. 2009. *Is God a Mathematician?* New York: Simon and Schuster.

Lloyd, Genevieve. 2008. *Providence Lost*. Cambridge, Mass.: Harvard University Press.

Löfving, Staffan, ed. 2005. *Peopled Economies: Conversations with Stephen Gudeman*. Uppsala, Sweden: Interface.

Lutzker, Adam, and Judy Rosenthal. 2001. "The Unheimlich Manoeuvre." *American Ethnologist* 28 (no. 4): 909–23.

MacIntyre, Alasdair C. 1981. *After Virtue: A Study in Moral Theory*. Notre Dame, Ind.: University of Notre Dame Press.

MacKenzie, Donald, Fabian Muniesa, and Lucia Siu. 2007. *Do Economists Make Markets?* Princeton, N.J.: Princeton University Press.

Mackie, J. M. 1943. Letter to the Chief Secretary to the Government. April 18 (C.S.O. 26, 36895 Vol. III). National Archives, Ibadan, Nigeria.

Mallard, Alexandre. 2007. "Performance Testing: Dissection of a Consumerist Experiment." In *Market Devices*, ed. Michel Callon, Yuval Millo, and Fabian Muniesa, 152–72. Oxford: Blackwell.

Malmkjaer, Kirsten. 2002. *The Linguistics Encyclopedia*. New York: Routledge.

Malthus, Thomas. (1798) 1992. *An Essay on the Principle of Population*. Cambridge Texts in the History of Political Thought. Cambridge: Cambridge University Press.

Marshall, A. G. 1942. Letter to Major Kirk. September 22 (C.S.O. 26, 37909/C-18). National Archives, Ibadan, Nigeria.

Marshall, Alfred. 1890. *Principles of Economics*. Library of Economics and Liberty. www.econlib.org.

Matthews, William. 1987. *Foreseeable Futures: Poems*. Boston: Houghton Mifflin.

Maurer, Bill. 1999. "Forget Locke? From Proprietor to Risk-Bearer in New Logics of Finance." *Public Culture* 11 (no. 2): 365–85.

———. 2002. "Repressed Futures: Financial Derivatives' Theological Unconscious." *Economy and Society* 31 (no. 1): 15–36.

———. 2005a. "Chronotopes of the Alternative." Paper presented at the conference "Hope in the Economy," Cornell University.

———. 2005b. "Finance." In *Handbook of Economic Anthropology*, ed. James Carrier, 176–93. Cheltenham UK: Edward Elgar.

———. 2005c. *Mutual Life, Limited: Islamic Banking, Alternative Currencies, Lateral Reason*. Princeton, N.J.: Princeton University Press.

———. 2006. "The Anthropology of Money." *Annual Review of Anthropology* 35: 15–36.

———. 2007. Incalculable Payments: Money, Scale, and the South African Offshore Grey Money Amnesty. *African Studies Review* 50 (no. 2): 125–38.

———. 2011a. "Mobile Money, Money Magic, Purse Limits and Pins: Tracing Monetary Pragmatics." *Journal of Cultural Economy* 4: 349–59.

———. 2011b. "Money Nutters." *Economic Sociology: The European Electronic Newsletter* 12 (no. 3): 5–12.

———. 2012a. "Mobile Money: Communication, Consumption and Change in the Payments Space." *Journal of Development Studies* 45 (no. 5): 589–604.

———. 2012b. "Payments." *Cambridge Anthropology* 30 (no. 2): 15–35.

Mauss, Marcel. 1990. *The Gift*, trans. W. D. Halls. New York: W. W. Norton.

Mbembe, Achille. 2001. *On the Postcolony*. Berkeley: University of California Press.

———. 2011. "Theory from the Antipodes: Notes on Jean and John Comaroff's *Theory from the South*." Manuscript.

Mead, Margaret. 1944. "Food as a Basis for International Cooperation." *Africa* 14 (no. 5): 258–64.

Merry, Sally. 2011. "Measuring the World: Indicators, Human Rights, and Global Governance." *Current Anthropology* 52 (supplementary issue no. 3): S83–S93.

Meyer, Birgit. 1999. *Translating the Devil: Religion and Modernity among the Ewe in Ghana*. Edinburgh: Edinburgh University Press for the International African Institute.

Mihm, S. 2007. *A Nation of Counterfeiters: Capitalists, Con Men, and the Making of the United States*. Cambridge, Mass.: Harvard University Press.

Miller, Rich. 2005. "Too Much Money: The Surprising Consequences of a Global Savings Glut." *Business Week*, July 11, pp. 48–56.

Mintz, Sidney. 1960. *Worker in the Cane: A Puerto Rican Life History*. New Haven, Conn.: Yale University Press.

———. 1964. "Currency Problems in Eighteenth Century Jamaica and Gresham's Law." In *Process and Patterns in Culture*, ed. Robert A. Manners, 248–65. Chicago: Aldine.

———. 1974. *Caribbean Transformations*. Chicago: Aldine.

———. 1985. *Sweetness and Power*. New York: Viking.

Mirowski, Philip. 2000. "Exploring the Fault Lines: Introduction to the Minisymposium on the History of Economic Anthropology." *History of Political Economy* 32 (no. 2): 919–32.

———. 2004. *The Effortless Economy of Science?* Durham, N.C.: Duke University Press.

Mitchell, Timothy. 2002. *Rule of Experts: Egypt, Techno-politics, Modernity*. Berkeley: University of California Press.

———. 2011. *Carbon Democracy. Political Power in the Age of Oil*. London: Verso.

Miyazaki, Hirokazu. 2003. "The Temporalities of the Market." *American Anthropologist* 105 (no. 2): 255–65.

———. 2004. *The Method of Hope: Anthropology, Philosophy, and Fijian Knowledge*. Stanford, Calif.: Stanford University Press.

———. 2012. *Arbitraging Japan: Dreams of Capitalism at the End of Finance*. Berkeley: University of California Press.

Modigliani, Franco. 1966. "The Life Cycle Hypothesis of Saving, the Demand for Wealth and the Supply of Capital." *Social Research* 33 (no. 1): 160–217.

———. 1986. "Life Cycle, Individual Thrift and the Wealth of Nations." *American Economic Review* 76: 297–313.

Mokuwa, E., M. Voors, E. Bulte, and P. Richards. 2011. "Peasant Grievance and Insurgency in Sierra Leone: Judicial Serfdom as a Driver of Conflict." *African Affairs* 110 (no. 440): 339–66.

Morgan, Lewis Henry. 1877. *Ancient Society*. New York: H. Holt

Moore, Sally Falk. 1978. *Law as Process: An Anthropological Approach*. London: Routledge and Kegan Paul.

———. 1986. *Social Facts and Fabrications. "Customary" Law on Kilimanjaro, 1880–1980*. Cambridge, UK: Cambridge University Press.

Muniesa, Fabian. 2014. *The Provoked Economy: Economic Reality and the Performative Turn*. Oxford: Taylor and Francis.

Munn, Nancy. 1992. "The Cultural Anthropology of Time: A Critical Essay." *Annual Review of Anthropology* 21: 93–123.

NAS (National Academy of Sciences). 2013. *Measuring What We Spend: Toward a New Consumer Expenditure Survey*, ed. Don A. Dillman and Carol C. House. Washington D.C., National Academies Press.

Neiburg, Federico. 2010. "Sick Currencies and Public Numbers." *Anthropological Theory* 10 (nos. 1–2): 96–102.

Newbreed. 1993. "Budget of Deceit: Old Wine in New Bottles." March 8, pp. 4–15.

Newswatch. 1987. November 30, cover.

———. 1988. July 25, p. 36.

———. 1989. "Sap Not Evil Speech." June 19, p. 20.

Ni, Peimin. 2002. *On Reid*. Belmont, Calif.: Wadsworth.

Nigerian Economist. 1987. January 6–19, p. 10.

———. 1988. "It's Spending Ease in '88." January 6–19, 13–14.

Nigerian Hand Book Review. 1992. 119–20.

Nixon, Simon. 2014. "A British Solution for EU's Corporate Debts." Europe File. *Wall Street Journal*, August 7.

Nordstrom, C. 2008. *Global Outlaws: Crime, Money and Power in the Contemporary World.* Berkeley, Calif.: University of California Press.

Obey, Ebenezer, and His Inter-Reformers Band. 1984. *Austerity.* (Jacket copy of phonograph recording). Lagos: Decca (West Africa).

Obukhova, Elena. 2002. "Living and Trusting in the Economy of Debt: The Distribution of Newspapers and Magazines in Ibadan." In *Money Struggles and City Life: Devaluation in Ibadan and Other Urban Centers in Southern Nigeria, 1986–1996*, ed. J. I. Guyer, L. Denzer, and A. Agbaje, 147–72. Portsmouth N.H.: Heinemann.

Olaniyan, Tejumola. 2004. *Arrest the Music! Fela and His Rebel Art and Politics.* Bloomington: Indiana University Press.

Omokhodion, Lawson, and Victor Iduwe. 1987. "A String of Deficit Budgets." *Thisweek.* February 2, pp. 24–25.

Orr, John Boyd. 1936. *Food, Health and Income.* London: Macmillan.

Orr, John Boyd, and David Lubbock. 1940. *Feeding the People in War-Time.* London: Macmillan.

Ortiz, Horacio. 2014. *Valeur financière et verité: Enquête d'anthropologie politique sur l'évaluation des entreprises cotées en bourse.* Paris: SciencesPo, Les Presses.

Ostrom, Elinor. 1990. *Governing the Commons: The Evolution of Institutions for Collective Action.* Cambridge: Cambridge University Press.

Oyewole, A. 1987. *Historical Dictionary of Nigeria.* London: Scarecrow.

Packard, Randall M. 1989 "The 'Healthy Reserve' and the 'Dressed Native': Discourses on Black Health and the Language of Legitimation in South Africa." *American Ethnologist* 16: 686–703.

Partridge, Damani J., Marina Welker, and Rebecca Hardin, eds. 2011. "Corporate Lives: New Perspectives on the Social Life of the Corporate Form." *Current Anthropology* 52 (supplementary issue no. 3). Wenner-Gren Symposium Series.

Patterson, Orlando. 1991. *Freedom.* New York: Basic Books.

Peebles, Gustav. 2010. "The Anthropology of Credit and Debt." *Annual Review of Anthropology* 39: 225–40.

———. 2011. *The Euro and Its Rivals. Currency and the Construction of a Transnational City.* Bloomington: Indiana University Press.

Peirce, Charles Sanders. 1905. "Issues of Pragmatism." *Monist* 15 (no. 4): 481–99.

Peters, Pauline E. 2013. "Conflicts over Land and Threats to Customary Tenure in Africa." *African Affairs* 112 (no. 449): 543–62.

Phelps-Brown, E. H., and Sheila Hopkins. 1956. "Seven Centuries of the Prices of Consumables Compared with Builders' Wage-Rates." *Economica* 23 (no. 92): 296–314.

Phillips, Kate, and Julie Bosman. 2006. "A Failure to Communicate? Big Oil Thinks It Has a Message, but It Isn't Reaching Consumers." *New York Times*, May 3, p. C1.

Piketty, Thomas. 2014. *Capital in the Twenty-First Century.* Cambridge, Mass.: Harvard University Press.

Polanyi, Karl. 1944. *The Great Transformation: The Political and Economic Origins of Our Time.* Boston: Beacon.

———. 1964. "Sortings and 'Ounce Trade' in the West African Slave Trade." *Journal of African History* 5: 381–93.

———. 1977. *The Livelihood of Man.* New York: Academic Press.

Polanyi, Karl, Conrad M. Arensberg, and Harry W. Pearson, eds. 1957. *Trade and Markets in the Early Empires: Economies in History and Theory.* New York: Free Press.

Poole, Robert, Frank Ptacek, and Randal Verbrugge. 2005. *Treatment of Owner-Occupied*

Housing in the CPI. Washington, D.C.: Bureau of Labor Statistics, Office of Prices and Living Conditions.

Poovey, M. 2008. *Genres of Credit Economy: Mediating Value in Eighteenth- and Nineteenth-Century Britain.* Chicago: University of Chicago Press.

Post Express. 1996a. "Antimonies of a Fiscal Policy." August 15.

———. 1996b. "1996 Budget Still Off-Target." November 27.

Povinelli, Elizabeth. 2011. *Economies of Abandonment: Social Belonging and Endurance in Late Liberalism.* Durham, N.C.: Duke University Press.

Produce Department. 1940. Memo titled "Cassava Starch," addressed to the District Administrator, Lagos. September 30. (C.S.0.26 36895 vol I). National Archives, Ibadan. Nigeria.

Ptacek, Frank, and Robert M. Baskin. 1996. 1998 CPI Revision: Housing Sample. Monthly Labor Review. http://www.bls.gov/cpi/cpifp001.pdf (accessed August 2013).

Putnam, Robert D. 2013. "Crumbling American Dreams." *New York Times,* August 3.

Ralph, Michael, 2015. *Forensics of Capital. Risk and Liability, Citizenship and Sovereignty, in Senegal.* Chicago, Ill.: University of Chicago Press

Rawls, John. 2001. *Justice as Fairness: A Restatement.* Cambridge, Mass.: Belknap, Harvard University Press.

Reid, Thomas. (1785) 1997. *An Enquiry into the Human Mind: On the Principles of Common Sense.* Edinburgh: Edinburgh University Press.

Richards, Paul. 1985. *Indigenous Agricultural Revolution.* London: Hutchinson.

Riles, Annelise. 2006. *Documents: Artifacts of Modern Knowledge.* Ann Arbor: University of Michigan Press.

———. 2012 "Is This Still Capitalism? And If Not, What Is It?" Special entry, "Do We Need an Anthropology of Finance?" ed. Bill Maurer. *Cultural Anthropology,* May 14, online.

———. 2011. *Collateral Knowledge.* Chicago: University of Chicago Press.

Robbins, Joel. 2004. *Becoming Sinners: Christianity and Moral Torment in a Papua New Guinea Society.* Berkeley: University of California Press.

Robertson, Alexander F. 1984. *People and the State. An Anthropology of Planned Development.* Cambridge, UK: Cambridge University Press.

Roitman, Janet. 2005. *Fiscal Disobedience: An Anthropology of Economic Regulation in Central Africa.* Princeton N.J.: Princeton University Press.

Rostow. W. W. (1960) 1965. *The Stages of Economic Growth: A Non-Communist Manifesto.* Cambridge, UK: Cambridge University Press.

———. 1990. *Theorists of Economic Growth from David Hume to the Present. With a Perspective on the Next Century.* New York: Oxford University Press.

Rotman, Brian. 1987. *Signifying Nothing: The Semiotics of Zero.* New York: Macmillan.

Sahlins, Marshall. 1972. *Stone Age Economics.* Hawthorne, N.Y.: Aldine De Gruyter.

Samuelson, Paul. 1948. *Economics: An Introductory Analysis.* McGraw-Hill.

The Saturday Newspaper. 1996. "The Budget of Faith." February 17, pp. 12–13.

Schuler, Kurt. 2006. Classifying Exchange Rates. http://users.erols. com/kurrency/classifying.pdf.

Schumpeter, Joseph A. (1960) 1961. *The Theory of Economic Development: An Inquiry into Profits, Capital, Credit, Interest, and the Business Cycle.* Translated by Redvers Opie. New York: Oxford University Press.

Scott, H. S. 1937. "Education and Nutrition in the Colonies." *Africa* 10 (no. 4): 458–71.

Seferis, George. Collected Poems. 1967. Translated by Edmund Keeley and Philip Sherrard. Princeton, N.J.: Princeton University Press.

Shipton, P. 2007. *The Nature of Entrustment: Intimacy, Exchange, and the Sacred in Africa*. New Haven, Conn.: Yale University Press.

Silverstein, Michael. 2003. *Talking Politics: The Substance of Style from Abe to "W."* Chicago: Paradigm.

Smith, Adam. (1776) 1927. *An Enquiry into the Nature and Causes of the Wealth of Nations*. New York: Modern Library.

Smith, Daniel Jordan. 2007. *A Culture of Corruption: Everyday Deception and Popular Discontent in Nigeria*. Princeton, N.J.: Princeton University Press.

Smith, Thomas. 1811. *An Essay on the Theory of Money and Exchange*. London: J. Hatchard. The Hutzler Collection, Sheridan Libraries, Johns Hopkins University.

Sobowale, Dele. 1996. "Budget '96: Much Ado about Nothing." *Sunday Vanguard*, February 18, p. 19.

Sommers, Marc. 2012. *Stuck: Rwandan Youth and the Struggle of Adulthood*. Athens: University of Georgia Press.

Sowell, Thomas. 2000. *Basic Economics: A Citizen's Guide to the Economy*. New York: Basic Books.

Sperber, Dan, and Deirdre Wilson. 1995. *Relevance: Communication and Cognition*. Oxford: Blackwell.

Springer, Yitzhok. 2003. "What the Rebbe Saw . . . What You Can Do." *New York Times*, April 16, p. A9.

Stansfield, Hamer. 1858. *An Appeal to the Working Classes: The Monopoly in Money. The Mere Instrument of Exchange; A Great Social Evil*. Pamphlet, the Hutzler Collection, Sheridan Libraries, Johns Hopkins University.

Stapleford, Thomas A. 2009. *The Cost of Living in America: A Political History of Economic Statistics, 1880–2000*. Cambridge, UK: Cambridge University Press.

Stedman Jones, Daniel. 2012. *Masters of the Universe: Hayek, Friedman, and the Birth of Neoliberal Politics*. Princeton, N.J.: Princeton University Press.

Stein, Judith. 2010. *Pivotal Decade: How the United States Traded Factories for Finance in the Seventies*. New Haven, Conn.: Yale University Press.

Steiner, F. 1999. "Notes on Comparative Economics." In *Orientpolitik, Value and Civilisation: F. B. Steiner Selected Writings*, ed. J. Adler and R. Fardon, 160–73. New York: Berghahn.

Stewart, Kathleen. 1996. *A Space at the Side of the Road*. Princeton, N.J.: Princeton University Press.

Stieb, Ernst W. 1966. *Drug Adulteration: Detection and Control in Nineteenth-Century Britain*. Madison: University of Wisconsin Press.

Stigler, George J. 1954. "Early History of Empirical Studies of Consumer Behavior." *Journal of Political Economy* 62 (no. 2): 95–113.

Stolper, Wolfgang. 1966. *Planning without Facts: Lessons in Resource Allocation from Nigeria's Development*. Cambridge, Mass.: Harvard University Press.

Strathern, Marilyn. 1996. "Cutting the Network." *Journal of the Royal Anthropological Institute* 2 (no. 3): 517–35.

———, ed. 2000. *Audit Cultures: Anthropological Studies in Accountability, Ethics, and the Academy*. London: Routledge.

———. 2002. "Externalities in Comparative Guise." *Economy and Society* 31 (no. 2): 250–67.

———. 2004. *Partial Connections*. New York: Rowman and Littlefield.

Suber, Peter. 1997. "The Great Chain of Being." Notes for the course "Rationalism and Empiricism." Department of Philosophy, Earlham College.

Swedberg, Richard, ed. 1991. *Joseph A. Schumpeter: The Economics and Sociology of Capitalism*. Princeton N.J.: Princeton University Press.

Tawney, R. H. 1913. "The Assessment of Wages in England by the Justices of the Peace." *Vierteljahrschrift für Sozial und Wirtschaftsgeschichte* 11 (no. 3): 307–37.

Tett, Gillian. 2009. *Fool's Gold: The Inside Story of J. P. Morgan and How Wall St. Greed Corrupted Its Bold Dream and Created a Financial Catastrophe*. New York: Free Press.

Thomas, Hugh. 1973. *John Strachey*. London: Harper and Row.

Thompson, E. P. 1967. "Time, Work-Discipline, and Industrial Capitalism." *Past and Present* 38: 56–97.

———. 1971. "The Moral Economy of the English Crowd in the Eighteenth Century." *Past and Present* 50: 76–136.

Thrift, N. 2001. "Finance, Geography of." *International Encyclopedia of the Social and Behavioral Sciences* 8: 5655–57. Oxford: Pergamon.

Tillyard, E. M. 1942. *The Elizabethan World Picture: A Study of the Idea of Order in the Age of Shakespeare*. London: Donne and Milton.

Trouillot, Michel-Rolph. 1989. "Discourses of Rule and the Acknowledgment of the Peasantry in Dominica, W.I., 1838–1928." *American Ethnologist* 16: 704–18.

Tsing, Anna Lowenhaupt. 2005. *Friction: An Ethnography of Global Connection*. Princeton, N.J.: Princeton University Press.

Tupper, Mark, and Murray Rudd. n.d. *Economics: Determining the Non-Extractive Value of Coral Reef "Icon Species."* University of Guam Marine Laboratory.

Turner, Victor. 1967. *The Forest of Symbols: Aspects of Ndembu Ritual*. Ithaca, N.Y.: Cornell University Press.

Udry, Chris and Hyungi Woo. 2007. "Households and the Social Organization of Consumption in Southern Ghana." *African Studies Review* 50 (no. 2): 139–53.

Ugor, Paul U. 2013. "Survival Strategies and Citizenship Claims: Youth and the Underground Oil Economy in Post-Amnesty Niger Delta." *Africa* 83 (no. 2): 270–92.

United Nations. 2009. *Practical Guide to Producing Consumer Price Indices*. Geneva, Switzerland.

U.S. General Accountability Office. 2010. *GAO Citizen's Guide to the 2010 Financial Report of the United States Government*. Washington, D.C.

Uzor, Mike. 1995. Another Lost Year. *Policy*. December 11, p. 37.

Vaggi, Gianni, and Peter Groenewegen. 2003. *A Concise History of Economic Thought, From Mercantilism to Monetarism*. New York: Macmillan.

Vaughan, Rice. 1675. *A Treatise of Money: Or a Discourse of Coin and Coinage*. London: Printed by T. Dawkes.

Veblen, Thorstein. 1899. *The Theory of the Leisure Class: An Economic Study in the Evolution of Institutions*. London: Macmillan.

Verbrugge, Randal. 2008. "The Puzzling Divergence of Rents and User Costs, 1980–2004." *Review of Income and Wealth* 54 (no.4): 671–99.

Verran, Helen. 2001. *Science and an African Logic*. Chicago: Chicago University Press

———. 2007. "The Telling Challenge of Africa's Economies." *African Studies Review* 50 (no. 2): 163–82.

———. 2010. "Number as an Inventive Frontier in Knowing and Working Australia's Water Resources." *Anthropological Theory* 10 (no. 102): 171–78.

———. 2012. "A Political Arithmetic of Australia's Fish? Articulating the Performativities of Numbers Embedded in Australian Environmental Policy." Paper for London conference titled "The New Numeracy," February 16 and 17.

Wallerstein, Immanuel, Randall Collins, Michael Mann, Georgi Derluguian, and Craig Calhoun. 2013. *Does Capitalism Have a Future?* Oxford: Oxford University Press.

Wallis, Jim. 2005. *God's Politics. Why the Right Gets It Wrong and the Left Doesn't Get It.* New York: HarperCollins.

Wallman, Sandra, ed. 1992. *Contemporary Futures: Perspectives from Social Anthropology.* London: Routledge.

Watts, Michael J. 1987. "Brittle Trade: A Political Economy of Food Supply in Kano". In *Feeding African Cities: Studies in Regional Social History,* ed. J. I. Guyer, 55–111. Manchester, UK: Manchester University Press for the International African Institute.

Webb, Sidney, and Beatrice Webb. (1922) 1963. *The Development of English Local Government, 1689–1835.* London: Oxford University Press.

West Africa. 1991. "Financial Discipline." January 14–20, pp. 12–13.

Williams, Brett. 2004. *Debt for Sale: A Social History of the Credit Trap.* Philadelphia: University of Pennsylvania Press.

Wolf, Eric R. 1988. "Inventing Society." *American Ethnologist* 15: 752–61.

Wright, Robert. 2005. "The Market Shall Set You Free." *New York Times,* January 28, http://www.nytimes.com/2005/01/28/opinion/28wright.html?pagewanted=1.

Yearley, S. 2001. "Risk, Sociology and Politics of." *International Encyclopedia of the Social and Behavioral Sciences* 20: 13360–64. Oxford: Pergamon.

Yotopoulos, P. 2006. "Asymmetric Globalization: Impact on the Third World." Stanford Center for International Development Working Paper No. 270.

Young, James Harvey. 1989. *Pure Food: Securing the Federal Food and Drugs Act of 1906.* Princeton, N.J.: Princeton University Press.

Yuran, Noam. 2014. *What Money Wants: An Economy of Desire.* Stanford, Calif.: Stanford University Press.

Zaloom, Caitlin. 2004. "The Productivity of Risk." *Cultural Anthropology* 19 (no. 3): 365–91.

———. 2005. "The Discipline of the Speculator." In *Global Assemblages: Technology, Politics and Ethics as Anthropological Problems,* ed. Aihwa Ong and Stephen Collier, 253–69. Malden, Mass.: Blackwell.

———. 2010. *Out of the Pits: Traders and Technology from Chicago to London.* Chicago: University of Chicago Press.

Zelizer, V. 1995. *The Social Meaning of Money.* New York: Basic Books.